Lost
Initiatives

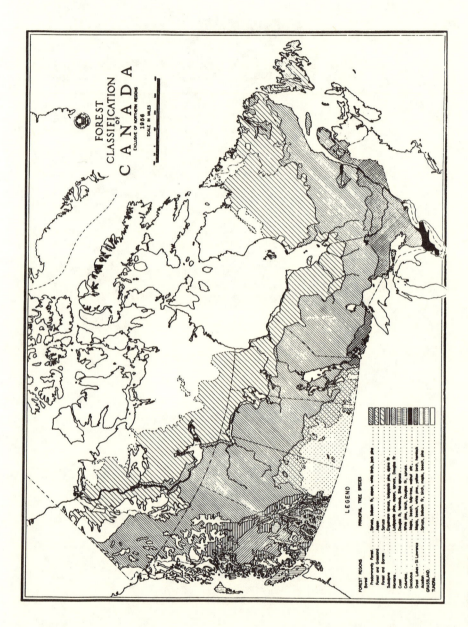

The forest classification of Canada (printed by permission of the National Map Collection, Public Archives of Canada).

Lost Initiatives

Canada's Forest Industries, Forest Policy and Forest Conservation

R. Peter Gillis AND **Thomas R. Roach**

Contributions in Economics and Economic
History, Number 69

Greenwood Press
New York • Westport, Connecticut • London

The Forest History Society is a nonprofit, educational institution dedicated to the advancement of historical understanding of man's interaction with the North American forest environment. It was established in 1946. Interpretations and conclusions in publications prepared by the Forest History Society are those of authors; the Society takes responsibility for the selection of topics, the competence of the authors, and their freedom of inquiry.

Work on this book and its publication were supported by grants to the Forest History Society.

Library of Congress Cataloging-in-Publication Data

Gillis, R. Peter.
    Lost Initiatives.

    (Contributions in economics and economic history, ISSN 0084-9235 ; no. 69)
    Bibliography: p.
    Includes index.
    1. Forest policy—Canada.   2. Forest products industry—Canada.   3. Forest conservation—Canada.
I. Roach, Thomas R.   II. Title.   III. Series.
HD9764.C3G55 1986   333.75'0971   86-3122
ISBN 0-313-25415-X (lib. bdg. : alk. paper)

Library of Congress Catalog Card Number: 86-3122
ISBN: 0-313-25415-X
ISSN: 0084-9235

First published in 1986

Greenwood Press, Inc.
88 Post Road West, Westport, Connecticut 06881

Printed in the United States of America

The paper used in this book complies with the
Permanent Paper Standard issued by the National
Information Standards Organization (Z39.48-1984).

10 9 8 7 6 5 4 3 2 1

To
Ernest H. Finlayson
Canadian Forester and Conservationist

Contents

Illustrations

Conversions

Readers might like to note that the following conversion factors have been used in this book:

1 square kilometre	0.386 square miles
1 acre	0.405 hectares
1 metre	3.28 feet
1 kilometre	0.621 miles
1 cord	3.625 cubic metres
1 cubic foot	0.0283 cubic metres
1 Mf bm	2.3764 cubic metres

SOURCE: P. J. Rennie, *Measure for Measure* (Ottawa, Canada Department of Forestry, Forest Research Branch, 1963), pp. 9, 10, 12, 14, 15.

Acknowledgments

We would like to thank our spouses, Sandra Gillis and Lucie Edwards, and the following individuals and organizations for their help and assistance in preparing this work: Graeme Wynn, Terry Cook, Bruce Hodgins, Gabrielle Blais, Henny Kahwa, Richard Judd, and Pete Steen. The staffs of the Public Archives of Canada, the National Library of Canada, the Public Archives of Ontario, the Forest History Society, and the Environment Canada Library have all been incredibly cooperative. We also wish to acknowledge the financial support of the government of Canada through the Canadian Studies Directorate of the Department of the Secretary of State of Canada.

Lost
Initiatives

CHAPTER 1

Close and Natural Ties: The British North American Timber Industry and Government Regulation, 1800–1870

Modern Canadians have an indistinct and distant perception of their country's forests. They are envisaged as relatively hostile environments, suitable for adventurous vacations but not for full-time residence. Only for canoeists and other outdoor enthusiasts are the forests a haven from the hustle and bustle of industrial civilization. For an ever-decreasing number of individuals, the woods are a workplace and a source of livelihood. For the vast majority of Canadians, living in a largely urban, industrial society, these areas are no longer an integral part of everyday life. With the loss of this experience has gone a crucial understanding of the forest's tremendous importance to the country's social and economic existence.

This change in perception of the forest is a relatively modern phenomenon. It was not true at the time of Confederation. Travelling from Saint John, New Brunswick, to the western end of Lake Superior in the 1860s, a citizen might have remarked on the fine farms and the promise of nascent industry in burgeoning urban centres. But, wherever he went, the observer would have noted the activities of lumbermen. Whether it was sawmills, log-rafts powered by sails on the St. Lawrence, or loggers out on a spree, lumbering was the one general and pervasive activity common to all of British North America.

In this period nearly half of Canada's adult male population was involved one way or another with the timber and lumber industry. It rivalled agriculture in importance and, in 1871, accounted for $29 million worth of exports, an immense sum for the period. Across what is now eastern Canada were dotted a myriad of towns relying on the trade for their well-being. Besides serving as supply centres for lumber camps spread yet farther into the hinterland, many towns had their own sawmills feeding planks and deals into the apparently insatiable markets of Britain and the United States.[1] The bulky nature of woods products meant they were difficult to transport in the years before the full development of railways and, much later, roads and diesel-driven trucks. Thus Canada's lumber industry remained oriented toward lake and river systems until well into the 1950s.

In the colony of New Brunswick the valleys of the Saint John and Miramichi rivers developed as major lumber-producing regions. There, during the decades from settlement to Confederation, loggers had early sought the white and red pine, although, by the 1850s, they were concentrating on white and red spruce which found its prime market in Great Britain. White spruce was also abundant along the shores of the St. Lawrence river and its tributaries stretching northward toward the dark and mysterious boreal forest. Farther west in the immense area of the greater St. Lawrence rivershed, white pine was king and supplies of this valuable species appeared to be inexhaustible. Towering fifty or more metres above the forest floor, these naturally grown giants were prized above all other materials in North America for construction and decorative purposes. In searching out high-quality groves of pine, the industry established itself on the intricate river systems of southern Ontario and had spread out along the shores of the Great Lakes. During the nineteenth century and into the Edwardian era, pine was sawn in Ontario towns such as Desoronto, Peterborough, Fenelon Falls, Seneca, Owen Sound, Midland, and Ottawa and was shipped south across the Great Lakes or the St. Lawrence to American freshwater ports such as Burlington, Oswego, or Tonawanda and on to the prime markets of New York and Boston.

The centre of this trade, before which all other regions paled in comparison, was the valley of the Ottawa river. Running north from the St. Lawrence, a short distance west of Montreal, it encompassed some 640,000 square kilometres of territory. From its mouth to its sources in the major lakes of the northern forest just south of James Bay was roughly 1,100 kilometres. The Ottawa had many major tributaries of which the Rouge, Gatineau, Coulonge, Dumoine, Mississippi, Madawaska, Bonnechere, and Petawawa all came to figure prominently in the trade. An incredulous Henry Franklin Bronson, surveying the area in 1849 to determine if his firm should relocate in Bytown (Ottawa), reported to his partners in northern New York State that the valley was a "sea of pine". By 1870 lumbermen "on the Ottawa" were producing some 615,000 cubic metres of sawn lumber annually. H. F. Bronson had undoubtedly made the right decision to move two decades earlier; his firm, the Bronsons and Weston Company, led production in the Valley, sawing nearly 60,000 cubic metres of lumber alone. It was all shipped south to committed markets in the northeastern United States via the company's wholesalers in Whitehall and Painted Post, New York.[2]

The pine lumber industry, which became Canada's third great staple trade after the fur trade and the cod fishery, had its origins in the throes of war. The European explorers of eastern Canada in the sixteenth and seventeenth centuries encountered a heavily forested land. They shared the attitude of the explorers and settlers of the thirteen colonies to the south that trees had little commercial value, simply serving as impediments to travel and rapid settlement. But, by the seventeenth century, Britain had so over-cut her own forests that she had to import increasing quantities of naval stores and wood. The forests of the Baltic coasts were a more economical and convenient source of supply than any of the small trans-Atlantic colonies, and a trade with Russia and Scandinavia soon developed. This changed during the Anglo-Dutch War, fought from 1652 to 1654. The Commonwealth government in England started to purchase some naval stores from New England, and subsidies were put in place to maintain production. In the same way, the government of France attempted to encourage some production of timber from its colony of New France with the mercantilist policy of Jean-Baptiste Colbert.

In 1721 Britain took the strategic step of reserving North American white pine for naval use through its "broad arrow" policy. This system extended to the newly acquired colony of Nova Scotia (then including New Brunswick) and, following the 1763 Treaty of Paris, to Quebec. It was not until the settlement of New Brunswick by Loyalists, following their evacuation from the United States, that the northern colonies became a prime source of masting material for Britain. Prior to the 1780s, Nova Scotians and New Englanders alike illegally cut the pine but found their export markets restricted by competition from the Baltic ports. Paradoxically, following the acquisition of Quebec by the British Crown, the local demand for lumber was filled by loggers in the forest of northern Vermont.[3]

By the end of the eighteenth century the British lumber merchants and the loggers and sawmillers along the Baltic coast had established exceptionally intimate relationships. British merchants sent their sons to the east as apprentices in the mills with which their fathers did business. Marriages between the families often followed. Not unnaturally, British merchants quickly became biased against the products from Canadian forests. This bias was assisted by the marketing conditions found in England where each merchant supplied a few users and there was no such thing as standard dimensions. Only in the production of masts was New Brunswick seen to be better than the Baltic, and generally mast contracts were let directly by the Crown. All through the nineteenth century and well into the 1930s Canadian lumber faced this bias. Only the unnatural economic circumstances created by war or by heavy countervailing duties forced British merchants to take Canadian square timber and lumber seriously.

The first of a long series of wars to affect Canada's forest industries was that of the American Revolution. The Admiralty had long been used to dealing directly with merchants in New England for their masts, and this conflict sundered these links. The necessity of a continued supply of masts resulted in a move to the forests of the Saint John river valley. Admiralty contracts proved a boon to the financially strapped loyalist refugees and helped found a lively trade in naval stores and, later, ship building.

Revolution in France, and that country's determination to export the condition to the rest of Europe after 1793, brought it into conflict with Britain. British success in the conflict depended on her navy. At first, naval dockyards appeared to have adequate supplies, and the Baltic Sea remained accessible and open until a series of events, commencing in the year 1798, shook British confidence in the security of its wood supplies. In that year Russia caused a momentary crisis by cutting off exports of timber, but an exemption was quickly negotiated by Britain for its supplies of masts and naval timber. Then, in 1800, various Baltic nations allied against Britain and once more the flow of naval supplies was briefly terminated. British business then demonstrated its overwhelming patriotism through a nefarious body known as the "Timber Trust". It worked to control the amount of timber still available in order to further drive up the prices being paid by the Navy Board. The result of these two crises was that the Royal dockyards suddenly faced potential shortages that would have made it extremely difficult to maintain the fleet.

His Majesty's Government responded in two ways to the situation in which it found itself. It increased existing contracts for masts from New Brunswick, and it enlarged the contracts to include naval stores. Because the forests of New Brunswick were already depleted of trees for the best and longest masts and spars, the government decided to move into Quebec. In 1804 the Navy Board awarded a contract to Scott, Idles and Company to exploit the banks of the St. Lawrence river and its tributaries. The contract was made through an agent in Quebec City, Messrs. Joliffe and Muir. To ensure the stability of this new colonial trade and to maintain a competitive edge over the Baltic trade should it ever recover, all duties on timber from the North American colonies were dropped, and, in 1804 and 1806, levies on foreign imported timber were raised to £1/5/0 per load of 50 cubic feet. This tariff structure was retained and expanded. During the years 1813 to 1821 the duties on imported, non-colonial timber jumped to and remained at the extraordinary high rate of £3/5/0 per load. This was equal to an *ad valorum* rate that varied from 81 percent to 130 percent of the value of the imported deals and timbers. At these rates then, it is no wonder that the few loads of Baltic lumber that made their way to the shore of England during this period were priced right out of the market. Nor is it any wonder that this system of discriminatory duties, known as the "colonial preference," resulted in a rapid expansion of Great Britain's trade with its colonies in British North America.[4]

It was not until after Napoleon's successful Baltic campaign of 1807 that the flow of wood to England from the Baltic totally ceased. In November of that year the French emperor signed a treaty with Russia closing the Baltic ports to British traders. The resulting trade embargo was expanded into the "Continental System" of trade by Napoleon through pressure on his European neighbours. The embargo was broadened when the United States joined it, although independent-minded Vermonters still slipped considerable quantities of timber across the border, taking advantage of high wartime prices. The Continental System endured until December 1810 when Russia broke free of the alliance. During these years, very little timber or naval stores reached the beleaguered island from eastern Europe. Great Britain had to scour the world for the supplies it needed to maintain its fleet. Scotland, Ireland, and Portugal all contributed, but the most important source became British North America.

In both New Brunswick and Canada, ever larger contracts were let by the Admiralty and continued after the lifting of the embargo in 1810 through to the opening of hostilities with the United States in 1812. The Saint John and Miramichi rivers both developed bustling timber trades during these years, but the great entrepôt of the trade became Quebec City. During the embargo, about 75 percent of exports from British North America were naval stores and about 90 percent of these passed through Quebec. One merchant participating in the trade, Irishman George Hamilton, estimated that the value of naval contracts in 1809 alone was £2,500,000.[5]

The original firm of Scott, Idles and Company supposedly controlled all Canadian contracts up to 1814. Others, such as the Hamiltons and Henry Usborne and Company, manufactured stores that the Navy Board purchased, even though they had not been cut under legal contract. This illicit harvesting grew in importance as a non-military trade developed with the mother country. This trade was built on construction materials including white elm and oak, square timber, and deals (planks about 80mm thick, 225mm to 275mm wide, and of varying lengths). R. G. Albion has claimed that "for every ship which took masts and naval timber to the Royal Dockyard, dozens of cargoes of lumber left Quebec for Liverpool, Bristol and London". As Sandra Gillis has emphasized, most of this timber was not cut on private lands, such as the large seigneurial holdings of Quebec, but rather was taken illegally by trespass on the Crown domain.[6]

The practice of cutting timber on Crown land without a legal contract was common to New Brunswick. Local officials often turned a blind eye to the activities of loggers, occasionally levying their own licence fees to provide an independent source of revenue. The effect of the colonial preference was generally beneficial. It attracted traders to North America and gave the agricultural colonies a "place" in the Imperial system. Many farmers "made timber" in these years and profited mightily as the market rose. The canny settler put his money into his farm or into a primitive sawmill realizing that the timber market might be fickle especially as it became more and more difficult to find the desired high-quality white pine. Some settlers, however, made the mistake of ignoring their farms and other business opportunities and relying totally on the timber trade for their livelihoods. Often they lost everything when the market crashed.

The declaration of war with the United States in 1812 had a negative effect on the prosperity of the timber trade even though the market in Britain remained protected by a high tariff. This occurred because the hostilities ended the large-scale importation of American foodstuffs necessary to supply the lumber camps. As a result, production costs rose, a situation worsened by the increased cost of marine insurance due to the effect of the war at sea. The advantage given to Canadian forest products by the colonial preference was thereby eliminated. Many ships, which had been engaged in the trans-Atlantic timber trade, now switched back to the Baltic in the spring of 1813. The British North American trade fell into a depression. Despite a doubling of the tariff, to the rate discussed above, exports of pine fell to 59 percent of their pre-war average. New Brunswick was less badly hit than Quebec, but the cycle of boom followed by bust, a characteristic of the industry to this day, was felt in the colonies for the first time.

An end to the war with the United States was finally arranged in 1815. With peace in Europe already established and the Continental System a thing of the past, British North America's lumbermen felt doubly uncertain about their future. Would Great Britain revert to the trade policies that existed before the American war? Or would it maintain the colonial preference? The answer had actually begun to unfold early in 1813 for those who were perceptive enough to see it. In that year, Russia had asked the British government to abolish the colonial preference. Merchants with substantial investments in North America also formed a powerful counter lobby, the Committee of Merchants Interested in the Trade and Fisheries of North America. It had been quick to petition the Colonial Office that large amounts of capital had been invested in the colonies on the understanding that the conditions needed to develop the trade would remain in place.[7] From the point of view of the British government, there was no doubt that a self-contained empire had shown itself to have definite benefits under the strategic threat created by the Continental System. To the relief of the merchants, their petitions were accepted. The Canadian timber trade was saved. British ships would carry immigrants and merchandise across the sea to the New World and return laden with timber in a policy that soon came to be characterized as "ships, colonies and commerce". The colonial preference was to remain and, if necessary, be increased. As Donald Creighton has put it, the British North American timber trade "had been born of the war and blockade; it was maintained and continued by all the devices of a reanimated and intransigent commercial imperialism".[8] The colonial preference remained at protective levels until 1841 when it was lowered by the Tory administration of Sir Robert Peel and then eventually largely phased out between 1846 and 1849.

That the preference lasted for some thirty years does not mean that it had total acceptance by British politicians. Commencing immediately after the Napoleonic Wars, Britain entered a period of uneven economic growth. It was as if the country were on an economic roller coaster. Each dip in the economy brought stronger cries for free trade from parliamentary supporters of the cause. They were joined, naturally, by business interests involved with the Baltic timber trade. Besides using economic arguments, these lumber merchants assailed North American imports for their poor quality of manufacture. This was a false criticism since, at this time, most developments in sawmilling technology originated in England where mills concentrated on the careful resawing of the squared timbers and deals into the multitude of dimensions of lumber required by the particular customers of each firm. The criticisms, however, resulted in the extreme precision and resulting waste with which timber was "squared" in the bush and then refaced in the coves of Quebec. British lumber merchants familiar with the Baltic trade also used other methods to belittle North American products. Each mill in Russia and Scandinavia had its own grading standards and most ports, their own measurement systems. British merchants required that North American material meet the standards of the company in the east with which they personally were aligned. The resulting plethora of undefined terms and jargon left many a Canadian angry and confused.

The alliance of free-traders and certain British timber merchants resulted in the gradual growth of free-trade sentiment within the trade. Free-traders, however, had an uphill struggle. During the life of the colonial preference there were many parliamentary debates and reports before actual changes were made. Each engendered a rush of hurried meetings as supporters of colonial trade drafted petitions in defence of the preferences. In British North America, each debate sent the industry into frantic overproduction, which was followed by a depression as the market absorbed the surplus. This overproduction of timber only exaggerated the effect of the existing economic slumps and resulted in the timber trade being severely depressed during the years 1819–1821, 1825–1826, the mid–1830s, and the early and mid–1840s. In the hinterland in particular, the recessions drove many to bankruptcy as creditors sought payment for the goods they had advanced the loggers.

The preference was linked in the British North American mind with the very survival of the economies of New Brunswick and the Canadas. The British North American commercial community never had any trouble filling their petitions with signatures or passing resolutions by the small constituent assemblies. They were even from time to time able to attract the largely anti-commercial French Canadian elite in the Assembly of Lower Canada to their cause. As one colonial free-trade advocate, John Neilson of the *Quebec Gazette*, put it in an editorial supporting the preference: "whenever there is a good crop in Europe, we shall have nothing to export but a few furs. Without exportation, all importation must cease, and the strongest link of connexion between the colony and Great Britain be broken".[9] While British politicians were not sure that their country had made an open-ended commitment to subsidize the colonial trade, these arguments were enough to turn back the free trade wave and allow British North American lumbering to develop as a thriving industry.

Thus by 1815 there existed in New Brunswick and Canada the foundation of the square timber and deal trade that was to last into the twentieth century. In the beginning, the timber trade was organized along lines similar to those of the Hudson's Bay Company in its early days. The merchants from the English houses set themselves up in their coves at Quebec, on the edge of the hinterland. Here they waited for the "natives", the Canadian loggers, to appear with "furs" or rafts of logs. At Quebec, Saint John, and a few other places, such as at the mouth of the Miramichi river, were the facilities, or coves, of the timber merchants. A cove was basically a flat beach where the rafts could be drawn up at high tide and broken up, and the timbers refinished. There were also loading facilities for the ships engaged in the trans-Atlantic trade. The activities in each cove were usually supervised by a representative of the wealthy trading house in Great Britain that had organized the cutting and shipping of the timber from the interior. This house shipped its wood across the ocean, stored the timbers in its yards in England, and then put the deals and logs up for auction.

The Hamilton firm in Quebec City was typical. It had its own cove at Quebec City, managed by a family member, and named New Liverpool. The family ran its British business from headquarters in Liverpool, England, while the bush work was looked after by yet another member of the family living at Hawkesbury in the Ottawa valley. Here a deal mill was located, the contracts for timber were negotiated, and the teams of shantymen were hired and sent off into the hinterland with a winter's supplies. It was an organization very similar to that of the Russian and Scandinavian logging firms. The major differences were, of course, the large size of the country in which the Hamiltons worked and its wilderness nature.[10]

The timber merchants fulfilled two vital roles. First, in the fall of each year, they extended lines of credit into the hinterland. The credit occasionally went directly to the up-country lumbermen who would be making the timber. More usually, it went to merchants living in communities in or close to the forest who would act as middlemen in timber-making contracts. In a frontier society where cash was very scarce, this credit was essential for the carrying on of all trade. Second, in the spring when the timber was brought downstream to the merchant's port facilities, these men determined the prices paid for it. Using commercial intelligence obtained from England, they purchased the annual cut, refinished it, and contracted with the timber ships for its transportation across the Atlantic.

The merchants were often the "bêtes noires" of the up-country contractors and river drivers. They complained about the quality of the timber and the lack of skill in finishing it.[11] They shaved prices wherever they could and often demanded instant repayment of loans. Many were the epitome of the imperial interloper, staying in the particular colony only as long as prices were good and timber was plentiful. Arthur Lower records that, once the pine square timber trade was finished in Canada, some of these men moved to other parts of the Empire, transferring their skills to other climes, races, and species of wood. As a result, up to World War II squared hardwood timber was regularly imported to England from countries other than Canada.[12] Others, like the Prices, Hamiltons, Sharples, Gilmours, and Cunards, remained to found merchant and manufacturing dynasties synonymous with British North American economic progress. All practiced a conservative ideology dedicated to the health of trade, the mercantilist system, and the British connection.[13]

The up-country entrepreneurs and lumbermen dependent on the timber merchants were a far less wealthy group. In the early days of the trade it was normal, as Arthur Lower and Graeme Wynn have both described, for gangs of men, working for a farmer-businessman, to go into the woods to make a small amount of timber. Supplies were obtained, on credit of course, from the local storekeeper, and the men lived in a rudimentary shanty during the winter. This was how a settler augmented his subsistence farming with some cash income. Under these circumstances, logging became characterized by its extravagant waste of the forest resource. Only the best trees were felled and, from these, only the largest and best logs were taken. Over a third of each tree was left in the woods as hewings. No attempt was made to curb this senseless waste until much later in the 1860s when higher government dues combined with increasing shortages of knot-free logs started the move to "waney" timber and, eventually, the disappearance of the square timber trade.[14]

Without a doubt, a major factor contributing to the waste and general mess of nineteenth-century logging, and especially square timber making, was the insecurity of the trade. The lumberman and his associates were most affected. The trade had an element of gambling to it although, when the market was good, large profits could be made. The overhead needed for putting in a timber camp was limited, and would-be lumber-kings were often tempted into the bush having no idea as to the condition of the market far away across the sea. In the following spring, the long strings of logs inexorably made their way down the creeks and small rivers. There was no way the process could be stopped. Often the hard-won logs were dumped onto a market already crumbling and were left to rot on the shores of some merchant's cove.

Despite the high risk of the trade, by the 1820s there were developing in the up-country major entrepreneurs who were prospering from it: men such as William Harper and John Ward of New Brunswick, Joseph Aumond, Patrick McGoey, Peter Aylen, and George Hamilton on the Ottawa, and the Stricklands on the Trent. These lumbermen operated out of small centres in the hinterland and, at this stage, were still dependent on the timber merchants for support. Moreover, they were slowly achieving a measure of economic independence and political power. They were engaged in a business notorious for its volatility, fiercely competitive and basically illegal—the Crown still had not opened access to its lands for loggers even though it relied on them for supplies. These men experienced the violence and economic uncertainty of the lumbering community at first hand.

As they amassed relatively large investments in their organizations, larger, more established lumbermen began to call for increased regulatory control over the resource. In so doing, they began the conflict that has continually characterized the Canadian frontier. On the one hand, the independent settler sought an immediate living from the forest while, on the other, business enterprise wished to monopolize the resource with firm regulations to protect investment. This conflict between users of the forest continues to this day even though environmentalists and urban users have, in some part, replaced the original farmers and settlers, expressing aims that are not generally exploitive in nature. Although many would argue that the Canadian public currently has a large influence on provincial land use policy, and that, in the beginning, government policy emphasized agricultural settlement, lumbermen have more or less had their own way in forest regulation. The best illustration of how early lumbermen influenced government can be found in the careers of two men: Thomas Baillie in New Brunswick and George Hamilton in the Ottawa valley.

The regulation of forestry in Canada really started in New Brunswick. The town of Saint John had a sawmill as early as 1766. The arrival of the loyalists twenty years later resulted in a boom in construction materials, and this was quickly converted into trade with the West Indies, the New England States, and, of course, Great Britain. By 1792 the colony's government at Fredericton was issuing regulations governing the use of the Saint John river by loggers, even though the majority of the logs must have been illegally cut on Crown lands. In 1816 the colonial government formally took over timber regulation from imperial authorities, and a rudimentary system of licences was introduced. These required loggers to define the area in which they were going to operate and specified that they must be British subjects. Lumbermen were supposed to get their licences from deputy timber surveyors appointed, naturally, by the Crown. It was, however, a typical early colonial system with no personnel assigned to control the activities of the deputy timber surveyors. One of its few small successes was that some Americans were caught and prosecuted for trespass.[15]

In March, 1818, the Lieutenant Governor of New Brunswick proclaimed the levy of the first official timber dues of one shilling per ton on all licences. Although the reaction from the lumbermen was outrage, the point was established that the Crown had control over unalienated lands and the resources on or under their surfaces. During the next two years, the Executive Council in New Brunswick reformed the regulations creating a relatively comprehensive system of forest administration. To many, this represented a restriction of opportunity on the public domain, but, as was to happen in Canada, the forest was actually being integrated into the revenue collection network of the colonial administration. In the long run, this was particularly important because government quickly saw that it had a stake in the continued well-being of the young industry. In the short run, the collection of Crown dues became a point of conflict as the struggle for responsible government heightened because of tension between the executive and the assembly. The executive used the timber dues it collected to underwrite the civil list in order to avoid requesting the assembly to pass money measures.

The real problem for the colonial government, however, was that there was no effective control over activities in the forest from the seat of government in Fredericton. To end this inefficency and to collect missing revenues, the Colonial Office in London appointed, in 1824, an outsider to the position of Commissioner of Crown Lands for New Brunswick. Thomas Baillie has been described as a "brash Irishman" who had experience in estate management in his native land. Throughout the later 1820s and the 1830s Baillie worked to increase the revenue from timber, to improve the inspection system and to encourage capital investment in his adopted home. Whereas, in the Canadas, the impetus to control violence and provide business stability on the timber frontier came directly from the entrepreneurs while the government officials contributed relatively few ideas until the late 1840s, in New Brunswick, it was a government official who promoted these ideas in direct opposition to a large segment of the colony's entrepreneurs.[16]

Baillie's methods were successful in that they fostered the growth of large, well-capitalized lumber companies in the province, such as the Cunard interests in northeast New Brunswick. This was achieved, the Commissioner's enemies charged, through favouritism to those allied with Baillie's political faction and at the expense of the small operator—the farmer-lumberman who looked to the forest for a cash supplement to his livelihood. In 1828 Baillie began to advocate the disposal of timber berths by auction and, in 1833 and 1835, he raised timber dues substantially. He concentrated almost exclusively on the collection of revenues from forest resources and the prevention of trespass. Moreover, the Commissioner used new land granting instructions from Britain in 1827 to initiate land sales, including timberlands, some of which were to Americans. Public opinion was outraged when rumours spread that a Boston consortium had been formed to take control of timberlands and mill sites on the Penobscot, St. Croix, and Saint John rivers. Baillie further encouraged large-scale investment in the timber trade in 1831 by offering private reserves of timberland to entrepreneurs, like Cunard, who would invest in the improvement of waterways or guarantee annual cuts from new areas.

This threat of timberlands falling into private hands was used by rival merchant-lumber interests centred on Saint John, and led by Speaker of the Assembly Charles Simonds to open an economic and political war with Baillie and his powerful father-in-law William F. Odell, the Provincial Secretary. This group made representations to Britain and had the private reserves disallowed in 1833. Baillie countered in 1835, however, with five-year licences to cover the same areas as the reserves and to be given on roughly the same terms. He went on to include in the Civil List Bill of 1837 a provision to let licences by public auction with no preference in the second year to the original licencee. This was too much for the Saint John merchants and smaller operators who opposed Baillie's regulations; even Joseph Cunard turned against his former benefactor. The Assembly overturned the Civil List Act and stipulated that the Lieutenant-Governor and the Council were empowered to grant timber licences immediately upon application, and renewal rights were given. This battle in New Brunswick was fought ostensibly to beat back monopoly of timberlands and give smaller lumberers a chance. In reality, it was conducted to defeat Baillie's personal ambitions but accept his goals.

As W. S. MacNutt points out: "The victory of 1837 made remaining discontents seem of trifling importance. For it inaugurated the rule of victorious timber-barons who held the seats of an all-powerful legislature".[17] By the late 1840s, the large operators, who were mostly merchant-wholesalers, were firmly in control of lumbering and the timber markets. Unlike in Canada with its more diversified economy, they were a powerful single interest to which all other interests in the colony were tied. There was in New Brunswick a judicious alliance between those merchant interests that already had some capital and those who would use the forest to create capital, a true community of timber interests. Little was to change until Confederation when the new Dominion government assumed control of the timber export tax. This required changes in the leasing arrangements for timber, a process not accomplished by the province until 1874.

In contrast to the lumbermen in New Brunswick, those in Upper and Lower Canada faced a government that was less inclined to intervene directly in the industry. Other factors intruded as well. For a start, the scale of the country was enormous when compared to that of the Baltic states or New Brunswick. Only a few families of English timber merchants ventured into the wilderness, attempting to establish a family concern that looked after their own logs from the time they were felled and "made" until the time when they were sold in Great Britain. The real rise of the Canadian lumber king did not take place until after trade was opened with the United States in the 1840s. Prior to that date, all who tried logging in the Canadian Shield suffered from the wild swings of the market in faraway England. Making a living in a market subject to fluctuations in demand and price required careful control of contractors and employees as well as political acuteness. These

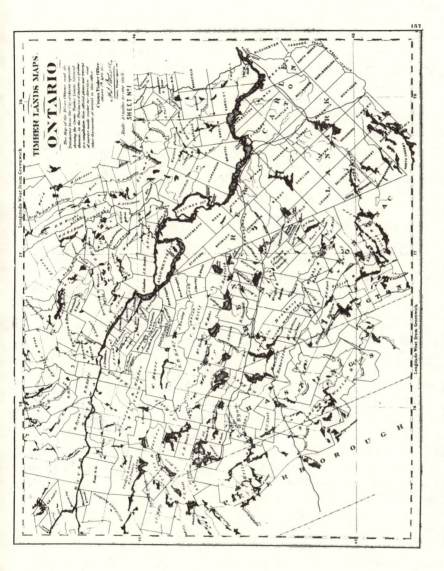

1875 timber berth map of the Algonquin Park area of Ontario and the Mattawa river to Hull area of western Quebec (printed by permission of the National Map Collection, Public Archives of Canada).

attributes are all well-demonstrated by the members of one British family lumbering firm, the Hamiltons, who came to Canada and made a successful living from the pine of the Ottawa valley. The members of this family exerted great influence on the political scene in Canada and played a large part in the creation of the colony's first forest regulations.

The Hamiltons were a Scots-Irish merchant family that had been involved in the Baltic timber trade. Following Napoleon's embargo of 1807, the company of George and William Hamilton transferred operations to Quebec City to take part in the timber trade under naval contract. In common with other British merchants, they established themselves at a cove on the North Shore and waited for the rafts of logs to float down to them. In a break from the traditional mode of operation, the firm advanced credit to a deal mill operation being started by two American immigrants, Thomas Mears and David Pattee, at the lower Ottawa valley settlement of Hawkesbury. In 1812, Mears and Pattee defaulted on their loan and the Hamiltons assumed control of the mill, thus becoming involved in the up-country side of the business. William Hamilton moved to Hawkesbury to take charge of the mill and its associated lumbering operations. At that time the felling operations were conducted primarily along the Rideau river, a tributary of the Ottawa which flows through what is now the capital of Canada. William's brother George remained at Quebec City as a salaried agent of the firm responsible for negotiating timber purchases and sales and securing naval contracts.[18]

Shortly, the family had to decide whether or not to stay in the British North American timber trade. The Continental System collapsed and war broke out with the United States coincidentally with the Hamiltons' acquisition of the Hawkesbury mill. Inevitably, the bottom fell out of the timber market as British merchants returned, wholesale, to their beloved contacts in the Baltic states. These unfortunate economic conditions were compounded by the destruction of the Hawkesbury mill by a fire that the family suspected to be the result of arson. The loss of the mill and piled deals was partially offset by insurance while the undamaged square timber that was waiting to be sawn was shipped to market. Rebuilding the mill in the late summer of 1812 stretched the resources of the firm, but it was completed on an expanded scale, and logging plans were made for the winter. In the fall of 1812, the firm had its men in the woods making timber and, in the following spring, over 8,500 cubic metres of timber, staves, and deals were successfully sold on the Quebec market. The Hamiltons were in the Ottawa valley trade to stay.

On William Hamilton's retirement from the firm in 1816, George Hamilton moved to Hawkesbury. He took over the management of the up-country operations while two other brothers, John and Robert, acted as agents in Quebec City and Liverpool, England, respectively. The firm was now organized on the same lines as the successful companies operating out of the Baltic. The mill at Hawkesbury cut the squared logs into deals of sizes that filled the idiosyncratic demands of the merchants and building construction companies purchasing them in Liverpool. These firms had a long history of dealing with the Hamiltons who knew fully their requirements. Members of the Hamilton family oversaw the passage of the logs or lumber at certain crucial points during transport from the forest to the market to ensure that losses were low and that the product reached its destination in top condition.

Once ensconced at Hawkesbury, George showed the business drive for which he was soon to become noted. The mill occupied an excellent site at the head of the Long Sault rapids on the Ottawa and was within easy distance of fine timber along the Rouge and Rideau rivers. The rapids were a major obstacle to timber rafts coming downstream, and many lumbermen were willing to sell to George Hamilton rather than continue the long journey to Quebec. In addition, the land around Hawkesbury was highly suited for farming and was being actively settled. This meant that not only did Hamilton have a market at his door for lumber, but also that he was able to purchase logs directly from settlers clearing land. Much of this trade was carried out on credit and involved a store Hamilton had established to supply his logging contractors.

Thus in the years after 1816 the firm developed into what was for its day a fully integrated lumbering company. In 1818 it was reported that George Hamilton employed eighty men, a large number for the time, and had forty saws in operation.[19] As was often the experience of Canadian lumber companies of the period, the firm's prosperity was destroyed by a downturn in trade in 1821 and the premature death of Robert Hamilton in Liverpool the following year. In the type of partnership arrangement typical of the Canadian forest industry up to about 1900, the death or defaulting of a partner could be devastating. This was the case with the Hamiltons, who were driven into temporary bankruptcy by Robert's demise. The company did not fully recover until 1830 when George Hamilton was able to form a new partnership with a long-time employee, Charles A. Low. This infusion of entrepreneurship and capital provided the basis for further expansion of the business. By 1835 the new partnership was producing 16,639 cubic metres of pine lumber annually, valued at £30,000. Its source of timber was vast privileges on the Gatineau and Rouge rivers as well as private lands in Plantagenet, Clarence, and Cumberland townships in Upper Canada.[20]

All this, however, is by way of setting the scene for the more important role George Hamilton played in developing Canada's timber industry. It was a role that went far beyond the day-to-day problems of managing a large, integrated lumber company. He found that the welfare of his business investments required him to take an intense interest in the public regulation of the timber resource and hence in the political affairs of both Upper and Lower Canada. In this, he was one of the first of Canada's lumber barons to play an influential part in Canadian public life. As an ultra-conservative in his political and social views and an active political partisan, George Hamilton became a quarrelsome and controversial figure in the Valley. He took as his model the British aristocracy. He refused to actually sit in the legislature of either Upper or Lower Canada, but this did not stop him from attempting to influence political events. He served as Judge of the District Court and Chairman of the Quarter-Sessions. As well, Hamilton was the local Lieutenant-Colonel of the militia and a vocal proponent of readiness to counter either American incursions into the country or unrest and subversion by the community of Yankee immigrants living near him at Hawkesbury. From these appointed offices, and through the economic influence he could wield, George Hamilton waged an energetic campaign to enforce his own version of social and economic order on the Ottawa valley. Inevitably, he came to equate good government with measures that promoted the welfare of his own firm, in particular, and the well-being of the timber trade, in general.[21]

For George Hamilton and the other entrepreneurs in British North America, the most troublesome feature of the timber trade at this stage of its development was its illegal nature. Theoretically, any timber taken for sale to the public was to be cut from lands under private ownership. On the timber frontier, far from the eye of public officials, this regulation was ignored. Most of the timber felled and floated down the Ottawa river during this period was cut by trespassing on Crown lands. Some half-hearted attempts were made to enforce the Crown's privilege. Timber known to have been taken by trespass was occasionally seized, but the trade was deemed to be so important to the economic success of the colony that total enforcement was judged unadvisable.

The Hamiltons were not above taking timber by trespass on Crown lands. It was often charged that George Hamilton and his associate, Charles Low, were two of the greatest offenders in such matters and also in violently defending their right to do so. As John Hamilton of Quebec explained before a Select Committee of the British House of Lords in 1820, the standing timber in the forest was "not of much value" and theft, therefore, was not a "matter of much importance".[22] Even if theft was the principal means by which the industry survived, participating in it did not mean acceptance or approval of the situation. George Hamilton became convinced that if access to Crown timber was legalized the trade would become stabilized. Financing would become easier to arrange, and small operators would not be able to commence operations at will contributing to reckless overproduction, breeding violence in the lumber camps of the Ottawa valley, and resulting in an uncontrolled rush to cut the best timber.[23]

After the War of 1812, there was a distinct possibility that the colonial preference would be dropped by the British government. At the same time, the colonial administration of Lower Canada, seated in Quebec City, found itself increasingly alienated from the elected Legislative Assembly. The Assembly expressed its displeasure with the appointed executive by refusing to cooperate in the passage of money bills. To avoid confrontations, the

Executive Council looked around for sources of revenue that were outside of the legislature's prerogative to control. These sources the Executive Council could regulate by Orders in Council and the signature of the Governor-General. As in New Brunswick, the Crown had the prerogative to set regulations for the removal of timber from its lands in this manner and to collect fines from those who disobeyed them. To increase its revenue, the Council moved to fine trespassers cutting its timber. More rafts than ever before were seized after 1824. The seized rafts were sold, usually back to their original owners, and the money received was turned over to the Governor-General.[24]

George Hamilton, because he was a District Court Judge, felt politically vulnerable in this situation. He feared being exposed as a trespasser in his own court. To his credit, he refrained from cutting on Crown lands to the extent that the forestlands he owned outright became "pretty bare having kept on them for the last two or three years to avoid difficulty." This need to "avoid difficulty" confirmed Hamilton in his belief that the timber trade needed more social and economic stability. Certainly his attitude in the "Shiner's War" of the mid–1830s was in marked contrast to the rough and tumble methods he had employed ten to fifteen years earlier. In the Shiner's War one faction of lumbermen tried to use Irish Catholic labourers to violently obtain control of the trade in the whole Ottawa valley. Hamilton condemned the violence and counselled economic and business accord to bring peace and prosperity.[25]

The enforcement of the Crown's privilege after 1824 had a devastating effect on the Ottawa trade. The lumbermen had no idea if their rafts might be seized or under what pretext because its application was capricious. The seizures combined with a depression in the trade, and bankruptcies and forfeitures to creditors resulted. The governments of both Upper and Lower Canada were finally told by the lumbermen that the illegal status of lumbering had to end. Either timberlands had to be alienated to private ownership or licences had to be let for cutting on Crown lands. There was a general agreement among lumbermen that the latter arrangement would be more satisfactory. Canadian lumbermen preferred licences to ownership of land for a number of reasons. Perhaps foremost was the nature of the shield country in which, by this date, the majority operated. It was generally acknowledged that once an area was cut-over there was no reason for the operator to continue to hold control. If he owned the land, he would want to sell it when cutting was finished so as to recoup more on the capital he had invested in the purchase. The shield was clearly unsuitable for farming, which meant that settlers were unlikely to purchase rocky cut-over forest. Properly constituted licences moreover were just as usable as collateral for loans as were deeds of ownership, and they had the added advantage of not requiring capital to obtain them. Hence, the owners of the small lumber companies thought licences would enable them to remain in the trade under much the same conditions as they were already enjoying. Larger firms, like the Hamiltons', were equally reluctant to lay out money for land and thought that the licence system would enable them to control large areas for the payment of a minimum fee. The licence could then be used as collateral to raise capital in Quebec City, Montreal, or Great Britain. Thus, two venerable tenets of Canada's forest industry were born—Crown control of timberlands and their use as collateral for financing private enterprise.[26]

It was the possibility of revenue that finally convinced the colonial administration to legalize the trade. As Lord Dalhousie candidly wrote to Lieutenant Governor Maitland of Upper Canada in 1826, attempts to stop trespassing on Crown lands on the Ottawa had been "without any other effect, than to create expense and embarrass the trade." He was under pressure from many sources to adopt "some course, by which the cutting of timber on Crown Lands may be regulated and turned to advantage since it cannot be prevented." The governments of both colonies appointed Surveyor Generals of Woods and Forests—John Davidson for Lower Canada in 1826 and Peter Robinson for Upper Canada in 1827. They were instructed to survey the forests and reserve areas for the cutting of naval stores. They were also told to define the areas in which each year licences were to be granted, specify the quantity to be cut, establish an upset price for each licence, and dispose of it at public auction. Unfortunately, these instructions immediately fell foul of the facts of Canadian geography and, showing themselves to be unworkable, were largely ignored.[27]

In the Ottawa valley the result of the government's initiative was that an intimate relationship grew up between the Crown Timber Agent and the lumbermen as the agent tried to make the regulations fit the situation in the "bush." In the late 1820s, the regulations were amended by the Executive Council in Quebec. The new rules governing auctions and the prepayment of fees proved just as unworkable as the old, in more than one instance driving the lumbermen to drastically overbid on the berths to reduce competition but often leaving themselves liable to pay dues on the unrealistic figure. George Hamilton became the leading critic of the new system and the prime advocate of a more orderly set of regulations to replace it. He argued that the 1828 rules encouraged men of no means to enter the trade and destroy the market, the quality of the product, and the stability of revenue. His new regulations, adopted by Charles Shireff, the acting Crown Timber Agent at Bytown, called for a lumberman to apply for a limit (usually 7.8 square kilometres), describing its boundaries and the quantity of timber proposed to be cut. The operator would be required to pay duties on the amount of timber proposed to be cut, whether or not it was actually taken; a limit would be auctioned off only when two or more applications were made for it. A quarter of the dues would be required as a down payment at the time of application, and the balance was to be paid in theory when the timber passed Bytown in the spring but in practice at Quebec. Hamilton's system reversed the onus on the lumberman. It was now to his advantage to underestimate his expected cut in order to minimize the payment he made in the fall, a time when all his cash resources were needed to finance the winter's operations. Hamilton postulated that the required down payments would keep speculators and non-professional operators out of the trade. He argued to Lord Aylmer, in December, 1832, that the proposed regulations would prevent the introduction of middlemen into the industry who would speculate on cutting privileges and put the trade into the "Hands of Capitalists" like himself.[28]

With the support of Shireff, these regulations were adopted by Lower Canada in 1832 and followed in a slightly modified form in Upper Canada. Thus George Hamilton had his impact on the first realistic licencing system in Upper and Lower Canada. Not unexpectedly it was favourable to the trade but did not negate in any major way the requirement of the colonial governments for revenue. As well, the regulations were oriented to the large operators whom Hamilton believed would bring economic order to the trade and social control to the Valley. He was to carry these principles forward in his leadership of the larger lumbermen in the battle for the Gatineau Privilege.

The Gatineau river is the largest tributary of the Ottawa below the Chaudière falls, entering the main stream from the north or Quebec side just east of the present city of Hull. By the late 1820s, its excellent stands of white and red pine had become the centre of the timber-making industry of the Valley. To control the access to the forest on the watershed of the Gatineau, the holders of the larger limits formed an association. Its members included Philemon Wright and Sons, C. C. Wright, Peter Aylen, Thomas McGoey, and, of course, Hamilton and Low. Besides grabbing control of the timber available from the watershed, the association expended some £2,000 on improvements to the river to ease the delivery of supplies to their camps and the driving of logs down the river.[29]

Owners of the smaller companies in the Ottawa valley, who were not members of the association, refused to refrain from operating on the Gatineau. Members of the association were enraged to discover that the lumbermen were cutting without licences and with the acknowledged support of the officials and the Bytown Crown Timber Office. George Hamilton attempted to change this situation by using his influence with the officials in the Commissioner of Crown Lands Office in Quebec and by petitioning the Governor General. His efforts were successful in spite of the complaints of the smaller companies. He obtained an Order in Council that gave the members of the association the exclusive right to cut in the watershed of the Gatineau river for two years. The owners of the small logging companies of the area, most of whom lived in Bytown, were livid at the usurpation of their privileges, especially as many of them had already started operations in the watershed. Local citizens joined in the agitation and succeeded, in

January, 1832, in obtaining a Commission of Inquiry into the whole matter of logging privileges granted by Order in Council. The commission of inquiry issued a report supporting the existence of the Gatineau Privilege. Indeed, it had little choice considering that such grants lay completely within the Royal prerogative and that the grantees had actually invested in improvements as they had promised to do. The Privilege was repeatedly renewed until 1843, and Hamilton and Low obtained a similar privilege on the Rouge river. The owners of the large companies had won in the political arena, bringing closer to achievement George Hamilton's goal of control of the trade by the larger firms.

George Hamilton died in 1839 leaving behind him a substantial reputation. A somewhat forgotten part of that reputation was his success in persuading colonial governments to cooperate with larger lumber firms in the control of a lucrative trade. Within the timber trade of Upper and Lower Canada, he was actively disliked by the smaller operators who viewed his efforts at securing government regulation as blatant attempts to shut them out of the industry. There was a great deal of resentment at the dues charged by the Crown and the methods of collection, especially the deposits that had to be made in the fall before operations started. On the other hand, there can be no doubt that the two governments concerned were happy to have found a way to tap the timber trade. In Upper Canada, for example, revenues from timber rose from $10,612 in 1826 to $57,209 a decade later.[30]

Discontent centred on the administration of the timber regulations and their promotion of monopoly conditions. There were other abuses as well, and these were criticised by Lord Durham in his report made after the rebellion of 1837–1838. His assistant, Charles Buller, found the regulations had been a source of much criticism because there had been a reckless and profuse alienation of the resources, especially to friends of officials. These same people were allowed to cut timber without paying dues. Neither were timber thieves, who took up settlement land under false pretenses and stripped it of trees before abandoning it, prosecuted. Finally, there was no adequate inspection or control of licences.[31]

These remained grievances as the two colonies of Upper and Lower Canada were united under a single administration in 1841. The administration of the trade in the Ottawa valley was centred, as before, at Bytown. One of the first actions of the new regime was to attempt to open the industry to a larger number of individuals thus promoting more competition to counter the charges of favouritism. The Timber Office showed its determination to rid the trade of monopolies by revoking the licences on all berths not being operated on. New regulations were announced that required all operators to cut a minimum amount regardless of whether they could sell it. The effect of these regulations was actually to increase the discretionary powers of the agents who took it on themselves to turn a blind eye to certain infractions. The new agent at Bytown, James Stevenson, for instance, tended to renew licences even if no timber was removed as long as annual "improvements" were made to them.[32]

Eventually, the role of lobbyist, played by George Hamilton when he was alive, was taken over by the peppery former leader of the Shiners, Peter Aylen. Never in accord with Hamilton's views, it was Aylen who was to lead a counteroffensive on behalf of the small lumbermen. He sponsored a petition on the behalf of the smaller companies calling for the dismissal of Stevenson for capricious use of his discretionary powers in granting licences and for several other reforms, particularly the public advertisement of the surveyors' descriptions of licenced berths. In August, 1846, the Aylen petition resulted in yet another commission of inquiry that, in turn, led to changes in the regulations as well as instructions to the timber agent at Bytown not to amend his instructions without permission from the government. The amendments had little effect on the trade except in one instance. The licences ceased to be transferrable. This act immediately removed their usefulness as collateral for loans and meant that a lumberman, wishing to close down his business, could not realize the capital he had invested in licences or improvements. Dissatisfaction with the amended regulations increased in the logging year 1846–1847 as it became clear that the British market was severely depressed and that the requirements to take out a minimum cut or forfeit the licence were only exacerbating the situation. The industry, with the support of the Bytown agent, once again descended on the provincial administration.[33]

The basic problem was that the Crown Lands Department, like its counterpart in New Brunswick, had shown itself to be totally preoccupied with increasing its revenues. It had attempted to do this through a strict regulation which was detrimental to the industry. At the same time, officials had attempted to meet Aylen's concerns regarding monopoly in a rudimentary fashion. All the Department had accomplished was to offend all factions, and, feeling political pressure from the lumbermen, the government compromised by keeping the regulations in place but lifting their application for each year through to 1849. This policy relieved the industry of its immediate financial problems while the government retained the option of applying a greater level of taxation when the economy picked up in the future. The relief was a temporary respite from the Executive Council's shortsighted and essentially selfish approach to an industry that more than paid its way. The trade welcomed the concessions, although A. J. Russell, the Assistant Timber Agent at Bytown, feared that such action served only to destroy "confidence in the regulations" on the part of the industry. Finally, in 1849, the Crown's Commissioner of Lands in the Union Government was persuaded to introduce a "Timber Bill" into the Legislative Assembly. For the first time in forty years of fiddling with the industry through regulations, the government was moving away from Orders in Council. This action, like the New Brunswick Legislature's rejection of the Civil List Act in 1837, is a landmark in the development of Canadian forestry policy. It testifies to the growing importance of the timber trade in the economy of the United Provinces as well as to the difficulty of the political problems that had become associated with the industry.[34]

As a result of the efforts of Members of the Legislative Assembly from ridings in which the lumber trade was an important economic factor, a Select Committee was struck by the Assembly. The committee was chaired by the member for Bytown, John Scott. It was charged with inquiring into the "state of the Lumber Trade, the cause of its present depression, the protection of the forests from unnecessary destruction and upon all other matters connected with the lumbering interest of this province." The committee heard from a number of lumbermen from the Ottawa valley as well as from A. J. Russell.[35] The committee's bias toward the trade was clear and untrammelled. Unanimously, it blamed the depression on overproduction stimulated by the high prices prevailing before 1846 as well as the decline in demand in Britain and a regulation that required a minimum amount be cut from each limit under the threat of forfeiture. The witnesses thought that some relief might result from enlightened (i.e., business-oriented) regulations. They stressed that regulations should be flexible so operators could respond to market fluctuations. Yet, they also wanted security of tenure, a guarantee against forfeiture, and protection from trespassers. Owners of the small companies were adamant that the new system prevent the creation of monopolies, and, finally, the government wanted the system to ensure a constant supply of revenue to it.

Two other important matters were raised for the first time by lumbermen appearing before the Committee. Objection was made to protecting smaller trees by higher duties. It was contended that this was inequitable especially if an operator had a berth with many small trees on it. The lumbermen also pointed out that the small trees were often mature; their major growth was finished. If they were not cut, the merchantable timber in them would fall victim to fire and would be wasted. These opinions show that the concept of the unharvested tree being wasted when it dies was already formed at this early date and also hints that forest fires following logging were already commonplace. Unfortunately, there was little testimony to balance against the exploitive ethic espoused by these entrepreneurs.

A second issue introduced before the Select Committee was to grow in intensity throughout North America in the following decades. At this date, all governments in North America had a policy that favored the creation of agriculturally based economies. As a result, it was relatively easy for a prospective settler to obtain preemption rights to a parcel of land regardless of the suitability of the land for farming. In some parts of North America, the alienation of land for any other purpose was impossible and so lumbermen used pseudo-settlers to obtain land for them which they then cut-over and abandoned. In the Canadas, pseudo-settlers obtained the rights to forestlands, cut the timber on them under the pretense of clearing the land for farming, sold the logs, and then abandoned the lot. The problem was that the acquisition of a lot by a settler had legal precedence over the lumberman's licence to the timber on the land. An operator might therefore licence a fine stand of timber and arrive on it in the fall to find a "settler" had already installed himself and was busy felling trees and legally making timber. As long as the settler paid the Crown dues on the timber he sold, there was nothing the licencee could do to obtain redress. As will be discussed in the next chapter, this legal fact of life was to become a major motivator in creating industry support for the early conservation movement.

The report of the Select Committee of 1849 failed to discuss the volatile political problems of control over settlement or the issue of trespass on licenced timber limits. Instead, it restricted itself to reiterating the views of the witnesses about the timber duties and the administration at Bytown. Finally, in a demonstration of the power the Executive Council had over the Legislature, the Committee failed to make public any recommendations. Not surprisingly, therefore, when the Executive Council presented the first Crown Timber Act to the Legislature later in the year, key areas of power continued to remain the privilege of the Crown. These included timber duties, occupation of limits, and the renewal of rights.[36]

In their *History of Crown Timber Regulations in Ontario*, published in 1899, Thomas Southworth and Aubrey White suggested that the 1849 regulations were a giant step forward "to rectify abuses and prevent over-production."[37] This overstates the case. The Crown Timber Act of 1849 clearly shows that the Crown was not ready to surrender some of its powers to the Legislature especially as this would have meant losing control over income. Neither were the Ottawa lumbermen, supported by Russell in the Bytown Timber Office, satisfied with the government's response. It was not until the appointment of a new Commissioner of Crown Lands, John Rolph, that their demands were listened to and included in the regulations by Orders in Council in 1851 and 1852. Then a ground rent system was finally established, and the dues paid for timber were based on the measurement of each stick by cullers at Quebec.

The ground rent system was an essential step toward giving the lumbermen some security of tenure on the land occupied by their berths. It was a move toward the eventual repeal of the settler's right to preemption, and it made the berths more attractive as collateral. Ground rents also helped concentrate limits in fewer hands because only major companies could afford to pay the rent on large areas, and large berths were becoming the norm at the government's timber berth auctions. Thus, in the end, George Hamilton's desire to control overproduction and keep the smaller "non-professional" operators out of the trade was achieved to some considerable degree despite the strong counterattack launched by the smaller operators in the later 1840s.[38]

In spite of Rolph's reforms, the licence system remained primarily a means of revenue collection for the executive branch of government, which largely abandoned its attempt to regulate the business structure of the industry. The regulations, as they stood in 1852, were also a successful compromise between the forest industry and the government of the United Provinces. This success is demonstrated by the fact that these regulations remained essentially the basis for timber management in both Ontario and Quebec until the end of the nineteenth century and were copied by other jurisdictions in Canada after Confederation in 1867.

Besides the evolution of regulations, the British North American timber trade went through another radical change in the years before Confederation. The period from 1846 to 1849 witnessed the end of the system of colonial preference. This resulted in an orientation of the lumber trade in Canada East and Canada West, as well as New Brunswick, toward the American market. At first, colonial timber interests in Britain and North America were extremely alarmed at the phasing out of the protective duties. Though these timber interests fought a rearguard action on the matter, the Peel government in Great Britain had one irrefutable argument on its side. Imports of timber from British North America had actually increased in 1842 in the teeth of a reduced tariff. The free-trade argument was further bolstered by new political support from British shipowners who until 1842 had traditionally supported the preference. Their shipbuilding costs had been reduced by the revisions, and they were convinced that the free entry of wood was now to their advantage. With this defection, the end of the colonial preference was in sight by 1845.

With free trade in forest products about to be announced, the industry in British North America reacted in a very predictable manner. It attempted to export as much timber as possible to Britain while the preference was still in force. Despite warnings that British demand was likely to remain steady, amateur and professional timbermen delivered immense quantities of timber to the ports. At Quebec in 1846, over 49,000 cubic metres of square timber were left unsold. The British market collapsed from the glut of imported timber in 1847, and the problem of disposing of the surpluses in Canada remained until 1849. The result in the hinterland was bankruptcy and hardship so severe that a number of Ottawa valley lumbermen pledged they would combine to limit production, something they had never contemplated before.[39]

The removal of the preference represented an economic setback to the industry, but it did not destroy the trade. What it really represented was a psychological barrier that, once overcome, would leave the industry in a healthier state. For a start, the British market grew rapidly after 1849. Immense amounts of wood were needed for railways and other construction including shipbuilding.[40] Experience was to prove that, while British North America's share of the market fell, the actual tonnage increased until about

1866. New Brunswick, in particular, remained oriented to the British market with mills cutting deals to the custom sizes required by the importers. In all of British North America, the pain of losing a traditional market was rapidly erased in the 1850s by the emergence of a new and potent replacement—the sawn lumber trade with the United States.

Until the late 1820s, the northeastern United States had been able to supply itself with lumber and even export some timber. By the late 1830s these forests were becoming exhausted, and American lumbermen began to cut out rich timber areas of Maine and the new west, such as in the Adirondacks of northern New York State. Naturally the transportation costs of wood from these areas was higher than before, and it put supplies from Canada in a competitive position. In addition, it quickly became clear that these new areas of exploitation were not large enough to supply the rapidly growing urban and industrial markets of New England and New York. With the forests of Michigan and Wisconsin not yet accessible, the lumbermen of New York turned north for both timber supplies and new lumbering opportunities.

As already mentioned, after 1827 lumber was shipped from Canadian sawmills by barge down the Oswego river to the Erie Canal as well as by way of the Richelieu river to the New York City area. This trade continued despite a 30 percent tariff on manufactured products applied by the United States government. At about the same time, Yankees began to speculate in New Brunswick timberlands and to join a host of sawmilling companies which had existed in the province from an early date.[41] In Canada, the industry's preoccupation with square timber and deals as the products of the forest had not prevented the establishment of small sawmills manufacturing lumber for the domestic market. Naturally, when the price was right, these mills were happy to export their products to the south, especially as the Americans did not share the British concern with a multitude of dimension standards. An example of this type of entrepreneur was Samuel Dickson, who emigrated from Ireland to Peterborough, Upper Canada, in 1830 and rented a mill on the Otonabee river in 1839. In the 1840s he produced both square timber and about 1,920 cubic metres of lumber for the local market and for export across the Great Lakes. By 1851, Dickson's production of lumber had grown to well over 2,376 cubic metres.[42]

Another phenomenon of the 1850s was the immigration of American lumberman into the forests of Canada. They brought with them a sawmilling technology well in advance of that then in use in Canada. Early British North American sawmills used British technology developed to saw deals and planks from squared timber. American technology, in contrast, was developed to saw lumber in a variety of sizes from logs without the intermediate step of squaring. At this stage in their development, American mills employed circular saws characterized by a wide kerf, which did not produce as accurate and precise a product as did the best British mills. The benefits they gave to the industry in the competitive North American market were higher speed and lower cost of production. In addition, as their use became common, the cost of the mill dropped. As the North American market changed and started to demand accurately cut, finely finished products, mill machinery manufacturers on this side of the Atlantic borrowed the band saw from Britain and precision-made planing and "matching" machines from Germany. These they developed to suit the requirements of the local industry—low cost, high speed, and operability by relatively low-skilled employees.

James Merrill Currier is an example of this type of American emigrant. He came to the Ottawa valley in 1837 from North Troy, Vermont, to take up employment in his cousin's sawmill at Templeton, Lower Canada. He later became manager of the extensive Bigelow deal mill at Buckingham and McKay and McKinnon's lumber mill in New Edinburgh on the banks of the Rideau river near Bytown. In 1853, Currier went into the lumber business on his own account, establishing a very large enterprise at Bytown. He served on the Bytown Council and, in 1863, was returned to represent the riding in the Legislative Assembly. Elected in 1867 to the first parliament following Confederation, he served as a member of Parliament for Ottawa until 1882 and was a key spokesman for the Ottawa valley lumber interests. Other entrepreneurs were lured north by the promise of the Canadian lumber frontier. General economic interest in Canada was also made manifest by the decision of Boston capitalists to connect their metropolis directly with the Ottawa valley by means of a railway line.[43]

Dickson and Currier were representative of countless individuals who began to sense the possibilities of a trade with the United States. At the same time, there was also an effort to attract American lumbermen to move to British North America. The most noteworthy of these ventures occurred in Bytown. Mayor R. W. Scott and his council, supported by several local businessmen, petitioned the Union government to survey and divide the hydraulic lots at the Chaudière Falls on the Ottawa river and to construct a dam there for mill purposes. New Hampshire, Vermont, and New York lumbermen were already showing interest in the site for the location of new mills. After persuading the government to act, Scott publicly promised these business interests that if they would bid on the lots and locate in Bytown, he would ensure competition would not drive the cost of the lots much above the £50 upset price. The firms of Harris and Bronson, William Goodhue Perley and Gordon B. Pattee, A. H. Baldwin and Company, and Captain Levi Young all jumped at the opportunity to purchase lots at very reasonable prices between 1853 and 1857.[44]

Bytown's "American community" was shortly joined by two very remarkable men. The first was a Canadian, John Rudolphus Booth, a native of the Eastern townships in Lower Canada. He came to the area in 1852 as a millwright to help construct the new mills and stayed to build, through remarkable entrepreneurial effort, one of the largest lumber manufacturing operations in the world. The second was Ezra Butler Eddy, a Vermonter who set up his match factory in Hull, Lower Canada, and eventually established a lumber and pulp and paper empire on the Philemon Wright properties there. Together with the so-called American community in Ottawa, these men and other entrepreneurs, who came to be known as the "lumber kings" of the Ottawa valley, wielded tremendous economic and political power in late-19th-century Canada.[45] They had their counterparts in New Brunswick—the Snowballs, Glasiers, and "Boss" Gibson.

The sawn lumber trade with the United States would have been a lot slower in developing if it had not been for the Reciprocity Treaty that came into effect in February, 1855. The treaty permitted the free movement of agricultural and wood products as raw materials, or in the first stages of manufacture, between the United States and British North America. It was a measure that had been advocated for nearly ten years by members of the forest industry in the colonies. It was felt that if Britain adopted free trade in timber, then so must Canada.

The event symbolizing the final break by Britain from the old colonial system was the repeal of the Navigation Laws. This coincided with its political break from the direct control of the colonies in the granting of responsible government and the signing of the Rebellion Losses Act. These two actions so stunned many in the colonial merchant community that they turned to riot and active support of the movement for annexation by the United States. When calm was restored, British North America decided not to seek political union with the United States but to obtain reciprocal trade relations with it. From their viewpoint, Americans saw advantages in obtaining cheap lumber and other commodities from British North America. As a result, the Reciprocity Treaty remained in place until 1866, the year before Confederation.[46]

The Reciprocity Treaty was the turning point for the forest industry of nascent Canada. A spectacular flood of sawn lumber poured out of British North America following the lifting of the duties. By 1866, 95,000 cubic metres of Canadian lumber had passed through the port of Oswego alone. Development was so rapid and extensive that some lumbermen even came to the conclusion that it was unhealthy and dangerous to both the industry and the forest. The Treaty and the trade that it promoted came at an opportune time for the industry. In the older timber districts of Canada and New Brunswick, lumbermen were finding it increasingly difficult to find the trees capable of producing prime square timber for the overly fastidious British market. Americans, on the other hand, were prepared to accept almost any grade of lumber that the Canadian mills churned out. As the production of squared timber and deals dropped, the sawing of lumber increased. For several decades in the second half of the nineteenth century, Canada's forest industry was actually independent of a single market. As a result, it gained a stability and confidence it has rarely had since.[47]

Perhaps the most important aspect of the new sawn lumber industry was the ease with which it fitted over the basic framework of the earlier square timber trade. This does not mean that square timber operators switched en masse to sawmilling. In reality, few made the transition to sawlogs; most continued to export square timber. In the Bytown area, for instance, only the Gilmours re-tooled completely for the new trade. They built a new, large mill and began to re-cut their square timber limits on the Gatineau river. The Boyd family, located on the Trent river system, did the same thing. Later, James Skead, a square timber man on the Ottawa, tried a similar transition only to fall prey to the 1873 depression. Many of the square timber men, who already had mills, expanded this side of their operation. It is also true that some of the sawn lumber operators, such as J. R. Booth, cut square timber for the British market. The normal trend, however, was for the new sawmill enterprises to move in alongside existing square timber operations. Often, limits already cut for square timber were re-cut for saw-logs; those of Peter Aylen and John Egan in Algonquin Park are particularly well-known examples of this activity.[48]

The influx of American lumbermen into Canada at this time reveals another interesting phenomenon. Not only was the system of licences and berths adopted from the square timber trade, but the newcomers also adapted to it with ease. The Yankee operators worried at first about the security of their tenure, but they quickly recognized the advantages of not having to put capital into lands that would be difficult to sell once they were cut over. The new lumbermen were soon lobbying the government for more and larger limits to secure their supply of timber and enable them to borrow more capital. The traditional yearly cycle of the woods operations was little disturbed by the influx of sawmills and the growth of trade with the United States. The major change was in the small communities, scattered across the country, where the new mills were located. These towns acquired an industrial aspect from the mill, piling grounds, a transportation network, and the now permanent homes of the sawyers, millwrights, and other workers needed to run the plant. In eastern Canada, the mills worked feverishly through the summer, fall, and early winter to produce the roughly sawn lumber for shipment, usually by barge or ship, to American entry ports along the border or Atlantic seaboard. Along the Great Lakes, the lumber went from these ports to the companies' refinishing mills and wholesale yards located in towns like Albany, New York, and Burlington, Vermont. The new entrepreneurs were soon experimenting in joint ventures such as steamboat and river improvement companies as well as railway lines to ease their transportation problems. In short, the sawn lumbermen gave the Canadian forest industry a new corporate organization, based on a dedication to developing and producing for expanding international markets, which continues to this day.

By 1866, a close relationship had developed between the forest industries of British North America and the governments of the individual colonies.

The Reciprocity period had been a bonanza for industry and government alike; as production soared so had the income to the public treasuries. In 1854 and 1863, legislative committees in the Province of Canada had the opportunity to change the system. This they declined to do despite the urging of influential public figures, such as Alexander Tilloch Galt, and the railway companies to copy the United States' policy of cash sales of timberland. Each time, the lumber community successfully defended the licence system. As had been earlier argued, sales mitigated against the smaller operators, who, the lumber barons contended, encouraged speculation. The lumbermen also pointed out that removal of the system would threaten government control and the constant flow of revenue to the administration.[49] These arguments were posed to protect, on behalf of large, relatively well-capitalized companies, a system that regulated access to a valuable natural resource. This relationship was developed even further after Confederation when the income from the forest industries became a major part of provincial revenues. Whenever they needed money for public improvements, such as just before an election, provincial administrations threw a few prime limits onto the market. At such timber auctions, it was almost guaranteed that bonuses would be bid up to fabulous amounts above the upset price particularly when first-class pine timber became scarce toward the end of the century. In short, what existed by 1870 was a close political-economic alliance between the lumbermen and politicians at both the provincial and federal levels in Canada.

Regardless of the success of this system, there were signs that all was not well in forestry. The very fact that a large industry had developed in the new Dominion meant that sizable investments had been made by the business community. For example, Perley and Pattee in Ottawa had mill facilities valued at $450,000 and employed 250 men. Perley and Pattee were only one of five or six companies in the area with similar holdings, and some of them were considerably larger.[50] With this amount of capital involved, businessmen were beginning to demand more security of tenure and protection for their basic collateral, the timberlands. Lumbermen did not wish any longer to be considered temporary tenants, always just one step ahead of the farmers. Though often characterized as "rapacious buccaneers", lumbermen could and did recognize the rapidly declining quality of the logs cut from the forest. The calls for government action concentrated on two issues: the need to remove timberlands from settlement and the need to establish some means of forest protection. It was, however, not only the self-interested concerns of lumbermen that emerged in the decades after Confederation; others had become alarmed at the devastation of the forest that followed the over-cutting stimulated by the Reciprocity Treaty. In May, 1862, John Langton, a native of the heavily lumbered Trent watershed in Ontario who was to become the first Auditor General of Canada, deplored this destruction in a paper read before the influential Literary Society of Quebec.[51] The paper proposed some form of forest reservation policy, a move by industry away from the wasteful square timber trade, and a study of tree growth.

Although the free trade in sawn timber ceased in 1866, there was only a pause in exports before they climbed to new record levels. Canadian lumbermen found that it was still profitable to ship lumber south over the border. It became increasingly obvious that the accessible forest in Canada was receding at an alarming rate. The condition was so serious that it led a usually unconcerned Prime Minister John A. Macdonald to muse in 1871 that

The sight of immense masses of timber passing my windows every morning suggests to my mind the absolute necessity for looking into the future of this great trade. We are recklessly destroying the timber of Canada and there is scarcely a possibility of replacing it.[52]

Perhaps Macdonald was influenced by his colleague from Kingston, Alexander Campbell, who served as the last Commissioner of Crown Lands under the Union constitution. Campbell expressed the first definite conservationist attitude in Canadian public policy. He slowed the sale of timber limits and moved to find acceptable ways to prevent mills from clogging the rivers and streams with their waste and picked up earlier initiatives to investigate ways of preventing forest fires. In the case of mill waste, the most that could be done was to install machines that reduced the waste to a fine sawdust. In his annual report of 1865, Campbell advocated the cropping of timber on a rotation basis as was done in Europe and Scandinavia.[53] All these initiatives, unfortunately, were lost in the debates and negotiations leading to Confederation in 1867. Almost immediately thereafter, the exceptionally severe worldwide depression resulting from the American stock crash of 1873 devastated Canada's lumber industry postponing these harbingers of change for a decade. It was not until the 1880s that the exploitive ethic was to be seriously challenged, and with this challenge came the birth of the forest conservation movement.

CHAPTER 2

The Beginnings of a Movement: The Montreal Congress and Its Aftermath, 1880–1896

The rise of the North American conservation movement and of forestry as an art, a science, and a political movement dates from the 1860s and the work of a Vermont naturalist. George Marsh's widely read and discussed work, *Man and Nature*, was one of a number of books that led North Americans to rethink their conception of society and its relationship with the natural environment. When John Astin Warder founded the American Forestry Association in 1875, the movement coalesced into a group of diverse correspondents scattered across North America. From its founding, the American Forestry Association had a small Canadian membership. The Canadians benefitted greatly from the suggestions and support they received from their correspondents in the United States. This led to what Paul Pross has termed a "ferment of ideas" in eastern Canada, which brought the issue of forest conservation to the notice of the public and the government. In Canada, the proponents of conservation came from three distinct sections of society, each with a unique approach to the concept.[1]

From Canada's fledgling scientific community, arborculturists and entomologists joined with members of the scientific farming movements to form organizations such as the Ontario Fruit Growers Association. From its foundation the Association was oriented toward practical and efficient resource management. Most of the members of this Association lived and worked in central and southwestern Ontario and were interested in improving the agrarian environment which had suffered greatly by deforestation through the settlement process.

A second group comprised a number of lumbermen from eastern Ontario and Quebec who were concerned that the quality and quantity of the trees they were felling were declining yearly. Was the limit of the exploitable forest being reached? Should the trees, and the forest, be treated as if they were inexhaustable, or was there a better way? Was there a method of management that would not require operators to be forever moving farther and farther into the hinterland?

A third group, environmental preservationists, ably represented in the United States by John Muir and his followers, was present in Canada in small numbers. Coming mainly from the country's educated, largely urban elite, they became important later after their number had increased. Eventually representing a broad cross-section of Canada's new, reasonably affluent middle class, they were to provide the movement with a popular base. This group was active in supporting the establishment of Algonquin National Park by the Ontario government in 1893. As in the United States, Canada's preservationists were initially attracted by the idea of resource conservation but were eventually repelled by the practical, utilitarian nature of the forest conservation movement and consequently played only a small role in its organization and promotion.[2] For this reason, early leadership for the conservation movement in Canada was provided by the scientific farmers and the lumbermen. From these groups came influential men who pushed for the introduction of some elementary improvements in the way the forest resource was treated in Canada. Eventually they were successful in persuading the federal and provincial governments to take some rudimentary steps toward a more responsible and provident forest policy. In doing so, they left their mark not only on Canada but also on the whole North American conservation movement.

In Canada the concept of forest conservation had to be properly publicized in order to have much impact on public policy and general public opinion. The first publicity the movement received came from the Dominion and provincial government departments responsible for agricultural resources. In their annual reports these departments provided space which played educational and information-distribution roles in the decades before World War I. The reports had a noncritical, positive tone that limited their usefulness to any reform-minded movement. No government, no matter how sympathetic to the aims of the conservation movement, was going to publish critical material that might scare away potential settlers or upset the voting public. Through the years, this negative aspect of government assistance was experienced by many of the proponents of conservation. The movement therefore began to publish its own journals as well as use the public and trade press to its own advantage.

While some government departments regarded the resources for which they were responsible from a strictly exploitive viewpoint, others were more enlightened. In the Province of Ontario, it was the department responsible for agriculture and the arts that supported the work of the Fruit Growers Association and published the reports of its annual meeting. Thus it was this department that first spread the ideas of the movement and became involved in forest conservation. Following this tradition, Ontario's Depart-

ment of Agriculture and Arts hired the first of a number of official propa-
gandists who advocated scientific forest management of woodlands.[3]

By no means were the members of the Ontario Fruit Growers Association
all orchard owners; many were farmers whose main interest was the general
advance of agriculture. In the 1870s a lack of extension services, chemical
pesticides, fungicides, and fertilizers restricted the ability of farmers and
fruit growers alike to react to pathogens and other difficulties encountered
in the growing of crops. The Association first took on the task of collecting
and disseminating information about the pests commonly found on Ontario
farms. The approach of the scientists who prepared information for the
Association was to look for ways to manipulate the environment of the crops
and thus control pests by natural means. Publication of the results of their
studies allowed members of the Association, and the public having access
to the reports, to identify and tackle the problems they faced.

It is not surprising that the Fruit Growers quickly became interested in
all aspects of "farming". The protection of their fields from wind damage
or water erosion and the realization that many beneficial animals lived in
wooded areas led to an interest in farm woodlots. From there it was but a
short step to advocating the reforestation, by planting, of farms abandoned
because the land was unsuitable for agriculture. They viewed with alarm
the wastes of sand dunes left after the forest had been removed in such
southwestern Ontario counties as Norfolk and Simcoe. The Fruit Growers
saw the proper maintenance of woodlots in economic as well as environmental
terms. The Association's reports carried articles discussing how a woodlot
could be managed to yield income as well as provide any fuelwood and
fencing material required by its owner. Much to the concern of these early
environmentalists, many farmers were selling the woodlots for cash payments
that were well below the real value of the logs.[4] From an interest in farm
woodlots and their efficient exploitation, it was only a short step for the
members of the Fruit Growers Association to become interested in the fate
of Canada's forests. This concern resulted in an alliance in the late 1870s
with several of the lumbermen of Quebec and the Ottawa valley. This
alliance was tremendously important to the future of forestry in Canada, and
without it, the conservation movement would have had very little impact on
public opinion or policy.

The lumbermen, who found a common cause with the Fruit Growers,
were dynamic and powerful men. They represented an industry that, by
this date, had been recognized by government as essential to the country's
prosperity. While some modern writers have characterized them as "rapacious
buccaneers" who had already creamed off the best timber and now wished
to play "forester among the stumps", they genuinely sought a more stable
basis for the investments they had made. Viewed by the political ideology
of the time as the instruments by which land was stripped of trees for
settlement purposes, they now saw themselves as permanent features on

the country's economic landscape. These men were in the process of forming a powerful lobby to plead for studies of the limits of economic agriculture and the creation of a permanent forest dedicated solely to lumber production.[5]

On the lumbermen's side of the conservation movement were a father and son, James and William Little. James Little had gotten his start in the trade by exploiting the pine stands along the Grand river in southwestern Ontario. He exported quantities of lumber cut from the forests of the watershed during the early years of the Reciprocity Treaty. By 1860 he had moved on to Georgian Bay where untouched stands of pine had been discovered. These stands were soon thinned by Little and other lumbermen, and Little, by now in his late sixties, once again had to move on. In 1873, at the age of seventy, he was in Montreal with his oldest son, William, overseeing the family's new limits and timber brokerage business, concentrated in the St. Maurice district of Quebec. This lifetime experience of movement to new forests and their subsequent abandonment once cut-over had a profound effect on James Little. At first, he blamed the Reciprocity Treaty for stimulating overproduction, but further thought led him to see the problem in a wider context. His correspondence with conservationists in the United States, who were members of Dr. Warder's American Forestry Association, helped to clarify his thinking.[6]

In 1872 and 1876, James Little published the first call from industry for forest conservation in Canada. The two pamphlets warned that the timber resources of Canada and the United States were being destroyed by fire and over-cutting. He called for strict regulations, to be enforced by government, requiring that the forest be managed on a sustained yield basis. His greatest worry was that, once the forest of the eastern states had been depleted, the United States would turn to Canada for its supply of logs. Based on his own experience, he forecast that if this happened the forests of Ontario and Quebec would be quickly devastated. As a start to forest management, Little wanted to see forest fires controlled, minimum cutting diameters established, and lands classified to keep settlers out of nonagricultural but forested areas. With controls like these, he thought the forests would be safe from over-cutting even if a large growth in demand occurred.[7]

The pamphlets published by James Little received a mixed reception. His ideas had a sympathetic hearing from lumbermen, even though many disagreed with his hypothesis that the United States would become totally dependent on Canada for its lumber requirements. His views were widely published in the press of the day, but unfortunately many of the public were lured into a false sense of security by the widely held belief that Canada's forests stretched on and on forever. Fortunately, the active members in the Ontario Fruit Growers Association recognized James Little as a kindred spirit. They too had observed the decimation of the forests that had once grown on the uplands bordering, to the north, the farmlands of central Ontario and on the sandy areas of the southwestern portion of the province.

Thus, by 1880, there was a group of informed people in Ontario and Quebec who were interested in the welfare of the nation's forests. Within the nascent conservation movement, James Little was the most publicly prominent man on the strength of the pamphlets he had published and distributed. The leaders of the Fruit Growers Association, however, had more political influence because of their relationship with the Ontario Department of Agriculture and the Arts and because they represented a discernible political interest. These people, particularly James Little, shared their opinions with the members of the American Forestry Association; together, they made up a network of correspondents numbering fewer than a hundred people. It therefore came as something of a surprise to both American and Canadian members of the American Forestry Association when, in late 1881, they received invitations from Cincinnati, Ohio, to take part in the formation of the American Forestry Congress by attending its inaugural meeting in April, 1882.[8]

The reasons for the sudden creation of the American Forestry Congress have never become completely clear. According to a young forester, Bernhard Fernow, who had recently moved to the United States, it was a purely municipal affair. Fernow, who was later to become the first professional forester to be hired by the United States government and the first Dean of the University of Toronto's School of Forestry, was convinced that local politicians planned to use the occasion to enhance their reputations within the city, perhaps by honouring a visiting German forester, Richard von Steuben. The organizers were sincere in their interest in the issue, however, and were probably pleasantly surprised at the broad general interest engendered by their meeting and at the resulting events.

In Canada, the American Forestry Congress attracted the immediate attention of the Fruit Growers, and, at their annual meeting in December 1881, they decided to ask the provincial government of Ontario to support a delegation to the gathering. This request was granted, and James Gills, P. C. Dempsey, and Thomas Beall, all farmers or orchardmen, joined Professor William Saunders, an entomologist at the University of Toronto's Ontario Agricultural College at Guelph, to form a delegation led by the Secretary of the Fruit Growers Association, D. W. Beadle. In Cincinnati, Ohio, they met three men who had travelled from Montreal at their own expense: James and William Little and A. T. Drummond, a Montreal financier, lawyer, and author of articles about Canadian forests and forestry. The Quebec men joined the Ontario delegation and named Beadle as their official spokesman, although James Little, because of his reputation as a lumberman advocating forest conservation, fulfilled the organizers' invitation to give the keynote address to the meeting.

The opening session of the Congress was not auspicious: only 250 people attended, scattering themselves amongst the seats for 2,000 in Cincinnati's Music Hall, which had been hired for the occasion. The meeting picked up momentum, however, with its first public session when the hall was filled to overflowing and the audience was divided into sections according to the topics of the papers being read. The importance of the Canadian group was recognized when its members were given specific roles to play in the conference proceedings. James Little and D. W. Beadle joined the committee discussing the future of the Congress. Because this was the first time that so many of the correspondents had met, this committee was discussing, by implication, the future of the forest conservation movement in North America.[9]

Two major problems faced this committee. The first was how to maintain and build on the momentum given to the movement by the meeting, and the second was how to ensure a united effort. Either the Congress should become a part of Warder's American Forestry Association, which still had fewer than one hundred members, or Warder should surrender leadership to the new body. This problem was more than the committee could resolve, so it moved on to name the time and place of the next meeting of the Congress. Beadle proposed that, instead of waiting a full year, they should take advantage of the upcoming concurrent meetings of the American Association for the Advancement of Science and the Society for the Promotion of Agricultural Science scheduled for August, 1882, in Montreal. The committee agreed, and Beadle issued an invitation to the members of the Congress on behalf of the Canadian delegation. This invitation was enthusiastically accepted by those attending the Congress, and thus the initiative for action in the young movement passed to Canada.[10]

Because the next meeting of the Congress was to be held in Montreal, the hometown of the Little family, it was agreed that William Little would organize the meeting. On his return home, William started to work on the program and to promote the August meeting. As Fernow had noted, the Cincinnati gathering had included botanists, entomologists, and professors of agricultural science, but only a few woodlot owners or lumbermen.[11] The Littles decided that the Montreal meeting had to attract significant numbers of men from the leadership of the forest industries for it to be a success and gain political momentum for the movement in Canada.

It soon became apparent that this task was to be easier than William or James Little had expected. Many Quebec lumbermen were in the mood to organize and lobby. Their logging teams were reaching the northern limits of the pine along the shores of the headwater lakes of the Ottawa river. They knew their forests contained proportionally more spruce than did the forests of Ontario, and this was making it increasingly difficult for them to obtain the timber they required. A complicating factor was that the lumbermen found themselves coming into competititon for forest lands with the powerful colonization movement backed by the Roman Catholic clergy: colons and lumbermen were vying for the remaining stands of pine. Another major source of anxiety for the holders of limits in Quebec arose from their lease contracts. Those in force in 1868 had been granted for twenty or twenty-one years, renewable annually, with the timber dues fixed for the lease period.[12] Such licences covered the great majority of accessible timberland. The lumbermen naturally supported the continuation of this policy since it gave considerable security of tenure. The provincial government was oblivious to the advantages such a system could have in timber management, and, by the 1880s, was worried that the fixed timber dues prevented it from quickly increasing government revenue from timber duties. It wished to eliminate long-term fixed licences in favour of a system that would enable it to raise rates immediately as the value of timber increased. In the forefront of the battle on the lumbermen's side was the Quebec Limitholders' Association. It was not long before this organization realized that the meeting of the American Forestry Congress was a means by which it could meet with the public and present its own point of view on land classification and the proper tenure for forest management.[13]

The Quebec Limitholders' Association was only partially successful in its attempt to dominate the proceedings of the American Forestry Congress because of the integrity of the Littles and their ability to see the issues in the widest context. The Littles guided the meeting into a discussion of a more general programme of forest conservation rather than into the particular interests of the lumbermen while ensuring the proceedings maintained a practical bent.

The Littles were immeasurably assisted in their preparations when they were joined by Henri Gustave Joly, the Seigneur of Lotbinière, a gentleman who quickly became a leader of the movement. Elected to the Legislature of Canada some six years before Confederation, Joly had taken part in all the major debates of the intervening years. Consistent with his Protestant religion and European education, he was a Liberal in political affiliation and personal philosophy. He thus complemented the Littles' Tory inclinations and added a political balance to the Congress. Joly was also a major landowner and a very wealthy man—factors which gave him a considerable degree of independence in thought and action. Joly had wide interests. In the 1880s he was President or Vice President of six societies concerned with agriculture, forestry, and the advancement of industry, as well as the Royal Humane Society of British North America. He was president of a railway company; he had turned down an offer to become a federal Minister of Agriculture in the administration of Alexander MacKenzie (1873–1878); and briefly he had been the Premier of his province and was now the leader of the Opposition. Later in his career, he would join Sir Wilfred Laurier's cabinet, would be granted a knighthood, and would become Lieutenant Governor of British Columbia. More germane to the meetings were perhaps Joly's experimentations with European forestry techniques on his own lands and, in 1875, his publishing of the first forest survey of the Dominion, which had been undertaken as a project funded by the federal government. In this publication, he had called for more conservative use of the forest resource. With his moderate liberal stance and his modern views on the utilization of natural resources, he was a favourite of many in Quebec's anglophone minority. It would have been difficult for William Little to have found a more experienced, tactful, and dignified personage to propose as chairman for the upcoming congress.[14]

The Quebec Limitholders' Association promoted the meeting of the Congress within its membership and arranged for its most influential members to present their views to the public. Included among these were the Honourable George Bryson Sr., Franklin H. Bronson, William C. Edwards, John R. Booth, and Peter White, M.P. All these men were prominent in the forest industry of the Ottawa valley. White, who was from Pembroke, Ontario, sat as the Tory member for the federal riding of Renfrew North. His major political role in the House was as the unofficial spokesman of the lumber industry. Enjoying the confidence of the Ottawa valley lumbermen, White continued to play the part of spokesman for them at the meeting of the Congress. In this role, he was supported by George Bryson, the patriarch of a family deeply involved in a lumber business based in the Pontiac district on the opposite side of the Ottawa river from Pembroke.[15] The Quebec lumbermen were most concerned that the Congress have something to say about the problem of settlers encroaching on forest land and causing forest fires. The problem, primarily a local issue, could be approached only indirectly at a meeting that was to be attended by a wide variety of participants from all over North America. As events were to show, Joly adroitly handled this problem and, by doing so, avoided alienating the representatives of the forest industry.

With Joly available to handle the delicate negotiations with the lumber interests, William Little was free to tackle the difficult issue of organization. By now, the membership of the American Forestry Congress was larger than that of the Forestry Association, and it gave the appearance of being a continued success. The organizers of the Congress were all concerned that the efforts of the forest conservation movement not be divided between two organizations that might compete for attention. From their point of view, it was logical that Warder's American Forestry Association dissolve itself by joining the Congress. They hoped to achieve this objective by persuading Dr. Warder to agree to the merger. With this aim in view, a meeting was held with Warder when he arrived in Montreal the day before the Congress opened. Warder met B. E. Fernow, F. B. Hough, Chief of the Division of Forestry in the United States Department of Agriculture, and William and James Little. After much persuasion, Warder acquiesced to the arguments of Fernow and James Little and agreed that his association would merge with the Congress before the meeting opened.[16]

With this auspicious beginning, the Congress convened on 21 August 1882 in the office area of the Littles' company, which had been especially renovated and renamed "Forestry Hall" for the occasion. The opening session was dedicated to business, and its main purpose was to organize several committees that would make reports to the final session. The room was crowded. In addition to a great many well-known people from the Quebec and Ottawa valley lumber trade, there was an expanded official delegation from the Ontario Fruit Growers Association. The government of Quebec was officially represented by G. B. Cooper, C. E. Bell, Eugene Renault, and, most notably, Minister of Crown Lands Dr. W. W. Lynch, accompanied by two major officials from his department, E. E. Taché and A. J. Russell. Federal members of Parliament and members of the provincial legislature also attended; whatever empty spaces remained in the Hall were filled by Canadian and American members of the two organizations.[17]

Henri Joly was named chairman of the proceedings, and the first major item of business discussed was the damage done to the forests by fire. Because this was the topic dearest to the hearts of the lumbermen in the room, Little and Joly expected it to be the one most difficult to handle in the context of an international gathering. The problem was how to allow the men most directly involved in the issue to have their say without their monopolizing the proceedings. Fortuitously, a committee struck at the Cincinnati meeting to study the problem of forest fires had failed to present a report, and this enabled Joly to make a motion from the chair that a new committee be formed to study the issue. This committee would be instructed to complete its work in time to present recommendations to the final business session of the meeting. If accepted, these recommendations were then to be presented as a petition to all the levels of government concerned. Those nominated to the committee to represent Canada included Joly, Peter White, George Bryson, Sr., William Little, and J. K. Ward, a Montreal-based lumberman. These men had direct economic and political interests in the topics to be discussed by the committee: settler encroachments and the problems of forest fires. Representing the American members were Dr. F. B. Hough, Professor C. S. Sargeant, Dr. C. Mohr, E. D. Becker, and B. E. Fernow—a much more academically oriented group that would end up following the lead of the Canadians.[18]

Other committees struck at the opening session gave those in attendance the feeling that the movement was off to a dynamic start. There was so much business to attend to that the third and final business session was postponed half a day. At this meeting, the first report presented was the much-awaited recommendations from the forest fire committee. The chairman of the committee, George Bryson, recommended that governments, on behalf of the public represented by the Congress, be urged to enact effective

regulations to combat forest fires. Specifically, the proposals were that reserves of forestland unfit for agriculture be established, that brush burning
be prohibited in certain months of the year when the danger of wildfire was
high, and that some kind of police force be created to enforce regulations
and to organize fire suppression activities when necessary. The cost of the
policing force was to be borne by a tax on the industry. These recommendations, which were accepted unanimously by the assembled members, were
to be of tremendous importance in the future. Not only were they to form
the basis of legislation passed by several governments in Canada, but they
also resulted in the movement's gaining the support of industry. The recommendations were exactly what the Quebec Lumbermen's Association
wanted from the Congress and, by not alienating this group, the Littles and
Joly secured the support of many influential men for the cause of forest
conservation.[19]

At the conclusion of the Congress, James Little was appropriately singled
out for praise by the assembly. He was given the honorific of "Nestor in
American Forests", an allusion to the advisory role played by the Greek
chieftain Nestor during the siege of Troy, as recorded by Homer in *The Iliad*.
The Montreal press was quick to label the meeting of the Congress a success
even though they looked at it from a narrow viewpoint as just one of the
"Three Great Congresses" that had brought large numbers of people to the
city. Bernhard Fernow, however, was less enthusiastic in his analysis of the
gathering. He had been impressed with the Canadians he had met and had
become friends with Henri Joly, a man whom he had come to admire, but
Fernow considered that only a few of the papers he had listened to took a
"scientific" approach to forestry. Also, there was too much interest in tree
planting and arboriculture for his taste and not enough discussion about
commercial forest management. These were complaints he was to voice
frequently about future Canadian forestry meetings.[20]

From a Canadian perspective, the events of the following years were to
show that the meeting had been very successful. For a start, the Congress
now had a membership of 184, 103 of whom were Canadians. A third of the
Canadian members were prominent men in the lumber trade of Ontario and
Quebec. At this stage in its development, the American Forestry Congress
was very much a Canadian affair and appears to have had something meaningful to say to industry. The two most important positions on the executive
council of the Congress were firmly in the hands of Canadians committed
to the cause, Henri Joly and William Little. This represented a Canadian
"coup" of sorts. It is a pity that this situation did not last longer than to the
next meeting of the Congress. In 1883, Joly, Little, and a handful of Canadians attended the annual meeting held that year in Minneapolis, Minnesota. At this meeting, the Congress returned to being a totally "American"
body, which eventually evolved into the present-day American Forestry
Association. This turn of events indicates that the Montreal Congress was

designed to serve uniquely Canadian political ends by its organizers. It was an effort by the small forest conservation movement in Canada to demonstrate that it could attract the interest of both the public and the forest industry. The Congress pushed the movement from an almost exclusive focus on the environmental issues of the effect of forests on climate and the role of deforestation in the creation of desert wastes to one of practical business concerns of forest fire protection, land classification, and forest reserves. In retrospect, the view of the Quebec and Ottawa valley lumbermen that, if adequate fire protection were given to the forest, regeneration would occur naturally seems somewhat naive. It would have been much more fruitful for Canadian forestry if the environmentalists and the lumber interests could have found more common ground. Only one paper at the Congress discussed how rudimentary silviculture could be used to improve forest production and growth, and so, from another aspect, certainly foresters like Fernow found little to support at the proceedings. Nevertheless, an enduring partnershhip had been forged—one that is tremendously important to the understanding of public forestry policies in Canada for, as would become obvious over the next decades, it was only when the forest industry, or a substantial part of it, was willing to support conservation measures that progress was made. The alliance between the more traditional environmentalist or preservationist wing and the industry, formed in Montreal, was shaky at best, but it did continue in such mutually advantageous fields as watershed conservation and, until World War I, the environmentalists seemed largely content to let industry's concern over fire protection and forest reservation become the political rallying cry of the movement. These, in turn, fitted easily into the wider interest in resource planning and efficiency in utilization which occupied the North American conservation movement as a public issue after 1900. At first, however, Little and Joly sought more limited gains from the impetus created by the Montreal Congress. From this time on, even though the number varied, there would always be a section of the forest industry in Canada that was helpful and sympathetic to the cause. This support was to be vital to conservation in Canada because it helped ensure its survival in the tough times that lay ahead while ensuring the movement remained relevant to the problems faced by the industry.

From the point of view of its supporters, the immediate success or failure of the Montreal meeting was gauged by governments' responses to the resolutions of the forest fire committee. Little and Joly had been given an initiative, and the question waiting to be answered was what they would do with it. Both were impressive men. Both had come out of the meeting with their reputations enhanced. As Bernhard Fernow noted, he would be surprised if "our Canadian friends do not in a short time eclipse their cousins over the line in this field of political economy". The young German was right when he noted that conservation movement had finally moved into the battleground of politics, government administration, and practical economics.[21]

Once the meeting of the American Forestry Congress was over, William Little added the duties of corresponding secretary for the organization to his already heavy workload as a businessman. The Canadian members of the forest fire committee wanted him to begin lobbying for the adoption of their resolution by writing to the Dominion and provincial administrations of Canada. Quebec was the first to react to the policy proposals circulated by Little. This is not surprising considering that the Congress had met in Montreal and that it had been well attended by many politically important people from that province. In the legislative session of 1883, the province's Conservative government enacted laws that provided for the hiring of forest rangers to patrol timber limits under the supervision of a special superintendent. This system was entirely paid for by the limitholders concerned. More important, provincial Commissioner of Crown Lands Dr. W. W. Lynch, who had attended the meeting, was persuaded to establish the nation's first forest reserve. This reserve covered a large area east of the Ottawa river that was drained by many of the Ottawa's tributaries. This land was set aside solely for timber production; settlers were not allowed, in the future, to locate lots within its boundaries. Both of these measures were directly related to the resolutions generated by the Congress's forest fire committee.[22]

The lumbermen of Quebec expressed delight with these new government initiatives, attributing them to the direct influence of the Congress. From their point of view, the forest reserve effectively separated the settlers from the loggers. But the setting up of the reserve had a dire political consequence that was not foreseen by those who advocated it and welcomed its establishment. The creation of the reserve and the effective withdrawal of land from settlement incensed the supporters of the colonization movement. In their eyes, the reserve prevented their access to a large area of land suitable for settlement. In actual fact, settlement of such areas was ill-advised as most of the area was within the Canadian Shield. Politically, Lynch's action drew lines of division between the government and one wing of its traditional support, the Ultramontanists or "Castor" group whose members tended to combine French Canadian nationalism with religious conservatism. The Ultramontanists considered the welfare of the colons to be more important than that of the dues-paying, but largely English speaking, lumbermen. This division combined with other political events inside and outside of the province and became a factor in the ouster of the provincial Tories from power. One of the symbolic and ideological acts of the Parti National administration that replaced the Tories in 1886 was the cancellation of the forest reserve.[23]

The Ontario government was slower to act than its counterpart in Quebec City, but the measures it enacted were more enduring. The government's first response to the resolution of the Congress was made in 1883 when it hired a forestry publicist, a former journalist, Robert W. Phipps. Phipps filled a newly created position in the bureaucracy: Clerk of Forestry in the Department of Agriculture and the Arts. By implication this recognized the influence and importance of the Fruit Growers Association. The action also showed that the government of Ontario interpreted "forestry" as a term related to the more traditional idea of woodlot management and the reforestation of abandoned farm lands. This interpretation is confirmed by the fact that the Clerk had nothing to do with the office responsible for the disposal of timber limits and the collection of timber dues, which remained in the domain of the Commissioner of Crown Lands.[24] Phipps, conscious that he was the Clerk of Forestry in the Department of Agriculture and the Arts, issued an extensive series of publications discussing, among other things, the settlement and subsequent abandonment of lands unfit for farming and their suitability for reforestation. With reference to the management of the province's extensive forests, conservationists in Ontario would have to wait some years before their government took its first tentative steps in that direction. Phipps was to prove to be the first in a long line of civil servants who laboured under the government's conception that forestry was part and parcel of farm management.

Meaningful action by the Ontario government on the Congress's recommendations had to wait three years. Ontario Commissioner of Crown Lands Timothy Pardee had promised in his report of 1882 that he would give sympathetic consideration to the recommendations of the Congress on their receipt. In spite of this, the reaction of the Liberal government of the province when it heard from William Little was to order that they be studied further. Pardee accomplished this by giving them to a new employee in the Woods and Forests Branch of his department, Aubrey White. White's previous experience as a woods ranger and Crown Land Agent in the Bracebridge area of the province did not seem to speed up his deliberations materially. The new clerk took his time, and it was not until March, 1885, that he presented his superior with a long memorandum.[25] In spite of this delay, White's proposals went no further than the original recommendations he had received thirty months previously. Essentially, he suggested that rangers be appointed to patrol the districts at risk during the fire season. The rangers would organize fire-fighting efforts and educate the public to the risks of being careless with fire while in the forests. The cost of the program was to be shared between the government and all limitholders. White's report was accepted, the companies were polled to nominate candidates for the positions, and thirty-seven men were hired during the summer of 1885. This legislation served as the basis of fire protection in Ontario for many years.[26]

The Dominion government took the smallest step in the wake of the Montreal Congress. In 1882, Canada had stretched "from sea to sea" for some eleven years. The federal government controlled the land and natural resources in the North-West Territories, including Manitoba and the future provinces of Saskatchewan and Alberta, as well as a strip of land, forty miles wide, following the route of the proposed transcontinental railway through British Columbia. It was probably the largest area of unalienated land controlled by one government on the continent. The Prime Minister of Canada, Sir John A. Macdonald, had received the petition from William Little in February 1883, just before the speech from the throne opening the first session of the fifth Parliament. Macdonald was acutely conscious of the depletion of timber supplies in the Ottawa valley, but, since the natural resources in that area were under provincial jurisdiction, he was limited to action in the Canadian west.[27]

For this reason, while the provincial governments of Ontario and Quebec reacted to William Little's memorandum with increased awareness of the risk of forest fires to standing licenced timber, Macdonald made a different interpretation. Like the earlier government of Reform Prime Minister Alexander Mackenzie, which had initiated an early but ineffective tree-planting programme in 1876, he was worried that the lack of trees on the prairies was inhibiting their settlement. Instead of opting for legislation based on the recommendations from the Congress, Macdonald decided to initiate a study of the problem as he saw it. In a memorandum sent to the Privy Council in February, 1883, he noted that the Congress had agreed it was important, for the welfare of the Dominion, that steps be taken "not only for the protection of present forests but also for the planting of forest trees in an extensive area". In order to further this "desirable end", the memorandum recommended that "a competent person be employed to inquire into and report upon the whole subject", the desired result being concerted action on the part of both the Dominion and provincial governments. The memorandum ended by recommending Joseph H. Morgan of Anderdon, Ontario, for the job.[28]

The memorandum is significant because it reveals much about attitudes toward conservation within the Dominion government at the time. In terms of control over logging practices and the lumbermen, clearly the federal government was not prepared to go any further than had the provincial governments. This was a policy that was followed until control over natural resources was turned over to the provinces concerned in the 1930s. At the time of the memorandum, and until the turn of the century, the barrenness of Canada's prairies was a continuous worry to federal politicians who were convinced that this was the reason why they were not being settled.[29] At the root of this concern was that a major portion of the income of the Canadian Pacific Railway was supposed to come from servicing settlements along its right-of-way through the prairies. Nominally a private company completely independent of government, the Canadian Pacific Railway had actually been built with the aid of heavy cash subsidies as well as immense land grants from the federal government. In addition, there were close links between the management of the company and the leaders of both political parties in Ottawa. The railway thus had no difficulty in ensuring that its concern over a lack of customers on the long haul from Manitoba to British Columbia was shared with the Dominion government of the day.

This concern about settlers restricted the Dominion government's response to the resolution from the American Forestry Congress in a number of ways. In the lands of the Dominion-owned Railway Belt of British Columbia there was already a conflict between settlers and lumbermen. If reserves were created or if restrictions were placed on burning brush, the settlers would be angered, and their conflict with lumbermen would be intensified. Moreover, in 1882, the government had created the Timber, Mineral and Grazing Lands Office in the Department of the Interior. This office, copying the policy of Ontario, had set up a system of leased timber berths that required bids on top of "upset prices" as well as the payment of royalties for the volume of timber cut.[30] The office also supervised the leases and permits for the exploitation of other resources on federal lands in western Canada. The few small sawmills in Manitoba, British Columbia, and western Alberta already resented having to pay for logs which previously they had obtained for free, and they would accept very little additional regulation. In this respect, the appointment of Morgan in late February, 1883, was, in the opinion of the Prime Minister, exactly the right kind of political response. It had several precedents, and its objectives were limited so they would not conflict with established interest groups.

The criterion for choosing Morgan for the task of producing a report was simply that he was a faithful Tory. But, even though the Congress and the ideals of the conservation movement were completely new to him, he embarked on his task with enthusiasm. He read widely and made an exploratory trip to the West. In March, 1884, he presented Macdonald with a report he described as "preliminary", suggesting that a tree-planting programme on the prairies was feasible and desirable.[31] Government apathy toward the West, however, prevented Morgan's plans from being followed. Finally, in the spring and summer of 1885, the North-West Rebellion led by Louis Riel intervened, and Morgan's work lay forgotten.

After the rebellion had been put down and the railway had been completed to the Pacific in 1886, the issues investigated by Morgan surfaced once again. The need for prairie settlement was considered to be even more pressing, and Macdonald therefore turned once more to Morgan. In July, 1887, an Order in Council gave him the title of Forestry Commissioner, and he received virtually the same instructions that he had received four years earlier. In addition, he was to consider ways of "preserving and protecting the forests of the Dominion". It was a hint that for the first time the federal government was considering the issue in somewhat wider terms. Morgan presented yet another positive report on tree planting and on the need to protect the headwaters of rivers in the Rockies through fire prevention and forest reservation. On the strength of this, his appointment was continued through 1889. Then, in the spring of 1890, he once more made his way westward and was in northern Saskatchewan in July when he was informed that his services had been terminated! By bureaucratic oversight or, more likely due to friction between Morgan and his superior, Deputy Minister of the Department of the Interior A. M. Burgess,[32] funds for Morgan's work had been omitted from the department's estimates for the year. Disconsolate, Morgan paid his own expenses for his trip home to Amherstburg, Ontario. That he then had to spend several years petitioning the government for reimbursement for these expenses is a comment on the amount of real interest there was in his activities.[33]

The only result of Morgan's efforts, other than giving moral support to western tree plantings, was one change in the Dominion Lands Act. Passed in 1884, this amendment provided for the "preservation of forest trees on crests and slopes of the Rocky Mountains, and the proper maintenance, throughout the year, of the volume of water in the rivers and streams" having the slopes as their sources. This amendment deserves some discussion because effectively it was the Dominion government's first step toward the creation of the forest reserve system that, in turn, led to the first flowering of forestry in Canada. The amendment was a direct result of Macdonald's desire to do everything possible to encourage the settlement of the western lands. Southern Alberta and Saskatchewan had a very dry climate. In spite of this, the land appeared suitable for ranching and some agriculture as long as water supplies were maintained. A convenient source of water were the rivers and streams of the eastern slopes of the Rocky Mountains. The government was warned that the forests played an important role in the storage of water. Forest preservation thus figured prominently in plans for the development of these semiarid lands.[34] From this combination of forest preservation and land and general watershed conservation, federal forest policy was to grow.

Unfortunately, once these amendments to the Dominion Lands Act were in place, federal policy toward its forests languished. It was another decade before any number of reserves were named, and it took a change of governing party before anything significant was done to administer them. The boundaries of the initial Rocky Mountain reserve were established, on paper, and adjacent treed areas were added to it. The responsibility for the area was given to the Timber, Mineral and Grazing Lands Office, which was known by the semiofficial sobriquet, "Timber and Grazing Branch". The Branch had one problem with the reserves—and this was that it had already leased considerable areas inside their boundaries. The leases for these timber berths were renewable annually in perpetuity as long as the lessor paid the ground rents and stumpage. Beyond ensuring that no further timber berths were let inside the boundaries of the reserved areas and some token attempts were made to warn operators about the danger of fires, the Branch did absolutely nothing with the areas. It did not even try to halt the inevitable trespassing by the operators, the illegal squatting by settlers, or the wildfires that swept across the hills. Effectively, the government of Canada had hardly paid lip-service to the ideals of the early forest conservation movement.

Of the Dominion and six provincial governments governing in Canada in the last decades of the nineteenth century, only Ontario and Quebec had actively responded to the requests of the American Forestry Congress meeting of 1882. The gains in Quebec unfortunately did not last long. The Conservative party in that province retained power until the furor following the trial and execution of Louis Riel in 1885 split the party. In the provincial election of October, 1886, Honoré Mercier led the newly formed Parti National to power. The lumbermen of Quebec now found themselves with a government openly sympathetic to the emotional issues then sweeping through the province. In particular, this included fullhearted support of the colonization movement and its desire to have access to all of the unalienated lands of Quebec. Mercier championed the colons' cause and, after having the case of those on the forest reserve lands heard before the full Cabinet in early 1887, set out a policy for abolishing the provincial forest reserves. Mercier kept this promise in 1888, although he allowed the legislation establishing the fire patrols to stand and settled licence tenures for a period up to 1900.

The case prompting the Premier's action was an emotional battle in court between the Gilmour Lumber Company and a group of colons led by the activist priest Father Charles Paradis. The settlers, located in the Gatineau river valley, had challenged the action of the company when it had seized logs they had cut on their lots located within the boundaries of the forest reserve and began to harvest all standing timber as well. The legal case was fought, with the active support of the provincial government, all the way to Britain's Judicial Committee of the Privy Council, the highest court of appeal in the Empire. In 1889, this body upheld the case for the settlers.[35]

The defeat in Quebec coincided with difficult times for the Canadian lumber industry as a whole. During the late 1880s and early 1890s, the economic situation was depressed. The impetus of the conservation movement lay dormant as lumbermen sought to hedge against low profit margins by cutting costs and high-grading the remaining forests. Careless operating practices were compounded by forest fires. The effect of these and over-cutting on the accessible forest of eastern Canada became more and more noticeable as cut-overs failed to regenerate in a satisfactory manner and soil erosion and flooding became rife. For all those who had participated in the Montreal Congress there came the increasing realization that there were real limits to the size of the exploitable forest. The Canadian leaders of the Congress pointed to these effects and advocated ways to conserve the remaining forest but generally found politicians of all persuasions and at all levels of government uninterested in their agenda.

The one bright spot during this period was the establishment of Algonquin

National Park by the government of Ontario. First proposed in 1885 and finally created in 1893, the rationale behind the park was to remove a large area of white pine forest from the threat of settlement. At the same time, the forest cover of the watersheds of several major tributaries of the Ottawa as well as Muskoka area rivers would be protected. A feature of the act setting aside the park was that the berths leased by the lumber companies were allowed to remain. Public opinion was brought to the side of the park, which was really a forest reserve, by some adroit publicity that touted it as a nature sanctuary and recreation area. In retrospect, the only people to suffer from the creation of Algonquin Park were a few trappers and pseudo-settlers since the land was undeniably unsuitable for agricultural development. Many of these individuals quickly found lucrative employment as fishing and canoe trip guides for the groups of tourists who soon invaded the area.[36] The establishment of Algonquin National Park was emulated two years later by Quebec, when two more "national" parks, Laurentides and Mont Tremblant, were founded, shutting extensive areas off from settlement, setting up game preserves, and, like Algonquin, leaving the timber licences in place.[37]

By the 1890s, however, the preservationist's definition of a park was well understood in North America, and the dual role for the three national parks created by the governments of Ontario and Quebec was viewed with some scepticism. The scepticism grew to open criticism as large numbers of tourists overcame the isolation of the areas and saw for themselves the beauty of the forest and the horror of logging methods. This brought a new dimension to the forest conservation movement in Canada adding a stronger preservationist wing based largely in the rising educated urban elite of the major cities of the east. As the new century approached, pressure from this group resulted in a political reorientation in Ontario, and the conservation movement found itself once more with political power culminating in the founding of the Canadian Forestry Association and the hiring of professional foresters by various jurisdictions.

In retrospect, the fifteen years following the meeting of the American Forestry Congress in Montreal in August, 1882, were mixed ones for the nascent movement. On the negative side was the fact the movement showed it was affected by the state of the economy. When economic times were difficult, the forest industry lost interest in implementing conservation measures, concentrating instead on cutting operating costs. Down to the present, this attitude has prevailed with short-term economies winning over more risky and longer term advantages. In a way, it is as if a predominant part of the industry has never abandoned the nineteenth-century notion of the limitless forest. The loss of the nation's first forest reserve was also a setback because it demonstrated that conservation could be usurped by populist causes. That Ontario chose to treat conservation more as a publicity venture rather than implement new timber-management policies was also to cause difficulties in the future. By doing this, the government showed it considered that its definition of forestry had little to do with forest management in direct contrast to then already well-established European practice. It was a policy emulated many times over in Canada in following years.

On the positive side, the movement captured the attention and sympathy of many influential people, including Henri Joly, who, for the rest of his life, was to play a role of quiet leadership and provide an example of forest management on his estate that was effective precisely because it was not public. The years also witnessed the acceptance by two provinces of the recommendations of the forest fire committee of the Congress and a minimal start on a forestry policy by the Dominion government. In fact, it can be argued that the conservation movement achieved a success just by staying alive in the difficult years of the depression of the early 1890s. Some long-term accomplishments during this difficult period also can be identified. For instance, after Ontario created Algonquin National Park, it was much more difficult for governments to create a reserve restricted to the exploitive activities of one industrial group; the interests of the public had to be taken into consideration. From this period forward, forest reserves would be created at both the federal and provincial levels in Canada. Their intent would be to promote scientific forest management, and often attached to this activity, to realize such other goals as protection of game, water control, preservation of natural beauty, and promotion of the area for recreational purposes, all of which went beyond simple forest industry demands. Once the public saw logging at first hand, it lost some of its sentimental aura, and conservationists found themselves supported by a growing and diverse group stretching from outright environmental preservationists to modern businessmen concerned with efficient resource development. After the Congress, forest conservation had moved from being the interest of a few individuals into the storm and fury of politics and economics. The next fifteen years saw it evolve into a progressive reform movement that was to be actively courted by the major players on Canada's political scene.

CHAPTER 3

The Laurier Liberals and Conservation, 1899–1911

In Canada, as in the United States, there is a tendency among historians and conservationists to look on the years from 1899 to 1911 with unwarranted nostalgia. It is true that in the two nations great strides were made in conservation and that there was an awakening of interest and concern among the public. It is probable that the opportunities were seen and grasped to a greater extent in the United States than in Canada, but to Canadian conservationists, who had waited out the early years of the 1890s, these twelve years saw gains at the federal level they had long thought unattainable. Of course there were also failures and drawbacks in the policies that were adopted in these years and in the initiatives that were not taken. Politicians of the period showed themselves capable of both altruism and shameless expediency when faced with decisions concerning the management of natural resources.

The revival of conservation as a political issue at the federal level in Canada really began slowly after 1893, with a revitalization of the forest reserve surveys and the creation of Moose Mountain Reserve in present-day southeastern Saskatchewan in 1894. Then, in the general election of 1896, the Conservatives, long in power, were toppled from office and the Liberals, led by Wilfrid Laurier, formed the government. The Liberal party under Laurier was an amalgam of interest groups and ideologies stretching from the Prime Minister's rather traditional laissez-faire liberalism, tempered with total political expediency, to his Minister of the Interior, Clifford Sifton's, clear-headed, calculated dedication to material progress where government should give dynamic leadership in guiding private enterprise, through strict regulation if necessary, to serve the public interest.[1]

Regardless of ideological orientation, the Liberals had as a priority the speeding up of the economic development of Canada, particularly the West, where they thought the use of efficient and enlightened resource policies would aid the settlement process. Just as with the Conservative party before them, these policies did not prevent Liberal politicians from directing patronage in an overt effort to ensure their party won the next election. This included granting cutting rights to timber, without public competition, to their friends and supporters. In the Edwardian era in Canada, political feuds were very partisan, often personal in nature, and friends expected to be rewarded. Sifton, indeed, was notorious in this respect, and the Opposition often charged that he helped his political friends to free resource tenures and even lined his own pockets through speculation in timber leases. Such charges were never proven, but the era had definite affinities to the "Great Barbecue" in the United States which contributed to the rise of the Progressive movement.[2] Nevertheless, the Liberals were determined to proceed with some progressive resource policies if these could aid western development and bring a national prosperity with which the party could identify itself. Their ideas made possible the adoption of major forest conservation initiatives by the Dominion government. Eventually, a federal forestry organization was established that eclipsed provincial efforts and led the nation in defining what forestry and conservation meant in practical terms. Three specific acts of the Liberal government contributed to this process: the founding of the Forestry Branch in Canada's Department of the Interior; the passing of the Dominion Forest Reserve Acts of 1906 and 1911; and, in 1909 at the instigation of President Theodore Roosevelt, the founding of Canada's Commission of Conservation.

Many of the ideas for conservation-oriented policies came from civil service employees within the Department of the Interior and had been in gestation during the Tory years. Crucial to the acceptance of the ideas and their development into policy was the new Minister of the Interior, Clifford Sifton. Sifton held strong views on the need for a centralized direction of public lands policy as it concerned the prairie farmlands and western forest. An interested observer of American trends, the Minister well appreciated the mounting popularity of scientific forestry in that country and the economic arguments provided by men such as Gifford Pinchot to support a new, efficient basis for resource use. In addition, Sifton had no qualms about moving quickly by Order in Council to establish new regulatory systems if these served his overall goals. He moved immediately in 1896 to get more Crown Timber Agents on the ground by adding these duties to several existing land agents; in addition, homestead inspectors doubled as forest rangers, and two North-West Mounted Police (NWMP) officers were made responsible for controlling trespasses by Americans on Canadian timber along the boundary. Finally, a few fire guards were established for the timber reserves. The Minister had in mind, however, a more comprehensive policy, and for this he turned to proposals by federal officials that were of immediate interest to the new government.

Recommendations for improving the management system of the forests of western Canada originated with William Pearce, Superintendent of Mines in Calgary, North-West Territories, and E. F. Stephenson, Inspector of Crown Timber Agents, based in Winnipeg, Manitoba. Pearce was interested in forest reserves to preserve water needed for irrigation. Stephenson controlled the men responsible for scaling the timber cut on Dominion timber berths but was also interested in classifying forestland for local settlement needs. He suggested that more and larger forest reserves should be created in the West and that their management should go beyond the preservation of timber for watershed protection. He proposed that protection of woodlands could be achieved while, at the same time, making timber available for settlement and commercial purposes. To bolster his arguments, the Inspector addressed a questionnaire to town reeves and prominent settlers throughout the West. The returns indicated a concern about the disappearance of local forest resources and their devastation by fire as well as the general need for forest reservations to aid settlers. In his report to Sifton, the Chief Inspector concluded that the appointment of a Commissioner was desirable to "go thoroughly into the whole subject of forest management, to look into forest protection, the matter of forest reserves and their influence on climate and water supply, to look into planting trees on agriculturally unproductive land, to look into means of preventing prairie fires, and to collect information to enable the government to frame its future timber policy."[3]

Stephenson's proposals received a positive reaction from the Laurier government, resulting in an Order in Council, issued on 24 July 1899, which created the post of Chief Inspector of Timber and Forestry under the Chief Clerk of the Timber and Grazing Branch. Besides reporting on the state of the western forest reserves, the inspector was to survey new areas and investigate the wildfire situation on all Dominion lands. A second section in the order altered the timber berth leasing regulations. Besides establishing a minimum diameter limit of ten inches on all timber cut, it required operators to pay half the cost of fire prevention and suppression on their berths. In what was intended to be a reformist move, sealed tenders were henceforward required for bids on timber berths. This system, centralized at headquarters in Ottawa, unfortunately proved to be open to manipulation and politically motivated chicanery.

The Order in Council was divided into two sections, probably for administrative ease. The division was to have long-term effects in that it effectively established the responsibilities of the two offices within the Department of the Interior that eventually became responsible for forest management on Dominion lands. From the Chief Inspector's office grew the Forestry Branch, the precursor of the present-day Canadian Forestry Service. Until the transfer of the natural resources from federal to provincial control in 1930, it was responsible for all fire fighting on Dominion forestland and for the management of the reserve system. The Timber and Grazing Branch, on the other hand, continued to be responsible for the leasing of Dominion land for

purposes of timber production. This division of responsibilities, which emulated Ontario's system, was to have unfortunate effects on the forest conservation movement in Canada.

The Liberals made a fortunate choice in the man they appointed as their
first Inspector of Timber and Forestry. Elihu Stewart was a land surveyor
with extensive experience, some ambition, and excellent political connections. He made his home in Collingwood, Ontario, and, according to Sifton,
he had had some practical experience with forest surveys. He took up his
office in July, 1899, after some outcry about his partisan proclivities, but he
showed that, besides having good "Reform" credentials, he was a sound
administrator and had an amateur's avid enthusiasm for his new-found vo-
cation. In his first eighteen months as Inspector, Stewart worked on his own
doing practically the same job as had J. H. Morgan when he had been Forestry
Commissioner. He also successfully reinterpreted his rather vague commission to be the creation of "a judicious system of forestry in Canada" based
on "the encouragement of [tree] planting on the plains of Manitoba and the
North-West Territories" and, as the Minister indicated in the House, the
establishment of more forest reserves. He also worked hard to separate
himself as much as possible from his superior, the Chief Clerk of the Timber
and Grazing Branch.[4]

In 1899 there was heavy public pressure on the Dominion government to
pursue some policy actively with regard to the lack of trees on the prairies.
Boards of Trade of the major western centres had memorialized Clifford
Sifton and the Prime Minister for a tree-planting programme. The rationale
had, by this time, moved from the aesthetic view that trees would alleviate
the bleakness of the plains to the more practical objectives of reducing crop
damage and water evaporation through the proper placement of windbreaks.
Tree planting was expected to increase a farm's productivity as well as
enhance its beauty. Stewart drew his inspiration for a tree-planting programme from the United States Bureau of Forestry as well as from projects
started by the midwestern states. In March, 1901, Stewart was joined by an
assistant, Norman M. Ross, the first professional forester hired by the Canadian government. Ross was a graduate of the University of Toronto's
Ontario Agricultural College at Guelph and of Carl A. Schenck's Biltmore
Forest School where he was considered one of the best students. Indeed,
at this time, Schenck was asked to complete a report on Canadian forestry
in which he vehemently advocated government support for tree planting
through provision of seedling stock. As a result of this work, Stewart's title
was formally changed to Superintendent of Forestry for Canada, which
marked the creation of a Forestry Branch independent of the Chief Clerk
of the Timber and Grazing Branch.[5]

The new Branch was given the task of assisting farmers with their tree-
planting efforts and of cooperating with municipalities and such other organizations as railroad companies. In addition, Stewart retained his earlier

responsibilities with regard to wildfires. The tree-planting programme started quickly when Ross and an assistant moved out to the Dominion Indian Head Experimental Farm in Saskatchewan and established a tree nursery. While the assistant, A. P. Stevenson, inspected farms in Manitoba and gave advice to the owners, Ross worked in Saskatchewan and Alberta. The programme of cooperative agreements proved popular and rapidly expanded in size. Ross managed it until his retirement in the 1920s.[6]

At the end of 1901, Stewart was well on the way to becoming the leading representative of Canadian forestry. Ironically, his confidence and position were bolstered by the failure of the Ottawa valley lumbermen to influence the governments of Ontario and Quebec. These men wanted current forest conservation measures to be applied to the forests in which they operated. With the failure of their efforts, which is detailed in following chapters, this influential group became interested in federal efforts in the hope that this leadership would act as a demonstration to their errant provincial governments. Many were Liberals, and they became faithful supporters of Laurier's conservation programme. Through men such as lumberman W. C. Edwards, who was a confidant of Wilfrid Laurier, they soon had direct access to the Prime Minister. It was this support that aided the expansion of the Forestry Branch in the years to come, moving it from practical efforts aiding western settlement to advocacy of a national forestry movement.

This shift in policy occurred slowly over a number of years with due regard to political conditions in western Canada. In contrast to policy in the older provinces, there was at first a consensus between some settlers, especially in the southwest portion of the West, and federal officials that existing forested areas had to be preserved. Living in a fragile, largely treeless environment, the connection between forest conservation and soil protection was readily apparent to these settlers. There existed a prairie lumber industry serving the needs of local farmers and providing materials for railway construction and mining, but, though the area of forest let for timber limits was extensive, it was scattered. Only west of the prairies in parts of the Railway Belt of British Columbia was there any real competition for timberland. A lack of waterways on the scale of the eastern rivers limited the trade's development. As a result, the settlers' demand for lumber was largely filled by mills operating on the west coast of the United States and Canada. In western Canada, experience was to show that it was not the local lumber interests that supported forest conservation, but rather a paternal federal government supported to a large degree by substantial eastern lumbermen, who recognized forestry as the basis of the resource planning techniques needed for increased settlement and rational national development.

The key that would open the door to Stewart's ambitions proved to be the reserve system. Since 1884, when Sir John A. Macdonald's Conservatives had started creating forest reserves, the number had been slowly increasing until, by 1906, they totalled over 1.2 million hectares. At first, reserves were restricted to the eastern slopes of the Rocky Mountains, but soon they encompassed many of the small islands of timber found on the prairies and, eventually, even included parts of the northern tree belt. Stewart desired to be given responsibility for the reserves—to establish a system of management on them and to extend their area to include all forested land in the vast region. He had shamelessly drawn this ambition from his dynamic American counterpart, Gifford Pinchot, chief of the Forestry Bureau in the United States Department of Agriculture.[7]

One of Stewart's first actions after taking office in July, 1899, was to write to Pinchot asking him to forward information and publications about forestry to Ottawa. Stewart recognized the American's expertise in a field in which he was a novice, and he also knew that the Dominion government drew on United States' examples for its own administration in other areas. The letter was the first of a series that culminated in Stewart's visiting Washington, D. C., in the late fall of 1899. Pinchot was flattered at this attention and told his admirer that he was lucky to be starting out from a new beginning. He advised Stewart on two points that were to become important guideposts in the development of Canadian policy. First, he pointed out that the administration of federal forests in his own country was then divided between three government organizations with a resulting loss of efficiency and an increase in conflict. Second, he contended that the reservation of all remaining government-held forestland in the North-West Territories and British Columbia was all important.[8]

Pinchot's well-founded advice was a precursor to the habit Canada's federal foresters soon developed of using American experience as a guide for their own actions. They used American experience because they believed the two countries had more in common than they actually did and because they looked on the United States Forest Service as a successful prototype. Their lack of appreciation for the political, constitutional, and cultural differences between the two nations was to be the source of a number of crucial policy miscalculations in the future.

When Stewart and Pinchot first met, Pinchot was just starting on the campaign that was to see him successfully unite federal forest management under the control of his service. It was a goal that Stewart was to adopt as his own, and it was Pinchot's methods he used in the attempt. Ironically, it was a relatively limited initiative to promote agricultural tree planting that was to set this campaign in motion. A meeting originally organized to discuss this topic led to the most important public gathering of forestry supporters in Canada since the American Forestry Congress held in Montreal in August, 1882. Just before Christmas, 1899, Stewart received a letter from his new Deputy Minister, James Smart, who was Sifton's old friend from Brandon, Manitoba, and the Minister's confidant. Smart suggested that Stewart bring together all those interested in tree planting on the prairies and draw up a plan of work. Stewart replied that he would "ask a few gentlemen to meet some evening for the purpose of starting a Canadian Forestry Association" which, he was convinced, would be a "useful factor" in furthering the cause of prairie tree planting. Stewart also committed himself to discussing the idea with the first chairman of the American Forestry Congress, Sir Henri Joly de Lotbinière, then serving as the Minister of Inland Revenue in Sir Wilfrid Laurier's cabinet.[9]

Stewart moved swiftly on the project, and sent out a circular letter on January 8, 1900, calling for a meeting in his office on January 15. Invited to attend were Sir Henri Joly; J. R. Booth, the influential Ottawa lumber baron; James Smart; Dr. William Saunders, of the Dominion Department of Agriculture; Professor John Macoun, of the Geological Survey; W. T. Macoun, of the Dominion Experimental Farm; William Little, the organizer of the Montreal meeting of the American Forestry Congress; Thomas Southworth, Clerk of Forestry for Ontario; Sydney Fisher, Dominion Minister of Agriculture and a leading supporter of conservation ideas; and Thomas C. Keefer and Charles H. Keefer, two well-known engineers based in Ottawa. All, except Fisher, were able to attend. After appointing Little as Chairman and Stewart as Secretary, the group named a committee to write a constitution for a forestry association, expressly modeled on the American Forestry Association, and then settled down to listen to a presentation by Dr. Saunders about conditions on the prairies.[10] The importance of this meeting cannot be overemphasized. It united the old leadership of the American Forestry Congress, which had influenced legislators throughout the 1880s, with a new group led by provincial and federal officials and politicians determined to advance the conservation cause in Canada by direct government intervention.

With permission readily granted by Smart for Stewart to use the resources of the Department of the Interior, a public meeting was organized to inaugurate the new Association. Stewart drafted a second circular letter stating that the purpose of the Canadian Forestry Association was "the encouragement of the growth and cultivation of trees on our North-Western plains." Thomas Southworth, as a crucial provincial representative, reviewed this draft and, recognizing the full potential of the new organization, advised that prairie tree planting would not interest many people in Ontario, the province expected to make up the bulk of the membership. Southworth suggested a new theme:

The time has arrived when the efforts being made by our various governments for the adoption of national forestry methods should be assisted and guided by intelligent public opinion. This can best be done by the formation of such an Association as we have in view, composed of men who are interested in forest preservation.[11]

This theme was accepted, and the circular letter was sent out using mailing lists provided by Southworth and others.

The response to the circular letter was very gratifying. Those attending the meeting filled the Railway Committee Rooms in the East Block of the Parliament Buildings on the March 8, 1900. As with the 1882 meeting of the American Forestry Congress, a relatively short business meeting was followed by a series of papers about forestry conditions in Canada. Those present accepted a proposal from a Montreal publisher that the newly founded sportsman's magazine, *Rod and Gun in Canada*, provide space for news about the Association and for articles written by its members. The meeting also saw the official establishment of the relationship that continues to this day between the Association and the Canadian Forestry Service. Appropriately, the meeting recognized the older leadership of the forestry movement by making Sir Henri Joly de Lotbinière, President, and William Little, Vice President. To show the national scope of the organization, a slate of Vice Presidents was elected to represent the provinces, although the Board of Directors largely represented Ottawa and Toronto.[12]

The inaugural meeting of the Canadian Forestry Association created a unique amalgam of politicians, bureaucrats, and the private sector. The Association became dedicated to the popularization of scientific forestry and conservation. From the start, it was politically influential and was an effective lobby for the adoption of forest conservation at all levels of government. Through its meetings and published reports, its own magazine (after 1905), and the use of *Rod and Gun in Canada*, the Association pushed for increased fire protection, more forest reserves, control of pulpwood harvesting, land classification, and the adoption of forest management plans. Rarely did the Association speak with one voice. Its approximately 400 members represented too many diverse interests for that to occur, but it did serve as a powerful general lobby for forestry measures. After World War I, the Association suffered as more specialized organizations undermined its position as a voice for those interested in the scientific and managerial aspects of forestry. The Association reacted by narrowing its role to the dissemination of fire prevention propaganda amongst the public as a whole—a necessary task but also one designed not to offend the forest industries which increasingly formed an important part of its membership.

The influence of the Canadian Forestry Association undoubtedly supported Stewart in his efforts to increase the power and prestige of his Forestry Branch. In early 1905 the Dominion government formally recognized the need for cooperation between the forestry and timber-leasing parts of its administration. Robert H. Campbell, who worked well with Stewart, was appointed Chief Clerk of the Timber and Grazing Branch under the general direction of Stewart. It was the step Pinchot had talked about in 1899—the vital move toward consolidation. It had taken Stewart six years to move himself and the branch he headed from being subservient to the Chief Clerk of the Timber and Grazing Branch to a position of authority over that office. Without a doubt, this success, achieved through political gamesmanship, did not increase Stewart's popularity with some officials in the Department of the Interior and did create a powerful opposition to further efforts. It was also a fleeting victory and was to prove to be the closest he ever came to achieving the goals urged on him by Pinchot.

In early 1905, political events dimmed Stewart's hopes. Clifford Sifton, who had proved to be a dynamic supporter of conservation measures, resigned from his cabinet post. His Deputy Minister, James Smart, resigned soon after. The major reason for the Minister's resignation was his opposition to French language education in the public school system of the new provinces of Saskatchewan and Alberta, then being created. Sifton was also ill from nervous tension caused by overwork, and he had earlier discussed resigning. He thought his main work in the Department of the Interior was finished, he wanted new responsibilities, and he was becoming increasingly frustrated with Laurier's lack of decisive leadership and his failure to give greater western representation in the federal cabinet. Other, perhaps more speculative reasons, suggest a possible scandalous alliance with another man's wife and Sifton's increasingly obvious wealth garnered from his many questionable dealings in western development projects. The major issue of the moment, however, was the North-West schools question and it was to rob federal conservation efforts of their dynamic leadership.[13]

Sifton's replacement was Frank Oliver, an independent Liberal M.P. from Edmonton, Alberta. The founder and publisher of the *Edmonton Bulletin*, a newspaper which espoused the preeminence of local issues,[14] Oliver was an efficient and consummate politician. On his own, he had built a political organization in the northern half of Alberta that supported the Liberal cause and had showed itself to have influence outside of its immediate boundaries. Laurier was thus in considerable debt to Oliver even though, in the House, Oliver took a strong independent stance.

Oliver and Sifton were ideologically opposed. Whereas Sifton had advocated centralized planning and development of the North-West, which Oliver interpreted as a further attempt by the East to dictate to the free West. The new Minister advocated decentralized and unrestrained western development and supported farmers and small businessmen who were then settling the area. Oliver was not a supporter of the federal forestry initiatives, except to the extent that wildfires should be controlled. As a believer in laissez-faire free enterprise, he rejected government regulation of lumbering activity especially when applied to the prairies.

With the departure of Sifton, the Canadian Forestry Association increased in importance as a supporting organization for Stewart. Most important, it lent its good auspices to sponsoring an event intended to move forestry to the forefront of public issues in Canada. This was the convening, by the Prime Minister, of a Canadian Forestry Convention to meet in Ottawa on January 10–12, 1906. The idea for a convention received a positive response within the government. On the political plane, it was a carefully arranged attempt by Sir Wilfrid Laurier and the Liberal party to identify themselves with the popular issue of conservation. The actions of the parties involved leave one with little doubt that they were attempting to copy the successful efforts toward this end undertaken by Gifford Pinchot and President Theodore Roosevelt.[15]

The announcement of the Convention was received enthusiastically in all parts of Canada, although the majority of the attendees came from the urban areas of Ontario. The meeting, opened by Governor-General of Canada Lord Grey, featured many presentations by people well known in the conservation movement in Canada. Their presentations contained suggestions for increased fire protection and more forest reserves and advocated better forestry education, tree planting, and artificial regeneration.[16] Those attending the convention also experienced something of the tensions lurking close to the surface of the country's conservation movement when they listened to speeches from the Minister of the Interior, the Prime Minister, and the leader of the Opposition. The Prime Minister, who potentially had the most to gain or lose politically from the convention, chose a careful path between supporting forest preservation and reforestation without either placing the blame on the lumbermen for the devastation or giving them the responsibility for rebuilding stocks. Robert Borden, the leader of the Opposition, was buoyed by an enthusiasm for forestry and, seeing an opportunity to publicly criticise the government, selected a more activist stance. He cited statements by Bernhard Fernow, who was becoming a popular scientific figure in Canada, regarding uncontrolled exploitation of the country's forests, and he advocated increased government involvement in forest management. But, as if to underline the completely political nature of the conservation idea, both leaders were overshadowed by the keynote speaker of the meeting, Gifford Pinchot.

Pinchot had recently successfully managed the 1905 American Forestry Congress. Resolutions had been passed to assist the passage of a bill in the United States Congress transferring the administration of public lands from the General Land Office of the Department of the Interior to Pinchot's bureau in the Department of Agriculture. In his autobiography, Pinchot revealed his happiness with the meeting in terms that undoubtedly expressed Stewart's hopes for the Canadian Forestry Convention: "The American Forestry Congress issued the call, but the meeting was planned, organized and conducted for the specific purpose of the transfer by the Bureau of Forestry".[17] Passage of the Transfer Act followed shortly, and this legislation, along with the Appropriations Act of March, 1905, gave the newly named United States Forest Service wide powers. In particular, the Service was enabled to use the funds gained from the sale of forest products for the Service's own uses and to engage in the marketing of products; furthermore, its officers were empowered to arrest those suspected of violating forestry regulations.[18]

In his speech, Pinchot called for Canada to adopt an organized national forest policy; to undertake the evaluation of land before settlement and the reservation of all nonagricultural forest areas; to promote the management of reserves by trained government employees; to improve federal fire-fighting efforts, including legislation to secure the cooperation of railway companies in controlling fires during construction and operation; and to encourage tree planting on the prairies.[19] These five points, repeated by almost every speaker at the Convention, represent the theme of the meeting. With Pinchot's help, the resolutions passed by those attending covered several activities in which the federal government was already involved. The main thrust, however, called for increased Dominion action in forest conservation and a single forestry service. The resolutions defined the issue for the federal government and gave it support to enact them. The question now was how far Laurier and Frank Oliver were willing to go. This became clear on 26 March 1906, when Oliver introduced the Dominion Forest Reserves Act.[20]

The bill governing the forest reserves had been planned for a long time, and it is clear that Stewart intended the Convention to garner support for it. The bill was conceived in November, 1904, just three months before Sifton's resignation. It followed inquiries by Stewart about Ontario's practices and method of creating forest reserves. In the Dominion system, although reserves were set up by Order in Council, they lacked a comprehensive unique legislative base for their creation and management. Stewart desired a Forest Reserve Act which gave him control of these areas but retained the designation process as a simple Order in Council which would speed up the process of reserving nonagricultural areas in the West regardless of whether they were under a current timber licence or other lease. It was the type of powerful, single-purpose legislation of which Gifford Pinchot would have wholeheartedly approved. Sifton agreed, and the Secretary to the Department of the Interior was instructed to draft suitable amendments to the existing Dominion Lands Act. By January, 1905, Sifton was being asked to endorse a complete revamping of the Act including sections protecting wildlife, but he was not able to consider the matter because of his resignation. Instead, the draft legislation was passed to the Prime Minister, as acting Minister of the Interior, who was not prepared to take action until he had appointed a new Minister. In this way, Stewart's proposals came before Frank Oliver, a man not favourably predisposed toward Stewart's objectives.[21]

Not surprisingly, the bill was held over for a year, ostensibly because Oliver considered that parts of it interfered with provincial jurisdiction, particularly the provisions regarding the protection of game within forest reserves. At the heart of the matter, however, lay the basic philosophical differences between Sifton's men and Oliver. While Sifton had agreed that regulation through Order in Council was advantageous, Oliver was strongly opposed to it. Where Sifton would expropriate private property, whether leasehold or freehold, or apply regulations governing its use, Oliver supported the rights of the individual over government and considered the alteration of a lease to be a breach of contract. What is clear is that the departure of Sifton and the arrival of Oliver radically altered the balance of power within the Department. Stewart had learned to bypass the senior civil servants in the Department of the Interior by going directly to James Smart or Clifford Sifton with his ideas or requests. The methods employed in proposing the amendments to the Dominion Lands Act and the way in which the Forest Reserves Act was first drafted are examples of Stewart's technique. Naturally, this created antagonisms. When James Smart was replaced as Deputy Minister by W. W. Cory, a Sifton appointee from the Yukon but a man who knew he must get along with Oliver, T. G. Rothwell, the Department's Solicitor, who appears to have been a leading personal opponent of the Superintendent, found an ally against Stewart. In the months of March and April following the bill's first reading in the House, drafts were passed back and forth between these two men with occasional requests to Stewart to justify or clarify a point.[22]

While these delaying tactics were going on, a political crisis was brewing in the West. It had its roots in the way in which the western lumber trade had developed. After 1900, the rate of prairie settlement had increased dramatically. Coincidentally, from 1898 to 1906/7, the average price of lumber in eastern Canada rose from an index of 99 to an index of 165. At the same time, in the United States, it rose from a base index of 100 to a peak of 210, at an average annual rate of increase of 2.4 percent above the average annual cost of all commodities.[23] Prairie purchasers of lumber were in a peculiar position. Most of their wood came from the western coasts of Canada and the United States and was delivered in returning railcars that otherwise would have been empty. Deliveries of lumber tended to be tied to decreases in demand for the product on the eastern seaboard. In other words, the prairies were convenient dumping grounds for the surpluses of western lumbermen. "Local" producers, who were owners of mills in the eastern Rocky Mountains, found it hard to compete in a market where prices fluctuated wildly in response to the activities of west coast mill owners. In an attempt to retain a portion of the market for themselves under these circumstances, local producers habitually priced their product at up to four dollars per Mfbm below the wholesale price of their coastal competitors. Another favoured tactic of these mill owners was to close their mills and await the return of better times. Because of its instability and its higher growth, compared to general commodity prices, the cost of lumber became a touchy topic with westerners. This was especially true during late 1905 and early 1906 when lumber prices peaked and then were driven upward by the disastrous earthquake and fire that destroyed San Francisco in April, 1906.[24]

In the next eighteen months, the demand for lumber to rebuild the city set virtually every mill on the Pacific coast operating twenty-four hours a day. The demand was so great and the prices were so high that Vancouver's building boom was interrupted. The United States government reacted to the situation in California by removing the 2 percent tariff on lumber imported from British Columbia. Mills on the coast of the province boomed. The supply of logs on the open market disappeared, and all lumber shipments inland ceased. This left the prairie market wide open to mill owners in the mountain regions of British Columbia and Alberta.[25]

Year after year, these men had watched as trainloads of lumber passed eastward. Now, seeing the chance to make a good profit in a business that was notoriously fickle, these operators entered into alliances with lumber dealers' associations on the prairies. While the Forest Reserves Act was being debated in the House, prairie lumber prices rose precipitously, eventually reaching nearly twice their 1905 levels in some areas. Farmers and settlers in the region, who claimed that the values were artificially high, created such a furor in Ottawa that, in late 1906, the Commons struck a Select Committee to investigate the facts. Chairmanship of the Committee was given to Thomas Greenway, one-time Liberal Premier of the Province of Manitoba and now federal member for Lisgar. The committee produced a final report in April, 1907, which charged that lumber manufacturers, dealers and other interested parties were acting in combination to hold lumber prices at a high level. Although it did not have a direct effect on the price of lumber on the prairies, the investigations leading to the report did have a tremendous negative influence on the Forestry Branch's efforts to garner political support for a new Forest Reserves Act which, common rumour had it, would impose controls on local lumbermen and make it more difficult for them to get access to timber thus supporting the high lumber prices paid by settlers and farmers.[26]

In the period between the first reading of the Forest Reserves Act and its second appearance before the House, Stewart lobbied all his contacts to counteract these negative factors, not hesitating to write directly to Laurier, Oliver, and Sifton. In spite of these efforts, it was an emasculated bill that was placed before the House in early May for its second reading and consideration by Committee of the Whole. Although it appeared to follow closely the resolutions passed by the Convention in January, vital clauses exempted timber leaseholders from Forestry Branch control. Also omitted were clauses drafted by Stewart that would have enabled the creation of the forest reserves themselves and management regulations by Order in Council. Clearly, the Liberal administration was not about to create a new, all-powerful forestry organization. In spite of its limitations, the bill took an extremely important step when it transferred the control of the forest reserves from the Timber and Grazing Branch to the Superintendent of Forestry.[27]

That the government recognized the bill contradicted some of the ideas expressed at the Canadian Forestry Convention was revealed by Laurier in his speech supporting the measure. He claimed the bill would allow the government to set regulations directly over all Dominion forest land—a claim that was reiterated by Oliver in Committee of the Whole. Opposition members, led by Borden, showed this claim to be inaccurate by forcing Oliver to read out the standard clauses of a lease. When Oliver did this, it became obvious that leaseholders effectively held their land indefinitely with no restrictions and that the bill upheld this position. Eventually, an embarrassed Laurier conceded the point to Borden, confirming that to change the terms of a lease would entail a breach of faith with its holder. The fallacy of this position was pointed out by John Haggart, the Conservative M.P. from Lanark South in Ontario. Haggart indicated that the federal government was simply following provincial tendencies not to interfere with existing, almost perpetual leases, and he reminded the government that it had the legal power to do so if it desired—the question of whether or not to use the power was solely a moral issue.[28]

Attacks by Borden, Haggart, and other opposition members from Ontario probably reinforced Oliver's attitude toward eastern Canada. In the end, with the vocal support of other members from the West, such as the M.P. for Assinaboia, John Turriff, it was Oliver's interpretation of the rights of established timber leaseholders that prevailed. The sole concession was that, when a leased timber berth was cut-over, its return to the Crown would be expedited. This policy statement represented the end of the hopes of Stewart and the conservationists to obtain total control over all federal forestland. The Forestry Branch was denied regulatory authority over working leases and would be able to take them over only when they had been denuded of merchantable timber. It was progress but hardly a stunning victory for forestry in Canada. The debate was repeated five years later when the Forest Reserves Act was amended to become the Forest Reserves and National Parks Act of 1911.[29]

This latter Act is generally considered to be the culmination of the Liberal government's efforts in resource conservation. The bill definitely originated in the Liberals' attempt to identify their party with this popular movement in preparation for the rapidly approaching federal election of that year. It has been generally interpreted as a victory for the conservation movement on the basis of the definite mandate given to the National Parks Branch and the establishment of a separate Parks Service.[30] This interpretation does have validity but, in larger terms, the bill represented a step backward for the conservation movement as a whole in Canada. Hidden within the objectives behind the bill, and inspired by Frank Oliver, lay the first real challenge to the ideals of the conservation movement. If he had had his way, the Forestry Branch, the flagship of the movement, would have been crippled. Thus, the debate and political manoeuvering that went on behind the scenes reveals both the fragility of the concept of forest conservation in the pre–World War I period and the ambivalence of the Laurier administration toward it.

As introduced, the Forest Reserves and National Parks Act of 1911 amounted to a complete revision of its predecessor. In the debates in the House over the measure, a number of familiar themes reappeared. Politicians representing western constituencies split with those from the East. A type of prairie populism emphasizing local control was once more pitted against the concept of scientific planning and the controlled use of natural resources. This happened primarily because, in the West, Oliver was subjected to pressure from three distinct groups.

Farmers and wealthy ranch owners in southern Alberta wanted the forest reserves on the eastern slopes of the Rocky Mountains to be enlarged. As in 1906, their concern was that the forest cover be maintained thus preserving the watershed that provided them with water supplies for their cattle and for irrigation. Western lumbermen, in contrast, were worried that their precarious position within the industry would be jeopardized. They were better organized than in 1906 and put new arguments before the Minister. As they saw it, the Forestry Branch would set regulations that would increase their costs and drive them out of business if it were given responsibility for supervision of their leased timber berths. Finally, the position of the prairie settlers and farmers was unchanged since 1906–1907. Even though the retail price of lumber had dropped in the intervening years, they still considered it too high. As a group, the farmers could be guaranteed to oppose any measure they were convinced might increase the price of this commodity. Thus, while some settlers had originally supported the idea of forest reserves, there was now an innate suspicion of where government policy and regulation was now attempting to go. Their basic negative attitude toward the Forestry Branch was increased by dissatisfaction arising from the eviction of squatters from the forest reserves following the 1906 Act. Unfortunately, their anger was not counterbalanced by the popularity of the shelter-belt planting programme being carried out by Norman Ross.[31]

These pressures were all taken into account by Oliver in the drafting of the new bill. His main objective was to give the Dominion's parks the same legal status as the forest reserves, to enlarge the area of the Rocky Mountain Reserve, and to ensure continued utilization of the forests. On the other hand, the Forestry Branch saw the bill as an opportunity to achieve some long-planned objectives with regard to increasing its control over logging on timber berths leased by the Timber and Grazing Branch but actually located within the forest reserves.[32] Oliver, however, asserted his authority by rejecting a draft of the legislation prepared by the Branch. As finally tabled, the bill actually increased the security of tenure of leaseholders. The amended Act was "not to affect or prejudice any right or interest" acquired by leaseholders to log under Timber and Grazing Branch regulations. In a letter accompanying the bill, the Assistant Secretary to the Minister of the Interior, L. Pereira, emphasized this was a significant change from the 1906 legislation.[33] Oliver made other changes as well, especially limiting the government's right of expropriation of land held in fee—simply on the grounds that the cost of compensating leaseholders would be too high.[34]

For the Forestry Branch, the good news in the Act was that the reserved areas were increased from twenty-one with an area of 1,351,680 hectares to thirty-six with an area of 6,704,256 hectares. The government boasted that this expansion of reserved land proved its dedication to wise resource planning, and, indeed, the extent of the new areas was impressive despite the flaws in the legislation. Support for expansion of the reserves had been perhaps most consistently advocated within the government by Sydney Fisher, the Minister of Agriculture and the strongest conservation advocate after the departure of Joly and Sifton from the cabinet. With these new responsibilities came a considerable increase in funding for the Branch and an increased ability to set fire regulations and restrict public access to the reserved areas. Unfortunately, at the same time the Forestry Branch lost its preeminent position in the wider conservation cause when the Act transferred responsibility for the preservation of wildlife to the new Parks Branch. This development, which indicated the diversification of the conservation ethic in Canada, was to become symptomatic of the fragmentation that was occurring in federal conservation organizations. It was a break with the older conservationist ethic, which had tended to see reserve areas or watersheds primarily as an ecological whole. Given the basis of government policy of the time, however, such a change was inevitable.

The new Parks Branch was given its independence and freedom of administration so it could develop along lines not dominated by the utilitarian forestry viewpoint. Furthermore, Oliver himself stated that the two Branches were included in the same bill with the same regulations so that forest reserves could easily become parks. But the Minister cannily omitted that the reverse was also true; logging could just as easily be carried out in the parks under Forestry Branch supervision if the demand were to warrant it. Effectively, the only difference between a forest reserve and a park was that public access to the latter was guaranteed. Indeed, the Act revised the area of the Rocky Mountain Forest Reserve to include all land above 1,220 metres along the eastern slope of the mountains from the international boundary to a point 161 kilometres north of Jasper, some 46,620 square kilometres. But, as well, the limits of the two existing national parks, Banff and Jasper, were considerably reduced in size. Oliver's wish was to have available as much area as possible for general development of lumbering, mining, grazing, and water power, though, in this instance, under more controlled conditions. The growth of tourism and the popular urge to protect the natural beauty of certain areas had convinced the federal government to recognize the preservationist impulse for flora and fauna in legislation but only to a limited extent. Only in 1914 would the pressure of public opinion restore the park boundaries.[35]

Forestry advocates would have viewed these changes more optimistically if the Minister had declared his government's full commitment to conservation measures. In the debates in the House of Commons early in 1911, Frank Oliver summarized what were his real objectives behind the bill. The points he chose to emphasize in his speeches were not concerned with conservation but rather with protecting established rights. Time and again he ignored calls from eastern M.P.'s for increased control over logging practices. In a statement that would be familiar to present-day conservationists, Oliver said that

In a great measure the public requirements are met by holders of timber licences inside and outside the forest reserves, but our purpose, in dealing with the timber in the reserves is, first, the economic utilization of the timber which is useful for economic purposes and, next, the reproduction of timber so that there shall be a continuous supply.

To which he added that it must be remembered that timber had two values, one of which was in dollars per thousand board feet, and that he did not think the public would allow cutting to be stopped altogether because "we have to meet the immediate pressure of public opinion of the settler who wants wood and who wants building logs."[36] In this, Oliver clearly was stating the government's enduring position. While existing business rights and interests, exemplified by holders of timber leases, were to be protected and nurtured, their ability to exploit the situation and raise prices was to be held in check by easy access to the timber on the reserves granted to farmers and settlers. This policy was not conservation oriented but it was popular, persuasive, and long lasting. In the last *Timber Disposal Manual* issued by the Forestry Branch in 1929, the priority given to the reasons for cutting trees on the reserves was as follows:

1. Timber cut for administrative purposes only
2. Free use to settlers or for social improvements
3. At non-competitive rates for local development purposes
4. At non-competitive rates for commercial purposes
5. At competitive rates for commercial purposes.[37]

Only as a last resort, when there was a surplus over and above local needs, was the timber to be put up for sale at public auction. The role of the timber reserves was effectively to act as a drag on price increases by keeping the value of the raw material at a low level. Unfortunately, this acted to delay the application of conservationist practices on the part of industry. Why invest in a resource when its owner actively pursued a policy of keeping its value low?

As mentioned previously, the debate over the Forest Reserves and National Parks Bill of 1911 exacerbated divisions already existing within Canada.

Ontario M.P.'s, such as Thomas Sproule from East Grey, were worried that, by leaving a few trees after cutting, leaseholders could retain their leased holdings forever, with the rental and royalty rates unchanged and the berth increasing in value as it reforested naturally. This was a situation he had noted happening in Ontario where the activities of speculators had resulted in a loss of income to the Crown. In general, members from ridings in Manitoba and eastern Canada, who had seen the results of "cut-and-get-out" woods operations, showed the most concern. On the other hand, western M.P.'s tended to see the resource either as limitless or a source of free building material for their constituents. Unfortunately, there was little intellectual understanding in either group that a properly managed forest resource would provide a self-perpetuating supply of timber at reasonable prices. Such an understanding might have acted to unite the members because the two aims are not contradictory. The fact was that western-eastern enmity and distrust had effectively driven a wedge between the two groups.[38]

The debate over the bill did not raise new controversies so far as the western lumbermen were concerned; rather, it acted on their existing apprehensions. Their attitude can best be understood as fear of the unknown. They owned and operated small companies cutting stands that were marginal compared with their Pacific Coast competition, which was capable of flooding the prairie market with low-priced surplus stock. These entrepreneurs thought many of the forestry regulations were arbitrary in nature. They feared that the cost of slash and brush disposal, advocated by the Forestry Branch after 1907, would drive them out of business. Not unnaturally, they strongly resisted all attempts by the Forestry Branch to supervise all the forest controlled by the Dominion.

From the point of view of the Forestry Branch and the forest conservation movement in Canada, the situation was far from ideal. Proper forest management and conservation had been shown to be vulnerable to political necessity. A point well understood by Oliver, it proved to be the governing limit of the Laurier government's support of the conservation cause. It was prepared to provide ample funding for the Forestry Branch, but it was not prepared to bear either the political difficulties or the additional expense of bringing the productive timber lands of the West under intensive forest management. Nor was the government prepared to regulate the western lumber industry. Like most of the provincial governments, the Laurier administration found the creation and enlargement of forest reserves to be an excellent political compromise especially when "vested interests" could, at the same time, be adequately protected.[39] The policy gave the appearance of adopting modern resource management ideas in regard to land classification without actually interrupting the headlong rush of resource exploitation. The Acts of 1906 and 1911 meant that the Dominion Forestry Branch was responsible for fire fighting on Dominion forest lands outside the reserves, but also that it had no control over existing lumber companies carrying on logging. Furthermore, although the issuing of timber leases practically stopped after 1907, few timber rights were ever leased by the Forestry Branch itself because the area of berths, already under the control of the Timber and Grazing Branch, was so extensive that there was never any demand for access to the reserved lands. Worse still, these existing leased areas were scattered throughout the reserves, including those on the eastern slopes of the Rocky Mountains. These leases encompassed the pockets of superior, accessible timber, leaving to the Forestry Branch most of the unproductive forest—stands that were either too young or not economically exploitable. Because it never obtained control over a substantial area of productive forest, the Branch was never able to demonstrate properly what forest management could achieve. As a result, Stewart and his successors effectively became foresters without axes.

It is only with hindsight, unfortunately, that the restricted mandate of the Forestry Branch can be truly appreciated and criticised. At the time, the officers of the Branch were optimistic that additional progress would be made if they could galvanize the leadership of the conservation movement into pushing for new measures. In this sense, the first five years of the Branch, between 1906 and 1911, were crucial to its future performance and reputation.

When Elihu Stewart stepped down as Superintendent on 1 March 1907, he could point to the reserve system and the fire-fighting responsibilities as important beginnings for a federal forestry organization—all of which had been advocated by the Canadian Forestry Association.[40] Stewart, himself, did not say farewell to forestry; he left to take up the Vice Presidency of Spruce Falls Power and Paper Company at Kapuskasing, Ontario, and at his departure his influence with the Laurier Liberals remained high enough that he could dictate the choice of his successor. This was Robert Henry Campbell, who had been Chief of the Timber and Grazing Branch in the few months before the passage of the 1906 Act when it had been nominally under the Forestry Branch's control. He had also assisted in the formation of the Canadian Forestry Association, and he was solidly committed to working toward a stable and progressive forest policy. Like Stewart, he had had no formal scientific training. As an individual, Campbell was the epitome of the Ottawa civil servant of the era. His father, James Campbell, worked in the Parliamentary Library. Robert graduated from Ottawa Collegiate in 1887, and a career in government seemed natural. He joined the Department of the Secretary of State at the age of twenty and rose rapidly through the ranks. He showed "earnestness, good judgement and capacity for work" and was also literate, bilingual, and an able speaker. Contemporaries describe him as "retiring" in disposition and, in fact, he remained a bachelor all his life. More than Stewart, Campbell was considered a "good tactician" because of the way in which he was able to get his opinions accepted by his bureaucratic and political masters. It was this quality, more than any other, that enabled him to guide the Branch successfully through a difficult period of development up to the end of World War I.[41]

Campbell's first task in his new position was to carry out the requirement in the Forest Reserves Act of 1906 that settlers illegally squatting within the boundaries of the forest reserves be evicted. The majority of the squatters were compensated for their losses, but, even so, the Branch lost much of the good will it had gathered from its shelter-belt programme. Most of the complaints came from Manitoba and parts of Saskatchewan where small islands of treed hills and gullies had been given reserved status to protect their fragile environments. Virtually each one of these small reserves had groups of settlers living on its borders who wanted the land thrown open for settlement by their friends and relations. Typically in such situations, a local merchant organized a petition that ended up in the files of the Branch with a memo to the Minister attached. The Branch tended to give unsympathetic responses on the grounds the merchant either had an eye to increasing the number of potential customers or was interested in cutting whatever timber was growing on the broken land.[42] In all cases, a good deal of rancour resulted before the case was settled.

A second major task for Campbell, and for the staff of foresters he was slowly managing to hire, was drafting and implementing new logging regulations. Study of the regulations resulted from renewed charges by the Conservative Opposition that officials of the Department of the Interior had corruptly dealt with western timber berths. There were charges that Sifton's brother-in-law, T. A. Burrows, on his own and through companies and legal intermediaries, had conspired from 1899 through 1906 to fix bids for licences. Attempts were made to implicate Sifton himself through charges that he had amended the timber regulations in 1903 to give licence holders virtually perpetual rights as long as there was merchantable timber on the limit. Nothing was proven absolutely, but it did appear that Burrows and the Imperial Pulp Company, with which he was associated, gained rights to about 250,911 hectares of western timberland under particularly shady circumstances during Sifton's tenure as Minister. Sifton was not very convincing in his own defence in these matters, and the episode remains a major blot on his public career. The 1903 amendment, however, was not a particularly blatant piece of corruption. It provided that so long as the licencee complied with the regulations he would be entitled to a renewal of his licence from year to year while merchantable timber was available on it. It simply made renewal more certain than the previous licencing system of 1889 and brought it clearly into line with the system used in Ontario. Nevertheless, the Liberals wished to give the impression that they were moving to improve the management of forest leases in western Canada. The result was the new regulations of 1907 which were produced by the experts in the Forestry Branch in cooperation with the Timber and Grazing Branch. The regulations required that berths be properly cruised before being opened for auction, that a minimum diameter be set for cutting, and that all logs cut on Dominion lands be manufactured in Canada. Two other major provisions were included. The first sprung directly from the recommendations of the Select Committee headed by Greenway and revised the way in which royalties were paid to the Crown.[43] Up to 1907, the regulations required mills converting logs cut from Dominion berths present reports on the volume of lumber the logs yielded. This was a system clearly open to manipulation, and mills habitually reported only a portion of the volume they sawed. Henceforth, logs could be scaled in the bush before they were removed from the landings if the Branches so desired, and, most important, all operators cutting on Dominion lands were required to dispose of their slash in a manner prescribed by the officers of the Department of the Interior.[44]

These new regulations were binding on both the Forestry Branch and the Timber and Grazing Branch. Although they represented an advance for control over forestry activities on Dominion lands, they did not go much further than the best existing provincial regulations. For the Forestry Branch, they were the minimum requirements for a forest management programme, and it soon changed them as its techniques grew more sophisticated. The Timber and Grazing Branch, which was the main offender in the Opposition charges of 1906–1907, viewed the regulations as the maximum required and often allowed exceptions when pressed. It made no substantial alterations to the regulations from the time they were promulgated in 1907 to the Branch's disbandment in 1930. For instance, while operators cutting under Forestry's control had their logs scaled in the bush, those whose logs came from Timber Branch berths continued to provide this Branch with sworn statements based on the output of their mills. While Forestry conducted considerable research into the cheapest and best way to dispose of slash and then required its operators to follow its directions, Timber issued no directives and ignored advice from Forestry. As a result, Timber and Grazing Branch berths proved to be fire traps until, after seventeen intensive years of lobbying, it relented and required its operators to lop and scatter felling slash.

In summary, Forestry used the regulations to control woods activities so lumbering conformed to what the Branch's foresters thought would achieve their ideal: efficient utilization of the resource while ensuring its continued productivity and regeneration. The Timber and Grazing Branch, which controlled all the significant logging operations, simply noted that the regulations required the loggers follow the directions of one of its officers and that, if no directions were given, the logger could do as he pleased. From Timber's point of view, Forestry's regulations and objectives were just so much unproved theory that should be ignored by "practical men". This rift in attitude and policy was a direct reflection of the divisions so apparent in the Order in Council of 1899—the same divisions that presented themselves again in the debate over the Forest Reserves Acts of 1906 and 1911 and would come to light again in the 1930s when Timber and Grazing Branch officials once more had a major influence on the policies that would be adopted.[45]

But, even if the debate over forestry and forest conservation in Canada in the first decade of the twentieth century had its own unique national aspects, it could not escape the dynamic American influence of Theodore Roosevelt and Gifford Pinchot, Roosevelt's Chief Forester. At this crucial period, when the federal conservation initiative was most in need of direction, Roosevelt and Pinchot leapt onto the Canadian scene offering once more American examples to guide its progress. Roosevelt was not the most popular American President north of the border after the dispute over the Alaska boundary but, with his usual aplomb, this did not stop him from foisting the needs of internal United States policy onto Canada and thereby affecting immeasurably the conservationist cause in this country.

In early 1908, when he had only one year remaining as President, it was clear to Roosevelt and his Chief Forester that certain figures, both inside and outside of Congress, were biding their time to undo much of the progress made by American conservationists. One way to restrict the freedom of action of the waiting wolves in sheep's clothing (as one cartoonist later depicted them)[46] was to form a permanent commission, free from congressional influence, that would act as a watchdog and provide reports on all matters of interest to the movement. The membership of the commission would have to be self-perpetuating, and it would need wide support within the nation. As a result, the individual states were to be involved.

The responsibility for the creation of the commission was assigned by Pinchot to F. H. Newell, then Chairman of the Inland Waterways Commission. In the summer of 1907, as described by Pinchot, after discussions between Newell and Roosevelt, the original idea for a permanent commission was transformed into a conference of Governors of the individual states with a limited number of experts in attendance. The Governors' Conference was held in May, 1908, with W. J. McGee, a civil servant and a figure well known in the conservation movement, as secretary. One of the resolutions of the successful three-day meeting called for the establishment of State Conservation Commissions and a national body based in Washington, D.C. Out of the then forty-six states in the union, forty-one complied with the resolution. In addition, the National Conservation Commission was created in June. The founding meeting of this Commission was attended by Robert Campbell and Senator W. C. Edwards, as Canadian delegates.[47]

Like all of Roosevelt's commissions, the National Conservation Commission relied on volunteer labor to collect its information and prepare a report. In spite of a lack of a professional staff, the Commission completed an inventory of the nation's natural resources in time for its first meeting held in early December, barely four months before the end of Roosevelt's second and last term. The speed with which this considerable task was done speaks volumes for the organizational abilities of the protagonists, and also for their understanding of the need for almost frantic haste to create a permanent body before Roosevelt's departure.[48] The creation of the Commission was not enough for Pinchot and the President, who thought it should have links outside of the country to give it greater legitimacy. On 24 December 1908, Roosevelt wrote, and immediately released to the press, letters to Governor-General Lord Grey of Canada and President Porfiro Diaz of Mexico, inviting them to send representatives to meet in mid-February 1909 with himself and Gifford Pinchot. These letters were not entrusted to normal diplomatic channels; Pinchot was to travel first to Canada and then to Mexico as the President's personal representative and deliver the letters in person. Pinchot left Washington for Ottawa on 28 December and arrived on the following day with only the shortest of advance warning.[49]

The North American Conservation Conference was intended to identify and discuss conservation issues common to the three countries. It was claimed that such issues existed because of Mexican and Canadian interest in the National Conservation Commission and the National Rivers and Harbors Congress. Pinchot's abrupt arrival in Ottawa caused something of a crisis. A special luncheon meeting of the Canadian Club had to be organized for Friday, 30 December, to accommodate the situation. In a speech to the lunchtime gathering, described by the Ottawa papers as being interrupted by "loud applause," Pinchot reviewed the work done by Roosevelt's congresses and commissions, stated that problems as well as resources knew no national boundaries, and called for a co-ordinated approach that would reap benefits for the whole continent.[50]

The reply to Pinchot's address was made by the Governor-General, who revealed that the letter Pinchot had just passed to him called for co-operation between Canada and the United States in "a common and joint endeavour to safeguard the interests of posterity and guard from further reckless waste and wanton destruction and to protect that great inheritance of natural resources with which providence has so bounteously endowed us."[51] Lord Grey pledged that his government completely supported the motivation for the letter and that his government would soon be choosing delegates to attend the meeting proposed by President Roosevelt. Inadvertently, Grey exceeded the bounds of constitutional limitations when he made this statement of policy. Laurier recognized this but sensed that an important political opportunity was in the making, and he let the matter slip, stating humorously that "the Governor General has told you of the action that his advisers intend to take" and which he, Laurier, endorsed.[52]

Thus Canada committed itself to a course of action that was really the result of the desire of Pinchot and Roosevelt to protect their policies from a noncooperative Congress and, to their minds, a less than enthusiastic President Taft. As David Hall, Sifton's biographer, points out, American progressive reform politics were being exported to the North American continent in that

concern for conservation also was part of the reform sentiment of the era. By application of utilitarian theory, scientific research, some government regulation, and moral suasion, it was thought that the machinery of society and government could be cleansed and renewed, while corruption, slums, greed and waste were controlled or eliminated. A clean, productive natural environment was essential for the proper functioning of the social . . . environment.[53]

Few governments needed such cleansing reform more than Laurier's, and subsequently Minister of Agriculture Sydney Fisher, who was very sympathetic to conservation issues, Clifford Sifton, and Henri S. Beland, a Liberal M.P. from Quebec who had spoken often in support of conservation measures for pulpwood, attended the conference as Canada's representatives. They were joined by F. H. Outerbridge, who represented the Colony of Newfoundland, four Mexicans, and three Americans led by Pinchot. The Conference identified five areas of common concern: public health, forests, water, lands, and minerals. Not surprisingly, it recommended that in each of the three countries and in the Colony of Newfoundland, a permanent conservation commission be created. The commissions were to be restricted to information collection and exchange and work toward common legislative goals. The thrust of the Conference was to stress interdependence of conservation measures for all natural resources and the need for government regulation over the private sector to protect the public's interest in such resources.[54]

The Conference completed its work less than two weeks before Taft's inauguration. Almost immediately the plans made by the participants fell apart. Newfoundland and Mexico were never able to get their commissions organized. In the United States, Congress removed the item allocating funds to the National Conservation Commission from the budget and Taft did nothing to reinstate it thereby forcing the Commission to convert itself into a public association. Only in Canada, where Laurier perceived the idea as a good political measure for a government long in office and a little short of ideas, was a permanent commission created.[55]

The creation of a permanent commission required an act of Parliament. The bill would have to be carefully written because it was clear, from the outset, that the body would be in danger of encroaching on provincial jurisdiction. Sifton, as the most knowledgeable individual in the field and the one most sympathetic to the conservationist ethic, was given the job by Laurier of drafting the legislation. In April 1909 Sydney Fisher introduced a bill to Parliament to create a commission that would investigate and report on questions and problems that were referred to it or which it defined for itself while it lacked any administrative responsibility or executive powers.

The bill put the opposition in something of an embarrassing position. During the 1908 general election, Robert Borden had tried to catch a popular issue and advocated conservation and the rational development of natural resources as part of the Conservative party's election plank. Following the election, Borden and the opposition had successfully badgered the government into striking new Standing Committees of the House relating to Marine and Fisheries, Mines and Minerals, as well as Forests, Waterways, and Water-powers. Not wishing to abandon these achievements, Borden pushed for an expanded role for these committees. Fisher, however, argued that poor attendance at the meetings of these Standing Committees showed they were ineffective and that they were not the right vehicles for the tasks of information gathering and dissemination and public education intended for the new commission. In addition, Fisher, somewhat unfairly and inaccurately, criticized the Canadian Forestry Association for becoming too scientifically oriented and for not playing a role of publicly advocating conservation.[56]

In the end, the Opposition allowed the bill an easy passage since, in actual fact, they favored the establishment of a body dedicated to the advocacy of conservation measures. Thus, the government ended up with the best of all worlds—a commission that would investigate difficult issues of great popular concern but which could only make recommendations that were not binding on the government. Laurier, who, as stated above, was not at home with a larger regulatory role for government, had once again found a policy compromise satisfactory to his own particular views. Subsequently, the government named Clifford Sifton as Chairman of the new organization, and Sifton named a committee to guide the Commission in its work. Among the members of this committee were some of the country's leading supporters of conservation such as W. C. Edwards and Professor Fernow, supplemented by ex-officio representatives of the governments from each province and some business figures, such as E. B. Osler and Sir Sanford Fleming. Sifton, who himself remained a Member of Parliament, had hoped that the Liberals would be relatively nonpartisan in their appointments and pick men of vision and knowledge, but he was only partially successful in securing such nominations. In practice, although the Commission could investigate a wide range of topics, it was at first careful to restrict itself to an advisory role on questions referred to it.

The Commission of Conservation was rather a peculiar organization for Canada at this period of the country's development. It was really the forerunner of such agencies as the National Research Council, although it was more independent of government. It was the epitome of Pinchot's multidisciplinary approach to conservation, embracing a wide range of resource, environmental, and health issues and advocating the use of inventory and research to derive common coordinated solutions to evironmental and social problems. The Commission's wide mandate and multilevel nature meant that it was not constrained by constitutional niceties as were Commons committees or government departments although it was funded by the Dominion government and reported to Parliament through the Minister of Agriculture.[57]

Under the leadership of Sifton and the Commission's energetic permanent secretary, James White, the Commission of Conservation soon developed a reputation for independent and accurate research. Many bright individuals worked as researchers hired by the body to investigate problems. An excellent example is Roland D. Craig who pioneered techniques for modern forest surveys with his inventory of the forests of British Columbia. Such projects were initiated by the provinces concerned, carried out by independent investigators, but paid for by the federal government. On its own initiative, the Commission hired Thomas Adams to produce reports on town planning and moved into investigating the location of water resources and power sites across Canada. Public health and the preservation of the country's game populations were also topics investigated and introduced to public scrutiny for the first time.[58]

As time went by, the staff at the Commission became more and more frustrated by not having a direct impact on public policy. The negotiation of cooperative research agreements with the provincial governments was an attempt to overcome this situation, as was the successful promotion in 1912 of the creation of effective fire prevention patrols by the railway companies under an American forester, Clyde Leavitt. In the beginning, the Commission actively sought cooperation with the Forestry Branch as the two organizations shared many ideas and points of view. The Commission, at Sifton's direction, supported the Forestry Branch by criticizing, in print, the lack of forest management initiatives by the Timber and Grazing Branch and pointing out the need for all forest authorities in Canada to employ professional foresters in timber administration. Timber responded with a scathing attack on the training, experience, and personality of the foresters of the Forestry Branch in general and of Professor Fernow in particular, who, now at the University of Toronto, was perceived to be their mentor. The internal memorandum, forwarded by Leavitt to the Forestry Branch for its comments, did nothing to help feelings between the two organizations within the Department of the Interior. In addition, the Commission supported the Forestry Branch's requests for additional funding and Campbell's failed attempt to expand the role of his branch in the Forest Reserves and National Parks Act of 1911.[59]

The early years of World War I brought problems to this happy relationship. The Forestry Branch was given the authority to carry out forest products research and work on the problems associated with controlling the supply of lumber and pulpwood needed for the war effort. Thus, slowly, the Branch found itself moving away from being an organization solely concerned with the management of Dominion forest reserves and forest fire suppression. After the war, this national role for the Forestry Branch expanded greatly when the Branch began to develop its own research capability and represented Canada at the Imperial Forestry Conferences. These developments expressed new ambitions on the part of the Forestry Branch which led it to cast covetous eyes toward the cooperative projects developed by the Commission of Conservation in silvicultural research and forest inventory. By the end of the war, what had started as a minor irritation had become a major breach, and the Forestry Branch was prepared to turn on its old friend and ally, the Commission of Conservation, and work toward its demise.

Canada's Commission of Conservation shows how peculiar and ironical was the development of official conservation policy in Canada. It will be recalled that in 1899 Gifford Pinchot emphasized to Elihu Stewart the importance of there being only one body in Canada to carry out all aspects of Dominion forestry policy. This principle was reinforced in the White House Conference of 1909 where the interdependence of all conservation measures was stressed. Yet, after 1911, there were in Canada's federal government four organizations involved in aspects of forest management alone and these were divided between two Ministries: the Forestry Branch, Parks Branch, and Timber and Grazing Branch in the Department of the Interior, and the Commission of Conservation, which was loosely attached to the Department of Agriculture. In fact, it can be argued that Pinchot contributed to this diversity through his advocacy of the commission concept. The decentralization increased the need for co-operation between the organizations and made the effective practice of forest conservation harder to achieve. In addition, it gave politicians such as Frank Oliver, who had little sympathy for forest conservation measures, the opportunity to "divide and rule" —an opportunity Oliver was not slow to use to his advantage.

From the turn of the century to its disbandment in 1930, the Timber and Grazing Branch controlled practically all the merchantable forest under Dominion control and worked hard to ensure that loggers operated freely on it. In this period, conservation of natural resources, particularly as expressed in forestry and forest conservation, was a major political issue at the federal level in Canada. It was an issue that had its origins in the United States but was also popular in the Dominion, and it galvanized the Laurier government into undertaking some measures to manage what were rapidly coming to be perceived as valuable and increasingly scarce resources. But the issue also revealed the Laurier administration's lack of political will to face the vested interests in western Canada and bring forestry to the producing woodlands. Effectively, the federal government was careful to go no further than the minimum undertaken by the provincial governments, opting for forest reserves, fairly extensive in acreage but which, in fact, had excluded from them all of the commercial timberland under lease.

In this sense, its forest management programme was very limited in scope, and the political rhetoric of the Liberals supporting forest conservation was just so much window-dressing. In the background, some of the worst examples of nineteenth-century logging, being carried on under the benign eye of the same government, could be seen by those who cared to look hard enough. During the 1920s, official parties of foresters from every Dominion and colony in the British Empire were shown the Forestry Branch's neat demonstration plots and the magnificent western parks. They never saw the berths controlled by the Timber and Grazing Branch. The Laurier administration and later governments boasted that they had followed a number of progressive policies recommended by forestry advocates, but they never admitted that they ignored advice from their own expert officials on how to establish an effective forestry system on producing woodlands. Such policies were completely within the tradition of Canadian compromise. On the one hand, the government could appear to be taking action on serious national problems while, on the other, it could allow exploitation of valuable Dominion forestlands to go on relatively unfettered and avoid offending influential political interests in the West. Because the federal government failed to apply forestry to the producing woodlands under its control, it also failed to present the provinces with durable examples of leadership which they might have copied. This failure of statesmanship had a tremendous negative impact on the development of forest conservation in provinces. At best, it promoted diverse and partial solutions to the problem and, at worst, it gave a model for avoiding, in a politically satisfactory manner, effective policies.

CHAPTER 4

The Rise and Decline of Forest Conservation and Forestry Policy in Ontario, 1890–1940

Ontario had responded to the recommendations of the Montreal Congress by establishing a fire patrol system on licenced timberland on a shared-cost basis with the lumbermen. It had not gone as far as Quebec in legislating forest reserves, but neither had the province retreated from its commitments. Despite the province having the most diverse economy in the Dominion, the lumbermen in Ontario still were politically powerful. The leading eastern operators had supported the ideas expressed in Montreal because they were worried about their diminishing stocks of white pine. For this reason, they held the provincial government to its commitment to maintain and improve its fire protection system. As at the federal level, economic uncertainty into the 1890s retarded additional progress in forest conservation in Ontario. Smouldering as an issue, conservation could not be fanned into an open flame until it was caught up in the dramatic flow of economic and political events that combined to realign the province's forest industry between 1890 and 1920. These events were to lead Ontario to experiment in some very progressive forestry and forest conservation measures. Those measures were to thrust the province into a leadership position in the field before 1905 where, as we have seen, it provided important examples for the federal government. These successes were unfortunately short lived as the speculative bonanza connected with the development of northern Ontario led the province to reinstate the exploitive ethic as the mainstay of its timber policy. Ironically, by the late 1920s, the early leader in forestry was universally viewed as one of the most retrogressive provinces in Canada in regard to forest management practices. It was a situation which would not change until the 1940s as Ontario was the last major forest jurisdiction in the country to turn its timber over to professional foresters.

The decade following the Montreal Congress was difficult for the supporters of conservation in Ontario. By 1890, the advocates of greater control over the forest resource and increased security for the forest industries were reduced to the small groups that had originally championed the cause, especially the lumbermen of the Ottawa valley with their aging, cut-over limits. Even though some of these individuals were politically influential, they lacked the means to convince provincial politicians that new forestry measures would garner popular support and were thus worth adopting. In spite of this, economic forces on the continent were under way—forces that would soon renew forest conservation as a political issue in the province. Foremost amongst these in the years following the Congress was a significant change in the price of lumber in relation to the average value of other commodities. For the first time, the lumber prices started to rise steadily when compared to fluctuations in the index of average prices. Several events quickly followed this phenomenon. First, the use of lower grades of lumber increased which meant that a smaller proportion of each log was discarded as waste. Second, it became economically feasible to transport wood from greater distances to the geographic area of greatest demand: the seaboard of the northeastern United States. As the years to 1900 passed by, lumber was carried east from ever farther west and south until, in the first decade of the twentieth century, southern pine and western Douglas fir competed with each other in the lumber yards of New York City.[1]

The increasing value of lumber in the northeastern United States and the increased importation of Douglas fir and southern pine products had important effects on the lumber industry of Ontario. Ontario's lumbermen were forced to react to the actions taken by the owners of mills in Michigan and Wisconsin, the two states most affected by both the changing value of white pine lumber and the disastrous logging techniques of their woods industry. Loggers, who had started on the eastern boundary of Michigan, figuratively cut their way westward, then moved on. By 1900, the adjoining state of Wisconsin had taken the lead in production. Much of the money that had been made from the forests of Michigan was reinvested in Wisconsin and in holdings on the Pacific coast as well as in the forests of the south.[2]

In the late 1880s and early 1890s, the plight of Michigan's forests and the requirements of its lumbermen for new supplies were well known in Ontario. The situation was viewed by the province's business and political leaders with a peculiar combination of fear and speculative ambition. The ambivalence resulted from the policies of the Michigan lumbermen from the eastern portion of the state who had chosen not the follow the movement westward. With their accessible stocks depleted, these men were turning their eyes northward. An appreciable number moved their mills to the Ontario shore and started cutting on limits leased from the Crown. This was the same type of migration that had drawn American mill owners to various parts of British North America in the late 1840s and the 1850s. By and large, these new arrivals were welcomed as the harbingers of economic growth.[3]

Other Michigan lumbermen took a different approach to solving their problems. Their mills were located conveniently close to good markets with excellent transportation facilities, and their capitalization costs had already been recovered. These men opted to divert the funds that otherwise might have been used for building a mill in a new location to paying for higher log extraction and transportation costs. These mill owners, and there were quite a few, chose to tow booms of logs across the Great Lakes from limits on the Canadian shore. This policy was not welcomed by the mill men of Ontario. There was a keen appreciation the province might obtain a larger share of the American lumber market even though Ontario lumbermen were aware they could not hope to fill the demands of the northeast. To attempt to do so, they were convinced, would denude the province's pine forests in less than a decade.[4] This was really the issue. Ontario lumbermen wanted to be able to feed a fairly constant supply of lumber into a steady market. Like most businessmen, they desired security of supply and of market. The mill men of Michigan threatened both sides of this equation. This essentially conservative quest for security breathed new life back into the forest conservation movement and pushed the issue back into the public political arena.

In the mid–1890s, the vast majority of Ontario's citizens lived in rural and semirural settings. Most voters were still farmers or were dependent on the fortunes of farming. Not unnaturally, a bias toward agriculture permeated the province's politicians. For example, the provincial government perceived the development of northern Ontario in terms of the extension of the agricultural frontier. Lumbering was still seen as a transient activity preparing the way for farms. Amongst the bureaucrats in Toronto, this belief was slowly changing. Led by the Clerk of Forestry, people were beginning to see the necessity for distinguishing between lands suitable for agriculture and those suitable for forestry. The most promising move in this direction was the establishment of Algonquin National Park by the province in 1893.[5] The continuing agricultural bias in the provinces's development policies, however, partially dimmed the provincial Liberal administration's understanding that northern Ontario was rapidly becoming a scene of operations for competing groups of lumbermen each driven by the changes occurring in the lumber markets of North America. Soon, each group would be making large political demands on the good auspices of the administration.

From the east came the Ottawa valley lumber barons. Since the early 1880s, they had noted the depletion of the high-quality logs on which their mills depended. Their response to the situation was to look to the forests of the north and west and to construct railway lines into these areas to preserve their large investments in mills and marketing facilities. Lines were constructed northward into the Gatineau Hills and northwestward up the Ottawa River to North Bay, thence due north following the east shore of Lake Temiskaming to Lake Kipawa. The most important and the most politically explosive line headed due west, right across central Ontario, toward Georgian Bay. Two men, J. R. Booth and William G. Perley, had established the

Canada Atlantic Railway in the years 1879 to 1882 as a faster, more direct route from the Ottawa valley to their markets in New York and Boston. After 1887, this line was pushed west and north to reach new stands of timber and to supply the camps and depots. While the original acquisitions had been carried out with financial help from Sir John A. Macdonald's federal Tory government in partial compensation for the discrimination shown the Ottawa valley lumber trade by the National Policy, the westward extension was built on a different basis. Booth and Perley brought in other Ottawa valley lumbermen as partners and managed to get the line classified as a colonization railway. As such, it was able to receive grants from Oliver Mowat's Liberal government in Toronto. Support for the new grant was arranged by Erskine H. Bronson, president of the Bronsons and Weston Lumber Company of Ottawa and the industry's representative in the Ontario legislature.[6] Bronson obtained the grant as part of a political effort to bind the Ottawa valley lumber community more firmly to the provincial Liberal cause.

Slowly the line was pushed through the Algonquin Park area toward the newly constructed port of Depot Harbor near Parry Sound. Construction, naturally enough, kept pace with the logging crews, and in 1896 the task was completed. The route chosen for the railway conveniently cut across the headwaters of all the rivers flowing south from the park and diverted the riches of their forest eastward to Ottawa. Elevators were constructed at Depot Harbor and Port Arthur once the line was completed, and a fleet of lake steamers was added to complete the ensemble. Soon the line was carrying loads of western grain as well as Ontario logs.[7]

The completion of the Canada Atlantic Railway meant that products from western Canada could travel on a shortened route to Montreal and the United States eastern seaboard. From the point of view of some businessmen in Toronto, who had invested heavily in lumber companies located on Georgian Bay, the roughly constructed line appeared to be the first part of a system that would completely bypass their city and tap the riches of northern Ontario and western Canada. This threat of a westward extension of Ottawa's business influence was viewed seriously by these men, who complained bitterly about the provincial government's support of the interests of the national capital. A battle was on for the riches of northern Ontario, and both groups were well aware of it. In spite of their investment in railway lines and their powerful influence in provincial and national political circles, it was a battle the Ottawa men were to lose. The political implications of this metropolitan competition came to a head in the mid–1890s with an acrimonious debate over how to prevent the Michigan mill men from exporting unprocessed logs across the Great Lakes.

By political inclination and economic ideology, lumbermen in Ontario had favored free trade in lumber products between Canada and the United States since the 1850s. From 1854 to 1866, they had prospered under the Reciprocity Treaty so much that William Little had blamed it for the devastation of the pine in western Ontario. From Confederation to 1890, a variety of tariff rates had been in place, though none had seriously affected the export of Canadian lumber to the United States. Support for free trade was especially strong amongst the lumbermen operating along the shores of Georgian Bay. Their spokesman, Liberal Member of Parliament John Charlton, began to lobby the United States Congress for a reduction in the import duties on sawn lumber.[8]

Charlton was an aggressive businessman and an avid speculator. An American by birth, he had business connections in Ottawa and Toronto. He also exported logs from the north shore of the Great Lakes to mills he owned in the United States along the south shore of Lake Erie. Reciprocal free trade in woods products was manifestly in his own interest. As a prominent lumberman and Liberal politician, Charlton was successful in bridging the gap between the western-dominated Ontario Lumbermen's Association, supported by the Toronto interests, and the Ottawa valley operators. Charlton persuaded eastern lumber barons, such as J. R. Booth, E. H. Bronson, W. C. Edwards, G. H. Perley, and E. B. Eddy, to renew their support for the Lumbermen's Association in its efforts to remove the tariff on lumber, arguing that such a turn of events would soon be of benefit to them through reciprocal tariff arrangements. Charlton also had influential contacts in the United States Senate and in the White House. Through these contacts, he lobbied for the reduction of the tariff and supported the Wilson-Gorman Tariff Act of 1894 which completely freed imported lumber of tariff. [9]

Unfortunately for the Canadian lumber industry, the years from 1891 to 1896 saw a drop in the demand for lumber in the United States. In spite of this depressed market, imports of Canadian lumber actually increased by an average of fifteen percent each year during this period because of the growing scarcity of cheap lake states wood. Also, during these years, increasing numbers of Michigan mill men made the move to Ontario and joined the Canadian exporters in shipping lumber into the United States. Increased imports of a finished product into a depressed market was not considered a positive benefit by many American mill men from the midwest who were also facing increased competition from western and southern lumber. One obvious step was to have the Wilson-Gorman legislation repealed. The Michigan men, who boomed their logs across the Great Lakes from the Ontario shore, were to the fore in advocating this step which would give them an advantage over their Canadian competition—a competition that had conveniently agreed to remove export taxes from Canadian sawlogs. With the active assistance of Senator Dingley of Alabama, the United States government was converted to protectionism after experiencing only three years of free trade. In so doing, they nicely finessed the lumbermen of western Ontario into an intolerable situation.[10]

The Dingley tariff of 1897 levied a duty of $2 per thousand board feet of finished lumber imported into the United States.[11] The Dingley tariff began to drive a wedge between the Georgian Bay lumbermen and the Ottawa valley mill owners. Located near the market for their lumber, operating established water-powered mills, and having their own direct rail line for shipping, the Ottawa mills could still sell their products at competitive rates admittedly with reduced profits. For them the solution was to stabilize their industry through measures to preserve the remaining timber and hopefully improve the quality of their lumber over the long term. On a more practical basis, they had also taken the precaution of filling their wholesale yards in the states of Vermont and New York with as much duty-free lumber as they could hold. In addition, the plight of the western Ontario mills presented an opportunity for the industry of the Ottawa valley to regain the leadership in white pine lumber production which had begun to slip to the western part of the province in 1886. The Ottawa valley interests therefore decided on a policy of cutting production and trusting in the Dominion government to reach a negotiated settlement that would preserve the trade and permit them to pursue their own political agenda perhaps, as Charlton was suggesting, through a Joint High Commission to settle trade problems. These lumber barons were also extremely afraid that any precipitous action by either the federal or Ontario provincial government would result in the McKinley administration opting for a higher retaliatory rate.[12]

For their part, the western Ontario lumbermen could not afford the luxury of waiting out the political and economic storm as could their eastern counterparts. They were being driven toward economic ruin. With smaller, newer mills and consequently proportionately higher overheads and debt charges, they had to maintain production and sales. Furthermore, their distance from market was greater than that of their nearest competition in the United States, the mills of the Michigan men who were towing booms of logs across the Great Lakes.[13]

The Canadian general election of June, 1896, resulted in the defeat of the Conservatives and the election of Wilfrid Laurier and the Liberals. Although the new government was sympathetic to the plight of the Ontario lumber industry, the retaliatory clauses in the Dingley tariff prevented any quick, effective response from being made. It requested the British embassy in Washington, D.C., which at that time represented Canadian interests, to lobby with the McKinley administration in the United States to remove, or at least reduce, the tariff. Failure of these efforts was due, at least partially, to British lack of interest in the issue, which further infuriated the lumbermen. Furthermore, the government of the United States was unsympathetic to a return to free trade because, following the imposition of the tariff, the economy of the country had bounded upward, and the new prosperity was popularly credited to Dingley.[14] A Joint High Commission did eventually meet in Quebec City to negotiate a number of issues between the two countries but with no success.[15]

These failures left the members of the Ontario Lumbermen's Association with only one desperate recourse—their provincial government. This was now under the premiership of Oliver Mowat's successor, Arthur Hardy, a former attorney general and an experienced, but skittish, politician from the western part of the province. The Georgian Bay lumbermen were happy to find themselves joined by an electorate who were thoroughly outraged at what was interpreted as American high-handedness and callousness and were ready to put political pressure on the Premier. To lead them in their approach to the provincial government, the members of the Association chose John Bertram, their President, and Edward Rathbun, a mill owner from Deseronto, a village along the eastern shore of Lake Ontario. Bertram was a Toronto Liberal with a variety of business interests including lumbering in the Georgian Bay area. Rathbun had Tory proclivities, but his work with Bertram, his experiments with increased utilization of wood, and his advocacy of conservation measures soon made him a favourite of the provincial Liberals.[16]

To accomplish their goals, these men combined private pressure on the Ontario Premier and public criticism of government inaction on the issue of the export of logs to the United States. It is not clear who conceived the idea of imposing a "manufacturing condition" which would require the conversion of logs cut on Crown lands to be made at mills in Ontario. Rathbun had written Laurier several times arguing that national and provincial economic policies required logs not be exported from the country in an unmanufactured state and that banning the export of whole logs was a conservation measure. Regardless of whoever was responsible for it, the idea developed in the public mind as a remedy to the problem of sawlog exports when renewed negotiations with the Americans proved fruitless.[17]

As the popularity of the manufacturing condition increased, Hardy found himself faced with a political problem emanating from his supporters in the Ottawa valley. In vain, Hardy appealed to the Ottawa operators, through his Minister of Crown Lands, J. M. Gibson, to make a case that could dissuade him from taking the position of the Ontario Lumbermen's Association or to offer a compromise solution. But the Ottawa valley men were visibly split on the merits of the Association's proposal and, instead of replying in a positive manner, chose to remain in the nation's capital darkly predicting dire results if some of their needs were not met but failing to propose an acceptable alternative course. With no organized opposition forthcoming from his Ottawa contacts, Hardy proceeded to place a restriction on the export of logs cut from provincial Crown lands. Hardy preferred the new controls take the form of an amendment to the Crown Lands Act which implicated the legislature as a whole. This amendment to the Act was given Royal Assent in November, 1897, and took effect at the end of April, 1898, when the annual cutting licences for the following winter's work were to be issued. This meant that the Michigan men had the cut of 1897–1898 to export and thus an additional six months to find an alternative supply.[18]

For the government of Ontario, the ban on the export of logs, which was subsequently supported by the courts, was a bold and politically popular exercise of autonomy and a move toward the creation of "Empire Ontario."[19] The imposition of the manufacturing condition also had some other, more subtle repercussions. It was public recognition that the Georgian Bay lumbermen were the winners, both economically and politically, of the metropolitan battle for the northern Ontario hinterland. The Ottawa valley operators had misplayed their hand and, from this period forward, lost a great deal of control over government resource policies. In the long run, this was bad news for those advocating effective forestry programmes in the province. The western operators were men who had just opened up a new frontier of pine. They had little of the experience of the Ottawa lumber barons who were nearing the productive limits of their berths and were undergoing a traumatic readjustment as they were forced to diversify their product lines or go out of business. Few of the western men would support meaningful controls over the use of the commercial pine forest to secure a sustained yield. The limit of their concern was articulated in the manufacturing condition itself—mill conversion should take place in Ontario for logs cut on Crown land. Without their support for sustained yield management, the issue eventually died because the Ottawa valley industry was not prepared and was probably incapable of forcing through this type of measure on its own. The reason for this was that all operators were convinced that forest management would add significantly to their costs of production. No portion of the industry in the province was, therefore, prepared to see its costs rise unless the burden was shared by all.

The members of the Ontario Lumbermen's Association found a fellow spirit in their attitude toward exploitation in James Pliny Whitney, the leader of the Conservative opposition in the Ontario legislature who was to defeat the provincial Liberals in 1905. Whitney promoted the unbridled development of "New Ontario." From the time he became Premier, the government of the province looked for advice on forestry matters to the lumbermen of the north and west and their financial backers in Toronto. But, if the western lumbermen emerged from the debate on the manufacturing condition with their position enhanced, they did not displace the advocates of conservation without a considerable struggle. Thus, the debate on the "condition" and its aftermath served to rekindle public interest in forest conservation and generate measures for increased fire protection, forest reserves, and experiments in replanting and silvicultural techniques.[20]

The Hardy government attempted to answer this pressure for forest conservation through statements that the imposition of the condition was part of a genuine forest conservation program. This was simply not accepted at face value by a growing segment of the public, who appreciated the value of the manufacturing condition as an economic policy, but was now sophisticated enough to be able to judge the real worth of any "conservation" measure and wished the government to move in this area. Neither was it accepted by the Ottawa valley lumber industry as it observed the disappearance of the pine forests from its region. For these business interests, the crux of the matter was the failure of the pine to regenerate itself. For this sector of the industry with established mills, an efficient transportation system, and a secure market, this was the real issue, much more so than any debate over the nationality of the processor of the logs. The skepticism of the lumbermen from the eastern part of the province posed a definite political problem for Hardy. Many of these businessmen had supported the provincial Liberals in the past and their future support was crucial to the party. The need to placate these influential critics and the political necessity to identify itself with the new conservation movement in preparation for an imminent provincial election caused the Hardy government to emphasize forestry policies that the administration had already been in the process of considering in a more desultory fashion.

As a result of this complex tangle of pressures and often contradictory reasons, the Hardy administration, eager to identify with the modern progressive policies gaining popularity in the United States and among federal Liberals, began moving toward a forest conservation policy that was potentially dynamic and all encompassing. The man chosen by the government to lead the effort was Thomas Southworth, who had become Clerk of Forestry for the province in 1895. Since 1883, this position had been in the Department of Agriculture and was totally concerned with farmers and their woodlots. Now it was transferred, with its new incumbent, to the Department of Crown Lands. The move to the Department of Crown Lands and the government's new policy meant a major change for Southworth. Soon his reports were reflecting an interest in timber management instead of farm woodlots. He began to stress the need for forest reserves, the observance of the thirty-three centimetre minimum diameter limit (in effect since 1871 but not enforced), and improved forest protection. He also began an informal study of white pine regeneration. The Hardy administration, after it had been safely reelected in 1898, complemented Southworth's efforts by enlarging his office and renaming it the Bureau of Forestry.[21]

In fulfilling his new role, Southworth wrote about the distinctive characteristics of the forests of Ontario's north and northwest and about the possibilities for the natural regeneration of pine. He began to reverse the myth of the agricultural frontier by pointing out that large parts of the northern region were unsuited for agriculture but were "excellently suited for the production of successive growth of timber if growing conditions were closely controlled".[22] Like the lumbermen, he regarded fire as a major threat to pine reproduction. At the same time, Southworth was determined to establish an independent government position on forest conservation and distanced himself from the operators by blaming them for carelessness and for leaving large areas of flammable slash lying in the forest.

Further government support came to Southworth when, in June, 1897, the Hardy government met his request for a Royal Commission to examine the subject of "restoring and preserving the growth of white pine and other timber trees upon the lands in the province which are not adapted for agricultural purposes or settlement".[23] The Commissioners included the administration's two new-found advisors, E. W. Rathbun and John Bertram, and, despite some fears on the part of the eastern lumbermen, the findings of the Commission largely coincided with the desires of the Ottawa valley industry. In its *Final Report* (1899), the Commission called for greater fire prevention efforts, including more fire-ranger patrols; tighter regulation of timber berth leases; the classification of land; and the promulgation of a larger minimum cutting diameter limit for white pine.[24]

The report of the Royal Commission was an important document for early forestry in Ontario because it supported many of the demands of the forest conservationists for new regulatory legislation. Nevertheless, the document had an unfortunate side which seriously flawed it as the basis for a new forest policy. In short, the Commission completely failed to understand the problem of white pine regeneration. Its erroneous conclusions resulted in the adoption of a policy toward regeneration that hindered the acceptance of forest management in the province at least into the 1940s.[25] The problem lay in the nature of the chief commercial species, white pine, and the failure of the Commissioners to make a careful study of the shortcomings of natural reproduction from current European sources. Essentially what was occurring as the successive waves of logging teams moved across the landscape of Ontario was that the composition of the forest was changing. Many observers were prepared to blame the decline of white pine on natural circumstances. The older, well-established companies were convinced that, if the forest were properly reserved and protected from fire, the pine would regenerate satisfactorily. The tasks given to Southworth were to determine whether the pine was in truth suffering as badly as was thought and, if possible, to arrive at a solution to the problem.[26]

Early in 1896, before the Royal Commission was announced, Southworth had chosen to study this problem by carrying out a sort of public opinion survey. He wrote to the provincial Crown Timber Agents and to selected lumbermen asking for their comments. From the replies he received, he concluded that in many areas of the province the pine was regenerating successfully, but he was also told that fire was destroying young growing trees and that after every fire the proportion of pine in the forest decreased. Based on this loosely gathered data, Southworth definitively concluded that the generally held belief that the pine was not regenerating was false, even though there was some "scientific authority" endorsing it. Southworth stated such views were based on "popular error" resulting from the observation of burnt areas where there was no regeneration because fire had destroyed the seed lying dormant in the layers of dead leaves and needles. If cut-over areas were not burnt, then the pine invariably regenerated itself, Southworth declared, and to ensure its regeneration "practically all that needs to be done in order to maintain our timber supply in perpetuity . . . is to retain in the possession of the Crown all such timbered land as is not adapted to agriculture, and to protect it from fire". If this were done, he continued, the expected shortage of white pine would not occur, and the amount of available pine would actually increase.[27]

In its comments about white pine regeneration, Southworth's report of 1896 is as important for the things it did not say as for the recommendations it made. Little mention was made of the idea that Ontario's forests be managed by professional foresters on the European model, as had been done by the British in their Indian empire. Southworth may not have been directly acquainted with these techniques, but a more complete investigation would have easily revealed them. Alexander Kirkwood, another Ontario public servant, during his investigation in support of Algonquin Provincial Park, had already amassed and published a considerable amount of information on the subject. Basically, the tone of the 1896 report indicates that Southworth was not ready to admit that professional management or regulations governing logging practices were needed. His declaration about fire protection was also ambiguous. If his findings about the effect of fire on regenerating cut-overs was correct, then industry and government should have made a major effort to protect these areas from wildfires. In practice, this was not done. Fire rangers only patrolled areas of mature forest. As fire suppression grew in importance within the provincial forestry service, a policy was evolved that gave the protection of property in standing timber the highest priority when fire-fighting decisions had to be made.

Southworth's conclusions appear to be have been somewhat self-fulfilling. Aware of Hardy's political exigencies, he was eager to secure policies embodying conventional forest conservation theory which stressed the protection and preservation of standing timber. These ideas were also supported by the majority of woods operators. Coincidentally, other proposals of more intensive forest management, supported by a few conservationists and by the small number of professional foresters then in North America, were not viewed favourably by the vast majority of the forest industry. It is these ideas that were omitted. Total emphasis was placed on the call for forest reserves and increased fire protection as the only steps necessary to preserve and regenerate the pine.[28] The narrow basis of this position was partially recognized by the Ontario Royal Commission on Forestry of 1897–1899, but, in the end, Southworth's views were accepted in its report. In fact, in 1904, Southworth, himself, noted that the problem was not as he had earlier described it when he recognized that the drastic alteration in species composition of the forest following logging, as well as fire, might in fact be playing a significant role. Unfortunately, he did not go beyond admitting that he did not fully understand the process and that properly trained foresters were required to understand the conundrum. In spite of Southworth's later doubts, the basic conclusions about natural regeneration were sustained and eventually came to dominate official forest management policy in Ontario for many years.[29]

Fortunately, Southworth's recommendation did lead directly to some new provincial forest conservation legislation. Ontario's Forest Reserve Act, passed in January, 1898, authorized the Lieutenant Governor in Council "to set apart from time to time such portions of the public domain as may be deemed advisable for the purposes of future timber supplies". Forestry enthusiasts welcomed the act as "the inauguration of a scientific forestry system in Ontario" and as "the initial step in preparing for a rational system of forestry intended to ensure proper harvesting of existing stands of timber and to provide a perpetual source of income for the province." Officials moved quickly to designate reserve areas once the Act was promulgated. The first area designated included 33,000 hectares of cut and burnt over land in the southeastern portion of the province; this was quickly followed by a smaller area of 18,000 hectares on the north shore of Lake Superior.[30]

Unfortunately, this move was not followed by the designation of additional areas in need of regeneration or the setting out of a management policy for the reserves. It was not until 1901 when, facing its next battle at the polls, the Liberal government, now under the leadership of George Ross, found it politic to make another gesture to the conservationists. A huge area of 5,720 square kilometres centred on Lake Temagami in northeastern Ontario comprising virgin timber was designated the Temagami Forest Reserve. Two years later, in response to the popularity of the initial declaration, the reserve was enlarged to 15,340 square kilometres. It was claimed this expansion would permit closer regulation of recreational activities and secure adequate conditions for fire protection.[31] In fact, what it did was bring the large areas of future supplies for several well-known timber barons under the protection of the Act, ensuring they would not be disturbed by settlers and that they would be regularly patrolled by fire rangers. After several years of indecision, the policy of the Liberal provincial government was clarified. It wished to remove prime forest areas from the likelihood of frontier agricultural development and subsequent wildfires through forest protection measures as well as, hopefully, other management measures. It thought that, by doing this, natural regeneration of the pine would follow the logging which it intended to allow to continue at what it hoped would be a measured pace. Thus, licences were let in the reserves once the timber was mature or if it had been damaged by wind or fire.

The lumbermen from the Ottawa valley and eastern Ontario, who had advocated greater investment in public forestlands, won a substantial forestry measure with the Forest Reserves Act. They also clearly indicated to the Liberal governments of Hardy and Ross that they were prepared to have their timber-harvesting activities regulated. The problem was that in the few short years available to the government before its defeat by the Conservatives, the Liberals rarely demonstrated the fortitude to carry out the stated intent of their forest reserve policy and establish a timber-harvest policy for those areas. This lack of fortitude resulted largely from the rapidly diminishing influence of the eastern timber barons after 1900 and their increasing inability to influence provincial policies. Their eclipse was aided in no small measure by criticism from the so-called progressive forces grouped around the Conservative leader, James Pliny Whitney. The Conservative party identified the larger timber corporations as "monopolists" who had persuaded the provincial Liberals to give the forest resources of Ontario, through the medium of forest reserves, into the hands of greedy capitalists. The Tories proposed policies they defined as being progressive, democratic, and reform oriented, but, in reality, conservation for them had more to do with popular control over the resources and access to them rather than with long-range planning and sustained yield management. It was, however, Whitney's view which increasingly caught the attention of the provincial electorate. In 1905, when Whitney and the Tories won the provincial election ending thirty-four years of Liberal rule in Ontario, the forestry advocates were effectively removed from any influence over resource policies, and the whole programme went into limbo.

All that remained in Ontario, as it ventured into the new era of pulp and paper production, were Southworth's few reforms in reserving timber for the pine lumber industry and these, as we have seen, had inherent weaknesses. It is unfair to blame Southworth as the sole source of the delusion that forest reservation and fire protection would result in adequate pine regeneration. He was a publicist turned policy formulator. The ideas he wrote about were widely held among conservationists and lumbermen in all of North America in his time, and it probably seemed to him the logical course to follow. Even though Southworth's proposals were no use as a remedy to the failure of the pine to regenerate, there was considerable merit in the establishment of the forest reserve system and the improvements in the province's fire suppression organization. The pity is that these measures were not followed by scientifically based management of the public resource. Research was desperately needed to discover the proper silvicultural treatment that would result in the desired regeneration. This Southworth only partially understood, and the government he served remained totally oblivious to the need, retaining a naive faith in natural regeneration of northern pine forests.[32]

For this error, Southworth and his associates must be faulted. He must also be criticized for his early conclusion that professional expertise was not necessary for the management of northern pine forests and his later failure to lobby harder against this misconception. It was the beginning of a long-enduring myth in Ontario. Too many people, especially the leaders of the woods industries, came to the convenient conclusion that timber regeneration could be secured with a minimum of investment in silvicultural practice.

From their point of view, Southworth had placed a seal of approval on bush methods as then practiced, had confirmed that European methods need not be introduced and, increasingly, had stated that suggestions to the contrary from professional foresters could be ignored. The results were to be disastrous in the years of the new century when the pulp and paper industry moved into the province. This industry started wide-scale exploitation of Ontario's northernmost forests carrying it out as cheaply as possible with little or no thought to the future.

The pulp and paper industry developed somewhat differently in Ontario than elsewhere in eastern Canada. By the turn of the century, only in Ontario was the white pine still king of the forests. Lumbering in this province meant cutting white or red pine and continued to do so for some decades. Nevertheless, the signs of wear on Ontario's pine forests were considerable, and lumbermen foresaw the need to shift to new timber stocks and to the opportunities presented by pulp and paper. Because Ontario's lumber industry existed side by side with pulp and paper until well into the 1930s, the province found itself with the most diversified forest industry in Canada. Modern foresters would see this as a golden opportunity for integrated harvesting. In fact, it was an opportunity that was recognized by early Canadian foresters but was completely ignored at the time by both the provincial government and industry.[33] The province applied to pulp and paper the same policy structure it had applied to the older lumber industry along with the same inherent contradictions and weaknesses.

The first modern pulp and paper plant in Ontario was established at Sault Ste. Marie by an American, Francis H. Clergue. The plant set several precedents and patterns for the industry, particularly with a hinterland location close to the source of wood fibre and its control of its own hydroelectric power source. The company owning the mill also represented a new form of corporate structure that was being brought to the forest industries by the pulp and paper manufacturers. Although Clergue fitted the image of the great entrepreneur, he was different from the older type of lumber baron. These lumbermen had managed their companies personally, having, at the most, partnerships with one or two other men. Their mill and woods managers were under their personal instruction. Typical of this style of management was that of John Rudolfus Booth, the most illustrious of these lumbermen. By the 1890s, he was running one of the largest lumber companies in the world. He conducted his business from his office close to his mills in Ottawa; his main partners and heirs were his sons. Clergue, on the other hand, was closer to the modern businessman. He led a corporation owned by a number of shareholders, the day-to-day management of which was executed by men with technical and bureaucratic expertise.[34]

The employment of technically trained men was the norm in the nascent pulp and paper industry. The mills were, and still are, costly to build and complex in regard to equipment. Some employees must have engineering training, and there is usually a chemist with a laboratory to determine the quality of the product.[35] The corporate and business structure of pulp and paper mills was much more complex than that of a lumber mill. This often made paper companies more competitive in such areas as marketing, but they became more financially vulnerable in times of difficult and depressed markets because of their higher capitalization costs.

Clergue's mill was also the first paper mill to enter into an agreement with a Crown Lands Department to obtain spruce wood supplies. Signed in 1892, the agreement stipulated that the company could cut spruce, poplar, tamarack, and jack pine, paying dues of twenty cents per cord for the privilege. The lease was for twenty-one years; Clergue was to post a cash bond and agree to spend $200,000 on construction before December, 1895, to bring into production a mill employing 300 men for ten months of the year.[36] This agreement set a pattern for others which were to follow. The twenty-one-year duration was an innovation designed to allow the entrepreneur to recover the heavy investment required to build the plant. The agreement allowed large-scale, uncontrolled pulpwood cutting in return for specific conditions requiring the location of a large plant in the northern forest. It was expected that the mill would lead to a vast new industrial development in the hinterland. Using Clergue's agreement as an example, Ontario's Liberal government signed a number of similar agreements with other promoters. Many of these men had nothing more than speculation in mind; this system created a type of corporate speculator whose only relationship with the forest was as an investment opportunity.[37] While speculators in timber limits had been around since the days of the square timber trade, this group of pulp and paper investors introduced a new relationship with government, one that was neither happy nor particularly honest. This policy emphasized immediate economic development at the expense of proper resource management, and it was largely determined by events in the United States.

Pulp and paper companies were innately very attractive to Ontario's politicians. They employed large numbers of workers, many of whom were skilled; they involved considerable capital investment; and they were universally identified as examples of dynamic economic growth. Their location in the hinterland of New Ontario brought reality to long-promised dreams of development. The provincial government's attitude toward the industry was thus promotional. When demands rose from paper manufacturers for the province to declare a manufacturing condition on pulpwood, similar to that which it had applied to sawlogs in 1898, the province embarked on a resource policy as exploitive as the one it had adopted for pine timber.

Starting in the late 1890s, there arose in the United States a conflict between paper manufacturers and the American Newspaper Publishers' Association over the price of newsprint. The publishers wanted the free import of paper in the belief that this would lower its price. Canadian paper manufacturers supported this stand, of course, and tried in September, 1898, to convince the federal Liberal government of Wilfrid Laurier to place a tariff on pulpwood exports. Their requests met with the same negative response as had the efforts of the lumbermen when they had earlier lobbied for a reaction to the Dingley tariff.[38] Like the lumbermen before them, the pulp and paper companies of Ontario then turned to their provincial administration for help. Both business and government were pleased with the effect of the manufacturing condition as applied to sawlogs in April 1898. Several American sawmills had chosen to relocate in northwestern Ontario, and no retaliatory action had been taken by the United States government. With this success in mind, Arthur Hardy's successor, George Ross, passed an Order in Council in 1900 imposing a manufacturing condition on all pulpwood logs cut on Crown lands in the province.[39]

Ross was worried, however, that this interventionist policy might disadvantage the province in its search for potential investors in pulp and paper manufacturing. Realizing perhaps that the shortage of wood supplies would eventually force the industry to relocate in the province, he procrastinated. The implementation of the Order in Council was delayed until an agreement was reached with Quebec that it would simultaneously impose a manufacturing condition on pulpwood. It would appear that the death of Quebec's Premier Marchand, just after agreement was reached on this point, ended this understanding. Quebec's new Premier, S. N. Parent, formerly Minister of Lands and Forests, found the pressure from powerful lumber interests exporting pulpwood and the colonization movement too strong for him to impose a manufacturing condition on pulpwood. The most Parent dared do was raise the royalties on all logs allowing a discount if the logs were converted in the province.[40]

The failure of Quebec to provide strong support was not enough to delay application of the popular manufacturing condition to pulpwood, and the government promoted it as a conservation initiative just as they had with the sawlogs measure. In doing so, Ross was trying to alleviate the political difficulties of his government just as Hardy had done in 1897–1898. This the policy failed to do, and the pulpwood concessions became part of a maelstrom that destroyed the provincial Liberals. In the years between 1898 and 1905, the Liberals suffered from a problem with their public image. It might have been eased if the new pulpwood concessions had been placed under effective management. But, the government, which had been in power since 1872, did little more than expand its reservation program so that reserves now included some pulpwood concessions. Fearful that the imposition of forest management conditions would discourage investment in a precarious new industry and unwilling to move beyond the exploitive ethic, the Ross administration maintained a "business-like" approach to resource matters which sanctioned speculation and uncontrolled exploitation. This policy reinforced the impression that the government was tired and lacked vision, while, at the same time, laying it open to accusations of corruption and of favouring closed deals with large monopolistic enterprises over smaller, local busi- nesses. Aware of the opportunity, Whitney kept up a constant barrage against Liberal forest policies, contending they should be more supportive of smaller operators and farmers.[41]

The most celebrated case was the original Spanish river pulpwood conces- sion negotiated in 1900 by a group of Ontario operators working with Amer- ican capitalists. Whitney demanded that the concession be revoked and placed on the market for an open auction with bids. The Liberal government, ably supported by its press, particularly the *Globe*, scoffed at this suggestion on the grounds that capital could not be induced to take part in the free- for-all of a public auction and that negotiation was the only means by which large concerns could be enticed to invest in pulp and paper operations. For a while, it was able to point to the success of the Clergue operations in Sault Ste. Marie as support for its approach. Then in 1903, a recession brought financial difficulties to Clergue, and the argument began to lose its validity. At the same time, the three firms that had completed negotiations for conces- sions and had actually started building mills went out of business, and dis- cussions on the remaining five pulpwood concessions languished as investors cannily waited for the market situation for newsprint to reach conditions to their liking before completing negotiations.[42]

The Liberal industrial development strategy, based on the possibilities of pulp and paper, was in shambles and was exposed as a speculative sham. The Ross government deserved better than it got, but it was hoist on its own petard. Whitney, the man from Prescott, pointed to a Conservative platform which advocated the necessity of having an inventory of timber resources, legislative control over leases, and public competition for all concessions. Finding electoral support slipping away from them, the Lib- erals, as they had in 1897–1898, once more looked to conservation-oriented policies to improve their position. After the election of 1903 placed them in a minority government, the government decided to bolster its "forestry" image by appointing its first professional forester, Judson F. Clark, a native of Prince Edward Island, as an assistant to Southworth.[43]

Ironically Ross was stymied even in his efforts at reform. Southworth remained charged with looking after the northern commercial forests of the province; Clark was made responsible for southern Ontario, which meant farm woodlot forestry and associated publicity duties. In this way professional advice was kept from the commercial forests and the seeds were sown for discord. While it appeared that Clark was well suited for a government forestry job, having studied at the Ontario Agricultural College in Guelph before obtaining masters and doctoral degrees in forestry under Fernow at Cornell, there was great potential for his becoming frustrated with his po- sition.[44] He had visited Europe extensively, had taught botany, and then had worked under Gifford Pinchot in the United States Bureau of Forestry. Clark, who had a youthful eagerness to introduce proper forest management to Ontario, could therefore easily recognize the inherent contradictions in Ontario's existing forest policy. Unfortunately, he lacked the political skills of Southworth and, within a few months of joining government service, he addressed the Canadian Forestry Association's annual meeting with remarks that had not been even remotely discussed as possible government policy. He advocated the cost of forest management be borne totally out of the revenue from timber sales—heresy to most politicians and lumbermen. Later, he criticized the Doyle Log Rule, which was in official use in Ontario, for inaccuracies favouring lumbermen.[45] Clark and Southworth were under the supervision of Assistant Commissioner of Crown Lands Aubrey White, the man who had introduced fire protection to the province and who had held this senior position since 1887. Clark's remarks certainly did not win the sympathy of White, whose prime responsibilities were the leasing of timber limits, the measurement of logs, and the collection of royalties. In fact, they served only to create enough controversy to further hinder Southworth in the bureaucratic struggle to get some kind of true forest management adopted as official policy on the reserves and, rather than winning kudos for Ross, heightened the criticism of the Liberal administration.

This imbroglio was the last gasp of the government's conservation initiatives which had appeared to hold so such promise and marked its ultimate failure to control pulp operations. Having reduced Ross's Liberals to a minority position in 1903, Whitney and the Tories won the provincial election of 1905 by branding the Ross administration as tired and corrupt. The new Minister of Lands, Forests and Mines, as the Department of Crown Lands had been renamed, was Frank Cochrane from Sudbury, Whitney's personal choice as his strong political arm in northern Ontario.[46] Cochrane's task was to devise a policy to fulfill the government's election promises of developing New Ontario as a resource frontier and an engine for the economic growth of the province as a whole. One of his first actions was to cancel the five pulpwood concession agreements on which the terms had not been filled. In what appeared to be a bold move, he then asked his forester, Judson Clark, to prepare a proposal for new regulations covering the leasing of pulpwood concessions. Clark's report emphasized the government's responsibility for ensuring an adequate supply of raw materials while providing leases long enough to justify the capital investments being made. In return, the investor was to be expected to care for the resource he was utilizing—to protect it from fire, pay his dues, and contribute in investment and jobs to the provincial economy. Clark also included the Tory campaign promise that all leases and concessions should be bid for in open, public competitions.[47] The new government had in hand a plan that could bring proper management to the northern forests.

Unfortunately, Whitney was not prepared to combine campaign promises with political fortitude. Clark's report was quite at variance with the opinions of some members of the woods industry, particularly new investors in northern pulp limits who did not want government regulation to interfere with their speculative enterprises and attempts to lure American capital into the area. This discontent was brought to the notice of Whitney and Cochrane who quickly indicated they were not about to open a new era of forest management in Ontario. They were more interested in visible, public reform of administrative processes than in scientific management of the forests. The pulpwood concessions were reoffered shortly after they were cancelled in February, 1905, under what the administration announced as its own version of a fair businesslike auction system. No mention was made of a resource inventory, the requirement of a utilization plan or conditions stipulating the care to be taken of the resource. The government blithely ignored the professional advice of its forester, and Whitney conveniently forgot about legislative control over the leases. Even though his "reforms" were praised in the industry's trade journal, the *Pulp and Paper Magazine*, for their openness and fairness, the result was a fiasco. The trade was depressed, and only two of the concessions attracted acceptable bids. Contemporary opinion gave Whitney credit for establishing a new negotiating system but considered that nothing more could be done until the American market opened to Canadian products.[48]

An even clearer demonstration of the new government's attitude toward conservation and management of the forests came when the Bureau of Forestry and Colonization was transferred back to the Department of Agriculture. Henceforth, it was to concentrate on promoting the settlement of new farmlands, mainly in New Ontario, and abandon plans for forest reserve management.[49] The Tories obviously defined forestry in its older meaning: a science related to arborculture, agriculture, and the reclamation and preservation of farmlands. Shortly after, Judson Clark resigned from his position. He felt rebuffed by the government's neglect of his report and the move back to the Department of Agriculture. Bernhard Fernow said of his one-time student that he was "an aggressive man, with decided opinions and views, and was bound to do something of a practical nature in forest work. But his efforts failed to bear fruit, perhaps because he was too advanced for the situation."[50] Clark moved to Vancouver and entered in a career of forest consulting. He became the professional forester for the British Columbia Timber and Forestry Chamber of Commerce and was an influential force in forest policy formation in that province before he moved on to California.[51]

Once he had unburdened himself of his forestry advisers, Frank Cochrane made no more changes in the senior staff responsible for timber sales, and the search for new investors in Ontario's northern forests went on apace. Aubrey White was named the Deputy Minister of the new department and set about reforming the existing timber scaling regulations in such a way as to promote local control of the situation. He did this by decentralizing the system, by increasing the importance of the culler or timber scaler, and by tying all payments to the volume of wood scaled in the bush. There were two potential problems to this approach. First, it depended on the honesty of the timber scaler. The scaler was a part-time, winter appointee of the government paid directly by the company whose cut he was scaling. Quite often companies employed their scalers in the summer as fire rangers or in other positions. As a result, they were not to prove to be impartial reporters of their companies' production. Second, despite criticism from Judson Clark, White maintained the Doyle Log Rule with its acknowledged inaccuracy when used on logs of small diameter.[52]

Along with this decentralized administration, Cochrane combined a populist approach to leasing new limits. The Minister knew the north well and was quite aware that settlers looked to the trees on their locations as being their first crop. He was concerned that the market for pulpwood, in particular, not become flooded by the opening of too many new limits. Thus relatively few areas were put up for public auction and these were of limited size. This was described by Cochrane as being a conservationist approach to leasing. Such a policy was viewed favourably by a southern electorate, who accepted the government's declaration that it was conservationist in orientation, while the Minister could reap political rewards in the north, where the policy was popular with groups not the slightest interested in conservation. Obviously, the settlers appreciated this effort to keep pulpwood prices at good levels. The policy also pleased the lumbermen of northwestern Ontario, many of whom did not have the funds available to invest in limits as large as a township; but smaller offerings could be located so as to pick out the best pine stands available in an area, then they could cut the best of the trees like mice nibbling away at a cheese. Indeed, the only positive steps that the Whitney government took to support forest management in the province were the creation of a School of Forestry at the University of Toronto in 1907 under Fernow's leadership and the setting aside of new reserve lands in Temagami and in the Quetico boundary area.[53]

The forest resource policy of the Conservative government, which was in reality a reinstatement of the exploitive ethic, was eventually saved from the harsh criticism levelled at its Liberal predecessor by events in the United States. By 1909 the consumption of newsprint by American newspapers almost exactly equalled domestic paper production.[54] The American Newspaper Publishers' Association, led by John Norris of the *New York Times*, opened a campaign against cartels and combinations in the paper-making industry and against the high tariff. The Association contended that the cartel and the tariff acted to keep newsprint prices artificially high. The story of this campaign has been told many times before and need not be repeated here.[55] It is sufficient to say that the manufacturing condition was put to a severe test after 1909 as the United States attempted to break it through the Payne-Aldrich tariff and that American efforts to obtain free access to Canadian pulpwood were at the heart of the Canadian election campaign of 1911, which resulted in the ultimate defeat of Sir Wilfrid Laurier over the Reciprocity issue. By 1910–1911, American investment in Canadian pulp and paper had reached $82 million. American investors were recognizing two points: the only remaining supplies of cheap wood fibre were in Canada and the tariff would inevitably be removed. After Laurier's defeat, President Taft unilaterally lowered the tariff, and it was eventually completely eliminated by Woodrow Wilson in 1913.

The movement of the newsprint industry into Canada probably owed more to the growth of demand for the product in North America as a whole than to the lifting of the tariff. The evolution of the trade resulted in large new investments in Ontario's forest industries adding a gloss of success to the Conservatives' forest administration. It was only a gloss, however, because this economic success masked a colossal failure in public policy. Ontario politicians did nothing to capitalize on the intense public interest in resource matters and the popularity of the conservation ethic. In contrast to other provincial governments, it decided not to invest in a forest administration based on forestry principles. If the government had tried to take this initiative in New Ontario, it would have discovered forest management was more easily imposed on the new pulp and paper industry than it was on the older and entrenched lumber industry. Forest conservation in central Canada thereby might have been given a new and stable base on which to grow and demonstrate its efficiency.

In 1911 Cochrane left the Ontario cabinet to take a portfolio in Robert Borden's new federal Conservative government. He was replaced by William Hearst, a northerner from Sault Ste. Marie who was less interested in the day-to-day details of resource administration than was Cochrane. With Cochrane's departure went the close supervision of the senior officials of the department; this looseness soon percolated down to the level of the cullers and scalers. Following Whitney's death in 1914, Hearst became Premier, and the Department of Lands, Forests and Mines came under the stewardship of Howard Ferguson. Hearst has been described as an "astonishingly inept... party chieftain" and the tone of his government is best summarized in the sobriquet used to describe it, the "Pink Tea Administration".[56] Meanwhile, Ferguson, a lawyer from Kemptville, Ontario, cultivated the image of a man who could get things done regardless of the opposition. Perhaps most important of all he combined with his portfolio the general responsibility for the party's electoral organization. After the death of Aubrey White in office in 1915, the last restraints were removed from this minister. White's replacement was Albert Grigg, an ineffectual figure who had been the Conservative M.P.P. for Algoma. Willy-nilly, he became a cipher for the wishes of Ferguson and his overbearing private secretary, Carroll Hele.[57]

This was a period of rapid growth in the forest industries of Ontario—a growth Ferguson wished to aid and abet. Although the traditional market for Ontario lumber languished during the war years, the demand for paper products created by the conflict more than made up the difference. North American demand grew so rapidly during this period that, at the end of the war, the federal government was forced to set quotas and regulate supplies so essential industries were not caught short.[58] The situation in the forests of Ontario was made to order for pork barrelling and boondoggling. Ferguson was friendly with a number of important individuals in the forest industry. Most prominent of these was Jim Mathieu, an American who had moved to Rainy River, Ontario, and had become the Conservative M.P.P. for the riding. Around this gentleman and Colonel Don Hogarth, a Conservative bagman, was to grow a powerful and malevolent body known as the "Old Tory Timber Ring".

The ring turned the timber leasing process of the province into a vast collection net for the Conservative party's campaign fund and contributed to a deterioration and at times outright corruption of the administration of timber regulations. Scalers became so inept that some mills converted more than twice the official scale. The system of open bids was quietly shelved and replaced by unpublicized sealed tenders. Auctions, when held, were given such a brief advertisement that only the companies with advance knowledge were able to bid. When manipulation of the bidding system was not enough, large quantities of wood were leased using the vehicle of permits usually restricted to small quantities of firewood or mine timbers. Over 2,600 square kilometres of timberland were leased by this method. Much of the timber and pulpwood cut by the members of the ring and their associates was shipped by Ferguson's friends in Rainy River across the border to United States factories in direct contravention of the province's manufacturing condition.[59]

Although their choice of forest policies revealed the Conservative party had not really changed its conception of forestry and conservation since the 1880s, the greater shame lay in the events that followed Judson Clark's resignation in 1906. The caution and resentment nurtured in Aubrey White toward the reforming zeal of his first provincial forester was enhanced by his later dealings with Clark's old professor, Dr. Fernow. In March, 1907, Fernow moved to Toronto to found the University of Toronto's School of Forestry. From the first, it was apparent that he and White were from such different backgrounds and were of such contrasting temperaments that agreement between the two would be difficult. Fernow believed passionately that the professional forester acted as an agent of the state and developed policies for forest administration for the benefit of the public based on scientific principles. This was the German model of the civil servant, professionally trained and serving the greater interests of the state.[60] White saw himself and his administrators and clerks as chief advisors on forest administration to the government. After offering advice, it was the duty of the advisors to accept and implement the policy chosen by the elected legislators of the province regardless of any good or bad effects on the forest environment. Thus, White interpreted the desires of the legislators with regard to forestry to be limited to the reforestation of abandoned lands in the southern regions of the province and the protection of commercial forests from fire. He was not prepared to impose a broader forestry policy, and, for this, he and his immediate successors were roundly criticized by Fernow, other forestry professors at Toronto, and by the profession in general.[61]

It is not surprising then that White studiously avoided choosing Fernow's forestry graduates as employees. He distrusted their European bias and their identification with the Dominion Forestry Branch's approach to solving problems. It was not until 1912 that the Deputy Minister found a forester who he considered had the correct approach, an understanding of the situation and the right Tory connections to make him acceptable as Clark's replacement. This man, Edward Zavitz, was hired to administer the Counties Reforestation Act passed in 1911. This Act's limited objective of reforesting abandoned farmlands, such as the sand dunes of Norfolk county in southwestern Ontario, fitted perfectly the Ontario government's conception of forestry.[62]

Zavitz had traditional roots in Ontario and was a graduate of the Ontario Agricultural College. He had attended (but had not graduated from) the Yale Forestry School before finally graduating with a masters degree in forestry from Michigan. From 1905, Zavitz had taught at the Agricultural College and had worked part-time for the Department of Agriculture. The new employee was given the title of Provincial Forester and a "Forestry Branch" was again created within the Department of Lands, Forests and Mines.[63] Zavitz's job as Provincial Forester was intentionally limited in scope. The only opening related to commercial forestry permitted his Branch, beyond reforestation of sand dunes, was in fire protection. Using this opportunity, Zavitz worked to get overall responsibility for fire suppression assigned to him. Eventually he was successful, but not until 1917 after the large fire at Matheson in northeastern Ontario. Slowly, Zavitz enlarged the responsibilities of his branch so that by 1940 it included research, forest inventory, and forest protection in the broad sense of including entomology and pathology. He also found that the Department was willing to hire a few professional foresters during the prosperous days of the 1920s.[64]

With equally dogged determination, the Tory administration kept foresters from the "timbering" end of the business. Up until reforms were carried out in 1942–1943, foresters fought Ontario's forest fires while clerks and cullers, working their way up through the ranks, "managed" the forests by administering timber leases. It was a system highly reminiscent of the situation with the Timber, Mines and Grazing Branch in the Dominion Department of the Interior before 1930 and represented the ultimate triumph of the "practical man". As a result, Ontario was one of the last jurisdictions in North America to place the management of its forests under professional care. Successive governments continued the policy because, while it was popular to employ foresters in protection and research, true forest management was resisted by a large part of the forest industry which feared that costs would be raised and its access to new timber restricted. This opposition set the limit to which the provincial government was prepared to go with its resource policy.[65]

From 1920 until 1940, the pulp and paper industry experienced falling prices while competition was intense because of over-production. High plant efficiency and low raw material costs had to be maintained by companies wishing to stay in business. Through its acquisition of the Riordan Paper Company assets in eastern Canada, International Paper obtained the most modern and efficient mills in this part of the country along with some of the best limits. This gave the company such an advantage in the struggle that, during these years, its mills ran at full capacity while production at the older mills of its competition fluctuated widely. As a result, International Paper led other mills in setting lower and lower prices for the supply of newsprint.[66] The lumber industry was in a different situation, but the effect was similar. Northwestern Ontario was the last frontier of the lumber industry because, by the start of World War I, the Ottawa valley trade was but a shadow of its former self. Lumbermen in the northwest were fully aware their resources were limited and they wished to high-grade the remaining white pine as cheaply as possible. Not expecting to stay long, their interest in sustained yield was, to say the least, generally limited. During the period from 1900 to 1940, many companies hired foresters, but their role quickly became that of forest engineers. Rarely were they required to manage harvesting, introduce silvicultural techniques to secure regeneration, or develop realistic plans for sustained yield on pulp limits. Their role was to lower the cost of exploitation, a fate they were aware of and not slow to bemoan to their fellow foresters.[67] By 1920, new business imperatives in the Ontario forest industry had, in large part, replaced the more public-spirited views of the lumber barons of the 1880s and 1890s.

The statistician for the American Lumbermen's Association, Wilson Compton, was generally representative of the industry when he claimed that shortages of lumber from one species were easily replaced with products from others, that over-cutting was not a problem in North America because the excess of over-mature stock was still too high, that the era of cheap wood had to come to an end because it was not a measure of national wealth but rather an historical accident, that the industry had generally done society a favour by creating cleared areas from the mine of the forest and that, because of expense to industry, if the public wanted these areas reforested, it should pay for it even if the land was privately owned.[68] Perhaps no better example of how industry now opposed the initiatives of the conservation movement is shown than in its response to ideas sent to the United Farmers of Ontario government by the Canadian Forestry Association. In December, 1919, just after the election of the Farmers and the defeat of the Tories, the Premier, E. C. Drury, received a document from the Canadian Forestry Association. Written by the secretary, Robson Black, the document was entitled "A Memorandum Respecting the Better Administration of the Crown Forests of Ontario".[69] Black, besides sending the memorandum to the Premier, forwarded copies to the Boards of Trade of various cities in the province asking for their endorsement. The document called for an increase in the efficiency of the province's fire-fighting service by removing "patronage considerations in making promotions" and by employing staff year round. Black contended this aim could be achieved and a necessary emphasis could be given to regeneration by giving Zavitz's Forestry Branch administrative control over the entire Crown forest. He recommended the Branch be expanded by hiring a number of technically qualified men. Policy decisions in forest administration might, it was suggested, be guided by a "Forestry Board" that brought together politicians, foresters, and industrialists.[70]

Black's ideas were quickly endorsed by the Kitchener and Toronto Boards of Trade but not by the forest industries. In mid-January, Drury received a letter from C. Jackson Booth, the son of the famed lumber baron, who spoke for all Ottawa valley lumber and pulp operators through the auspices of the Upper Ottawa Improvement Company, the same interests that had so eloquently supported conservation from 1882 to 1906. Booth contended that Black's memorandum had "never been submitted to, nor approved of, by the members or directors of the Canadian Forestry Association." Booth continued, giving Drury the distinct impression that the Ottawa valley operators would not support the recommendations. In a reply to John A. Gillies of the Gillies Bros. Lumber Company of Arnprior, who was chairman of the Ottawa Improvement Company, the Premier indicated, in the face of this vehement opposition, that he was not about to implement Black's ideas. Facing increased competition for markets and looking to control costs through cheap fibre and timber, the forest industry in Ontario disowned what support it had had for forestry and forest conservation. It was not until the 1920s were nearly over that the deterioration of much of the province's forests once again became a problem for the industry, and it began, once more, to support measures to sustain a diminishing resource.[71]

Drury and the United Farmers of Ontario represented the only real possibility for change and reform during this forty-year period of neglect. Although they failed to follow up on Black's initiative, they remained interested in forestry matters, especially if they could be employed to their own advantage against the Tories and Howard Ferguson. Drury's government investigated various charges of corruption and bad administration of the Crown forests made against the Hearst administration. Known as the Latchford-Riddell Commission, Drury's hopes for its investigations were two-fold: to root out corruption in the provincial civil service and to exorcise Ferguson from public life. Those supporting forestry and forest conservation also hoped that the Commission would gather enough evidence for a complete reform of forestry matters in province.[72]

The Commission amassed a great deal of evidence of improper administration of forest lands in general and against Ferguson in particular. It also heard from witnesses about the way in which the resource should be managed. One of these witnesses was Judson Clark who returned from San Francisco in 1922 and presented recommendations that were practically identical to those he had made in 1906.[73] Industry, however, gathered its strength and supported the Tory's policies and Howard Ferguson in a powerful series of counterattacks. They criticized Clark's and similar proposals with counterarguments based on economic considerations. Howard Ferguson also came to his own defense criticizing the Drury government for its sanctimonious attitude and for its own relationship with various companies. The attacks successfully smashed whatever desire the United Farmers had for reform and played their part in tumbling the party from office in disarray.[74]

Ferguson's defensive attack on the Latchford-Riddell Commission was followed by his election as leader of the Conservative party in Ontario and then, in July, 1923, his assumption of the premiership following his party's victory at the polls. With Ferguson in power there was no hope for basic changes in the province's natural resource policy. Criticisms from professional foresters at the University of Toronto and from federal government officials appeared in the press and in other forums such as reports of royal commissions, but the Tories showed no inclination to change. The only bright spot occurred late in this period when William Finlayson served as Minister of Lands and Forests from 1926 to 1934. He was the half brother of Ernest H. Finlayson who was, at the time, the Director of the Dominion Forestry Service. Drawing on this connection, the minister drafted a new Forest Act in 1927 which would have brought the foresters closer to the management of the commercial forest of the province.[75]

Part of the Act provided for a Forestry Board along the lines advocated by Black some eight years previously, although the Board was to advise on research needs instead of policy. The men appointed to the Board were E. J. Zavitz; Dr. C. D. Howe, Dean of the faculty of forestry at Toronto; B. F. Avery, forester for the Abitibi Power and Paper Company; and James A. Gillies of the same Gillies Bros. Lumber Company which, ironically, had opposed the proposals of the Canadian Forestry Association. The Board quickly expanded its role outside of research. It launched itself into the midst of Finlayson's attempts to write two new pieces of legislation, the Provincial Forests Act and the Pulpwood Conservation Act, in 1928 and 1929. It also kept pressure on the government to increase the stature of professional foresters employed by the province by increasing their pay and getting them more involved in timber and forest management activities. Even though the Board had the tacit support of industry, it appears to have pushed some of the traditional officials in the Department of Lands and Forests too far, too fast. Finlayson's initiatives ran out of steam and sank out of sight as the depression of the 1930s intensified. The final blow to official forestry in Ontario came in 1934 with the election of Mitchell Hepburn's Liberal administration. The new Liberal Premier was determined to cut the expense of government to the bone in the belief it would help the province recover economically from the depression. The Department of Lands and Forests was ravaged of many of its personnel. Particularly hard hit was the Forestry Branch, which lost a number of its professional foresters on the basis of the argument that a university degree was not a prerequisite to efficient fire fighting.[76]

By 1934, the forestry and conservation movement in Ontario had, to all intents and purposes, died so far as its influence in official circles was concerned. It had had an optimistic start in the 1880s when it was amply supported by industry. Government had taken up the cause, and Ontario began well with fire ranger patrols and, eventually, forest reserves. But, from 1905, the situation had deteriorated. It was as if there was a complete misunderstanding as to what conservation was all about. The theme of the movement was that the orderly use of existing resources ensured the economy would always have sufficient renewable raw materials. Scientific techniques combined with co-operation from industry were advocated as the means for government to achieve this beneficial end.

In Ontario from 1905 to 1942, almost all parts of this equation were missing. Within industry the uncontrolled exploitation of forest resources came to be emphasized as the engine for general economic growth regardless of any government or public desire to plan resource utilization on a sustained yield basis. The rise of a new class of entrepreneurs, connected with the pulp and paper industry, appears to have heavily influenced this process. Unlike the Ottawa valley men of the 1880s, their commitment to the forest seems to have been as small as their commitment to the balance sheets of their corporations was large. Because conservation appeared to involve increased costs, it was rejected in spite of the movement's dedication to business-like efficiency. Businessmen thought this would gain them higher short-term yields even though difficulties might arise in the future, as indeed they have. During this thirty-five-year period, conservation and forest management were never given a fair trial in the province. Not a single company was required to modify its extraction techniques to achieve a silvicultural end. No company voluntarily considered conducting its own forest management experiments although some did establish tree nurseries. Whereas other provinces, notably British Columbia and Quebec, at least attempted to impose professional, technical expertise on the management of their forests during this time, Ontario remained a backwater. It was unable or unwilling to deal effectively with the fragile, renewable resource of which it boasted so proudly and on which it based so much of its estimate of provincial wealth.

CHAPTER 5

Lessons from Europe: Forestry Policy in Quebec, 1900–1940

Although Ontario and Quebec shared many aspects of their early regulations concerning the alienation of lands and the leasing of timber berths, by the 1870s and 1880s, most of these early similarities had disappeared. Major policy differences between the two provinces, which had become discernible by this time, eventually led to quite a different approach to the management of the forest resource in Quebec. Quebec alone opted for a full-fledged management system based on European models. It has been argued that it was the threat of unrestricted American exploitation of Ontario's pineries that sparked the political debate that led to the first rudimentary attempts at forestry in Ontario. In contrast, the impetus toward resource management in Quebec came from its continuing efforts to reconcile differences between the colonization movement and a forest industry that was becoming increasingly important in the province's economic development.

As in Ontario, the lumbermen of Quebec exported logs that they had cut on Crown land to the United States. Although the trade was limited, it was lucrative, and the businessmen concerned could bring tremendous influence to bear on any provincial administration that threatened the trade. As a result, Quebec failed to support the efforts of Ontario lumbermen to institute a manufacturing condition until 1910 when pressure to attract American pulp and paper mills to the province was felt. The lumbermen were aided in their political efforts by Quebec's greater isolation from direct American forays into unlicenced Crown areas. Furthermore, the lumber industry had reached the limits of its expansion in the province at a relatively early point in the nineteenth century and, by the 1890s, was already being replaced by pulp and paper. By the turn of the century, the mills of Quebec supplied Canada with 80 percent of the paper made in the country.[1]

Geographic and social factors resulted in a unique pattern of settlement in Quebec, which affected the industry. The most heavily settled area of the province, with the minimum of available Crown Land, was south of the St. Lawrence river and eastward along its banks. As a result, by 1880 most logging activity took place in the part of the province north of the river. To take advantage of the available modes of transportation, conversion plants and, especially, the new pulp mills, were located at the intersection of the south flowing rivers with the east-west running railway lines.[2]

Far more than in Ontario, the production and export of pulpwood from privately owned lands was a big business in Quebec. Most of the logs came from private woodlots in the southern and eastern portions of the province, an area where access to railways was good. American companies also owned large acreages of private forest, mostly in the eastern part of Quebec. These forests had been obtained through the purchase of seigneurial lands. The relatively small quantity of wood that came from private lands to the north of the St. Lawrence was cut by colons who sold as much as they could of the trees they cut while clearing their lands. As in the settlement areas of northeastern Ontario, the lack of roads and other transportation difficulties restricted the amount each settler could haul to market.[3]

During the 1880s and 1890s, the clay belt area of northern Quebec, northeast of Lake Temiskaming, was not yet open to settlement. In this period, most settlement activity took place in regions just to the north of the province's major cities and in Matapédia and the Gaspé. It was here that the colonizers and the timber interests clashed. Before the rise of pulpwood as a valuable commodity, logs cut by farmers or settlers were sold to local sawmills. As the demand for pulpwood rose, owners of private wood could choose where to sell their logs and, as a result, the price of both rose. After 1900, even though Quebec became the premier centre in Canada for the manufacture of pulp, most privately cut wood sold for pulping was still being exported.

There were several reasons for this. First, most of the mills were located to the north of the settled areas where most of the pulp logs were cut. A lack of connecting rail lines made the northward movement of logs difficult and expensive. It was cheaper and easier to ship them south. Second, paper-producing companies in the United States paid more for wood than did their Canadian counterparts. A third factor, applicable to wood cut from woodlots on older farms, was that this wood consisted largely of poplar and other hardwoods. These woods were suitable only for pulping with the soda process, and practically the only soda mills nearby were in the northeastern United States.[4]

The species of trees cut by the colons north of the river were softwoods as were the trees cut from the eastern seigneuries. These logs were in demand for newsprint production and found a ready market in the United States. Some train loads were even shipped to Canadian mills in Nova Scotia or southern Ontario through the United States. This active market was a boost to the advancement of the colonization movement but also increased the activities of bogus settlers and land speculators. It was this development that was at the heart of the problem in Quebec and generated conflict between the advocates of colonization and woodlands operators. It sparked a long and intense political controversy in the province.[5] The conflict intensified as the new pulp and paper plants sprang up in the northern part of the province bringing with them a form of expansionary industrialization. The government was forced to react to the controversy in some relatively nonpartisan manner. Taking sides in the issue would alienate one or more important interest groups within the province. Quebec chose to solve this problem by taking over control of all woods activity, which led to some very advanced forestry regulations and real efforts at forest management.

Augmenting this political and socioeconomic situation was another factor. Quebec had long had the most reason to be concerned about its white pine stocks, and this concern resulted in the lumber industry's becoming more receptive to new ideas than its counterpart in Ontario. Quebec lumbermen pressured Quebec politicians to conserve as much as possible the pine growing on public lands. The less open nature of Quebec politics meant the large lumber interests could exert considerable influence on the provincial administration. This resulted in co-operation between business and government in creating as stable conditions as possible for the industry's exploitation of the resource, often, under extremely generous financial conditions.[6] But such concerns also led to pioneering efforts to keep the resource in relatively abundant supply. Thus, as early as 1868, Quebec had a regulation setting the minimum diameter limit at 30.5 centimetres in an effort to ensure regeneration. As well, the province hosted the American Forestry Congress in Montreal in 1882 and a further meeting on forestry in Quebec City in 1890. The province was also the first to experiment with forest reserves. An amendment to the Crown Lands Act in 1870 allowed the government to reserve timbered lands from sale or colonization after inspections had shown they were not suitable for agriculture. This legislation was never implemented properly, however, and it was replaced by Dr. W. W. Lynch's new amendment to the Act in 1883, which is discussed in Chapter 2.[7]

Quebec was also the first province to hire staff to carry out inspections of logging operations while they were in progress. Starting in 1873, the inspectors or "forest rangers" investigated trespass and checked scaled wood piled at landings. They strove to increase the accuracy of the returns and hence the income to the Crown. This was a natural result of the province's having opted for twenty-one-year leases after Confederation. The Crown dues could be altered only at stipulated periods in these lengthy contracts, and thus the only way to increase revenues to the Crown was to increase the efficiency of the scaling system. Although they were originally hired for relatively mundane duties, the rangers soon found their role expanded. Provincial administrators, like the venerable E. E. Taché, had other loftier goals

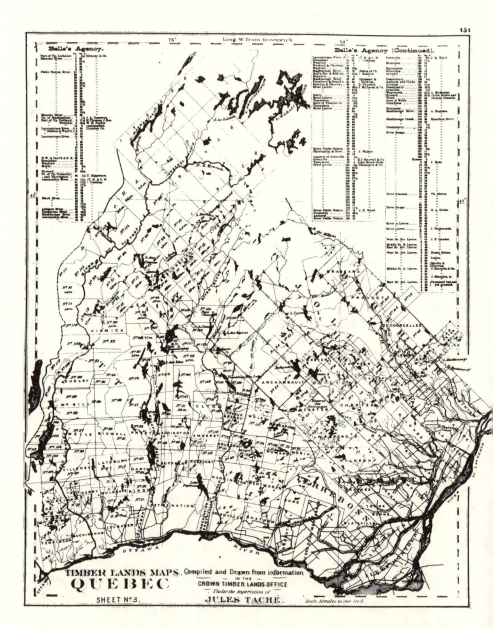

1875 timber berth map of west-central Quebec including the watersheds of the major tributaries of the Ottawa river. Berthierville is an unmarked community in the easternmost township of Berthier (printed by permission of the National Map Collection, Public Archives of Canada).

in mind than simply increasing the income from dues. They made the rangers responsible for overseeing a company's adherence to the diameter limits as well as for passing out information on fire prevention.[8] Unfortunately, it was not until the early twentieth century that the rangers were hired for more than just the winter. As was to happen later in Ontario, the logging companies were not slow to hire these men in the summer when logging was not in progress and thus earn their gratitude. As a result, as in Ontario, basically good legislation and regulations were less than effective in Quebec because the administration was often lax and, at times, outrightly corrupt.

Other limitations soon made themselves apparent. Following the 1882 Congress, the Commissioner for Crown Lands tried for several years to institute industry-government co-operation in fire protection. His efforts were unsuccessful, and he sorrowfully compared his province with Ontario where fire ranging efforts had started in 1885. But, obviously, for both the lumber interests and the forestry advocates, the major setback for forestry in the province was the repeal in 1888 of the Forest Reserve Act and the clause in the Land Act reserving merchantable pine on located lots if the lot was part of a timber limit. The passage of these pieces of legislation had been a major goal of the Quebec Limitholders' Association. To achieve this objective, the Association had formed the coalition with the conservationists that had made the 1882 meeting of the American Forestry Congress the success it was.[9]

The colonization movement was at the same time becoming a major force within provincial politics. Sponsored in large part by the province's Roman Catholic clergy and backed by French-Canadian Nationaliste politicians and journalists, it was a concerted attempt to reinforce the Catholic, agrarian ethic of French Canada in the face of burgeoning industrialization and urban growth. The colonization programme sought to open up the rugged, forested terrain of the Laurentians and Gaspé to agricultural settlers who would be drawn from the excess French-speaking population on settled lands and from families repatriated from the factory towns of the New England states. It was directed by people who passionately believed that French Canada had to strengthen its rural roots and resist the temptations of urban life in order to protect its culture. It was from this movement that opposition to the Reserve Act first emanated.

Settlers in Egan Township on the Gatineau river, led by Fr. Charles Paradis, an oblate missionary, challenged the large Gilmour Lumber Company of Ottawa-Hull over its exclusive right to cut timber on reserved forestland. The case was fought all the way to the Judicial Committee of the Privy Council, the highest court of appeal in the British Empire. In 1889 this body upheld the settlers ruling that timber on "located" lots in timber limits was the property of the location ticket holder and could be cut by the settler as long as Crown timber dues were paid to the provincial government.

Political trends also favoured the colonizers. The provincial Conservatives fell from power in the wake of the agitation over the hanging, in late 1885, of Louis Riel, the Metis leader of the North-West Rebellion, and were replaced by the Parti National under Honoré Mercier. The Mercier government was very sympathetic toward the rural, Catholic ethic espoused by the colonization movement. Partly in return for popular support in the electoral district of Hull (which included Egan Township), Mercier abolished the Reserve Act of 1883 though he retained the province's forest fire protection legislation. Quebec lumbermen thus lost their reserves and the right to remove timber from located lots within the boundaries of their limits.

The long-term results of these actions by Mercier were to be unfortunate, but at first they appeared to be a great success from the point of view of his supporters. There was a considerable increase in the alienation from the Crown of lands for settlement. Mercier had appointed the spiritual leader of the colonization movement, Father Labelle, to the position of Deputy Minister of Colonization. Labelle and other supporters of the movement praised highly the results produced by the new government's policy. What was often ignored was the fact that an increased portion of these sales was going to bogus settlers and land speculators. The Quebec lumbermen were assiduous in making this point but were dismissed as being interested parties. The Quebec Limitholders' Association was also not about to raise the issue of forest reserves with a government it knew to be violently opposed to them in principle. Its main concern was in negotiating a new dues structure to replace the twenty-one-year lease regulations due to expire in 1888.[10]

In 1886 and 1887, the issue of most immediate importance to the forest industries of Quebec was this one of setting the timber dues and retaining the rights to their licences without having them reopened for competition. They bent all their efforts towards negotiating an arrangement with the new government—an arrangement that would not upset their established position within the province. They were eventually successful, and a new deal on timber dues, to last until 1900, was struck in mid–1887. The arrangement was based on the lumber operators' willingness to accept higher rates of royalties payable to the Crown as long as it agreed to fix the rates over a suitably long period of time for all current and future leases and to renew the present licences without competition. Mercier accepted these terms and set out the agreement in an Order in Council which actually governed timber duties up to the revision by Premier Lomer Gouin in 1910.[11]

Even after reaching this quite satisfactory settlement over the tenure and timber dues issues, the Quebec lumbermen refrained from openly urging the Mercier government not to interfere with the forest reserves. This was a wise political move because the issue was an emotional one with the colonization movement and was one that could have been exploited by the Parti National for electoral purposes. Only after the nationalist premier was driven from power in 1892, as a result of the Baie de Chaleurs Railway scandal, and the Conservatives formed the provincial government, was pressure applied for the reinstitution of some form of land classification. In 1894 leading lumbermen quietly supported the formation of two national parks, Mont Tremblant and Laurentides, because, among other things, they served as forest reserves. The establishment of these parks did not, however, regain the position forestry had attained in the province through the influence of the lumber interests between 1882 and 1885. The colonization movement remained aggressive. It successfully kept the lumbermen on the defensive, challenging them politically by accusing them of having a corrupt relationship with the Conservative provincial government and generally agitating over the use of the public domain.[12]

Reports from the early years of the twentieth century reveal the sources of this conflict.[13] Once the surveyors had finished laying out land into lots for settlement, the company, in whose limit the lots were located, had only two months in which to remove the merchantable pine from them. Once a lot was taken up by a settler, all the trees on it were reserved for that man's use. This led to competition between the companies and the locatees as the company hurried to cut and mark as its own as much of the valuable timber on each lot as possible before the time limit expired. Bogus settlers, however, would locate on lots and start cutting immediately, claiming the time limit had already expired. As soon as they had sold the timber they had cut, they abandoned the lot and moved on. Speculators took lots, did the minimum work on them required to achieve title, and then sold the lot as "improved" when they were offered suitable prices. Often bogus settlers and speculators were actually settlers living a few miles away from the newly surveyed area, usually in the next township. They would take advantage of inside knowledge gained by their proximity to identify particularly good timber stands. It was not at all unusual for a settler or a farmer to have obtained false affidavits giving him power of attorney for nonexistent people or relatives living in the United States. In essence, every trick that was used by lumbermen in Michigan, Wisconsin, and the American Pacific coast to obtain open timberland was used by the Quebeçois settlers to raid standing timber.[14]

It was the continuing political conflict between the supporters of the colons and the defenders of the timber limits that eventually led to a renewal of forest reserves in Quebec. The Liberal party replaced the Conservatives in the provincial general election of 1897. Under the leadership of F. G. Marchand, the new government had, as one of its objectives, the growth of business enterprise in the province. While the Liberals professed some dedication to the colonization cause, many supporters of the movement doubted the government's sincerity, particularly after S. N. Parent, the Minister of Lands and Forests, replaced Marchand as Premier in 1900 on the latter's death. By 1902, opponents of the government were charging Parent with corruption, disrespect for the colonization movement, and favouritism to large forest companies. Their scepticism was reinforced when, as one of his first executive acts, Parent chose to dissolve the Department of Colonization and simply make the function an adjunct of Public Works. Henri Bourassa, the young reform leader of the nationaliste forces and a Liberal, was particularly incensed with this move and with the way in which sites suitable for electrical generation were sold off to private interests instead of being leased for a period of years and remaining part of the public domain.[15]

Sensing that this criticism might well be used to advantage by his political opponents, Premier Parent appointed a Colonization Commission in June 1902 to investigate the province's land and forest policies. The Commission initially got out of control of the government. Its most dynamic member was the wealthy and independent-thinking Montrealer, George Washington Stephens, a long-time supporter of forest conservation measures. His ostensible role on the Commission was to represent the capitalist elements of the province, but Stephens turned his position into an outspoken campaign against both the government and the colonization movement. This was politically unacceptable, and various Liberals advised Parent that "Stephens will turn against you if he discovers, or thinks he is discovering, some irregularities in the colonization policy."[16]

The death in 1903 of another Commission member, Judge Bourgeois, gave Parent the opportunity to reappoint the Commission without Stephens. At the suggestion of Wilfrid Laurier, the chairmanship of the new Commission was given to Senator J. H. Legris. Legris, who had served as the member for Maskinongé, had a keen interest in agricultural matters. With these qualifications and nationaliste sentiments, tempered with dedication to the Liberal party, the Senator was ideally suited for his position in the eyes of both the colonization movement and the Premier.[17]

Having doused one set of political fires, Parent was not about to turn the Commission over to the advocates of colonization and risk alienating the forest industries. The powerful position of secretary to the body had been given from the first to Chyrsotome Langelier, the representative of a prominent Liberal family and a friend of H. G. Joly de Lotbinière. He was a giant of a man who had served for many years in the provincial civil service, and he was a passionate advocate of better methods of resource management as well as an active member of the Canadian Forestry Association. The responsibility of the secretary was to obtain evidence and fashion a report with which the government could feel comfortable and could respond to with reasonably popular measures. Langelier's job was not made any easier by the colonization movement. Well organized since a massive Congress held in Montreal in 1898 and angered by the dissolution of the colonization department by Parent, it dogged the footsteps of the Commission as it travelled around the province, producing witnesses and encouraging them to stick to their testimony.[18]

During the presentation of evidence to the Commission, Langelier attempted to question witnesses on the operation of land speculators and the disastrous effects such activities had on forest lands and on the reputation of the colonization movement itself. As a result, he found himself accused of using his large bulk to dominate witnesses and bully them into giving answers that lent credence to his own views.[19] What slowly emerged from Commission hearings, however, was evidence that the government should champion true colonization while stopping speculative activities by revamping provincial Crown lands legislation. Despite this compromise position, there remained tension between Legris and Langelier, particularly over the latter's treatment of witnesses and the question of whether Henri Bourassa should be invited to appear before the Commission. In the event, the Chairman won his way with the support of the vocal colonizers and nationalistes. When the Commission returned to Montreal after its circuit of the province, Bourassa was invited to appear before it on 18 February 1903.[20]

Speaking to the Commission for two hours, Bourassa criticized the current colonization laws and regulations. He delved into the problem of conflict between the lumbermen and the colons. He described the situation as a battle usually won by the lumbermen because they were wealthy; they could hire lawyers and they had the ability to influence the government by lobbying for changes in the regulations backed up by contributions to the political party in power. In particular, Bourassa singled out the new pulp and paper industry which was owned by strangers from abroad who had little sympathy with the Quebecois way of life.[21] Bourassa ended his oration with a suggestion which must have pleased the harassed Langelier:

Separate the colonist and the lumberman, suppress this double right, these simultaneous ownerships, this source of unfriendliness. Reserve certain fertile townships for colonization to which the lumbermen have no access. The colonists and the lumbermen, each on their own land, can be neighbours to each other and aid each other for they have need of each other.[22]

The Quebec Limitholders' Association, whose representatives were present at the meeting, were quietly supportive of Bourassa and let him indulge in his closing remarks deploring the sale of water power sites to private interests. The reason for this is obvious. Bourassa, perhaps inadvertently, had supported the Association's long-held position of land classification and had given Langelier the basis for his report. Langelier must have realized this because he did not react to the criticisms of another witness appearing later in the day. This witness was Guillaume-Alphonse Nantel, a faithful follower of Curé Labelle, who raised the cry *"La Terre libré au colon libré"*. The secretary quietly left the public eye to compose a comprehensive report based on the evidence given before the Commission. It was a report which advocated better forest management practices more than it supported the demands of the colonization movement.[23] Released in 1904, it served Parent as the basis for a new forestry initiative in the province that was highly displeasing, for the most part, to the colonization movement. Claims that operators were ravishing the timber from areas open for settlement were dismissed out of hand. Instead, the report claimed that bona fide settlers had nothing to fear from the lumber industry and charged that only speculators objected to Crown timber regulations.[24]

The report adopted many suggestions from the witnesses the Commission had heard but turned the suggestions in a direction to support the development of the forest industries. It called for classification of lands into settlement and forestry areas, advocated forest reserves to keep settlers out of areas unsuitable for agriculture while guaranteeing timber revenues to the province, and advised that the regulations regarding the settlers' rights to timber on located lots be repealed. The report also supported the government's policy by advocating the sale of water power lots by public auction to the highest bidder. Finally, the Commission's report called on the government to encourage the expansion of the pulp and paper industry.[25]

Despite the accusation from the colonization movement that the government had sold out to the timber interests, Parent was determined to implement the recommendations of his commission. In order to give the recommendations an aura of veracity and respectability and to wash from them the taint of political expediency, the Premier had them reviewed by the Canadian Forestry Association. At the annual meeting of the Association held in Quebec City in March, 1905, the recommendations were publicly endorsed. This enabled Parent to go forward with a forestry programme which was fully supported by the forest industries and which would put Quebec on an equal footing with Ontario. He could now claim it had been blessed by a prominent nonpartisan body representing modern reform thought in the country on forestry matters, and he moved forward to put the recommendations into effect.[26]

Unfortunately for Parent, having made all the right political moves in a subtle and clever manner, he now badly misplayed his hand. The Premier introduced some of the reforms he had proposed but held back on others until after the federal general election of 1904 so as not to unduly raise the ire of the supporters of the colonization movement and prejudice the successful reelection of the Laurier government. Laurier was so strongly supported in Quebec during that election that Parent saw an opportunity for a political coup and promptly called an unexpected provincial election. The result was spectacular. The opposition was reduced to six seats. Unfortunately, the size of the victory and the basic corruptness of Parent had upset many Liberals. There was a feeling that the Premier had to be stopped. A movement grew in the Liberal party against the Premier, backed by among others Liberal supporters of the colonization movement, P. A. Choquette and J. H. Legris, the former Chairman of the Colonization Commission who now felt betrayed by Parent. The split in Liberal ranks occurred because of the Premier's apparent inability to hold the cabinet together, growing suspicion of corrupt links to various business interests, and his negative attitudes and policies toward the colonization movement. As a result, Parent was forced to resign as Premier and leader of the Liberal party. He was replaced by his Minister of Colonization and Public Works, Lomer Gouin. Gouin, a business-oriented Montreal politician, possessed better "reform" credentials than Parent, was somewhat "progressive" in his view of the proper role for the provincial government, and was generally supportive of measures to conserve natural resources and wildlife. Determined to end the political abuses of his predecessor, Gouin was committed to bringing wholesale changes to the forest administration of the province, but he was not yet quite sure what those changes should be. In any case, Gouin intended to be more circumspect in his approach than Parent had been. For the moment, he decided to continue to expand the major reform started by Parent in 1904—the expansion of the forest reserves.[27]

From 1904 to 1908, Premiers Parent and Gouin created a total of 429,283 square kilometres of forest reserves in Quebec. This impressive area was, for a short time, the pride and cornerstone of the province's nascent forest conservation programme. In contrast with the policies of the governments of the Dominion and Province of Ontario, Quebec consciously selected areas already held by licencees as well as areas that had been deforested and presented regeneration problems. It acknowledged that this classification programme was designed to aid the forest industries directly by ensuring that their limits were not subjected to pressure from those advocating alternative uses for the land. Thus the attitude of the Quebec government to its reserves was an activist one. Reserves were not "banks" of timber waiting to be cut sometime in the future. Further, in contrast to the Dominion government, Quebec did not have separate administrations for the sale of timber and the management of reserves. In Quebec, the operating areas were the ones reserved; one of the results of this policy was that soon foresters were attempting to institute management practices.[28]

The management of the reserves was placed in the hands of W. C. J. Hall, the Superintendent of Laurentides Park and an active member of the Canadian Forestry Association. Although Hall was concerned about the remaining white pine stands in the province, his conception of the forests of the province were as prime spruce production areas. Hall was convinced that Quebec's future lay with the production of pulp and paper, and he hoped that the reserves would help conserve the resources necessary for that industry. Like Southworth and Elihu Stewart, Hall was not a professional forester but rather a practical and interested layman who accepted and translated into his own idiom current popular ideas of conservation. Under his leadership Quebec had, by 1908, a system of reserves very similar to that of Ontario but of a much larger area. Hall's attitude to the problem of fire and regeneration in the reserves was, for instance, very close to that of

Southworth. He believed that if fire was kept out of the forest, cut-over areas would regenerate satisfactorily with the same species as had been there before logging. Quebec's forests would therefore retain their character indefinitely as long as fires were prevented. Hall saw the reserves as basic land classification units designed to separate the competing interests of lumbering and colonization. Not surprisingly, therefore, when Hall was promoted to Superintendent of the Forest Fire Protection Branch of the province's Department of Lands and Forests, in 1906, he took with him the control of the reserves, which emphasized his view that the reserves were primarily fire-control zones.[29]

While Ontario's approach to forestry and forest reserve management remained relatively static until the early 1940s, Quebec was soon experimenting with new ideas in which professional foresters played an important part. The formation of large forest reserves by the province was only the most visible sign of more far-reaching reforms designed to overhaul the rules and regulations governing Quebec's forests. Premier Gouin pushed into law a number of suggestions made by the Colonization Commission, including an amendment to the Department of Lands and Forests Act restoring the right of lumbermen to timber on lots located after the licence was granted.[30] The concession was a small one, but it did make the lumbermen happier and more willing to accept the changes that were to come.

It quickly became apparent that Premier Gouin had more ambitious plans than had Parent. He wished to place the management of Quebec's forest in the hands of professional foresters. He was convinced that they would bring the latest in scientific and engineering principles to the complex problem of resource use on Crown lands. He also hoped that the introduction of professional foresters would help erase the shadow of corruption that had hung for so long over the administration of forest lands in the province and calm the bitter debate that was continuing over land use. Premier Lomer Gouin was thus the first political leader in Canada to appreciate the need for the professionalization of his province's forestry administration and management. Ironically, the transfer in control of forest lands from appointees to professionals spelled the end of the system of large reserves.[31]

Gouin was influenced by Sir Henri Joly de Lotbinière and Monseigneur L. K. Laflamme, the rector of Quebec's Laval University, and perhaps, as well, by his exposure to forestry practices of the Laurentide Pulp and Paper Company. Both Joly and Laflamme were strong supporters of forestry in Canada and members of the Canadian Forestry Association. They both appreciated the extensive university-level training required for qualification in European forestry. By 1905 they had persuaded Gouin to sponsor two Quebeçois students to train as professional foresters. The two men nominated for the training were Gustave C. Piché and Avila Bédard. Piché, the elder of the two, had worked for the Canadian Pacific Railway and the Belgo-Canadian Pulp Company before studying at L'Ecole Polytechnique in Montreal. Piché was joined at Yale University's School of Forestry master of forestry programme by Bédard, who had just completed his B.A. The two studied under Henry S. Graves, who eventually replaced Pinchot as United States Forester, and graduated at the end of 1905. In the following year, both men went on a European tour before starting work with Quebec's Department of Lands, Mines and Fisheries—Piché as forest engineer and Bédard as his assistant.[32]

During 1907 and 1908, Piché founded the provincial tree nursery at Berthierville, a town on the north bank of the St. Lawrence about half way between Montreal and Trois Rivières. He and Bédard were also directly involved in founding Laval's School of Forestry which Bédard eventually took over. In 1907, the Department of Lands, Mines and Fisheries was reorganized. A Department of Lands and Forests was created, and Mines and Fisheries were separated from the department and combined with a new Department of Colonization. On 1 June 1909, Gouin announced a revised forest policy which was to form the main part of his reforms. The most publicized parts of his policy were the provisions that required all the pulpwood cut on Crown lands be manufactured into paper products in Canada. This policy had been rejected by Quebec in 1900 when it had been adopted by Ontario because of resistance from the colonization movement and some lumber interests. At the same time, the Premier declared a moratorium on the sale of timber berth leases in order to control timber supplies and to halt speculation in timberlands.[33]

A less commented on but much more important and prescient part of the new policy was, however, the creation of the Quebec Forestry Service. Within the Department of Lands and Forests, Piché created and headed a small section named the Forestry Service. To begin, the Service was made responsible for all the department's outside work in a block of seventeen townships northeast of Montreal in the foothills of the Laurentians, not far from Berthierville. Piché wanted to use this area for experimentation. He was to set up a rudimentary management system which would yield experience applicable to the rest of the province. The Service was to be the core of a new administrative organization that would eventually explore the unsurveyed northern territories, classify soils, supervise all lumbering on Crown lands, and manage reforestation. This courageous step had an appropriately cautious beginning, given the wide ambitions of the protagonists, but, most important, it was largely supported by the forest industries.[34]

An initial appraisal of the area showed that it contained 2,340 square kilometres of licensed Crown timberland as well as farmland, farm woodlots, and some wasteland. The general situation was much the same as reported for the province as a whole by the Colonization Commission. The problem facing Piché was therefore one of applying existing regulations. To do this, Piché organized his staff of rangers so that each patrolled a small district.

Each ranger was responsible for ensuring compliance with regulations relating to diameter limits, the piling of logs at landings to ease scaling, proper record keeping by shantymen, and the curtailment of trespassing.[35]

Piché's approach to the problems in his area indicates that he had a brilliant understanding of the provincial forest industry with which he had to work and whose activities he had to regulate. He brought to his new job a sound understanding of the European approach to forestry, but Piché realized it would not be accepted or work without a gradual and planned introduction. He also understood current North American practice. Under this regime, the first requirement for the proper introduction of forest management was considered to be a complete inventory of the forest followed by the development of silvicultural plans for each stand. Once the plans had been completed, the loggers would be instructed how and where to log. (This was the approach taken in British Columbia after 1912.) Piché, however, had neither the facilities nor the staff for such a survey. Furthermore, in a country where the people making their living from the forest saw it as a mass of trees waiting to be felled, change had to be slow. Revolution had to come on a small scale, a process of mutation leaving much that was familiar. Piché, therefore, moved first to ensure that the diameter limit was being adhered to, then that cutting was restricted to specific areas, preventing a shanty's teams from wandering through the forest picking suitable trees almost at random. Finally, he attempted to get the co-operation of the company owning the limit as well as that of the shantymen so that only those trees marked by foresters were felled. Only then, Piché knew, could silvicultural and management techniques be introduced.[36]

While he was organizing his rangers, Piché took on three apprentices from Laval's new forestry school. This started the tradition of hiring staff who were graduates of Laval University's Forestry School. Over the next decade or so, the majority of these graduates found employment in Quebec's Forest Service. This was in keeping with European practice where the forest services of France and Germany, as well as the British service in India, all had specific schools from which they drew their staff. It is also in direct contrast to events occurring in Ontario where Fernow found himself and his University of Toronto graduates excluded from the civil service until World War I.[37]

Perhaps the greatest asset of the Quebec Forest Service under Piché was its adaptability. Piché and his foresters insisted on building on what already existed rather than on starting large-scale projects that were expensive in both money and manpower. Thus, forest survey work was considered a long-term project that could be delayed. In the interim, Piché moved as quickly as possible to set up regulations providing for close regulation of all cutting operations. As more information on the silvicultural characteristics of the forest became available, the regulations could be modified. By the early 1920s, the Forest Service was beginning to demand from the larger lumber and pulp firms detailed inventories of their limits. Companies responded by investigating ways of fulfilling this requirement as cheaply and accurately as possible, and this led to the development of the use of aircraft and aerial photography in forest survey work. As well, annual cutting plans had to be filed with the Service. These plans detailed the silvicultural techniques the company planned to use to maintain yields. As a result, some pulp and paper companies established tree nurseries and carried out research to find the most efficient method of regenerating cut-overs.[38] The acceptance of these requirements by the forest industry of Quebec is shown by the legislation introduced in 1921 by the then Minister of the Department of Lands and Forests, Honoré Mercier. It required working plans be drawn up by the company and accepted by the Forest Service before an operation could start cutting for the year. This was the first time in Canada that such plans and their approval by government were legally required.

Unfortunately, these new procedures had much more effect on the pulp and paper industry than on the lumber industry. After 1919 this branch of woods operations in the province was in full and permanent decline.[39] The Forest Service seemed to be inclined to accept the fate of the white pine forest, putting aside for later the problem of its regeneration. The basic reason for this was that, in the 1920s, foresters recognized that the mechanics of pine regeneration had not been sufficiently studied in Canada to produce viable solutions. Early logging operations had left the forest in a condition where the pine were replaced by spruce and balsam fir, thus restricting current white pine operations to the remaining stands of virgin forest. These stands were increasingly over-mature and equally unsuccessful at reproducing themselves, thus causing the elimination of white pine lumbering in much of Quebec. It was not until the supply of this species in Ontario diminished in the late 1930s and 1940s that lumber production returned to Quebec. By then, however, it was not white pine that was cut, but white spruce. In the meantime, the Quebec Forest Service concentrated on the production of pulpwood. It also became interested in fire suppression but viewed it as a part of the larger world of forest management rather than as an objective in its own right.[40]

The use of a number of sophisticated forest management techniques pioneered by the Quebec Forest Service could not have happened without the co-operation of industry. A close working relationship between the Service and industry soon developed, and this eventually laid the Service open to charges of favouritism. While the Forest Service recognized a place for the state in protecting and enhancing forestlands, it also called on private firms holding limits to adhere to their obligations toward management, research, and the control of fire and insect pests. From this basis there developed a powerful state-corporate axis in the administration of the Crown domain that was criticized by opposition politicians as fundamentally corrupt and contrary to the public interest. Such criticism was to be expected from the colonization movement but, during the mid–1920s, the Service acquired a much more knowledgeable and troublesome critic in the person of a former employee, Thomas Maher.[41]

Siding with the colonization movement, Maher began his campaign by speaking at a colonization convention held in Montreal in 1923. He lambasted the Service for not properly controlling cutting over large areas and for permitting the pulp and paper companies to expand too rapidly. Further, he charged that in areas such as Bellechasse, Montmagny, L'Islet, Kamouraska, and Témiscouata the forest was almost completely gone. Erosion and decline of the water table threatened the remaining resources. The pine industry, he claimed, was in rapid decline in the Ottawa valley. In the pulpwood areas, Maher contended that large limits had been acquired by foreign firms solely for financial and speculative purposes. Piché defended the orientation of his Service's policies by claiming that larger pulp and paper companies, with sizeable investments in limits and factories, could be counted on to show concern about the maintenance of future wood supplies and would thus guarantee that improved forest management techniques would continue to be adopted. The example he cited most often was that of the Laurentide Pulp and Paper Company. This firm did have a professional forester in its employ and did some inventory and experimental work, but, unfortunately, it was one of the few companies to co-operate fully with the Service. In his heart, Piché knew that the battle would not be an easy one, but he put his faith in the Service's gradual regulatory approach rather than in revolutionary change.[42]

The commitment of the Service to scientific forestry led it to abandon the system of large forest reserves. It had grown more interested in and more capable of classifying land at the local rather than at the large-scale level. Simply put, the scientific justification for the maintenance of large reserved areas turned out not to exist, and, from 1910 on, the reserves were gradually dismantled. In the farming districts, land classification identified small areas for woodlots, and these were reserved for this use. Crown forests were set up near the sources of major rivers (for example, High St. Maurice, Bostannais, and Batiscan). These were designated for water conservation purposes and could be cut by forest operators only under direct and total supervision of the Forest Service. In most of the Laurentians and in the rocky zone of the Canadian Shield, however, the lack of agricultural land meant whole townships and counties were classified as forestland. This effectively meant no change for the woods industries whose limits lay in this zone. The only problem with this system was that forestland was not given legal status and could be reclassified if enough pressure was brought on the government. Piché proposed legislation to end this abuse, but it does not seem to have been adopted. In spite of this, industry accepted the disappearance of the reserves between 1910 and 1917 largely because the townships, once reserved, were classified as forestland and their limits remained relatively secure.[43]

The elimination of the reserves was an easy political concession for the Service to make to the colonization societies. Piché also suggested further concessions in the form of plans for opening the Abitibi clay belt along the line of the National Transcontinental Railway, then under construction. This new initiative was an astute political move and came at about the same time as the expectations of the colons were hardening. It was no longer possible for the societies to motivate people to go out into the wilderness with a minimum of support without knowing anything about the land on which their lot was located. Piché's proposal fitted in well with this change in attitude. By not allowing any large timber limits in the area, it was hoped the settlers could combine agriculture with pulpwood logging. The proposed area contained only one timber limit, leased to the Riordan Company some years before, and, by this date, owned by International Paper. Through this type of co-operation, the Quebec government anticipated that the forest industries and the colonizers would reach a compromise that would expand the economic base of the north and make settlement viable. The contribution of the Forest Service to this plan was the basic identification of suitable agricultural land and training and support in persuading the colons to manage their woodlots on a sustained yield basis.[44]

The only objection to the elimination of the reserves came from W. C. J. Hall, Chief of the Fire Protection Branch, who had been instrumental in their creation. He was effectively ignored, although the final blow to the reserve system was withheld until shortly after his retirement in 1918, when the Forest Protection Branch was absorbed by the Forest Service. At the same time, the administration of Laurentides, Mont Tremblant, and Gaspesian Parks (with the exception of the management of timber operations) was transferred to the Department of Colonization, Mines and Fisheries. Thus, in a relatively short period of eight years, Piché's Forest Service had managed to obtain control over all the Department's outside activities.[45]

Piché had not found the effort to introduce forestry measures to be easy, and it was not completely crowned with success. Although all the forest companies in the province complied with the regulations, very few were prepared to take initiatives of their own. Only the Laurentide Pulp and Paper Company and the Bronson Company, in addition to carrying out thorough inventories of their limits, actively attempted to reforest their cut-overs using their own nursery and tree-planting programmes.[46] But, by the end of World War I, it can be argued that the foundation for an effective forestry programme had been established in Quebec. One government authority was responsible for land classification, leasing, control of logging, forest protection, and regeneration. Further, the Forest Service was having an effect on the attitude of industry toward the resource. Even though the advance of forest management was slowed during the 1920s when the pulp and paper industry found itself in trouble, the progress made in Quebec was in marked contrast to what was happening in Ontario during the same period.

Indeed, by 1923, implementation of the new system was well under way. Yet, despite the Service's overt dedication to forestry principles, there was a growing criticism within Quebec over the administration of forestlands. Gouin's Liberal regime had had its reform side, but it never abandoned its dedication to a policy of economic growth through special concessions to new investors and only limited government interference with their activities. One of the great successes of this development strategy had been the pulp and paper industry. Giant corporations, mostly foreign owned, had obtained rights to immense tracts of spruce lands. They included such firms as Belgo-Canadian, Wayagamack, Saguenay Paper, Price Brothers, and International Paper. The jobs they provided were welcome, but the rapid growth of the industry after a short postwar slump occasioned a negative reaction from conservative elements that were worried about the erosion of French-Canadian culture in Quebec.

This criticism found its best expression through a nationalist organization called L'Action Française, which kept up a continuous critique of the administration of forest resources in the province during the 1920s. Although it lacked consistency in its approach, it called at one time or another for more stringent government regulation of timber cutting by foreign-controlled companies, reservation of timber and water rights for Quebeçois, and government encouragement of small-scale French-Canadian businesses, including forest industries. Maher's charges added fuel to this agitation.

Gouin had been replaced in 1920 by Louis-Alexandre Taschereau, an advocate of rapid industrial growth under the hegemony of big business (he would have called it a free-enterprise system). More than ever before, the legislature under the new Premier became a mill for private acts designed to dispense special rights and concessions to the resource industries. Patronage was used extensively in order to hold together the Liberal political machine. The most frequent charge against the Forest Service was that it was granting large tracts of land in perpetuity to pulp and paper companies. The outright sale of Anticosti Island in 1926 to a consortium of pulp and paper companies was also somewhat embarrassing to the Service. Nevertheless, in the sixteen years to 1936, when the Liberals were defeated in a provincial election, the Forest Service consolidated its position although, unfortunately, it was not able to take many new initiatives. Advances were made in inventory, in silvicultural research, and in formulating a philosophical basis for future activities. During these years, the Service worked closely with the pulp and paper companies in developing the working plans required by law after 1921. Although the financial restraints imposed by the depression of the 1930s and the production requirements of World War II reduced the effectiveness of this legislation, it led the way in Canada as an example of government-industry co-operation in forestry and conservation.[47]

In 1924, the Service underwent a minor reorganization when fire protection was once again made a separate section in the Department of Lands and Forests. The new Forest Protection Service had several divisions. One division coordinated the activities of the company-based cooperative forest protection associations which were required to adhere to strict government regulations and to be inspected regularly. These associations, funded and organized by groups of companies, were responsible for entomology and pathology problems as well as fire suppression. Piché resented the rise of corporate fire protection associations because he felt that the province was giving up a measure of control over all woods activities. He stoically accepted the change, however, realizing that both the politicians and the corporations were behind the move in an effort to cut costs and promote smaller government. Another division was responsible for the fire wardens who patrolled the colonization areas, issuing the fire permits that allowed settlers to burn their slash whenever conditions allowed. A third division in the Forest Protection Service was responsible for the protection of unlicenced Crown lands. By the 1930s this was a comparatively small area of the province's merchantable forest.[48]

That the remaining area of unleased forest was comparatively small by 1930 was the crux of the deteriorating situation. In 1924, the government resumed leasing new limits, prohibited since 1909. This was done at first to aid the expansion of the pulp and paper industry in the province and later, when over-production plagued the industry, to help it find stability. The new limits were used as financial collateral with banking institutions. The policy was adopted because Taschereau wanted to create a reasonably unfettered climate for industrial expansion. In spite of opposition from some colonizers, nationalistes, and other critics, it was a popular policy, particularly among the farmers and settlers of the clay-belt and elsewhere who not only sold their pulpwood to the companies but also found employment for themselves and their sons in the shanties. For better or for worse, by 1927, when the government stopped leasing limits once again, virtually all the potentially exploitable accessible forest had been licenced.[49]

By the late 1920s, the pulp and paper industry of Quebec found itself in considerable economic difficulty. This created problems for the Forest Service when the companies attempted to cut their production costs regardless of the consequences. In this period, Canada supplied the United States with large quantities of newsprint. Up to 80 percent of Canadian production was exported to the south. Since 1920, when newsprint sold for $135 per ton, the price had been steadily dropping. By 1934, when discounts and special deals were counted in, mills in Canada were receiving $30 to $35 per ton for their newsprint. At the same time, Americans, led by the conglomerate International Paper, had been acquiring Canadian mills. By 1928 this company had successfully purchased the newest and most efficient of the mills in eastern Canada. Canadian companies found themselves left with only the smaller, older, and least efficient plants.[50]

As a result of these tactics, International Paper was able to obtain a contract with the Hearst chain of newspapers to supply newsprint at prices from $7 to $10 dollars per ton below that of other companies. At this time, newsprint contracts contained clauses guaranteeing the buyer that the price he paid would conform to the lowest obtaining in the industry. As a result, International Paper was able to affect all newsprint contracts in North America through its price-cutting tactics. These tactics also enabled the company to obtain enough contracts to keep its mills operating at a steady and high enough rate that its production costs were covered. The effect of this on the remaining Canadian mills was quite devastating. Forced to lower prices in lock-step with International Paper and finding this company had obtained contracts with the steadiest purchasers, Canadian mills saw their production rates fluctuating monthly. As a result, a number of companies followed Abitibi Power and Paper into receivership. Twice, in 1924 and in October-November 1934, Premier Taschereau attempted through political pressure to force International Paper to raise its prices in order to relieve the Canadian mills of some of their problems. In both instances, his efforts were rebuffed.[51]

The Quebec Forest Service confronted many problems during this period of vicious competition. Economies were made by all the mills wherever they could. Laurentide Paper and Pulp Company gave its nursery to the Forest Service. The Bronson nursery was sold to International Paper as part of the firm's assets in Quebec and closed down. All regeneration plans were curtailed, and companies followed the example of their brethren in Ontario and relied on "natural" regeneration. Worse still, companies ceased to follow the silvicultural practices agreed upon between themselves and the Service. Where possible, the agreements were ignored on the grounds they were too expensive.[52]

The Service had its own problems with funding as well. In the relatively prosperous 1920s, income to the treasury from the forest was high. The Service shared in a portion of these funds, but appropriations failed to keep up with the expanding work load. By 1927 the Service was spread out very thinly indeed. Also, charges continued that provincial forestry officials had grown too close to the pulp and paper industry and simply danced to the tunes played by the international corporations and monopolists. Piché was willing to admit that his Service might have placed too much emphasis on pulpwood operations but not that it had been completely bought out by the companies. He contended that the Service was only attempting the art of the possible and joined the chorus of those pleading for financial assistance from the Dominion government, especially for land classification, protection, and research work. Even this dim hope was snatched from the Service after 1944, when Maurice Duplessis and the Union Nationale returned to power.

The new government consolidated its hold on the Province of Quebec through a strong nationalist stance which called for Quebec to go it alone in many fields. One of these, naturally, was forestry, but the government provided insufficient funding or political will to pioneer any new resource management policies. Even without nationalist complications, matters would have gotten worse during the depression of the 1930s. The government, which had taken and spent the large revenues from the forest in the boom years of the 1920s, did not hesitate to cut back on the Service's funding during the 1930s, even though it had not properly shared in the previous decades' heavy revenues. As a result, by the late 1930s, the Service had the reputation of being an ineffective, though professionally elite, body.[53]

There were other problems as well. By the beginning of World War II, the forest industry in the province was stagnant, and the companies were over-cutting the easily accessible areas of their limits and ignoring harvestable stands in more remote locations. The industry was effectively not fulfilling any role other than the economic ones defined by its owners. The Service would have preferred to see the pulp and paper mills playing a more active part in the social fabric of the north, but this was not to be. Some foresters even hypothesized that the industry should follow a European mode of development, where communities would make their living by exploiting all the resources available from a given area of the forest. Of course, the forest itself would be managed on a sustained-yield basis. In this scenario, industry exploited the fruits of the forest as they became ripe and were harvested. This was in contrast to the growing practice of industry to annually take from the forest what it required with little heed to what should have been taken.[54] It is unfortunate that the idea of a merger between the social and economic aims of forestry failed to become a reality in Quebec, since it was the one jurisdiction in Canada where European models may have had a chance of early success. By the 1940s the province had much of its forest industry scattered across its northland. The agricultural limitations of the clay-belt were having a greater and greater impact on the economic fortunes of the population of the area. With proper planning and control, the pulp and paper industry in the hinterland could have fulfilled a major social role. Of course, the economic fluctuations that the world has experienced in the last forty or fifty years might have intervened perhaps to hamstring this large-scale forestry experiment. At any rate, it was not given a chance because the major problem remained that North American industry was and is not organized to perform social functions within the economic boundaries of this continent. After a good start, which saw the development and implementation of many original ideas, Quebec's Forest Service was thereafter forced into the common mold of North American forestry. Quebec's example argues strongly that, despite the best of intentions, the economic environment often displaces public policy with regard to forestry. Expressed another way, the Quebec situation indicates that politicians are rarely courageous enough to deny, or to attempt to redirect, the economic claims of industry. The final judgment on Quebec in this period came from forester L. Z. Rousseau, who, in 1944, gloomily commented:

In searching for a means to exploit the territories bordering on the north and east of the actual economic forestry zone, we follow the path of the African peoples who, having used up the fertility of one tropical area, move their primitive exploitive agriculture to another corner of the forest. Likewise, our industry has not used the resource to its best advantage. It has perfected extraction methods but has ignored the elementary laws of economics. As a result, the large white pines have been disposed of to the detriment of our sawmills while the same policy will shortly lead to the deterioration of our spruce forests unless we bring order and regulation there immediately.[55]

CHAPTER 6

A Touch of Pinchotism: Forestry in British Columbia, 1912–1939

In forestry, as in so many other aspects of Canadian life, British Columbia is a special case in and of itself.[1] No other province has such a wide diversity of forest types, land forms, and climates, or a forest industry divided on geographic lines. The isolation of the bulk of the interior region of the province, combined with the giant size of the timber of the rain coast, resulted in the province's being the last timber frontier in Canada to be exploited. British Columbia required a different technology to utilize the forest and a different business structure for the industry.

Once British Columbia's forest industry became etablished, its size and power enabled it to dominate provincial politics. In addition, more than in any other province, except perhaps New Brunswick, it was not competition with other interests which marked the growth of the lumber industry but rather competition within the industry itself. This competition came to have a direct effect on the political scene and was ultimately connected with the development of forestry practice in the province. The arrival of forestry in British Columbia was comparatively late in terms of the general chronology we have been discussing here. This meant that the province's first forester had the opportunity to take advantage of the experience of others. As a result, foresters in British Columbia did not have to fight many of the battles fought by their counterparts in the east or at the federal level. To that extent, the system established in British Columbia is unique in the annals of the North American conservation movement. Yet, British Columbia's experience was also a logical extension of other similar events in the rest of Canada. The Forestry Branch, created by the province, inherited flaws in its administration and political control which ultimately made it only a little more successful than its eastern counterparts.

In British Columbia, the Cascade mountains, the north-south range of mountains immediately inland of the Coast range, geographically divides the province into two unequal portions. To the east of the mountains lies the interior—drier, with a more continental climate and a radically different forest from the coast. The coast area includes the relatively narrow strip of land bordering the sea, including the offshore islands. Characterized by a wet, mild, maritime climate and a rugged terrain with precipitous slopes descending into the sea, its forest was, and is, magnificent. The presence of giant Douglas fir, Sitka spruce, and cedars combined with the mountain slopes created an industry completely different from that of a few miles to the east. As a result, from its earliest days to the present, British Columbia has had two separate logging industries. Often they clashed, battling for control of the same market and making contradictory demands on the province's politicians. The division is such that comparisons between the sectors are not based on similarities but on contrasts. An understanding of this division is crucial for a proper analysis of the history of lumbering in British Columbia.[2]

The exploitation of the coastal forests of British Columbia predates the visits to the coast by European explorers. The large size of the trees gave the native people a material par excellence for artistic expression. The forest provided them with food, clothing, and building material. With the advent of European settlement, the trees were felled to build houses and to clear the relatively small areas of arable land, but, in spite of the later prominence of the industry in the economy of British Columbia, lumbering was not an important influence in the early development of the province. Like all the early administrations in North America, the objective of the colonial government of British Columbia was to establish a community based on agriculture.[3]

The physical characteristics of the colony did not make the implementation of this policy easy. The high mountain ranges restricted the arable land to the valley bottoms. The rivers, with their many rapids and gorges, made it difficult to use the waterways for transportation. The vast network of lakes and portages typical of eastern Canada was completely missing. Finally, the mineral riches discovered from 1850 onward were responsible for the creation of a mobile population, largely American, that lived in the interior. As a result, political pressure for the union of the mainland of the colony with the United States was always present. For its first Governor, James Douglas (1858–1864), the difficulties of establishing permanent agrarian settlements were compounded by the parsimony of the Colonial Office in London. The British government insisted that the money required for surveys and road construction be raised locally. Scattered mining camps and farms and ranches squatting on the pockets of arable land created insurmountable difficulties for surveyors, especially since a rough survey of the whole did not even exist. This problem was solved by establishing a pattern that was later transferred to the forest industry. Large areas of land were sold by the Crown to individuals. The terms of sale contained improvement requirements that, among other conditions, made the locatee responsible for the survey of his holding before title was fully transferred.[4]

Because of its policy, the government of the colony judged the trees of the forest to have a low value—an opinion then shared by the settlers and by the rest of North America. In spite of the quantities of excellent timber available close to the sea, or the timber being felled by those clearing land, most of the local demand for lumber during the time of Governor Douglas was filled by mills located in Puget Sound. It was for this reason that the earliest alienation of land, expressly for lumbering, did not occur until 1862. In that year, several tracts were granted outright to mill owners prepared to attempt to supply the Vancouver Island and Fraser river markets. At the same time, small portable mills appeared at convenient sites in the interior where lumber needed for a local mine or village was being cut.[5]

Land grants for timber extraction proved popular neither with the colonial government, with industry in its then early state of development, nor, after Confederation in 1871, with the electorate. Government soon discovered it had lost its right to receive revenue from granted lands, and industry found the ownership of logged-over hilly terrain to be a burden. Since most operators on the coast, before 1886, saw themselves staying at most twenty years in one location before extraction difficulties forced them to move, annually renewable leases on the Ontario pattern were introduced in 1865. Clauses, guaranteeing settlers' preemption rights, were included in the leases, reflecting the government's preoccupation with agricultural settlement.[6]

By the time British Columbia joined Canada in 1871, a logging and lumber production industry was well established on the coast. During this period, the population of the colony was scattered among mining towns in the interior with concentrations near Victoria, the capital on the southern tip of Vancouver Island, and Moodyville, a community of several hundred on the shores of Burrard Inlet on the mainland.[7] Because of the terrain, the sea provided the means of transportation between coastal communities. Therefore, before the completion of the Canadian Pacific Railway in 1886, mills were located where ease of access to the sea was combined with accessible stands of good timber. One such large site was Burrard Inlet, but many others existed like Port Alberni and New Westminster. At this time, the mills relied on the export of their lumber for the major portion of their income. In spite of the growth of a similar industry in the United States to the south, the operators of the coast of British Columbia were able to supply lumber to building booms in Australia, Hawaii, and, after 1873, in Chile and later Shanghai.[8]

The construction of the transcontinental railway consumed tremendous quantities of timber. In the interior, mills moved to concentrate along the right-of-way. On the coast, they opened on the banks of the lower Fraser river and around Burrard Inlet. This geographical realignment of the industry was to have results that lasted into the 1950s as, increasingly, the largest timber conversion plants were concentrated in the southwestern corner of the province. By 1891, five years after the Canadian Pacific Railway was completed, the city of Vancouver, located on the site of Moodyville, had replaced Victoria as the largest community in the province. Its population stood at 14,000 or 14 percent of the provincial total. By 1900 Vancouver was the financial capital of the area, holding control of the resource-rich hinterland to its north and east.[9]

After the completion of the Canadian Pacific Railway in 1886, the mills of British Columbia had access to their first real home-based market—the Canadian prairies. In the 1880s this small market was largely controlled by mills in Manitoba and northwestern Ontario as well as mills in Wisconsin, but it was destined to grow rapidly. When the railway gave the lumber industry of the interior access to the prairies, logging in the Railway Belt increased.

As discussed earlier, the Dominion government controlled the natural resources lying inside the belt. Dominion timber leases were administered by the Department of the Interior's notoriously lax Timber and Grazing Branch. The presence of an alternative system of leasing forestlands had a considerable effect on relations between the provincial government and the lumber industry. It provided the industry with a comparison with provincial regulations and the way in which they were enforced. Naturally enough, industry was not slow to exploit this opportunity and made many attempts to lower rates and ease conditions on the grounds that equivalence between the two sets of regulations had to be established. The berths made available by the Dominion had little effect on the realignment of the coastal industry that occurred after 1886 because the best of the limits had been quickly picked up on long-term leases when they had become available a few years earlier. The railway was also a mixed blessing to the mills of the interior since it gave government officials, based in Victoria, easy access to them. As a result of this, and an increase in lumber production, government regulation and revenue collection activities increased after 1886.[10]

With the largest sawmills increasingly concentrated in and around Chemainus on Vancouver Island and in the Vancouver–New Westminster area on the mainland, log supplies soon became a problem. The surrounding forest could not fill the demand, especially since the machinery had not yet been developed to log the forest-covered mountains some distance from the shore. Logs, therefore, had to come from the same source as before—the forest on the slopes accessible from the sea. To fell the trees and haul the logs in booms to the mills, a new group of operators, the independent loggers, arose in the industry.[11]

Soon the coastal mills and the loggers found themselves tied to a yearly cycle. The heavy winter rains on the coast curtailed logging, and it became traditional for the loggers to be let out of the camps in early December for a long Christmas holiday, which lasted until the end of the rains in the spring. As a result, the loggers spent the spring and early summer in the bush cutting logs, and it was not until midsummer that the first of the year's booms appeared at the mouth of Burrard Inlet. Thus in late summer and early fall the log market was glutted; in November and December there were days when gales interrupted towing; and, by late winter, all the booms would have to be brought in. In winter and spring, therefore, the cost of logs was high at Burrard Inlet and Chemainus. The sawmills would often shut down "for repairs" in concert at this time in an attempt to control the price of logs.[12]

The successful logger was, therefore, one who could produce a boom of logs when prices were at their highest, usually some months after logging had finished for the year and the logs were thrown into the sea. The depredations of the teredo worm, however, prevented logs from being stored for months at a time in salt water, and there were only a few places along the coast where logs could be held in fresh water away from the worms. Thus both the loggers and the mill owners on the coast of British Columbia found themselves tied together in a cycle of fluctuating supplies and prices that was set by a combination of human nature and natural phenomena.

The situation in the interior of the province was completely different. Here the mills were much smaller and, increasingly as the years rolled by, primitive compared to those of the coast. This was not solely because the trees were smaller. The mills in the interior typically operated only when they had orders to fill and generally cut their logs from areas of forest as close to their saws as possible. Once all the easily extractable logs had been hauled to the mill and converted to lumber, the mill was dismantled and moved. To make moving a mill a relatively simple task, the mills were constructed so that the largest single unit that had to be transported was the boiler for the engine. When the mill moved, the little community that had grown up around the plant moved too. The small size of these operations was symptomatic of the dearth of available capital and the instability of the market. As a result, economies of scale could not be employed by the mill men of the interior to lower operating costs. This further restricted the ability of mill owners to adjust to changes in situation. Thus, a typical response to any increase in the cost of logs or a decrease in the price of lumber was to close down the mill and passively wait for the situation to improve.[13]

Between 1890 and 1914, economic factors played a major role in the development of the industry, government legislation, and, eventually, forestry policy. British Columbia suffered with the rest of Canada through the long depression that plagued the latter half of the nineteenth century. During the early 1890s, the number of sawmills in the province dropped drastically.[14] In general, the industry languished until 1898 when the arrival of significant numbers of settlers on the prairies finally created an expanding demand for west coast lumber. All of Canada shared in the boom resulting from the demands of these settlers for farm machinery, manufactured goods and lumber. The picture of the settler's sod house is accurate, but it is often forgotten that his first farm building was a barn and this was generally made of wood. During the years in which the greatest number of settlers arrived, from 1901 to 1913, 65–75 percent of British Columbia's lumber production was shipped east, 5–17 percent was exported overseas, and the remainder was used in the province.[15]

The sudden expansion of this market led to growth of the industry in the interior and on the coast. Because of greater economies of scale, a higher grade of product and preferential railway tariffs, the coast mills, rather than the interior mills that were actually closer to the retail yards, came to control the trade. In order to maintain their share of the market, operators in inland districts were forced to price their products about $4 per thousand board feet below the prices charged by their brethren to the west. The demand for lumber on the prairies also fluctuated according to a seasonal cycle. Not unnaturally, farmers were loathe to purchase supplies of lumber until after their harvests were completed. As a result, in September and October the mills on the west coast found themselves flooded with orders for lumber to be shipped east. Providentially, this followed shortly after the period when the greatest proportion of booms of logs arrived in Burrard Inlet. Mill owners, therefore, found the peak time of demand for their products was the same as the peak of the supply of their raw material. With log prices low and lumber prices high, large profits could be made.[16]

This happy state of affairs led to the neglect of sectors of the industry's existing markets that were less profitable and harder to organize. While the sawmills of the interior had never been able to take part in the export of British Columbian forest products to the countries of the Pacific rim, this market had been important to the mills of the coast. They had been accustomed to using the export trade as a means of disposing of surplus stock. No mill specialized in exports, however, and all had neglected to make contacts with agents in such important centres as Seattle and San Francisco. From 1900 until 1913, while the demand for lumber in western Canada remained high, the export of lumber from the province decreased, and several potential overseas markets were lost. For example, at the turn of the century, New Zealand bought all of its imported wood from British Columbia, but by World War I it purchased practically none. Instead, it purchased its lumber from agents in the United States. These agents were known to actually buy Canadian lumber and restamp it as coming from American mills before selling it in markets that had been Canadian. The loss of the export trade was directly attributable to concentration on the domestic market combined with other factors such as the growth of the industry on the American Pacific coast, improvements in transportation through the use of steam ships instead of sail, and the activities of lumber brokers and agents.[17]

Besides altering the industry's markets, the completion of the railway also resulted in the imposition of government regulation as mentioned earlier. The first regulations actually date from 1865 and the creation of a leasing system. The government of the colony and, later, the province, began to realize, however, that leases in themselves did not create much revenue. But no changes were made until 1886—probably a reflection of the low value given to standing timber. Then, in that year, the government began to licence the small groups of loggers called hand-loggers, who were cutting timber along the seashore. These gangs traditionally used hand tools to fell the trees and roll the logs into the water, thus limiting their depredations. The hand-loggers had not bothered with licences because they moved to new areas each year. Because of the increasing demand for logs, however, the hand-loggers began to use machinery to extract logs. In addition, they were now staying for several seasons on the same location and were careless about whether the location was part of a lease or freehold. The government's General Timber or "Handloggers" Licence, instituted in 1886, allowed these gangs to continue operating as long as they restricted themselves to unlicenced Crown land and used only hand tools; steam-powered winches were strictly prohibited.[18]

In 1887 an important change in government attitude was signaled when the province's Land Act was amended. Instead of allowing a settler to preempt land already under lease, the onus was now placed on the settler to prove that his location was free from all encumbrance before a ticket was issued. Thus 1887 marks the point in time when standing timber in British Columbia came to have value in the eyes of the government. In the same amendment to the Land Act, a new form of timber licence was created. Called the Special Timber Licence (ST licence), it was intended to circumvent the requirements for a bid and upset price required by a lease for a berth. Valid for only one year at a time, at first, and for a given area (1,000 acres, later reduced to one square mile or 640 acres), the ST licences were to be used by the smaller companies who lacked the financial resources of the large firms. Although it took several years, ST licences came to be commonly used by the sawmills of the interior while leases became predominant with the coast industry. Although they required the payment of an annual fee, ST licences were not judged by the banks of the province to be suitable collateral for loans because they were not transferrable from one individual to another and because they were considered to give merely the legal right to the holder to remove the trees from a certain area. On the other hand, leases, which were transferrable and required the payment of a bid, were considered to grant a form of legal title to the trees.[19]

The licences and leases in place by 1887 established the basic system of regulating logging activity in British Columbia for many decades. Unlike Ontario and particularly Quebec, successive governments could not resist tinkering with the terms of the leases and licences. By 1900 the desire of

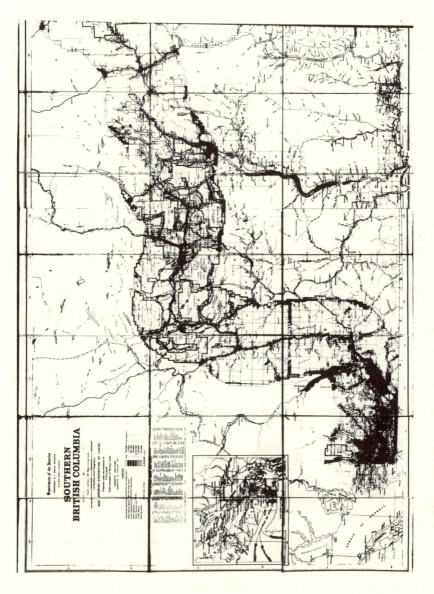

1914 map of southwestern British Columbia, immediately north of the border with the United States. The area within the shaded boundaries is the Dominion-owned Railway Belt (printed by permission of the National Map Collection, Public Archives of Canada).

provincial governments to obtain maximum income from the forests, consistent with the growth of a viable forest industry, had resulted in a plethora of revamped regulations. Leases and licences were valid for different lengths of time, depending on the regulations in force when they were issued. In addition, the annual payments and royalties varied from lease to lease, and those tracts that had been granted outright were exempt from all taxes, royalties, and later regulations governing the manufacture of logs cut in the province.[20] Clearly, the situation was now ripe for a major reform of the regulations. The impetus for this reform can be traced to a conflict between the loggers and the mill owners of the coast over the imposition of a manufacturing condition on logs cut anywhere in the province.

The manufacturing condition was a part of yet another amendment to the Land Act, this time in 1901. The confrontation between loggers and mill owners resulted from the situation of the independent loggers and hand-loggers in the province. The British Columbia Loggers' Association did its best to fix the price its members received for logs when it sold them to the mill owners. If a logger was not able to get a satisfactory price for his boom of logs, virtually his only recourse was to tow it to Puget Sound and sell it to an American mill. The mill owners and their organization, the British Columbia Lumber and Shingle Manufacturers' Association, had the upper hand largely because of the seasonal variation in the supply of logs and because towing booms to Puget Sound was expensive. The manufacturing condition was passed by the provincial legislature, as elsewhere in Canada, as a nationalistic economic and token conservation measure. In British Columbia, it profoundly affected one sector of the industry, the loggers, by removing their alternative market for logs.[21]

The logging companies quickly realized after 1901 that their very survival was at stake and that they had to avoid the manufacturing condition one way or another. Close scrutiny of the law revealed that there was in fact a loophole in it. Because of a drafting error, only logs cut on leased land or under ST licence were prohibited from being exported in raw form. Logs cut on privately owned land were of course exempt but so were those cut by hand-loggers. Logging companies quickly adopted the practice of operating with two separate teams. One team consisted of regular logging camps who cut on licenced or leased areas. The other team comprised a number of hand-loggers who cut on open Crown land one or two chains inland from the shore. Each group made up a separate boom, and it was not at all difficult for the boom's owner to arrange for logs he did not or could not sell locally to be in the boom at the hand-logger's camp waiting to be towed directly to American mills in Puget Sound. Of course, if questioned, he would claim that this boom contained only logs cut by his hand-loggers. The deception was made all the easier by the fact the Provincial Timber Inspector had only one tug for the long patrols up and down the coast.[22]

One of the largest logging operations engaged in this practice was owned by J. S. Emerson, the President of the British Columbia Loggers' Association, who was well known for his pugnacity and vociferousness. When the government discovered in 1904 that he was responsible for much of the illegal export of logs, public pressure was applied to force him and other loggers to stop. The loggers responded with an unsuccessful publicity campaign of their own and continued to slip their booms across the boundary. The government then seized one of Emerson's booms before it was exported and laid charges. Because no crime had been committed, Emerson easily had the case dismissed but the matter did not rest there. Two years later, in the 1906 legislative session, the province's Conservative government, led by Richard McBride, tried once more to control the export of logs. First, after a long and bitter debate, the law was amended to close the loophole, and the Timber Inspector was empowered to seize a boom if it appeared the intention was not to have the logs manufactured in the province. Following the passage of the act in late February, 1906, the Timber Inspector, Robert Skinner, took the government tug up the Strait of Georgia toward Emerson's booms. With Skinner were several sheriffs who were equipped with camping gear and supplied with food. Emerson's booms, which were still tied to the shore, were seized by Skinner in the name of the Crown and guarded by the sheriffs he left camped near them.[23]

Emerson reacted immediately by placing a cash bond for the booms with the Provincial Court and obtaining a restraining order. While the Provincial Attorney General was arguing the validity of both actions, the booms were broken open by timber thieves. In order to keep the booms intact, the government ordered them towed south, at its expense, to safer waters near Vancouver. At this point, Emerson went to the press and told them he was delighted that the government was saving him money by towing his booms closer to their eventual market. The Vancouver papers, never slow to poke fun at bumbling officials from Victoria, had a hilarious time with the story and successfully destroyed the Timber Inspector's credibility. Worse news for the government soon followed when Chief Justice Hunter of the British Columbia Supreme Court rejected the Crown's case on technical grounds.[24]

The way was now open for Emerson to seek redress through the courts; this he did by suing Skinner, as the Crown's representative, for illegal seizure. This civil action quickly went through the system to the full Supreme Court of the Province where, in July 1906, earlier decisions in favour of Emerson were upheld. The Crown asked leave to appeal to the Judicial Committee of the Privy Council in London, England. While the Court was considering the motion, Emerson broke up his boom, sold some of the logs locally, and exported the rest. At the same time, with considerable publicity, he brought another boom of logs south, stating it too had been made up by hand-loggers and was thus exportable. The Timber Inspector's efforts to thwart the export of this boom were easily evaded by Emerson. Acting on a tip, he towed the boom across the boundary waters, avoiding the government's tug. That same day, the Supreme Court gave the government leave, in the name of Robert Skinner, to appeal to the Privy Council. Cooler heads prevailed, however, and the appeal was never made. Emerson, triumphant, crowed to the Vancouver press how he had broken the law and had got off scot-free.[25]

The immediate result of all this skirmishing was that Robert Skinner lost his job. McBride's new Inspector, John Murray, moved to restore the government's control over the situation. He first warned the loggers that the technicalities employed by Emerson, which largely hinged on his claim that the logs had been cut before the law was signed by the Lieutenant Governor, were not valid in the upcoming logging season and exports must cease. This occurred in large measure and, as a result, the loggers lost what little control they had over their market. Thus the McBride government was initiated into the complexities of "timber politics" which had figured so prominently in other provincial legislatures in Canada. Facing political pressure, the Premier moved to redress some of the harm done to the loggers. In the previous year, 1905, at the request of the Loggers' Association, the government had pushed through legislation making the Timber Inspector responsible for timber scaling. Prior to this act, mill owners paid the loggers and made returns to the government, on the basis of the scale made by their own employees. Now, royalty payments had to be made on the scale provided by the government's own scalers. This action did not proceed without some harsh comment and controversy from the mill men, but the system was successfully operating in 1906–1907 after several months of patient negotiation by John Murray and the new Supervisor of Scalers, Andrew Haslan. The government then hired scalers who, besides measuring logs, also graded them according to criteria agreed to by the loggers and mill owners, thus creating a fair degree of standardization along the coast.[26]

Andrew Haslan's and John Murray's successful negotiation of the scaling agreements more than compensated for the government's loss of face over the Emerson affair. But both actions were important because of the precedents they set. Whereas the amendments to the Land Act of 1887 reflect the government's recognition of the value of the forests, those of 1905 and 1906 mark the government's move into an active role in the exploitation of the forests. For example, prior to these events, government revenue collection had come largely from leases and licences. Royalty collection efforts were haphazard and largely confined to the coast. It was not at all uncommon for several years to pass in which no revenue was collected from the mills of the interior.[27] The new Timber Measurement Act changed all this and led to further improvements in the next decade. Equally important was the way in which the government came to act as an arbitrator between sectors of the industry. This role became enlarged over the next few years and culminated in the creation of the Forest Branch of the British Columbia Department of Lands. Finally, the two confrontations were important because they established and confirmed the industry associations as representatives of their individual sectors in negotiations with the provincial government.

The confrontation described above involved only two of the three associations in the industry: the Loggers' Association and the Lumber and Shingle Manufacturers' Association. The group in the most precarious position, and the most vocal, were the loggers and their association. The Lumber and Shingle Manufacturers' Association was larger and more stable. It represented the owners of mills located in the coastal cities and towns concentrated in and around Vancouver and New Westminster. In 1905–1906 most mill men remained the owners of small or middle-sized mills in spite of several recent consolidations that had resulted in the formation of several large companies. The third and newest industry association in the province was the Mountain Lumbermen's Association whose members owned mills in the interior. Inasmuch as their mills were located far from Victoria and their markets even farther to the east, these men often found their voices lost in the general furor.

By 1905 then, the forest industry's trade associations were divided along structural and geographic lines. This division was paralleled by a similar one within the province's leasing and licencing regulations. By this date, practically all the leases were on the coast while, in the interior, the use of ST licences predominated. This situation changed when the McBride government demonstrated it had the same tendency to fiddle with the regulations as had earlier governments. In 1904 the government had made the ST licences transferrable from one party to another. In the following year, it extended the validity of the licences from five to twenty-one years. These two amendments gave ST licences some of the features heretofore restricted to leases.[28]

Ostensibly, these changes were made to increase the revenue to the Crown from the ST licences. There can be no doubt, however, that the government's real intention was to induce some good old-fashioned frontier speculation into the forest industry. At this time, Douglas fir lumber was rapidly increasing in value all along the Pacific coast as a result of the burgeoning market on the prairies north and south of the border. This meant that standing timber increased in value as well. The ease with which ST licences were obtained and, after 1905, their long validity and transferability made them attractive vehicles for timberland speculators. Each licence required the yearly payment of $140 if it was located on the coast and $115 if located in the interior. As the number of licences increased from the few hundred issued in 1905 to the 17,700 issued in 1907, money poured into the provincial treasury. Along with a generally expansive economy that created other sources of revenue, the money allowed the McBride government to embark on massive development plans.[29]

By allowing the licences to be used for speculation the government of

Richard McBride created a number of political and ethical problems for itself. For a start, the widespread ownership of ST licences created a new group within the industry: owners of licences who neither logged nor owned sawmills but held the licences for speculation. These men combined in 1907 with other ST licence owners who were sawmill owners and formed a fourth organization within the forest industry that had to be considered. In contrast to the three other associations, this new body, the British Columbia Timber and Forestry Chamber of Commerce, was a province-wide organization that represented licence holders from the interior and the coast. Despite its primary interest and the background of many of its members, it must be said that the Timber and Forestry Chamber of Commerce was in many ways the most modern and progressive of all the organizations in its outlook. For example, the organization hired a professional forester, Judson F. Clark, as its permanent secretary. Its members also had considerable financial and political clout even though they were not popular public figures.[30]

Perhaps the biggest problem for McBride and his Conservatives was that the boom in fir lumber prices did not last. It had been given a tremendous boost in April, 1906, when San Francisco was destroyed by an earthquake and the fire that followed. By mid–1907 this temporary stimulus had run its course and timber prices had started to collapse.[31] Almost all the good logging territory along the coast had either been leased or, as a result of frantic activities by the speculators, licenced. The loggers found their access to the forest severely limited because the ST licence holders demanded high prices for their stumpage. Worse for the loggers, in the 1906–1907 season, they had accidentally flooded the market for logs, prices had plummeted, and the speculators' demands were even further out of reach. To correct the situation by lowering the price of stumpage, the Loggers' Association campaigned to have the licence regulations changed so that many of the speculators would abandon their holdings. In their efforts, the loggers of the coast were supported by the majority of lumber and shingle manufacturers.[32]

Naturally, the Timber and Forestry Chamber of Commerce opposed the loggers. In this they were supported by the Mountain Lumbermen's Association whose members largely relied on the ST licences for their access to the resource. Both organizations wanted the licences made valid indefinitely. In this way, they argued, they would have more time to recoup their investment, the licences would become more acceptable to the banks as collateral for loans, and stumpage prices would fall. During the 1907–1908 session of the Legislature, these two groups had a very noisy confrontation that spilled over into the press. Neither group was prepared to move from its position and McBride firmly declined to take sides. All that his government did was to refuse to issue more new ST licences and state that the problem was under examination. As a result, the Premier faced the repetition of the heavy and contentious lobbying of 1907–1908 in the next session the following year and, to make matters worse, found himself facing the prospect of a provincial general election, with the problem unsolved. To defuse this situation, McBride's Finance Minister used his budget speech to announce the creation of a Royal Commission to study timber and forestry problems in the province.[33]

The membership of the Royal Commission on Timber and Forestry was named in June, 1909. The government's Minister of Lands, F. J. Fulton, was appointed chairman; the other members were A. S. Goodeve, the Conservative federal Member of Parliament for the interior riding of Rossland, and A.C. Flumerfelt of Victoria, a businessman who had extensive investments in mining and forestry. All were staunch Tories. The true role of the Commission, like that of the Colonization Commission in Quebec, was to calm the controversy by listening to all sides and then present the government with a workable consensus. Therefore, the Commissioners were people who understood the political problems facing Richard McBride and his Conservatives. The Commission, of course, needed a secretary to make the necessary travel and other arrangements and draft its reports. Providentially, a young man with considerable experience in the province's forest industry and a degree in mathematics from Cambridge had just presented himself before the Minister of Finance, Price Ellison. This young man was Martin Grainger and, even though, as he admitted himself, he lacked any political pull, he became secretary to the Royal Commission.[34] With this job, Martin Grainger began his association with government forestry in the province—an association that culminated, in 1916, in his becoming the province's second Chief Forester.

Grainger's immediate task was to help find a workable consensus within the forest sector. As a means of sampling public opinion, Royal Commissions were nothing new to the citizenry of British Columbia. The loggers' and lumbermen's associations were quite used to appearing before these bodies and so it is surprising that they let themselves be outmanoeuvered by the Timber and Forestry Chamber of Commerce in this instance. The Chamber hired a counsel, J. A. Harvey, who attended all the sittings of the Commission and questioned witnesses after they had made their presentations. Thus it was that, of all the interested parties appearing before the Commission, it was the timbermen whose views were most consistently and best represented.[35]

Fortunately, the Commissioners went farther than simply holding hearings in all the important logging communities around the province and listening to arguments made by various sectors of the industry. Impressed by American ideas about conservation and treatment of western timberlands, they attempted to find out more about these by attending the United States National Congress on Conservation and Natural Resources held in Seattle in August, 1909. Further, in December of the same year, Fulton, Goodeve, and Flumerfelt travelled east. They first visited Ottawa where they met with Robert

H. Campbell, the Dominion Director of Forestry. From Ottawa, the party then moved to Toronto for meetings with Professor B. E. Fernow, founder and Dean of the University of Toronto's School of Forestry, and Aubrey White, the Deputy Minister of Lands and Forests for Ontario. Finally, they visited Gifford Pinchot, Chief Forester of the United States Forest Service in Washington.[36] Thus the Commissioners absorbed a broader perspective than that of the immediate issue of ST licences given prominence by the questions of the Chamber of Commerce's legal counsel. Not only were they exposed to American thinking on the subject of forest conservation but they also met prominent individuals involved with the Canadian Forestry Association and the Commission of Conservation, who had a definite agenda for forestry in Canada.

Another important source of information proved to be Judson Clark. He presented a brief to the Commission of his own ideas that also went beyond the restricted issue of ST licences. Clark called for the appointment of a Provincial Chief Forester and the creation of a forest service free from political influence. The service would organize an efficient fire patrol system sharing the cost with industry. It would administer the collection of revenue and would carry out research on slash disposal and regeneration problems. Clark supported the extension of ST licences and proposed a royalty system that took account of fluctuations in the retail price of lumber. In short, the forester restated many of the ideas posed by Dr. Fernow and declared himself to be an ardent conservationist and a supporter of strict government regulation of logging practice. To his credit, virtually every one of his proposals was eventually incorporated in the Commission's *Final Report*. This must have pleased him in light of the neglect and insults he felt he had suffered at the hands of the Ontario government only a few years earlier.[37]

Clark made his presentation to the Commission in September, 1909, just before the provincial general election that led to major changes in the government and ushered in a new era for forestry in British Columbia. A major issue in the election campaign was the provision of government subsidies in the form of land grants to speed the construction of railroads. In fact, the Chairman of the Commission, F. J. Fulton, resigned from his cabinet position as Chief Commissioner of Lands because he strongly objected to the way one particular deal was handled by some of his colleagues. Following the election, which saw the Tories handily reelected, McBride appointed a member of the legislative assembly from his back benches to be his new Minister of Lands. The new Minister was William Roderick Ross, a forty-one-year-old lawyer who had represented the riding of Fernie as a Conservative since 1903. He had been born at Fort Chipewyan in the North-West Territories, a small settlement on the Athabasca river. Ross was the only son of the manager of the post, Ronald Ross Jr. His father, himself the son of a Hudson's Bay Company chief factor, died young leaving his orphaned nine-year-old son, William, to the care of Donald A. Smith (later Lord Strathcona) and an uncle, Roderick Ross. After graduating from St. John's College in Winnipeg, William Ross practiced law in Manitoba before moving to the interior of British Columbia in 1897. He was a respected and well-liked member of the legislative assembly. Following the landslide defeat of the Conservatives in 1916, he retained his seat until 1924 when he left politics. Ross, with his Hudson's Bay Company background, appears to have had different attitudes from many of his colleagues in McBride's cabinet. He did not collect a slate of directorships in various companies, for instance, and, when he retired in 1924, he moved to Vancouver and quietly started a law practice.[38]

When he was appointed to the cabinet in November, 1909, William Ross was faced with the problem of dealing with the province's forest industries. In spite of having had their say before the Commissioners, the associations were as obstreperous as ever. Ross became determined to solve the problem by using the ideas of the conservation movement as a guide. In so doing, he may be credited with being the leader in applying forestry ideas to British Columbia. His first step in the task was to introduce these ideas in a manner acceptable to all parties or the divided and argumentative loggers, sawmillers, and speculators would have rejected them with slight consideration. Of the means available to Ross, the most convenient was the Royal Commission, just then coming to the end of its public hearings. Ross set it on a new course and gave it a second year of work and study.

Therefore, it was not until January, 1911, that the Commission's *Final Report* was placed before the Provincial Legislature and subsequently released to the public. In the meantime, the Commissioners had released a guarded interim recommendation that ST licences be made valid indefinitely. This had been followed up by the government, and the regulations were amended as desired by the Chamber of Commerce and the Mountain Lumbermen's Association. Although this action took some of the heat out of the controversy, its effect on stumpage prices is questionable. At this time, there was a general fall in the value of standing timber all over the west coast associated with other factors.[39] Regardless, the amount of forest now within the financial reach of the independent loggers increased markedly, and they no longer felt themselves to be restricted. These events also left the Commissioners free to look at the problems of the industry from a broader perspective. They analyzed the situation much as had Clark and, as noted, included most of his ideas in their report. In fact, they went further than Clark in utilizing the ideas of the forest conservationists on some issues. For instance, they proposed that all income from the forests be put in a special fund. The fund would not be tapped; the government would use only the interest that accrued yearly until the fund grew large enough that withdrawals would not materially reduce the balance. Clearly, the Commission's exposure to the forest conservation movement had had an effect.

The Commission's report was well received in the province and across Canada. The demand for copies was enough to justify a second printing.

This favourable acceptance enabled William Ross to start on the next step, which was the preparation of the legislation to implement the recommendations. Ross moved the secretary to the Commission, Martin Grainger, to the Ministry of Lands and set him to work on reviewing the legislation already in force in the Province. Ross also corresponded with R. H. Campbell, Professor Fernow, and Gifford Pinchot to solicit advice and widen his knowledge. Finally, late in 1911 and again in early 1912, he travelled east to study at first-hand how other forestry services were organized.[40]

Assuming that his legislation would be passed by the legislature, Ross was committed to the establishment of a new bureau within his ministry. He, therefore, had major decisions to make with regard to its structure and, later, the choice of its senior personnel. To assist with the organizational details, he acted on the advice of Gifford Pinchot and hired a consultant, Overton Price, at that time Vice-President of the United States National Conservation Association. Price's previous job had been with the United States Forest Service where he was Associate Forester and Pinchot's trusted assistant and confidant. When Pinchot had been dismissed from his position by Taft following his controversy with the latter's Secretary of the Interior, Ballinger, Price had been forced to resign as well. It was from Price that practically all of the ideas for the plan of organization of the new bureau were to come.[41]

By June, 1911, William Ross was looking for a forester to head his new bureau. For advice on this matter, he turned to Henry S. Graves, the newly appointed Chief Forester of the United States. Graves recommended a man he described as being one of the most competent students to have passed through the Yale University faculty during his tenure as its first Dean. This was Harvey MacMillan, a native of Newmarket, Ontario, and a graduate of the University of Toronto's Ontario Agricultural College at Guelph. MacMillan had been valedictorian for his class when he graduated from Yale's Master of Forestry program in 1908, had worked on the Dominion government's forest surveys since 1905, and had joined the Dominion Forestry Branch on graduation as Assistant Inspector of Forest Reserves. When Ross approached him about becoming British Columbia's first Chief Forester, MacMillan was based in Alberta as an Assistant Director of the Forestry Branch, spending most of his time supervising activities in the Dominion's forest reserves in the foothills of the Rocky Mountains.[42] The young forester accepted with little hesitation.

Having secured MacMillan's appointment, Ross turned his attention to the bill which was to become the Forest Act of 1912. It was an omnibus piece of legislation, collecting under one roof all the relevant clauses from the Land, Bush Fires, Timber Manufacture, and Measurement of Timber Acts as well as sections of other acts governing rights-of-way and physical access to forestlands. Its comprehensive scope resolved a number of difficulties that had plagued other pioneering forestry administrations. These problems had been created by divided or incomplete jurisdictions. The bill also established a new system of timber leases, though it left existing leases and licences in force. Then, in a section lifted right from the Commission's recommendations, a forest protection fund was set up with contributions shared between industry and government. Last and most important, the bill established and empowered Ross's new bureau, the British Columbia Forest Branch.

The Branch's work was to be overseen by a Provincial Forest Board appointed by the Lieutenant Governor in Council and consisting of the heads of sections within the Branch. Through the Board, the Branch controlled and had jurisdiction over all matters relating to forestry in the province including revenue collection, fire protection and suppression, logging, and reforestation as well as regulating the trade in timber lands and logs and enforcing statutes. Below the level of the Board, the bill left the organization of the Branch undefined, giving Ross the flexibility to accept or ignore the recommendations of Overton Price. Finally, because the Board was ultimately responsible for enforcing the Act, it was given the power to summon witnesses and examine them under oath and lay charges for perjury and contempt. Also, the bill gave the personnel of the Branch wide powers to make regulations governing woods activities, particularly in areas connected with log scaling and fire protection. In practice, by using its powers in these two areas, the Branch was able to alter the cutting and waste-disposal methods of the loggers thereby increasing the utilization of the resource and enhancing natural regeneration. The act proved to be more powerful than was at first apparent.[43]

When the Forest Act was unveiled in the legislature in January, 1912, it was greeted with favourable comments in the press and from industry spokesmen. A member of the Commission, A. C. Flumerfelt, made it the topic of a laudatory address to the Vancouver Canadian Club. As might be expected from his business background and audience, Flumerfelt emphasized the positive effect on the value of timber holdings that would follow from the proposed improvements in fire protection.[44] In the legislature, however, William Ross and the Premier faced determined criticism from the minuscule two-member Liberal Opposition. The leader of the Opposition, Harlan Brewster, criticized the 1905 amendment for extending the life of the ST licences because it represented a major change in government policy. The Liberal leader then claimed that the new conditions outlined in the bill were nothing but a rehash of ideas his party had proposed some years before. It is fair to say, however, that Ross had gone much further with his proposals than Brewster suggested. Instead of defending government ownership of the resource on the grounds that its royalties provided needed income, he pointed out that "the perpetuation of the timber supply requires an investment stretching over generations and that sort of investment has hitherto been too long for private owner." The bill before the assembly therefore represented a "sane business-like policy of conservation, free from sentimental extravagance" which took "the many practical difficulties, impediments and risks" of the industry into account.[45]

Ross thus presented to the legislature some of the ideals of the forest conservation movement with which he had become directly involved. Instead of creating static forest reserves, as was occurring in many other jurisdictions in Canada, he intended to use government regulation and management as an active force in perpetuating a valuable resource and in this way maintain good condition for business investment. The government, he indicated, was going to make an investment in the forests in return for the $13 million that had already been produced for the treasury. Besides creating the Forest Branch, the government was going to fund it generously. Ross claimed that "the epoch of reckless devastation of the natural resources with which we, the people of this fair province, have been endowed by Providence" was coming to an end. With the Forest Branch in operation, the work of conservation was going to be advanced to protect this heritage for "all posterity".[46]

The Forest Act was a bold move on the part of Ross and the Conservative government. The lumber business was already well into the slump following the rebuilding of San Francisco, and in 1912 immigration to the Canadian prairies was also starting to level off. Part of the success of Ross's actions was due to the support he obtained from the powerful timbermen's lobby which was, in large part, molded by Judson Clark. These men stood to benefit not only from better fire protection but also from a provincial agency that promised to represent their economic opinions and encourage an increase in the utilization of the resource. In addition, licence holders saw their holdings increase in value because the bill confirmed that no new ST licences were to be issued while leaving those already issued untouched.[47]

The Minister of Lands left the task of answering Brewster's jibes to his Premier. Sir Richard McBride first claimed that, in 1905, economic conditions made it impossible to auction timberlands, a highly debatable point. As to speculators, the Premier opined: "In reality there are few people that were not speculators in one sense or another". Publicly, McBride was not criticized for these statements but, in private, things must have been different because, the following day, he took a conciliatory tack and admitted his government had been "severely taken to task" as a result of the amendments of 1904 and 1905. The Royal Commission, he continued, had done a tremendous job, and the current bill was the fruit of its labors. It was a nonpolitical measure and one on which every member could speak and be listened to.[48]

During the debates, the only open criticism of the bill came, paradoxically, from members representing rural constituencies. These M.L.A.'s, largely from ridings in the interior, were concerned that some farmers would find themselves stuck with a long fire season and with the regulations enforced by an unsympathetic fire warden. These were important concerns in a province where the majority of farmers were still clearing their land. Eventually,

Ross left the hiring of fire wardens to the Forest Board and promised the Legislature, and his Chief Forester, that only the best-trained men would be picked for service with the Branch.[49]

The Forest Act received Royal Assent on 27 February 1912. Its successful passage with no substantive amendments left Ross free to complete negotiations with the principal staff who would lead the new Branch. Harvey MacMillan now took the position of Acting Chief Forester, and a forester with the United States Forest Service, R. E. Benidict, moved north to become Chief of Operations, thus continuing the American influence within the new provincial organization. The other members of the team were Martin Grainger, who continued his civil service career by becoming Chief of Office; J. Lafon, Chief of Management; and H. K. Robinson, in charge of surveys.[50]

In the way it was created, in the policies that guided it, and in the way it behaved toward all users of the province's forests, the Forest Branch was a great credit to the early forest conservation movement in Canada. As a product of the ferment of ideas often called the Progressive Era, part of the Branch's success resulted from its being something of a late comer. The Dominion of Canada, the provinces of Ontario and Quebec and, of course, the United States had all experimented with forestry organizations by the time the Branch was founded. W. R. Ross was able to learn from others who had gone through similar difficulties before him, avoid the mistakes they were able to identify, and hire many of the young foresters they had trained. The Branch must therefore be considered a product of the early conservation movement in the mature phase of its development and, with the unique contribution of Overton Price, a direct offshoot of the ideals expounded by Gifford Pinchot for forestry in North America.

The act that created the Forest Branch shows this maturity in a number of ways. For one, it gave the new agency control over all forest activities in the province. An examination of the Forest Act shows that most of it is given over to this process of consolidation. It is clear that Martin Grainger spent a large part of his time during the summer of 1911 searching through the statutes of the province, identifying all that related to forestry. As a result, the battle for the consolidation of powers, which took up so much of Pinchot's time and energy and which he never completely won, did not take place in British Columbia. It was this same battle that had been fought and lost by Elihu Stewart of the Dominion Forestry Service and the foresters of Ontario, to the detriment of their organizations. As a result of Ross's determination and Grainger's work, Harvey MacMillan, from his first day at work as Chief Forester, was able to concentrate on the job he was hired to do.

Because it depended so closely on the ideas of Pinchot and Price, the structure of the Forest Branch indicates that government involvement in forestry, as advocated by these two men, must have had considerable support within the British Columbian forest industry. The four associations, each representing a different sector of the industry, could have banded together to form a powerful lobby against the bill. Yet, the Royal Commission's *Final Report* was well received, and the bill establishing the Branch passed through the legislature without public criticism from industry. Clearly the industry could see for itself that the new Branch would assist it even in times of decreasing demand and falling prices. Coincidentally, this positive attitude toward government involvement in forestry was also present in Washington and Oregon, the states immediately to the south of British Columbia where the forests were a predominant industrial sector. It must be assumed that the province's lumbermen were aware of this and possibly took their cues from their southern neighbours.[51]

MacMillan's first job as Chief Forester was to assemble a field staff. He accomplished this by hiring seventeen foresters primarily from the Dominion Forestry Branch and the United States Forest Service. By October, 1912, the Board had hired twenty-four foresters, and, in a letter to his old employer R. H. Campbell, MacMillan forecast he would soon have an annual budget of $400,000 to $500,000. At the end of 1912, the Branch stated in its first annual report that the "three great tasks" facing the new organization were "more efficient fire protection, the improvement of the forests by an active timber sales policy along conservation lines and the production of a steadily increasing revenue from the forest resource". This was an espousal of the ethics of the conservation movement; conservationists would have said that if points one and two were taken care of, the third would follow.[52]

While the Branch and industry appear to have been satisfied with the Forest Act of 1912, unfortunately the government was not. In order to maintain the high levels of expenditure undertaken between 1909 and 1912, more revenue was required to compensate for a tax base that was rapidly shrinking as the boom years passed. Improvements in scaling efficiency and royalty collection had been achieved by creating a Board of Scaling Examiners and requiring all the Branch's nonprofessional staff to be licenced scalers. This was not enough. Royalty rates had to be increased because of the decreasing cut. There were other factors as well. Increased timber royalties answered mounting public criticism that speculators were not contributing to the running of the province. This had been partially compensated for by increasing the dues paid into the fire protection fund which was interpreted as a measure that made the licence and lease owners pay more for their holdings. As a result of the need for more funds and because of public pressure, the Forest Act was amended, in a very clumsy manner, in 1913 and more successfully in 1914. With hindsight, it can be seen that the major flaw in the Forest Act was that it did not cancel all leases and licences held prior to 1912 and start afresh. Thus, for McBride, the problem he faced in 1913 and 1914 when he attempted to increase royalty rates was still the same as the one he had faced in the period from 1903 to 1907. The largest proportion of the province's annual harvest of timber was cut either on lands granted in the nineteenth century and exempt from royalties, or on old leases, dating from roughly the same period, on which the royalty rate was fixed by the contract of the lease. This situation applied particularly to a small number of the established large mills on the coast. Amendments to the 1912 act could, therefore, increase the rates only on logs cut from ST licences and the newer leases.[53]

The 1913 amendment to the Forest Act delayed the rate increase until 1916, but, even so, it caused so much unhappiness that, in the following year's session, it was repealed and replaced by a bill written for Ross by MacMillan himself. This bill proposed a formula for recalculating royalties once every five years based on the average selling price of lumber during the period. It was well received by industry, while the Vancouver press touted tying royalty rates to the price of lumber as "profit sharing" between industry and government. As an additional conservation measure, logs were to be graded, and the poorer quality grades were to be charged at a lower rate. Macmillan hoped this would encourage loggers to bring the lower grades out of the bush rather than leaving them behind to rot.[54] W. R. Ross, in a speech to the legislature introducing the second reading of the amendments, said that he expected the measure would help increase the stability of the industry, increase the utilization and hence conservation of the resource, and benefit the treasury. The amendment was passed into law in February, 1914, although it was not to come into effect until 1915. Its largest influence would be upon the industry of the interior which, as we have seen, largely used the ST licence to gain access to the resource. This sector of the industry was still as dependent upon markets in Alberta and Saskatchewan as it had ever been. In fact, these markets, and therefore the mills of the interior, had already been hurt by the decline in the prairie building boom that had begun in 1913.

Things worsened for all the forest industry in the province in July and August with rumours of the likelihood of war in Europe.[55] It took only this rumour of a European war to dry up the prairie market. The effect on the forest industry was immediate. Mills were shut down on very short notice, and loggers pulled their men out of the bush. A wave of cancelled orders swept on down through the service industries and transportation companies. Thousands of men were laid off, swelling the ranks of the unemployed in Vancouver. Within the Forest Branch, the declaration of war, coming at the end of the work season, had little effect at first. It was not until the spring of 1915 that it became apparent that a manpower shortage combined with a cutback in funds meant that the forest survey, needed for any future planning, would have to be severely curtailed. All the efforts of the Branch went into forest protection activities.[56]

By 1914 the forest industry of British Columbia dominated the economy of the province. With the declaration of war, the situation of the industry and therefore of the province became desperate. The worldwide shortage of shipping, which quickly developed, meant that the days of sending a speculative cargo overseas were gone. Furthermore, the industry had so neglected its contacts with agents in the United States that now the effort required to establish business links with these men was beyond the mill owners. With the collapse of the local and prairie markets and the lack of interest of eastern Canada in the province's lumber, the industry could do little but close down and await better times. In 1915–1916 MacMillan was named a Special Trade Commissioner on behalf of both the Dominion and British Columbian governments and was sent on a round-the-world tour to look for markets. He found that the demand for lumber and dimension timbers that could have come from British Columbia was being filled by a network of agents based in San Francisco. In fact, logs from British Columbia were regularly purchased by mills in Puget Sound where they were sawn and, as in the past, labelled as if they had come from trees grown in Oregon. What had happened to the industry in the province was that it had grown so used to selling directly to company-owned retail yards on the prairies that it had failed to develop the next, higher level of industrial organization, the broker-dealer. As a result, brokerage companies had become established in San Francisco, which had developed and eventually taken over the trade in lumber with all the Pacific rim countries as well as those on the west coast of Africa. MacMillan was able to secure some orders for British Columbia forest products while on his trip, but, unfortunately, lack of shipping and conflict between the companies prevented the delivery of most of these orders.[57]

Through 1915 the political and economic situation in British Columbia grew worse and worse for the Conservative government. In December, Sir Richard McBride resigned as Premier and left for London to become the province's Agent General. His place was taken by W. J. Bowser, the organizational genius and bagman behind the Conservative party's electoral successes. Another provincial election was in the offing, but Bowser delayed it until the fall of 1916. The Chief Forester arrived home just before the election. Apparently MacMillan could foresee the future because he resigned from his position just two days before the vote and the defeat of the government. After wartime service with the Canada Supply Board, MacMillan founded his own business, an export agency for British Columbian lumber and wood products. This eventually led to the founding of the corporate empire that became MacMillan Bloedel Ltd.[58]

The Conservative government that had held power in British Columbia since 1903 was soundly defeated at the polls by the Liberals in the 1916 election. Ross's place as Minister of Lands was taken by Thomas (Duff) Pattullo, later Premier of the province during the depression of the 1930s. In the Forest Branch, Martin Grainger became the new Chief Forester perpetuating, in part, the Canadian trend of putting self-trained, nonprofessional foresters in charge of forestry services. But, in the end, it mattered little since both men had to face the fact no money was available to carry out the projects started in 1912. With the call to arms reaching ever deeper into the ranks of Canada's young men, the staff of young foresters that had been hired was already depleted. It was not until after peace had been declared that the Branch would be able to expand beyond forest fire protection and turn, once more, to planning and implementing forest management practices.[59]

In many ways, the resignation of MacMillan represented the passing of an era in forestry in British Columbia. Certainly it was the end of the Branch's most optimistic period. This does not mean the years that followed saw neither growth nor development of forestry in the province. Through the 1920s the permanent and temporary staff of the Branch expanded. By 1930 when the province took over the control of the Dominion Railway Belt and the Peace River Block, the staff numbered 287 and over 150 well-trained rangers who helped fight fires in the summer months. Also, the province was the first to appoint its fire rangers by examination rather than through political patronage.[60] As its appropriations increased, the Branch embarked on an ambitious program of forest inventory. This job was not properly finished until after the development of aerial reconnaissance in the late 1930s. Another step taken toward intensive forest management was the reintroduction of forest reserves in the form of provincial forests. These were a precursor to the sustained yield limits or working circles. Although, at the time, the reintroduction of reserves was considered a positive step, it actually was a response to the frustrating situation in which the government's foresters found themselves. It was clear that the introduction of forest management to the province was going to be a long process. The expertise and technical knowledge of the foresters ran far ahead of the willingness and ability of government to implement their proposals. Aware of this, foresters responded by locating the reserves in relatively remote areas of good timber. The intention was that, by the time industry was ready to exploit the reserves, having cut out the holdings they then held, they would find themselves faced with a fait accompli. Long-established policies would hopefully force industry to operate in the reserves in the manner desired by the foresters. The idea was similar to the banking of timber that had been tried elsewhere and was inspired, in part, by the Dominion example. Of course the plan was never successfully completed although much of the reserved area did become part of the Public Sustained Yield Units created after World War II in response to the recommendations of the Sloan Commission.[61]

During the 1920s the Branch mechanized its fire-fighting efforts. It introduced gasoline pumps, replaced horses with automobiles, and put outboard motors onto the sterns of its canoes. Aircraft were hired for fire patrols and a radio network was established. A start was also made on researching regeneration, natural seed dispersal, stand makeup and growth, as well as the effect of controlled thinnings. Several attempts were made to coordinate research and fire-fighting activities with those of the Dominion Forestry Service.

While the Forest Service was expanding, the forest industry also underwent changes. The industry of the coast dominated the prairie market even more than it had done in the years before World War I. This was probably due to the results of government efforts to assist the coast industry in 1917 and 1918. The export corporation, created for the duration of the emergency, and the spectacular rise in the use of Sitka spruce lumber for aircraft construction allowed this sector to survive the war in comparatively good condition. Unfortunately, the war had a bad effect on the industry of the interior; it languished until the 1940s. At the same time, an average of 33 percent of the volume cut each year in the province continued to come from granted lands, particularly those of the Esquimalt and Nanaimo railway land grant, and thus were exempt from royalty payments. Another development within the industry was the growth of pulp and paper production. Pulp and paper mills were built during World War I, and by 1945, six were located on tidewater at the mouths of relatively isolated rivers. Unlike the industry of eastern Canada, these mills avoided the pitfalls of overproduction and reliance on a single product, newsprint, sold largely to one market, the United States. This industry successfully utilized its physical location to give it direct access to the markets of the Pacific rim countries, especially China, Japan, and Australia.[62]

It was, however, not all good news for forestry during the two decades between the wars. The funds given to the Branch by the government were unfortunately never sufficient to allow the development of a really effective regeneration program. Appropriations appear to have stayed at less than 30 percent of the income the province directly received from its forest resource. In particular, the 1920s saw a major alteration in the relationship between industry and government. This coincided with the founding of the Timber Industry Council of British Columbia, organized in 1921 by former Chief Forester Martin Grainger. The Council and the government debated the issue of timber royalties. Changes in the economic condition of the province, coupled with a drop in value (in real terms) of the Canadian dollar, meant that industry became convinced royalties were too high. The debate bypassed the officials of the Forest Branch as the Council dealt directly with the politicians, particularly Minister Pattullo. Finally in 1924, finding itself in a minority position and with an election imminent, the Liberal government of John Oliver abandoned the formulae of the 1914 act and accepted industry's demand for a fixed royalty rate. For the first time since the founding of the Forest Branch, industry demonstrated it could get its own way without using the foresters as intermediaries. That the industry was allowed to be successful in this way was unfortunate because the Branch, now under the intelligent and determined leadership of Peter Caverhill, had developed considerable expertise in forest management and was starting to apply it to the situation in the province.[63]

Other political difficulties acted to enhance the resurgence of industry's control over forestry policy. A series of disastrous fire years from 1918 to 1922 resulted in the depletion of the fire suppression fund. Besides raising its own contributions, the government increased the contribution rate for industry. Although it made the payments, industry, through its Council, complained bitterly that it was paying proportionally more for the protection of Crown land than for the land it owned or rented. As with the royalty rates, negotiations dragged on until 1924. In that year, the Forest Act was amended so that the ratio of government-to-industry contributions to the fund was three to two. In actual practice, however, this was never met. Government did not push the issue and, by 1927, the ratio approached five to three. Once again, this demonstrated that industry had political power and was not afraid to use it in its own interest.[64]

Thus, by 1928 the Forest Branch had had some success in introducing sustained yield management to the forests of the province. There had been progress, with the exception of the years during World War I, and indeed there was even public pressure to speed up the process. Yet the various sectors of the forest industry which had initially supported forestry regulation were now more restive and lobbied hard to decrease both the Crown's share of timber revenues and its regulatory influence. This opposition and the difficulties of the depression of the 1930s created a situation which, in the words of C. D. Orchard to the 1945 Royal Commission Relating to the Forest Resources of British Columbia, "mitigated strongly against continued progress in any line." The Forest Branch suffered large-scale staff reductions in the early 1930s, dropping to a low of 193 positions in 1935 from 287 positions in 1930. It did not benefit greatly from the "mini-New Deal" offered by now Premier Duff Pattullo and the provincial Liberals after 1933.[65] Indeed, by starting a number of relief and industrial welfare projects, the government actually ate into the revenues available for normal operations. Although the Premier pushed for more revenue sources to be turned over to the province in some sort of renewed federal structure, he was quite unsuccessful in influencing Prime Ministers R. B. Bennett and William Lyon Mackenzie King, and the province remained strapped for funds. The lack of revenue and manpower resulted in a scaling down of both timber management activities and, particularly, the regeneration studies then under way. Some aid was obtained for jobs requiring manual labour, such as road improvement and slash disposal, to aid forest protection and the development of provincial forest reserves. These were carried out through two province-inspired relief programmes: Forest Development Projects and the Youth Forestry Training Plan. But the Forest Branch had not been adequately funded during much of the 1920s, and the restraints and new tasks only doubled the burden. It was not surprising, therefore, that E. C. Manning, Provincial Forester, admitted candidly in the *Vancouver Sun* in 1937 that

Forestry, in simple language, means the replacing of old crops. . . . I contend that in that respect forestry in this province has been more of a fancy than a fact. We have been so engaged in collecting revenues and protecting present values in mature timber that a new crop has received insufficient attention through lack of funds and staff.[66]

This rather gloomy picture was reinforced a year later when the limited field crews available reported on the regeneration found on sites logged from 1921 to 1938. The results were truly alarming. Satisfactory regeneration rates were well below 10 percent for merchantable species. Older areas, logged before 1933, were getting better regeneration but still not over 10 percent. It was obvious that natural regeneration was not working in British Columbia and that there was a tremendous need for controls over logging and for silvicultural activity including reforestation. Manning was optimistic, however, because this adverse publicity and the easing of economic conditions resulted in an increase in funding and staff which could help the situation. In addition, on 9 August 1938, A. Wells Gray, the Minister of Lands, announced that facilities would be established to replant 10,000 acres of cutover land per year on Vancouver Island and the lower mainland. The next year also saw an increase in forest surveys and inventory work and a revival of extensive silvicultural research.[67]

In some parts of Canada, for a short time during the 1920s, the conservation movement was able take the initiative once more and for a few years begin to chart a new course. Unfortunately, forestry and forest conservation in British Columbia was able to join only marginally in this brief revival. The spirit that had led to the creation of the Forest Branch in 1912 was no longer present. The depression of the 1930s was a desperate period for conservationists all across Canada as governments fruitlessly looked to "business methods" for a solution to problems they confronted. Why forestry in British Columbia suffered so much is unclear. Perhaps the over-concentration of logging activity on privately held lands played a role. Perhaps the expansionist and pro-business mood of the province in the 1920s distracted those who might have cared. Certainly the 1912 legislation had been grafted onto a political jurisdiction more interested in exploitation than conservation. It promised to remove the rowdy lobbying tactics of the industry associations from the hallowed halls of the legislature where it was attracting altogether too much public attention. At the same time that forestry was a progressive idea that was publicly popular, it was also one that was never taken seriously by politicians. Certainly, funding for the Branch was never adequate even for the widely accepted cause of forest fire protection. Successive governments claimed that the population base in the province was not sufficient to sustain the taxation required to maintain all services including forestry.

Whatever the problem, even though the provincial treasury reaped millions of dollars annually from its forests, the Branch expanded and contracted according to the whims of the government of the day. In 1912 there had been eleven forest districts; in 1939 there were only five huge ones. By this later date, foresters were spread extremely thin on the ground, and the province was looking for federal subsidies for forestry activities.[68] Even more so than Quebec, by 1945, British Columbia had sunk to the level where forest conservation meant little more than a protective exercise to prevent fires and secure marginal regeneration.

Indeed, World War II disrupted even the limited work of the late 1930s. Once more, enlistments began to eat into the number of personnel available for any type of forestry work, and the Office of the Timber Controller pushed both the Branch and industry to emphasize production, which they did successfully; the province's cut reached approximately 8,775,000 cubic metres by the end of 1940. The requiem on many forestry projects during the early war period was "due to enlistments and transfers . . . programme activities are essentially on a maintenance basis." E. C. Manning, himself, was chosen by Harvey MacMillan as the Controller's Assistant on the Pacific coast. Unfortunately, the Chief Forester was killed in an aircraft accident while returning from Ottawa on 6 February 1941. A native of Selwyn, Ontario, and a 1912 graduate of the University of Toronto Forestry School, Manning had joined the Forest Service in 1918 after a three-year stint with the Dominion Forestry Service. Perhaps his most important contribution to British Columbia during his short five-year tenure as its Chief Forester was a clear understanding that effective forestry in the province had two main obstacles in its way. The first was politicians who consistently took a short-sighted attitude toward the forest resource. The second was business interests which automatically opposed any policy that might in any way reduce profits. It was left to Manning's successor, C. D. Orchard, to face the challenge presented by these two problems.[69]

Orchard was vocal in his efforts to obtain additional resources for forestry work. He stated in 1941 that,

realizing that every stick of timber cut must be recorded; that every logging operation must be inspected for compliance with "Forest Act" provisions and contract requirements; the hundreds of separate sales of Crown timber must be cruised, valued and sold; that all land applications must be inspected and classified; that preemptions must be inspected each year; [and] that fires must be fought[70]

with less personnel and money, it was a miracle that services had been maintained. Orchard was instrumental in pushing his minister, Gray, now part of a new Coalition administration which had replaced the Liberal government of Duff Pattullo, to approach Ottawa for financial aid. As will be seen, Ottawa was not ready for federal-provincial cooperation in forestry, and with that door shut for the duration of the war, any thought of creative forestry work was largely shelved. Some limited improvements were possible with the assistance of alternative service workers, but most hope was placed on plans for the Rehabilitation Council. These plans set out in detail the improvements needed in the various forest districts and the organization required to administer them.

Future planning was not, however, an adequate reply to the Cooperative Commonwealth Federation's opposition in British Columbia which by mid–1943 had launched a full-scale attack on forestry affairs in the province. As wartime production ground on, conditions which were already deteriorating became markedly worse. It was obvious that the better areas of accessible timber had been gutted while regeneration statistics remained distinctly unimpressive. To make matters worse, other stands of mature and aging timber had not been opened up to relieve the pressure on existing commercial areas. This fact was particularly galling to the province's forest industries which were publicly rumbling that they did not have the ready supplies or the security of tenure to underwrite the larger milling facilities required for expanding markets. The government now found itself in a very tight corner. Production of lumber had sunk from its wartime highs but was again edging upward with the promise of peace and, indeed, took off in 1947, increasing 2,376,400 cubic metres in a single year. At the same time, there was intensive political debate over the government's lack of progressive forestry measures. In the time-honoured tradition, Premier John Hart and his Coalition cabinet opted for a provincial Royal Commission to look into the matter.[71]

The sole commissioner was the Hon. Justice M. Gordon Sloan, a provincial judge and former provincial Attorney-General. Appointed in March, 1944, Sloan quickly came to the conclusion that all was not well with forest regeneration on the west coast. He heard alarming tales about how the timber had been cut out of areas in a few short years, leaving communities to collapse and disappear. C. D. Orchard told Sloan that in his opinion

up to date, forestry in British Columbia, insofar as actual practice in the woods has been concerned, has consisted in an inadequate, and consequently only partially successful attempt at protection from fire. There has been little attempt to practice sound silviculture. Such conservative legislation as we have has been appended to older concepts designed to protect the cash interest of the public in a resource.[72]

The judge expressed his opinion that the practices of the past had been completely unacceptable and could not be allowed to continue without grave consequences for the future of the province. His contention was that no longer could the forest industries rapidly cut-over areas and abandon them without any thought to the new growth of commercial timber species. This, Sloan affirmed, jeopardized the future of the industry itself, the economy of the province, and, by creating dislocation and unemployment, its social fabric as well. The proper solution to this situation, the commissioner urged, was a thoroughgoing sustained yield policy which would guarantee timber for the various mill communities in perpetuity.[73]

To obtain this new resource footing for the industry, Sloan proposed to divide timberland into privately- and publicly-controlled working areas or circles. Each type of area was to be managed on a sustained yield basis— the private areas by the company having the lease and the public areas by the British Columbia Forest Service. The details of these suggestions were considered by the Coalition government through 1946, and the Forest Act was amended at the session of 1947 to facilitate the practice of sustained yield management of the forest resource.

Orchard characterized this legislation as ranking "with the formation of the Forest Service thirty-five years previously in importance as a progressive step in the development and perpetuation of our forest resource". From this act developed the concept of tree farm licences which made timberland available on a long-term lease to larger operators who were willing in return to take on the duties of forest management. These licences were designed to overcome concerns about future timber supplies, random disposal of timber such as had occurred under the old timber sales licences set up as a result of the Royal Commission of 1910, and the failure to fund adequately public forest management activities. The tree farm licences, first called forest management licences, made the operator responsible for carrying out logging measures on a sustained yield basis and for preparing management plans, including reforestation programs, forest inventories, and calculations of allowable cut. These management plans were made subject to approval by the Forest Service. The reasoning behind the new system was that, if companies were given explicit security of tenure arrangements and then regulated on that basis, they would commence programmes to establish sustained yield production and long-term timber supply. The original licences were granted in perpetuity, but this was modified to a twenty-one-year lease when Sloan reviewed the province's forestry situation in another Royal Commission report in 1956. The other type of timber licencing that resulted from the 1947 amendments was the public sustained yield unit, which was to be applied to the remaining areas of Crown forest. These areas were to be managed by the Forest Service; disposal was to take place on an annual allowable cut basis under the existing timber sales licences. These units were conceived to be a flexible way by which the government could allocate timber to both large and small operators. The system was, however, particularly important in assigning supplies to smaller, independent operators.[74]

From 1948 on, these tenure systems were put into place in British Columbia. Through the direct control of the minister for both types of tenure, the Forest Service became responsible for assigning the types of timber each firm would obtain and the area in which it would operate. The long-term arrangements of the tree farm licences made them extremely popular with industry. By the time that Judge Sloan was once more commissioned in 1956 to reappraise the system he had recommended be put in place, twenty-three such licences had been approved. Most had gone to large integrated firms such as MacMillan-Bloedel and Crown-Zellerbach. All covered excellent timberland. Unfortunately, this in turn led to numerous complaints from smaller companies in the industry that they were restricted both by the government's foresters and the resource available to them from competing with the larger companies.[75] The old battle over the right to access to timber on the public domain was brought to the fore in British Columbia, and it has remained there to the present time. Nevertheless, British Columbia, with its extensive forest areas and persuasive timber industries, was in the forefront in establishing the new government-corporate axis which was to dominate Canadian forestry during its revival after World War II. It was a system that guaranteed security of tenure in exchange for corporate promises of forestry practices that would ensure sustained yield from the timberlands. In essence, it was the very type of agreement sought by Quebec and Ottawa valley lumbermen in the 1880s. It lacked, however, a strong commitment to a public interest in the forest to ensure its maintenance for posterity which William Ross had envisioned in 1912. The exploitive ethic was alive and well in the province, viewing its timber almost solely as a source of revenue and an engine of immediate, unbridled economic growth. Like so many other things started in Canada before 1914, forestry and forest conservation in British Columbia had been transformed from its progressive roots.

CHAPTER 7

The Dimensions of a Client Province: Forestry in New Brunswick to 1939

In 1943 the New Brunswick Committee on Reconstruction declared before the Special Committee of the House of Commons on Reconstruction and Re-establishment that "forestry, which is New Brunswick's most important industry in terms of dollar value of production, is relatively more important in New Brunswick than in any other province."[1] With the sole exception of British Columbia, this fact remains true today and certainly applied to the province in the nineteenth and early twentieth centuries. Lumbering was the preeminent occupation and touched virtually every aspect of life in New Brunswick. Thus in this province, as on the west coast, once agreement had been reached on a policy, it was simply adopted by the government. But New Brunswick is a limited physical area and has a relatively small population. Especially up to the 1890s, politics were extremely parochial; various local interest groups vied for power in a fluid party system that could rarely be classified in more precise terms than the "ins" and the "outs". After 1837, when Thomas Baillie's powers as Surveyor General were, in large part, transferred to the Legislative Assembly, the province came to resemble, as Hugh Thorburn has pointed out, the American pattern of government much more closely than the British one.[2] Committees of the Assembly overshadowed the executive because they controlled government spending, and members felt themselves to be free agents to drive good bargains for local constituents and friends. The public purse was emptied to pay for works of direct local benefit to those of influence. Within this system, local potentates, often lumbermen and merchants, enjoyed privileged positions of power, which they used to their own inclinations.[3]

With the government's authority drastically reduced, the various local lumbering interests could conspire to keep the leasing system rudimentary and timber royalties low. Indeed, much more than in the Canadas, major lumbermen suborned control of Crown lands policies and bent them to their own interests. In 1867 one prominent public official pointed out that the Crown was obtaining approximately five cents per thousand board feet for its timber, while private landowners were obtaining seventy-five cents to one dollar per thousand board feet for spruce and from one to two dollars for pine.[4]

This introduces another factor unique to New Brunswick in comparison to the other major timber-producing provinces. There was substantial private ownership of timberlands. Commencing with Baillie's move in the 1830s to raise revenues through land sales and his failure to discourage sale of prime timber areas, a sizable portion of the forest area in the province fell into private hands for speculative purposes. This was exacerbated in the period 1860–1880 when New Brunswick attempted to finance railway construction through land grants to various companies, the largest being the New Brunswick Land and Railway Company in the Saint John valley.[5] By 1923, 40 percent of the forest in the province was under private control.[6]

Private ownership hastened the closing of the timber frontier in New Brunswick. Substantial parts of the province were locked up for speculative purposes, and, with the relatively small land area involved and the long history of lumbering, most accessible Crown land was taken up under lease at a fairly early date. Certainly by the 1880s, there was little room for lumbermen to move to unfettered limits. They either had to purchase rights from fellow operators or buy private land or the wood from it. Unlike in Quebec, Ontario, and British Columbia, there was little hope of finding a new timber frontier in some other area of the province. Virgin timber still existed, but it was generally in the hands of another operator or a timber speculator. Thus the trend in New Brunswick was to exploit heavily existing limits for whatever variety of timber they would produce.

There was, proportionally, much less white pine in the province's forests. This species was under considerable production pressure by 1850 and had fallen to one third of the cut by 1870. Thus, the major species that would sustain the New Brunswick sawmilling industry through the second decade of the twentieth century was white spruce. It too, however, came under pressure as over-cutting of limits became evident and it was sought as pulp for new industrial enterprises. Failing to regenerate, spruce, in some considerable measure, gave way to balsam fir, which is the present staple species of the New Brunswick industry.[7] Such intensive cutting in forest areas changed not only the nature of the forest itself, but also the industry that used it.

As discussed in Chapter 1, better transportation routes and proximity to the British market led to a more diversified basis for early lumbering in New Brunswick than in the Canadas. Square timber was taken out, but there were also extensive deal mills, and American-type sawmills also appeared on a commercial basis. This continued into the 1840s when sawmilling and an orientation to the American market began to move to the fore as larger timber stocks declined.[8] Indeed, pressure on such stocks, felt by the late 1830s, contributed to the tensions in the Maine–New Brunswick boundary dispute and the incipient Aroostook War, as lumbermen feuded over the disputed areas.[9] As elsewhere in British North America, the Reciprocity Treaty of 1854 enabled extraordinary amounts of New Brunswick lumber to find its way south to the northeastern United States. But if the American market was important, it did not come to predominate the trade of the province as it did in the Canadas. The British market remained strong, especially from the Miramichi area and the northeast generally, and a good trade continued with the Caribbean.

At mid-century, New Brunswick stood proud and confident as a participant in world trade. Its timber was a sought-after commodity, and the sailing ships built from its wood were a valuable source of foreign exchange for its merchants.[10] Indeed, the period is looked upon with nostalgia by Maritime rights protagonists, who mark the area's entry into Confederation as the beginning of federal policies that dragged the province into economic dependence on central Canada. Historians and politicians are still debating this issue—an issue that cannot be resolved here.[11] It is sufficient to say that by 1866 and the end of the Reciprocity Treaty, trends in the world economy were working against New Brunswick. The age of steam was ending the age of the wooden sailing ship. Deterioration and decline were apparent in the province's pine forests, forcing a shift to spruce timber. At Confederation, the export tax on timber, the province's main source of revenue, along with customs duties, was turned over to the new Dominion government. In return, New Brunswick hoped to become the entrepôt through which goods left and entered the new nation and Maritime manufactured products could be shipped to the world. Indeed, rates on the Intercolonial Railway were intentionally fixed at low levels up to the post–World War I period in order to promote these developments. This hope was slowly dashed, however, and the province found itself becoming an economic colony of central Canada. These factors began an economic decline in New Brunswick, which its political and business leaders frantically and determinedly attempted to reverse.

These attempts to stimulate new industrial growth and economic activity included development of the forest sector. Activities such as these, usually in competition with other more resource-rich provinces, did not make New Brunswick particularly amenable to taxing or regulating the woods industry in any rigorous fashion. This meant that the province was often starved for revenue and depended on the federal subsidies negotiated as a basis for Confederation. As production pressure mounted after 1900, therefore, it was not surprising that this relatively poor province should negotiate federal aid to underwrite its forestry efforts and to enter cooperative agreements with its larger operators. There existed in New Brunswick in the period from 1860 to 1940 almost a client state perilously dependant on its forest industry.

A main government concern, after 1900, was to shore up a sawmilling industry which was visibly faltering as merchantable spruce disappeared and to provide a shift to pulp and paper manufacturing which would give a new industrial and employment base often dependent on American capital. In this effort, the ideas of the early North American forest conservation movement were to impinge on New Brunswick nurtured by federal support and example, and a province, which had traditionally followed a course of noninterference with its timber interests, attempted to adjust its client relationship with the industry to bring about a long-term stability that would be advantageous to both parties. In accomplishing this end, the New Brunswick forestry programme was only marginally successful before World War II. The reasons behind this failure are unique to the province itself and involve a complicated turn of events over a long period of time.

The sawmilling industry that developed in New Brunswick after 1840 was governed by a rudimentary licence system which was somewhat different from that in the Canadas. When the Assembly overturned the section of the Civil List Act inspired by Thomas Baillie in 1837, new legislation empowered the Lieutenant-Governor in Council to grant timber licences simply upon application. Renewal was granted if a new application was made before the expiry of the previous licence period, and auctions took place only when two or more applications for the same area were received on the same day.[12] It was a first-come first-served system tailored to those with political influence and inside knowledge and designed to aid timber speculation. In the nine-year period during which the system operated, there developed those very same large monoplies in timberland to which the members of the Assembly had ostensibly dealt a mortal blow in 1837. As Graeme Wynn points out, by 1846, there were petitions that there existed in New Brunswick a "monstrous monopoly", in which fourteen large interests were said to hold over half of the 2,300,000 hectares of licensed Crown land.[13]

In 1843–1844, the growing criticism by smaller operators and those who wished fairer, more competitive access to the public domain led the Assembly to consider a return to Baillie's plan of auctioning off leases, which were to be restricted to berths of between 3.2 and 16 square kilometres. An upset price of $1.25 per square kilometre was to be set and the stumpage dues raised. More important, in order to raise additional provincial revenue, an export tax would be placed on all timber shipped out of New Brunswick at a rate of 1 shilling per ton or per thousand feet, respectively.[14] The auction proposals were subjected to the same protests from the larger operators, namely that the economic burden would ruin the trade, and were thus delayed until 1846. In that year, the Assembly could not resist the ground swell of opposition that had arisen against the timber monopolists. It was apparent that the annual charge of 10 shillings for the right to exploit 2.6 square kilometres of timberland, as permitted under the 1837 conditions, was very low and permitted the wealthier merchants to grab large areas without competition. In order to buy off these gentlemen, there had been a 50 percent reduction in stumpage dues when compared with previous assessments and collection of the export duty was deferred by administrative arrangement until the timber was actually shipped. These advantages made the larger operators more quiescent and far less stubborn in their opposition to the auction system. On the other hand, New Brunswick politicians could argue that, by cutting the initial capital needed for entering the trade and by the auction system, the Assembly was meeting the complaints of the smaller lumbermen. As in Upper Canada, the 1840s witnessed a counter-attack against monopoly of the Crown's timberlands, and in New Brunswick, as well, a compromise was found which, while politically satisfactory, did not discriminate against the larger lumbermen. As Graeme Wynn contends:

unobtrusively, but nonetheless effectively, the evolving pattern of forest regulation in New Brunswick . . . reinforced an increasing domination of the timber trade by large, well-capitalized enterprises that were able to take advantage of technological improvements in the lumber industry and profit from the economies of scale and the enhanced economic stability confined by the extent of their interests.[15]

The compromise of 1844–1849 set the basis for the expansion of the sawmilling industry in the province into the late nineteenth century. The system was modified over the years both to serve the government's need for increased revenue and the lumberman's desire for greater security of tenure as more capital-intensive operations developed. Mill reserves were introduced in 1846 which allowed the government to lease for four years a mill site and up to 3,600 hectares of timberland, depending on the capacity of the mill constructed on the reserve. Such leases were independent of the auction system, and, while it appeared to be a good development policy, it did tend to help those who already had capital. On the revenue side, upset prices were increased in 1852 to $2.50 per square kilometre. It was not until 1874, when the province decided to introduce a new licencing system to replace monies lost through surrendering the export tax to the federal government, that major tensions between the lumbermen and the provincial administration arose over revenue and tenure. In that year, upset prices were doubled and the stumpage rate was set at 33.6 cents per cubic metre for spruce. The industry was willing to pay the increases in dues but wanted them fixed in long-term leases.

The provincial government was involved in promoting major railway development projects in an effort to stimulate new economic growth. Strapped for revenues, it was not willing to accede to the industry's demand. But the lumbermen had tremendous political influence, and they convinced the assembly to grant three-year licences with a $4 renewal charge. This recognition that the state had a role in providing a stable investment environment for the lumber trade started a process toward long-term timber leases in New Brunswick. In 1877 the licences were renewed for a period of five years and in 1883 for a period of ten years. After the election of 1890, the government of Andrew Blair found it necessary to seek the support of the four members from Miramachi in order to sustain itself in power. The agreement reached with these men became known as the "Northumberland Deal." Included in the deal was the understanding that stumpage rates would be reduced, regulations would be changed, and the leader of the group, Lemuel J. Tweedie, would be named Surveyor General. Blair moved quickly to reduce stumpage dues and then appointed a special Commission to study the lumbermen's suggestions for increasing the stability of the industry through longer-term leases and cheaper access to the resource. The Commission took two years to report but finally confirmed the reduced stumpage rate and recommended a twenty-five-year period for licences. Following this report, the licences were reoffered for sale in 1893 for a term of twenty-five years at a reduced upset price and stumpage. In most instances, existing licences were simply extended without even altering the dues let alone putting in new regulations relating to fire inspection or cutting or scaling supervision. Even in 1893, when the licences were actually re-opened for competition, no new requirements were imposed, and no major restructuring of limit-holdings occurred. This practice continued in the province until the 1970s.[16] By the late nineteenth century, New Brunswick was totally dependent on the lumber industry. Unable to reverse its relative economic decline, the provincial government was politically incapable of exacting anything even remotely resembling fair conditions from powerful lumber interests which could control a host of local members and held the province's economic destiny in their hands.

In 1845, 640 sawmills in the province employed some 8,400 men and produced lumber worth $900,000.[17] This is ample proof that a considerable milling industry was in place even before the Reciprocity Treaty of 1854, but the treaty itself added a tremendous stimulus for the province to push out beyond the British market. In the period from 1853 to 1865, the value of forest exports increased about two and a half times from £6,000 to £161,000.[18] What the treaty stimulated, the market opportunities created by the Civil War were to drive to fantastic proportions, and the United States was confirmed as an important market for New Brunswick throughout the nineteenth century.

It was this diversification which created the new business opportunities for lumbermen with capital to invest in sawmills and a few other ambitious entrepreneurs who, against incredible odds, would scramble up the slippery ladder of success to build lumbering empires. These men brought to the province new milling technology (e.g., the gang saw), more sophisticated business structures, larger enterprises than had been known before, and tremendous political influence. In this final respect, they were simply following an earlier generation of political fixers, but the very scope of their business interests made their title of "lumber kings" extremely appropriate, and in a client jurisidiction like New Brunswick their state was the province itself.

The lumber kings came from a mixture of old families and immigrant stock with no evident pattern. One of the Saint John valley lumber kings was John B. "the Main John" Glasier, the scion of a family involved in timber since 1777, whose firm in the 1850s employed over 600 men. His business started on the Shogemac and expanded to the upper Saint John River, above Grand Falls. He produced both ton timber and lumber.[19] Another lumber king was John A. Morrison, a shrewd Irishman who managed to set up a sawmill at Buctouche in 1858, then moved to Fredericton in the 1860s. His operations were diversified, with a speciality in cedar products, mostly clapboard and shingles. Unlike most other lumbermen, Morrison did not own either timber rights or lands; he either purchased logs or rented cutting rights.

The two main centres of the industry were Saint John and Fredericton. At Saint John, logs were driven down the river or later came by rail. Also, lumber came in from small ports and from Nova Scotia for transshipment. Most of the city's mills, sixteen in 1898, were not integrated companies. They contracted with up-country men in the old British manner for cutting and delivery of logs. Several mills were owned by Americans, who cut logs from northern Maine and sent their products to the United States duty free.[20] One of the largest Canadian millers was W. H. Murray, who sawed 40,040 cubic metres annually, mostly for the British market, and sold the remainder of his cut of 94,500 cubic metres to other firms.[21] He had 2,340 square kilometres of limits on the Big Black, St. Francis, and Main rivers as well as around the Temiscouata lakes. Murray was one of the most active lobbyists for the industry and was also a main organizer in cooperative business ventures to control transportation costs, such as the Saint John River Log Driving Company.[22] Other large Saint John operations included Purves and Murchie, Hilyard Brothers, Andre Cushing and Company, and the Randolph and Baker mill just outside the city at the company town of Randolph, which produced 49,600 cubic metres of lumber.[23] Saint John, however, was to see the heyday of its sawmills before 1900. After that date, transportation costs along with the declining quality of timber stocks forced mills to locate much farther upriver, closer to the sources of timber.[24]

Fredericton's most prominent sawmiller in the late ninteenth century was Donald Fraser. A latecomer to the industry, he did not immigrate to New Brunswick until 1873. In 1877 Fraser built a mill at River de Chute, and in 1884 he was able to expand to Fredericton where he built the Aberdeen Mill. Selling to both the British and American markets, the firm expanded again under Fraser's son, Archibald, into pulp and then paper. The company was one of the most integrated and successful forest firms in the province

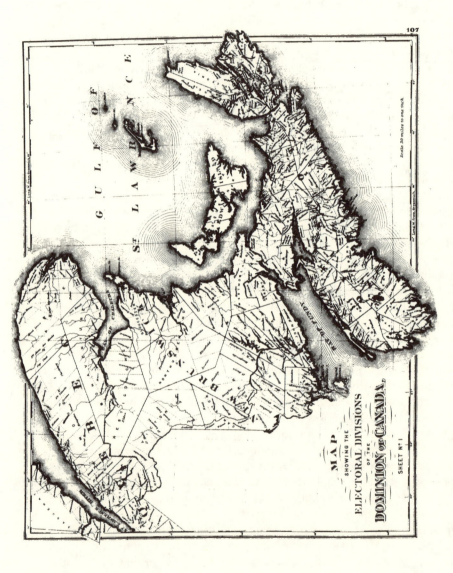

Political map of Maritime Canada in 1875—note the Northumberland area in central New Brunswick and Cape Breton Island at the extreme eastern end of Nova Scotia (printed by permission of the National Map Collection, Public Archives of Canada).

after 1900.[25] The Victoria Mill of Hale and Murchie was also located in Fredericton. The mill was owned by Frederick Bunting Hale, Conservative M.P. for Carleton, New Brunswick (1887–1891 and 1896–1904) and George Murchie, an American from Calais, Maine. The mill cut 28,500 cubic metres of spruce from the Tobique area for British and American markets.[26]

Finally, no description of the New Brunswick lumber industry in the nineteenth century would be complete without mention of Alexander "Boss" Gibson. If the others were kings, Gibson was the early emperor of the province. Indeed, his career is an almost complete reflection of the industry itself. Born in the village of Lepreau in 1819, Gibson worked as a lath sawer at Milltown. In partnership with his brother-in-law, he bought a mill and gambled with fate on the lower Nashwaak. After buying two financially troubled deal mills from the Rankin interests, he brought about economies in their operation and paid strict attention to quality standards.[27]

In 1863 the mills were producing 59,400 cubic metres of lumber per year and the company town of Marysville was founded. Along with an elaborate house for himself and schools, stores, and homes for his labourers, the Boss built lath and shingle mills as well as a cotton factory during the 1880s. The basis of his fortune was two large tracts known respectively as the "10,000 acres" and the "Bettle Block". Gibson's normal annual cut was 94,500 cubic metres. To anticipate his needs, he acquired the rights to large amounts of timber on the Keswick, Mactaquac, and Nackawick rivers to the west of the Nashwaak. Ahead of fellow lumbermen in the Canadas, the Boss investigated the use of railways to develop these timber areas. In 1866 he personally financed a survey of a route from the Nashwaak to Edmundston. The resulting railway company, the New Brunswick Land and Railway Company, managed to get 6,500 square kilometres of timberland from the province to finance its construction. The railway was completed in 1871, but the Boss fell out with his colleagues in the venture. Still, the shrewdness of his investment was shown by the $800,000 he received for his share of the land and stock of the company.[28] By the 1880s, Gibson sat astride the political and economic affairs of New Brunswick. He was involved in several other business investments, especially transportation companies. One of these was the Canada Eastern Railway which was designed to link Chatham with Fredericton. Gibson's partner in this venture was Jabez Bunting Snowball, a Chatham sawmiller and lumber exporter, who was to represent the area as a Liberal M.P. and Senator. Snowball's career ended with his services as Lieutenant-Governor of New Brunswick, where he played, along with his son, W. B. Snowball, a prominent role in introducing forest conservation ideas into the province.[29]

The Gibsons, Snowballs, and others were representative of how the diversification of lumber markets in New Brunswick had extended and aggrandized the power of the large timber firms. Older families had been joined by new entrepreneurs, who often bought out existing timber and mill rights and were willing to take other leases far up-country. These businessmen were now involved with capital-intensive investments which added enormously to their political power and influence. They represented one of the few successful economic sectors in a province which was vainly searching for the key to sustained industrial growth. Thus the client relationship between the provincial government and the industry was strengthened by the growth of sawmilling and the dependence during the 1880s on the fragile resource on which that industry was based.

Parallels can be drawn between New Brunswick and the Ottawa valley. Lumbering had been going on in both areas for a long time, and many limits had been reworked several times. An established group of businessmen dominated the industry and viewed it as an investment engine for new economic growth. In both regions, the lumbermen had considerable influence on and strong political ties with their respective provincial governments, though this was more pervasive in New Brunswick than in the more multifaceted economies of Quebec and Ontario. There were, however, also major differences, which partially explain the slowness of the New Brunswick lumbermen to support the forest conservation cause.

In the Ottawa valley, lumber operators were cutting white and red pine almost exclusively. By the 1880s they were beginning to find that the quantity and quality of those species were decreasing rapidly and were not regenerating satisfactorily. It was this threat to their investments and their industrial base that caused the Valley lumbermen to espouse the conservation cause. Its call for measures such as fire protection, land classification, and forest reserves all appealed to these businessmen because they would preserve standing timber and they gave some hope of regenerating the commercial species their mills were designed to harvest. In New Brunswick, however, pine was under heavy pressure from over-cutting by the 1850s, and by the 1870s it made up less than one-third of the provincial cut. Thus, the lumbermen had faced the possibility of running out of merchantable pine much earlier and made the transition to spruce. They now had a new resource base, which would not begin to show its exhaustion until 1900. In addition, New Brunswick was much less a settlement frontier by the 1880s than were Ontario and Quebec, where the north was still seen as an agricultural area. There was still some bush settlement, but the lumbermen, more used to dealing with private timberlands, simply bought up settler timber. In addition, if anything, the province complained about loss of its farmers' sons to the United States and the Canadian West. There were forest fires, but they were accompanied by less of the social tension between lumberer and settler than that which gripped settlement frontiers elsewhere. Not until after 1903, when timber stocks were considerably diminished, would the forest industry resort to the spectre of settlers' wildfires as a reason for initiating fire protection measures. The final major difference was the conservative, parochial nature of New Brunswick politics up to the 1890s, where issues were rarely viewed on a province-wide basis, and local power-brokers, especially lumbermen, arranged things pretty much as they pleased in their own areas.

For these reasons, the New Brunswick lumbermen, unlike their Ottawa valley counterparts, took little interest in the proceedings of the Montreal Congress of 1882. It cannot be determined whether William Little approached the provincial government to obtain action on the Congress's resolutions. It would be surprising if he did not, though it must be stated that Canadians in the early 1880s still had some difficulty in perceiving that the Dominion stretched beyond the eastern boundary of Quebec and had a penchant for ignoring the Maritimes. In any event, in 1882 New Brunswick was locked in a struggle to pass the provincial government from one power group to another. The winner of this struggle was Andrew G. Blair, who was beginning to shape a coalition of interests that would eventually emerge as the Liberal party in the province and control it until 1908.[30] During this period, Blair was much more interested in trimming government structures and controlling expenditures than in expanding any public role in fire protection and land classification.[31] The new Premier made his political peace with the lumber interests in 1883 by extending their licences without competition.

The government could not escape the fact that some concern was surfacing for increased protection of the province's forests. In 1880 the Surveyor General of the former regime had publicly raised the issue, and Blair felt it necessary to address the matter in his forest policy. He established New Brunswick's first diameter limit. This unique regulation prohibited the cutting of any trees that would fail to make logs less than 5.3 metres long and 23 centimetres in diameter at the top.[32] In typical fashion, no provision was made for government officers to enforce this rather strange rule. It was, nevertheless, the beginning of a long enchantment in the province with the diameter limit as a major forest management device. The limit changed over the years, dropping as the definition of merchantable logs was forced down in response to a decline in timber stocks. In 1917, the limit was a minimum of 30 centimetres at the stump for spruce and 23 centimetres for balsam.[33] New Brunswick retained the diameter limit much longer than other jurisdictions, but, as K. B. Brown, Assistant Chief Scaler of the Department of Lands and Mines, commented in 1941, such regulations remained difficult to apply and "did not prove to be an entirely satisfactory method of forest conservation for all types of forests under modern conditions."[34] In addition, the Blair government made a token attempt at providing some very rudimentary fire protection in 1885, but the system put in place was completely voluntary. In 1893, accompanying the licence renewal process, a provision was passed for special fire rangers on the Ontario model of equal cost-sharing between the government and the industry. The Blair administration unfortunately reduced its effectiveness by placing a cap of two thousand dollars on government expenditures.[35] This was to be the extent of New Brunswick forestry legislation until 1906.

There are really three reasons for New Brunswick's dramatic turn to forestry legislation after 1900. The first, as mentioned before, had to do with the nature of the forest itself. Soon after the turn of the century, the province's lumbermen found themselves facing a deteriorating timber supply. Essentially, they were facing the same situation faced by the Quebec and Ottawa valley operators after 1880. Indications of this decline are not hard to find. In 1911, 1,070,000 cubic metres of lumber were cut in New Brunswick; by the mid–1920s this had declined to about 830,000 cubic metres, although it must be noted that during World War I extremely heavy cuts of up to 1,422,000 cubic metres were taken.[36] Nevertheless, the sawmilling industry was beginning to suffer from acute supply problems, complicated by rising transportation costs, which hurt its ability to retain its traditional markets. Increasingly after 1900, operators began to complain of stiff competition from southern pine and western Douglas fir and to lament the distance of good timber from streams and mills. River driving became more uncertain as the removal of forest cover made the spring freshets more difficult to control. The lumbermen began to turn to more mechanized methods and railways to lower costs and also resorted to the traditional ploy of holding wages at a very low level.[37]

As elsewhere, the industry turned to pulp mills, as an alternative activity for using smaller logs and promoting new markets. The St. John Sulphite Company opened in Saint John in 1898 followed by six other pulp mills there and elsewhere in the province, in the period before 1910. Of these, the most prominent were the Maritime Chemical Pulp Company, the Dominion Pulp Company, and Cushing Sulphite Fiber.[38] These developments were accompanied by pulpwood cutting on both private and public lands for consumption by local mills and export to the northeastern United States. In 1910 the six mills were producing a gross value of goods of $1,199,313.20. Unfortunately, overexpansion and speculation was rife in these early ventures, and this, combined with the fact that no paper was produced in the province until 1923, caused the collapse of three of the operations by 1915. It was not until the 1930s that the number of mills in the province would climb back to the 1910 level.[39] Therefore, in the period before World War I, pulping held promise for industrial investment, but it was not yet any sort of salvation for the forest industry in New Brunswick. Rather, the lumber interests found themselves in a situation which one of their own characterized as one in which

the lands which are most accessible and cheapest to operate have been cut very hard—more in many instances than they should have been. On the other hand, the lands which are most remote, where the cost of cutting and driving lumber was materially greater, have not been cropped as they should have been, and, as a result, an enormous acreage must be allowed to rest for a long time before it can be of any value for the production of timber.[40]

Where before there had been little concern on the part of the lumbermen for fire protection, encroachment by settlers on timberland, and government regulations that stimulated over-cutting, these suddenly became issues in New Brunswick. There was particular agitation when there were rumours that the New Brunswick Land and Railway Company grants might be returned to the province to be opened for sale as settlement areas. Lumberers in the province, like their cohorts in Quebec and the Ottawa valley, began to look to their government to protect standing commercial timber, to plan its regeneration, and, generally, to protect their private investment as part of the public interest.

Another factor giving forest conservation ideas an urgency in the province, which they might not otherwise have had, was the national role played by the Canadian Forestry Association. By involving Members of Parliament from all regions, provincial politicians and officials, and business leaders, the Association portrayed a compelling national interest in the forestry cause. This was particularly true of New Brunswick where William B. Snowball, the son of Boss Gibson's erstwhile partner in railway building, heir to the Snowball timber operations in Chatham, and a prominent figure in federal and provincial Liberal circles, took an active part in both the Canadian Forestry Association and later the Commission of Conservation.[41] He interpreted the conservationist cause to fellow lumbermen in New Brunswick, who adapted it to the local political culture.

Finally, forest conservation was helped along in the province, as elsewhere, by the impact of American progressive ideas. New Brunswick did not escape from the immense popularity of conservationist ideas expressed most prominently by Theodore Roosevelt and Gifford Pinchot or from the crusading nature of progressive politics which promised to make government more honest, moral, efficient and an active agent for the public good. Indeed, some good muckraking, New Brunswick–style, was to push purity and progressivism to the forefront in politics and carry forestry and forest conservation with it as the province entered the most turbulent period of government it had ever experienced.

The movement for forest conservation in New Brunswick really began with Laurier's National Forestry Convention held in January, 1906, in Ottawa. The political and private delegates from New Brunswick who had been present returned with a sense of crisis and new ideas of how to proceed in forestry affairs. These ideas combined with the political situation in the province made it propitious for some action to be taken.

The loose coalition of interest groups which had rallied behind Andrew

Blair in 1883 was still in power and was now identified as the provincial Liberal party. Blair had left in 1896 for federal service, but, as was the practice in the province, he kept a strict hand on the local government from the federal capital until his resignation in 1903.[42] Mainly because of this control, Blair was followed by a series of steady but unspectacular Premiers. In 1906 the government, led by Lemuel J. Tweedie, the Northumberland man so prominent in the Northumberland Deal, was showing its political age and was desperately searching for issues that could erase its image of a tired and corrupt machine. The opposition was relentless in attacking the administration for laxness, boodling, and neglect of the welfare of the lumber industry. In the wake of the Ottawa convention, Tweedie moved to seize the initiative. A major bill, entitled, "An Act for the better preserving and protection of the public domain", was drafted and pushed through the assembly by the end of March, 1906.[43]

The new act was comprehensive in its adherence to the ideas expressed by the Canadian Forestry Association and by federal forestry advocates. It authorized a subcommittee of the Executive Council to employ officials to survey all Crown lands, to classify them as suitable for forest or agriculture, to divide them into districts, to estimate and inventory all timber, to report on watershed conservation and the log-driving capabilities of all areas, to identify areas of nonmerchantable timber, and to consider and report on other possible uses for public lands. The legislation further stipulated that, once the investigation was completed, regulations were to be issued "to properly protect and encourage the lumber industry and to preserve the various timber areas of the Province". To entice support from the lumbermen, provision was also made for regulations to be prepared "for the extension of existing licences for such areas as are reasonably necessary for the permanent carrying on of the existing lumber manufacturing industries". Other regulations were to govern the cutting of undersized or stunted timber, to provide better fire protection, and to regulate expropriation or other reservation of lands for watershed protection and to otherwise benefit the carrying on of the lumber trade.[44]

The act indicated Tweedie's good faith in recognizing the federal Liberal political objectives behind the Convention, but it was also window-dressing. It set out conditions to promote better forest management for a province that lacked even the simplest basis for this, and, as had happened in the past, there was no structure or funding to carry out the investigations so grandly announced. Despite this shortcoming, Tweedie boldly returned to the conservationist theme a year later in preparation for the uncoming provincial election. The Premier convened the New Brunswick Forestry Convention modelled on the federal event. He had seen Laurier's tactic of latching onto the rising popularity of the conservationist cause and intended to emulate it. The head table was full of dignitaries including Lieutenant-Governor Jabez B. Snowball. A great deal of puffery was indulged in, and

Tweedie warned direly of the importance of timber revenues to the province and chided the lumbermen for threatening these through wasteful business methods. Opposition Leader J. Douglas Hazen dwelt almost exclusively on the good work of the present fire rangers and the need to expand fire protection. Deputy Surveyor-General T. G. Loggie raised the issue of fraudulent applications for settlement lands. Others discussed the need for a forestry course at the provincial university.[45]

Of more lasting significance was a meeting on the following day which led to the founding of the New Brunswick Forestry Association. Here, as with the Canadian Forestry Association, there was a unique blend of lumbermen, academics, and members of the public interested in forestry matters. Its major objectives were to protect the forests of the province from "undue and unnecessary exhaustion in the process of lumbering and from destruction by fire" and to ensure reforestation of waste lands by private owners. The resolutions passed at this first meeting included better prevention of fire hazards created by the building and operation of railways, the creation of forest reserves in the province, the creation of a university course in forestry, better inspection of timber operations, the establishment of an organized fire protection service, and the prohibition of the export of sawlogs and pulpwood in an unmanufactured state.[46]

Its efforts at identifying with the forest conservation movement, however, could not save the Liberal government. It had for too long shown a dedication to a comfortable laxness and it fell to the popular and dynamic Douglas Hazen, who promised change, purity, and definite policy direction.[47] The new Premier, a lawyer and a businessman, had served as a director of the Eastern Trust Company and the New Brunswick Telephone Company.[48] His main promise was that he would bring an efficient, honest, and progressive administration to the province. Hazen had taken careful note of the movement for forest conservation. He was not yet ready to breathe life into the 1906 legislation, but he did move on two fronts which fitted in with his personal political philosophy. Needing additional revenue, Hazen tightened up the scaling of timber and appointed a provincial supervisor to oversee the diameter limit of 22.9 centimetres at the top of a five-metre log. The results were dramatic. In 1907 the government had collected $180,135 on 842,000 cubic metres scaled, but in 1910, under the new system, it collected $330,360 on 776,000 cubic metres scaled. In the same year, the Hazen government established a forestry department at the University of New Brunswick. Finally, in 1911, the Premier sponsored legislation to better protect the province from fires caused by railways, and, in order to cash in on the expected migration of American pulp and paper mills, he placed a prohibition on the exportation of all softwoods from Crown lands, except pine.[49] The latter issue had been discussed for some time in political circles, and there had been a fear that legislation would drive out American investment. Ultimately, when Quebec put in a full-scale manufacturing condition in 1910, New

Brunswick was forced to follow unless it wished to sit back and observe the uncontrolled export of its pulpwood.

These were all important measures, but they did not even vaguely represent a full conservation programme. Hazen was more interested in economic development projects such as the Saint John River Railway and the opening up of new coalfields and oil shales. He might have moved further with forestry measures, but in late 1911 he left the Premiership to become Minister of Marine and Fisheries and Minister of Naval Affairs in Robert L. Borden's newly elected Conservative government in Ottawa. His successor was James K. Flemming, a popular, small sawmill operator from the Woodstock area.[50] Hazen himself may well have soon encountered some political restiveness from the province's lumbermen. The new scaling practices were beginning to be felt and the industry was of the opinion that it had not got enough from the new political agenda of the Tories. Now, the operators were suspicious that Flemming, a small mill man, might be unfriendly to the larger timber interests. These suspicions were intensified when the Premier retained the post of Surveyor General. Flemming was able to sweep the province up in an initial enthusiasm for the Saint John River Railway to carry a snap election in June, 1912, but almost immediately afterward an agitated group of lumber kings confronted the Premier in Fredericton to request new guarantees of licence tenure.[51]

The issue at stake was a complex one. Licences, which had been reoffered for sale by the Blair government in 1893, were not due to expire until 1918. Changing sawmill technology and a decline in the size of timber being sought meant that a large number of smaller operators like Flemming were appearing in New Brunswick and were nibbling away at the edge of the limits held by the large operators. There was concern that the Premier would be sympathetic to these businesses and attempt to open additional timber limits to them. These fears were simply an extension of the ancient feud in New Brunswick between the large and small operators. Nevertheless, the industry demanded that the licences be extended without public competition.[52]

Other issues also lay behind the confrontation. The new scaling measures were biting into businesses which were now dedicated to controlling costs. Thus, the lumbermen were critical of the province's traditional policy of charging a flat rate for any particular species regardless of where it was located. This, they contended, caused over-cutting of accessible limits because costs were too great to harvest the more remote limits in any planned way. The industry argued for graduated rates. Finally, the lumbermen wished the timber administration of the province to be put on a more scientific and nonpartisan basis. Besides the licence extension, the lumber kings made six specific demands: (1) a complete survey of all forest areas to obtain growth data, (2) complete revision of stumpage rates to correspond with actual production costs, (3) repeal of the exportation prohibition on pulpwood to encourage thinning of stands, (4) control of settlement on nonagricultural lands,

(5) reduction of taxes on nonproductive lands so that collection took place when the trees were harvested, and (6) placing all forest lands under the supervision of a nonpartisan commission.[53]

Flemming had already indicated in 1911 that he was concerned about over-cutting provincial timberlands.[54] Now faced with a rebellion by the powerful forest industry, he was forced to act. The recommendations of the lumbermen were a combination of genuine forestry measures designed to conserve the resource and self-serving ideas to reduce the tax burden on their enterprises. In the session of 1913, the Premier introduced legislation which he hoped would salve the concerns of the lumber kings. The new act showed both some political ingenuity and sagacity. To meet the demands of the larger operators, Crown lands licences were divided into pulp and paper licences and sawmill licences, and each was extended for a further period of twenty years without competition. The licences were renewable from year to year upon meeting the various conditions, and one kind of licence could be exchanged for the other. The sawmill licences were eligible for a further ten-year extension and made subject to a manufacturing condition. Pulp and paper licences were also renewable from year to year and subject to a further extension of twenty years. The longer periods were justified by the larger investments needed for this type of operation, but special conditions were attached to the licences. The lessee had to have in operation, within three years, a pulp mill which was using on a continuous basis 50 percent of the timber cut on the licence area. In addition, within five years, it was necessary to have either a pulp and paper mill or another similar plant using 50 percent of the cut. The prohibition on the export of pulp was kept in effect. Outside the licencing provisions, the Act also provided for the survey, examination, and classification of Crown lands by experts and set down the requirement that, once this investigation had been completed, there would be a readjustment of limits to ensure a fair distribution of timber between large and small operators. Finally, stumpage rates were fixed for various species (spruce, pine, tamarack, and cedar paid $0.63 per cubic metre of sawn lumber), and bonuses were varied between $12.50 and $62.50 per square kilometre according to the location and quality of the timber.[55]

The 1913 legislation was a remarkable compromise document, considering that the government was facing a weak two-member opposition (both were Acadian Liberals who were inarticulate in English). It appeared that Flemming and the industry had negotiated a deal which would provide the basis for timber administration in the province for many years. There remained the issue of how the government would fund the forest survey, but the act appeared to be a good political mix which would create the basis for developing the type of forest administration in the province which had really been lacking since 1837. All of the political credit for the legislation had to be given to Premier Flemming, but what had at first seemed like sweet victory

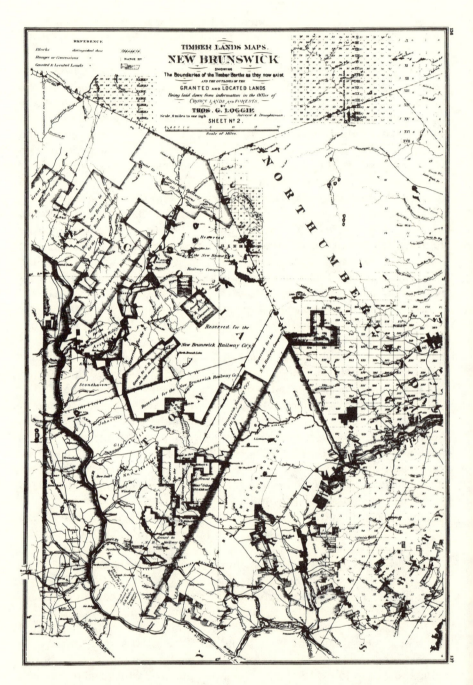

1875 timber berth map of the Northumberland region of central New Brunswick (printed by permission of the National Map Collection, Public Archives of Canada).

was soon an incredible disaster. The black side of New Brunswick politics, always present but elusive and shadowy, was suddenly thrust into the open and came to dominate the provincial scene.

The affair started innocently enough. Frank Carvell, a lawyer and Liberal Member of Parliament for Carleton, an *eminence grise* behind the weak opposition, and, coming as he did from Flemming's own area, the Premier's arch rival, was performing the duties of executor for the estate of a local lumberman, Timothy Lynch.[56] What he found was political dynamite. The negotiation over the licence renewal question in 1912–1913 had been far from nonpartisan. There was evidence that the lumber operators had paid substantial sums, perhaps as much as $100,000, in kickbacks to a Conservative political fund in return for renewals.[57] Carvell, a ruthless, tough, backroom politician, did some sleuthing. He found a definite link from the fund to W. H. Berry, a former employee of the Crown Lands Department, and a Mr. Brankley, who was the manager of the Miramichi Lumber Company. More important, the fund could be traced back to E. R. Teed, a Tory organizer in the province, and, circumstantially, to the Premier himself.[58]

This sensational issue was sprung on a stunned Premier in the Assembly. The government reeled, but Flemming maintained his absolute innocence in the matter. A Royal Commission was established to investigate the charges. The Tories hoped that they had found a "fixer" judge in the Hon. H. A. McKeown, a provincial Supreme Court Judge, to sway the other Commissioners in their favour.[59] As witness after witness appeared, however, it became apparent that the case was hopeless. Prominent lumbermen of all political stripes were paraded before the Commission to admit to contributing to the fund under coercion: Brankley stated he had collected $16,313 from nineteen lumber companies; Dominion Pulp had paid $4,500; W. B. Snowball told of reluctantly giving $7,200; and Angus MacLean, President of the Bathurst Lumber Company, indicated that Flemming had told him personally that Berry was the man for fixing bonuses.[60] It became obvious that such kickbacks had been the price the doing business in New Brunswick for a long time, but this was no salvation for the Premier. The Commission concluded that illegal methods had been involved in granting timber licences, and, although it claimed that no direct connection could be proved to Flemming, it was obvious his career as Premier was over.

Speaker George Clarke assumed the Premiership on a largely caretaker basis, and the Conservatives tried to pick up the pieces of their shattered government. James Murray became Surveyor General. His role was to try to get the forestry policy back on track. In 1914 the Surveyor General declared that

we [the province] cannot hope to propagate our forests if lumbering operations are allowed to be carried on from year to year practically over the same ground. Authority should be given to the Department to close out certain lands that have been hardcut for a stated length of time . . . [and] large sections of the Crown Lands are held and have been so held for years where no operations are conducted at all, resulting in serious loss . . . in stumpage dues.[61]

As always in New Brunswick there was an overriding emphasis on stumpage dues, but the government was willing to use its recently created forest survey to remedy some of the problems it now recognized. It had observed similar work on private lands held by the Pejebscot Paper Company which was based in Maine but owned extensive timberlands in New Brunswick. This seemed to indicate that the province could succeed in its endeavour. It did, however, need assistance, and this was arranged through the good auspices of the federal Conservatives who suggested that a cooperative venture be entered into with the Commission of Conservation. The Commission was already well versed in this type of survey work and saw it as an opportunity to establish a relationship with the province which would eventually also encompass research into insect problems, silviculture, and regeneration. For New Brunswick, the Commission was a source of expertise that could lessen costs.

The province hired its first professional forester, G. H. Prince, to run the survey. Prince, a graduate of the University of New Brunswick forestry course, had been working for the British Columbia Forest Service since its founding in 1912. He, in turn, contracted the services of Peter Z. Caverhill, a former federal forester working for British Columbia, to organize the survey between 1916 and 1918. Between 1916 and 1923, when budworm infestations caused cancellation of the project, provincial officials, supported at first by the Commission and later by federal forestry staff, took stock of 1,800,000 hectares (about 65 percent of all Crown lands). The survey classified and mapped areas by forest type and age class, studied growth and reproduction, and provided volumetric information. A unique effort at this early stage of Canadian forestry, it supplied valuable information on which New Brunswick officials were to base forest management policies up to World War II.[62]

It would, however, take a good deal more than the creation of a rather innovative forest survey for the Conservatives to escape the odour of scandal, which had not only involved forest administration but also the letting of railway construction contracts.[63] The provincial debt had skyrocketed to $16 million, and with these double weights the government fell decisively in the provincial election of 1917.

The new Liberal government under W. E. Foster now seemed to be the one possessing vibrant reform credentials. The province, despite its debt, was booming with the war economy, including its forest industry which was reaching record production. Foster, himself, has been dubbed by one commentator as the only "pure and unadulterated Premier the Province has ever acknowledged".[64] Certainly his government launched a whirlwind of reform to bring New Brunswick out of the dark ages. A Department of Health was formed to promote public health, pure milk, and food inspection, and Foster investigated the possibility of public ownership of hydroelectric power to control rates. In this atmosphere, the provincial forester hired to run the survey and those at the University of New Brunswick had a milieu in which their ideas were welcome. Thus, it is probable that forestry would have moved ahead under Foster in any case, but it was helped along by another minor scandal which had the potential of sullying the reputation of the new regime just after it took office.

The new Speaker of the Assembly was William Currie, a lumberman. The Conservative Opposition found a scaler, who had been dismissed from his job, who accused Currie of defrauding the government by bribing scalers to lessen their count. A Royal Commission appointed to investigate the charges determined that Currie had indeed conspired to defraud the government; that Murchie, the scaler, had routinely lied in all his reports in return for food and supply contracts to the lumber camps; and, most important, that the whole scaling business had become once more a farce. The Commission concluded that "the lumbermen, having things all their own way, with low stumpage and scalers to suit themselves, realizing no doubt that such a way of doing business cannot go on forever, have been cutting vast quantities of our timber".[65]

Currie was asked to step down as Speaker, and the Foster government took the advice of its forester, G. H. Prince, and decided to create a forest service. As an interim measure, the Surveyor General ordered that only trained men be given responsibility for scaling, and, to simplify the job, the diameter was set at 30.5 centimetres at the stump for spruce and 22.8 centimetres for balsam. Of a more enduring nature, the Forest Act and the Forest Fires Act were introduced into the Assembly. These acts provided for a consolidation of forestry functions including protection, timber administration, scaling, and game protection under a Forest Service within a Department of Lands and Mines. Radical as this was for New Brunswick, the legislation further required that the organization be staffed by permanent forest officers. Provision was also made for a forest protection fund supported by a tax on all licenced land as well as by consolidated revenues. Forest rangers were given powers to enforce strict fire regulations, and a role was envisioned for them in ensuring more complete utilization of timber on cutting operations. The first appropriation for the new fire protection service was $100,000. Finally, harking back to industry demands in 1912, the Forest Act set up an Advisory Board to guide the work of the new body. On the Board, the Minister of Lands and Mines served as Chairman. The first members were T. G. Loggie, Deputy Minister of Lands and Mines, G. H. Prince, Provincial Forester, D. J. Buckley, a private forest owner, and Archibald Fraser of the Fraser Companies.[66]

The 1918 legislation was drafted by G. H. Prince. It was simple, even rudimentary, but it had the essentials for being effective. New Brunswick had never had any type of forest administration with competent field staff to oversee timber operations, cruise limits or scale logs. This legislation gave promise of that, but, as it had to do given the circumstances, it stressed efficient dues collection and protection of standing timber in aid of conservation and regeneration. Trust was placed in the forest survey to push forward research, silviculture, and insect control work, hopefully with federal help. T. G. Loggie commented in 1918 "that the Forest Act and the Forest Fires Act are supposed to be the 'last word' in up-to-date legislation".[67] This was an exaggeration. It was a tremendous improvement which held some promise.

The new legislation was complemented by an annual licence system which had been promised off and on by provincial officials for some time to help smaller operators. These were experimental in nature, drawing on Prince's experience in British Columbia. The limits, which consisted of some 1,040 square kilometres of vacant timberland, were properly cruised and put up for auction under specific cutting conditions on a stumpage basis. The rates bid for these areas was considerably higher than for long-term licences, and the Forest Service was pleased with the results. But trouble loomed quickly on the horizon, and the system was discontinued in 1922. The official reasons given for the cancellation of annual licences were the difficulties encountered in supervising them, the depressed conditions in the industry, and the budworm devastation in the areas selected. This glossed over significant problems which went to the heart of how effectively the new Forest Service would be allowed to carry out its role in a client province.

A major job for the Forest Service was to organize the protection of standing and growing timber. It was to get a rough baptism on this front in the years between 1921 and 1924. Heavy cutting during the war years and immediately after had left a tremendous amount of waste and slash in the bush. This, combined with increased road access and very dry seasons, led to a record number of fires of a size rarely seen before in the province. In 1923 alone, the increase in Forest Service funds from $116,000 to $211,000 was due solely to fire-fighting costs.[68] The serious nature of the situation persuaded the government to spend fairly scarce resources on metal fire towers, fire roads, and other equipment fairly consistently throughout the 1920s and to promote cooperative efforts with the industry in protective work.[69]

These bad fire seasons, which required the rapid selling off of fire-killed timber before infestation, were combined with growing devastation by the budworm in both spruce and balsam fir. The two visitations were enough to cause a crisis in New Brunswick's forests, where it was estimated over 180 million cubic metres of wood had been damaged. By 1923, it was becoming obvious to some that the province was not going to be able to afford to maintain its forest resource alone. In response to this crisis, Pius Michaud, Member of Parliament for the Edmundston area, made a serious plea for federal-provincial cooperation in forestry matters during a Commons debate on the fire and insect situation in Quebec and Maritime Canada. His position was supported by both Arthur Meighen and W. S. Fielding.[70] As if to underline just how far New Brunswick had sagged in maintaining its forest resource, the Royal Commission on Pulpwood reported in 1924:

Without actual increase in the timber grown, lumber and pulp production cannot be maintained on the present scale, and some economic adjustment in consumption of the two industries is imperative.... The situation is veritably the occasion for the utmost concern if impending decline in the forest industry is to be forestalled, it can only be by the application of serious measures aimed at the curtailment of wastage ... [and] increase [of] the annual increment.[71]

The question throughout the rest of the 1920s and 1930s was whether New Brunswick could find the political support and financial resources to make this large but necessary effort.

The question of political support centred on the entrenched and powerful forest industry. It had backed forestry measures after 1900 as a method to protect declining spruce stocks and improve the efficiency of operations. During the 1920s, however, the province's lumber industry, which had experienced a boom during the war years, fell into a depressed state from which it never really recovered. By 1924 it was claimed that half the sawmills in New Brunswick were closed. The whole house of cards which had begun to shake at the turn of the century now came tumbling down. By the late 1930s, sawmill production was one quarter of what it had been in 1920.[72] The industry was in chaos. In the heady war years money had been borrowed which now could not be repaid. Declining quality in timber stocks and rising transportation and production costs were, once and for all, rendering all but the most stable companies noncompetitive against Pacific coast and Baltic timber in the North American and British markets, respectively. Sawmillers in New Brunswick were now fighting for survival. In desperate efforts to cut costs, they quickly abandoned forestry and opted for the traditional logrolling and political antics they had used throughout the nineteenth century to pressure the provincial government into reducing timber dues.

This was the message that Angus MacLean of the Bathurst Company, a leading spokesman for the New Brunswick Lumbermen's Association and formerly a firm supporter of the conservationist cause, took privately to the government. Pierre S. Veniot had replaced Foster as Premier in 1922. He was an Acadian who had toiled long and well in the Liberal ranks. His government had tied its development plans to the construction of a public power project at Grand Falls on the Saint John river. This was to provide power to International Paper, the Fraser Companies, and the Bathurst Company, all of which, the Premier claimed, would build new pulp and paper plants in the northern part of the province.[73] MacLean, who was a Liberal supporter, clearly told Veniot that, regardless of these plans, the lumber industry wanted relief from rate increases required by the Workmen's Compensation fund and a substantial reduction in stumpage rates from the current $1.68 per cubic metre to the Quebec rate of $1.13.[74] Reduction of government charges were necessary, MacLean indicated, in order to restore the competitive advantages of the industry.

Veniot ignored this advice. On 2 June 1925 the Lumbermen's Association met in conjunction with the New Brunswick Boards of Trade to make its demands official. It pledged to cut production by 35–50 percent in order to stimulate prices and demanded that the government reduce stumpage as described above and adopt the Quebec rule for scaling which would permit one-third more timber to be cut at the same stumpage rate. The lumbermen, abruptly and unceremoniously, gave the Premier one day in which to reply.

Basically, the lumbermen were holding the province up to ransom. The change would cost the government $200,000 in revenues annually. Veniot expressed his displeasure by remaining silent on the question for a month, but politically he could not afford to ignore the demand. He attempted a compromise by reducing the stumpage rate somewhat and indicated that the other changes could not be made by regulation but required legislation in the Assembly. The lumbermen, however, were not satisfied with this solution and met in Newcastle to condemn the Premier's actions. Following this gathering, MacLean formally met Veniot to inform him that the industry, in its entirety, would oppose him in the upcoming provincial election. MacLean, himself, became a leading campaigner for the Conservative Opposition under John Baxter. He called for caution on the Grand Falls project and placed advertisements in the press justifying the position of the province's lumbermen in regard to cutting costs, including wages, which MacLean charged the government was trying to hold at an artificially high level.[75]

Veniot was defeated, though the defeat probably had as much to do with his Acadian background as with the opposition from the timber interests. Nevertheless, with Veniot disappeared any slight hope of any government policy that might challenge the forest industry and push forward creative forestry measures in New Brunswick. Baxter was basically a laissez-faire liberal in his political philosophy. He reinforced the old client attitude when he cancelled the public contracts for the Grand Falls development and sold all the province's interests to the International Paper Company so that the facility could be built under private ownership. This development was completed in 1928 and was accompanied by the building of two new pulp and paper plants in the province: International Paper's mill at Dalhousie and the Fraser Companies' facility at Edmundston.[76] Uncertain markets in the 1920s and the effects of the depression meant that pulp and paper production did not really take off into sustained growth until the period of World War II. Baxter, however, was already laying the basis for the continuance of the provincial government's relationship with this new phase of the forest industry.

With the lumbermen abandoning the forestry cause, it became very difficult for the Forest Service to obtain funds to move beyond the protection role. Forest revenues remained an important part of the provincial budget for financing general items such as roads and other facilities and social benefits. Politicians were more concerned about expanding this type of spending than they were about increasing appropriations to further regulate the forest industry, especially when the lumbermen were proving more hostile to such measures and could well oppose them at the polls. Thus, for example, in 1923 the total income from the forest resource was $933,600, but disbursements to the Forest Service amounted only to $211,000; it rarely amounted to a quarter of revenues up to World War II.[77] It was this constraint on its budget, as well as opposition from the industry to higher timber dues, which led to abandonment in 1922 of the experimental annual licencing system patterned on the British Columbian system. It also contributed to the cancellation in 1923 of the forest survey, which had been heralded as the basis for a proper forestry programme. The survey was only 65 percent completed. A provincial forest nursery was established in 1923 to aid in replanting fire- and insect-ravaged areas, and Prince visited Europe to gain knowledge of planting methods. Work could only continue, however, with aid from the federal Advisory Council on Research (the forerunner of the National Research Council) and the federal Dominion Forestry Service.[78] Indeed, this became a pattern. New Brunswick provincial foresters concentrated mostly on timber administration and forest protection and looked to increasing federal support for silvicultural and regeneration research and advice on insect control. Provincial politicians argued that this was the only solution in forestry for a poor province with limited funds to spend in the field, regardless of how vital it might be to the provincial economy. On this basis, New Brunswick was to support efforts to obtain a more full-fledged federal-provincial cooperation in forestry matters. Such federal activity was not prolific in the 1920s and 1930s, but federally funded cooperative projects with private firms and the New Brunswick Forest Service itself enabled the compilation of data on rates of growth and reproduction, cutting methods, thinnings, and direct seeding. Support was given in these areas through the founding in 1934 of the Acadian Forest Research Station near Fredericton. In insect control, aid was given by the Entomological Branch of the federal Department of Agriculture.[79] The trend to federal support, started in 1916, was to continue to be an important strain in New Brunswick public forestry, as indicated by the fact that in 1958 twenty-three foresters were employed by the provincial government and twenty-four were employed by the federal government.[80]

Constrained by lack of funding, dependent on sputtering federal assistance for research support, and encountering an industry which was depressed and hostile, the Forest Service took the route of practicing forestry through forest protection. The only lasting expansion into other fields before World War II was the addition of forest inspectors to supervise logging areas to ensure that utilization regulations were obeyed, including those related to cutting undersized trees and the salvage of damaged timber.[81] Putting employees on the timber limits was a major move for New Brunswick, and the use of undersize cutting permits did hold some promise for some useful regulatory work in aid of forest maintenance and renewal.

The whole forestry problem in New Brunswick had been complicated by overreliance on diameter limits and long-tenure licences. The special regulations to govern the cutting of smaller trees were designed to aid the pulp and paper industry, which could exploit stands of black spruce which were dense and did not lend themselves to selective cutting. The regulations were also to apply to areas of slow and stunted growth. To qualify for such permits, larger licencees in the province were to complete a cruise of the area and submit a cutting report to the Forest Service. The plan and the area were then to be examined by a provincial forester and compared with inventory data to ensure the provincial goal of not cutting "an amount in excess of the estimated annual growth".[82] Such regulations, however, required sophisticated data on which to base growth statistics and close supervision of every area by trained personnel. Having abandoned its forest survey and having kept its Forest Service small, neither condition could be met in New Brunswick. Inevitably, there was pressure to grant undersize permits to sawmillers so that they could keep on exploiting accessible, over-cut stands. Unlike in Quebec where the situation was comparable, New Brunswick could not afford to abandon its sawmilling industry despite its pitiful situation. Quebec had benefited substantially from the pulp and paper expansion after the lifting of American tariffs and thus adapted quickly to the new industry. New Brunswick had had considerable but still less success. It still had to look after its sawmillers.

These circumstances, combined with overall forestry objectives, which stressed revenue and the furnishing of raw materials to mill communities dependent on the manufacture of forest products for employment, as were those in New Brunswick by the 1930s, resulted in major difficulties.[83] What had started as a promising policy evolved into the encouragement of undersize cutting to stimulate employment and to shore up redundant timber operations. Forest depletion was not checked because the annual cut probably regularly exceeded annual growth in these areas. Indeed, such undersize cutting may have helped create the single-species forests of balsam fir which even in the 1920s were seen as the prime breeding ground for the budworm devastations.[84] As a New Brunswick government forester admitted:

Methods of operating leave much to be desired from a silvicultural standpoint. Some areas are being clearcut which should be thinned or cut selectively. Some stands are being cut before they are mature while stands of mature timber, more expensive to operate, are being left standing with no production to net increment. Sizes of timber suitable for sawlogs are being made into pulpwood while in other localities small logs are being sawed into lumber with a large percentage of waste.[85]

This, in a sense, is the epitaph for forest conservation in New Brunswick before World War II. After a reasonably good and practical start in 1918, events had conspired to give the province the form but not the substance of a forestry programme. Strapped for funds and encumbered by a rapidly declining sawmill sector, the province's one attempt at sophisticated forest management could not be counted a success. The Baxter government was powerless when confronted by the searing edge of the Depression. It acceded to industry demands to further slash stumpage rates by one-half, and this, along with falling production as a result of evaporating markets, contributed to plummeting provincial revenues. The reductions were, in part, made up by federal funds given in 1930–1931 to replace the stumpage reductions and help in unemployment relief.[86]

C. D. Richards, who replaced Baxter as Premier in 1932, placed his faith in a presentation to the Imperial Economic Conference of proposals to secure a preferential treatment for New Brunswick timber in the British market.[87] Little relief was given from that quarter, and federal funds to replace reduced stumpage dues disappeared in 1933. In this gloomy atmosphere, the twenty-year sawmill licences, renewed in 1913, lapsed. Covering 19,985 square hectares of timberland, the government opened them for extension and renewal on a long-term basis in order to reassure the industry.[88] Also, many leases were converted to pulp licences. It was in this new industry that the Forest Service saw possibilities for forest management, but there was danger in the fact that the province was dominated by two powerful firms: the Fraser Group and International Paper controlled between them 55 percent of the leased forest. Though it could not admit it publicly, like Quebec, it was quietly writing off sawmill activities which, after their decimation in the 1920s and 1930s, were now small, dreadfully undercapitalized operations. The Forest Service retrenched like all other government agencies and settled down to wait out the storm.

The Liberal government of A. A. Dysart decisively swept the Conservatives from power in 1935 with the promise of more active, progressive management of the province. One of the areas in which the new administration wished to move was forestry, since there were fears that the timberlands had deteriorated even more since 1923–1924. The Crown Lands Act was amended in 1937 to require working plans governing timber extraction from the public domain. The act, in large part, put into law the old undersize permit system and remained oriented toward helping plan the growth of the pulp and paper industry. It stipulated that the Minister would only grant such permission "upon being satisfied that . . . [the] proposed management plan is in accordance with good forestry practice, having regard to the estimated annual growth and the principles of forest conservation and sustained yield."[89] The government also realized that the same weaknesses that had existed in New Brunswick before still existed. There was hope that the pulp and paper industry might more easily expand its client relationship with the government to accept forestry regulation. There was also recognition that a poorer, less populous province, like New Brunswick, could not hope in its current circumstances to finance such sophisticated policies on its own. For that reason, it was to become, during World War II, a champion for more federal-provincial cooperation in forest conservation matters.

CHAPTER 8

The Limits of National Leadership, 1911–1929

The forest conservation movement enjoyed considerable success before World War I, deriving much of its vitality from leadership provided at the federal level by legislative initiatives, from semiofficial sponsorship of the Canadian Forestry Association, and from the establishment of the Commission of Conservation.[1] This leadership survived the war, and the people involved attempted to employ the idealism resulting from the conflict to make conservation and forestry an essential part of postwar economic and social reconstruction. Their aims were actually little different from those of the leaders of a host of other causes. However, forestry supporters considered their cause to be better suited than many to be a leader in the process of reconstruction and rejuvenation. This was because of the close association of forestry with modern planning techniques, its support by a dedicated public service, and, as a discipline, its scientific base. Federal officials, striving to set national standards across the country, gave forestry an impetus during the first half of the decade of the 1920s. The Dominion Forestry Service and the Commission of Conservation tried to find constitutional and fiscal means to consolidate and expand forestry at both the national and provincial levels. This attempt to find a practical way in which to introduce forest management to all levels of jurisdiction in the nation brought the movement up against the hard realities of Canadian politics and, rather than establishing forestry and forest conservation as an essential part of Canadian public policy, pushed the movement into serious decline and nearly destroyed it as a national force.

One of the most heralded events in forestry in the prewar era occurred in 1912 when the Railway Act was amended. The amendment compelled all federally chartered lines to maintain adequate fire protection and suppression equipment and fire patrols along their right-of-ways and in construction areas.[2] This measure had been instigated by the Canadian Forestry Association, the Dominion Forestry Service, and the Commission of Conservation. The measure was hardly innovative since it had been proposed since the 1890s and several provinces already had similar legislation. The importance of the legislation was tied to the fact that most railway lines in Canada had federal rather than provincial charters so that this legislation had a greater effect. Responsibility for the supervision and enforcement of the regulations became part of the duties of the Board of Railway Commissioners. To carry out its new duties, the Board hired Clyde Leavitt, a young American forester who had studied under Fernow while he was at Cornell University in 1902 and who had subsequently worked for the Dominion Forestry Service and then served as Chief Forester of the Commission of Conservation.[3] Leavitt's links with the commission, the Service, and the Board eventually ensured a close relationship between railway fire suppression and all the other forestry organizations in the country. Links with the provinces were consolidated with the appointment of provincial foresters as regional commissioners of the Railway Board responsible for the implementation of the regulations in their respective provinces.[4] The implementation of the fire suppression amendment of the Railway Act thus inaugurated a new spirit of cooperation between the provinces and the Dominion government.

In 1913 the Dominion Forestry Service took another step toward becoming a national body rather than one concerned solely with the management of western lands. The Service was instructed to investigate the physical and structural properties of lumber from Canada's commercial tree species in order to encourage new industrial uses of wood. Methods of seasoning and handling lumber were to be investigated as well as the fibre and chemical characteristics of paper pulp. To carry out the work, a forest products laboratory was established in Montreal in association with McGill University.[5] A year later, the mandate was expanded to include the study of wood preservatives and the treatment of wood for building and construction purposes. These new responsibilities, given to the Service by the newly elected Tory government of Robert Borden, were intended to be federal aid to the lumber, paper, and construction industries in the form of research and product development. Coincidentally, the Service's expansion into forest products research took place just in time to be utilized for the war effort. Then, in 1919, in order to aid the Imperial Munitions Board in its selection of Sitka spruce for airplane construction, a second laboratory was constructed in Vancouver, in association with the University of British Columbia.[6]

Also as a result of the war, the Forestry Service was asked to assist the Canadian Army in handling their forestry problems on the Petawawa Military Reserve. Just north and west of the village of Petawawa, Ontario, the army had acquired a considerable area of uneconomic farmland and good timberland. The area was used as a military training ground from about 1916 on, and the army experienced considerable problems with wildfires starting from the explosion of ammunition and flares. These problems were compounded by the dry nature of the flat, sandy-soiled plain. The Service was brought in to employ its fire-fighting skills to control the fires. At the end of the war, military usage of the area all but ceased, but the Service remained responsible for fire suppression. The area was described as "a characteristic pine and spruce site" and the Service soon developed it as a forest experiment station. Besides providing basic data for use in management plans for the reserves, the station undertook experiments, in cooperation with the Council on Scientific and Industrial Research, into the yield and reproduction of eastern Canadian trees.[7] The development of a forest research station at Petawawa and the building and operation of two products laboratories represented the growth of the Service into a truly national body. In a more traditional mode, Dominion foresters continued to cruise and survey western lands, manage the reserves, and recommend new areas to be reserved. By the end of World War I, the Service had successfully reached a level of maturity where it was no longer satisfied with a field mandate centred on fire protection and reserve management. The corps of bright young men who had been recruited by R. H. Campbell were ready not only to involve their Service in the administration of all timberlands in western Canada, but also to see it become an active coordinating body for modern forestry in the rest of the country. These foresters were all acquainted with the best forestry techniques in use in Europe, the British Empire, and the United States. Aware of the difficulties created in Canada by the division of responsibility between federal and provincial governments, they, nevertheless, wanted to see sound forestry methods introduced across the country. These men were committed to conservation and forestry as an end in itself. They were convinced that efficient management of the forests would result in economies that would lead to greater profits for industry even though the initial implementation might be expensive. They were convinced that the way to reach this goal was to make the Service the sole voice for forestry matters in Canada. Thus, after 1918, a strong and confident Service stood ready to fight for this position which it felt was rightfully its own. The two rivals who stood in the way, the Commission of Conservation and the Timber, Mines and Grazing Branch, were soon to feel this challenge from the Dominion Forestry Service.[8]

It was this sense of destiny as well as a certain resentment, which is evident in a major report written by Ernest H. Finlayson after attending the first British Empire Forestry Conference held in London, England, in 1920.[9] Written with Campbell's blessing, the report is important because it sets a kind of agenda for the Service during the 1920s. Looking with hindsight at Finlayson's career in forestry, it is not surprising he was the author of so critical a piece. Finn, as he was nicknamed by his friends, was born in Toronto in 1887. He had studied for two years at the School of Practical Science at the University of Michigan before transferring to the University of Toronto where he received his B.Sc. in Forestry in 1912. His contemporaries, such as Abraham Knechtel and Peter Caverhill, noted his leadership and organizational abilities as well as his love for the outdoors and enthusiasm for forestry. His training at the University of Toronto under Professor Fernow had obviously convinced him of the the necessity of having a strong state agency dedicated to carrying out forestry work on a national scale. He confidently nominated his Service for this role.[10]

During his summer vacations from the University of Toronto's School of Forestry, Finlayson had worked for one year in Algonquin National Park and for two years on Forestry Service surveys in western Canada. When he graduated in 1911, he was employed as Inspector of Fire Rangers in the prairie provinces. Having shown initiative in reorganizing the forest fire patrols outside of the reserve areas, he was promoted and, just after the start of the war, became Inspector of Forest Reserves, the most important field position in the Forestry Service. Finn was transferred to Ottawa in early 1920 as Chief of the Forest Protection Division. One of his first major assignments was to take the place of fellow forester D. Roy Cameron, whose wife was ill, as Canada's representative at the Empire Forestry Conference in London.[11]

The British Empire Forestry Conference followed on the wartime Dominion's Royal Commission that had toured the Empire gathering information on an incredibly wide range of natural resource topics.[12] The conference was convened because the British government's new Forestry Commission had revealed the home islands had been cleared of mature timber, that a massive planting campaign was needed, and thus that Britain would have to rely on the Empire to fill the gap between demand and supply for some decades to come. The war had shown timber was still as strategically important as a war material as it had been a century earlier. The Conference was an effort to inventory Empire resources, determine strategic supply areas, and encourage their management. It was the first of a series of conferences that continue to this day as the Commonwealth Forestry Conferences.[13] The Canadian delegation to this first conference was particularly well qualified. Besides Finlayson, it included Robson Black, Secretary of the Canadian Forestry Association; Clyde Leavitt, Chief Forester of the Commission of Conservation; Ellwood Wilson, Chief Forester of the Laurentide Paper Company; Martin Grainger, Chief Forester for British Columbia; and Avila Bédard, Assistant Chief Forester, of the Province of Quebec.[14]

The programme of the Conference concentrated on the responsibility of the state for forest policy as well as management techniques and Empire forest resources. Inspired by these topics, Finlayson took the opportunity in his report to discuss the basic weaknesses of the Canadian system of divided responsibility as well as the need for a proper Dominion programme. In doing this, he leveled scathing criticism at the Commission of Conservation (still reporting through the Minister of Agriculture) and the Timber, Mines and Grazing Branch of his own Department of the Interior.[15]

By most accounts, the Commission of Conservation had done a great deal of worthwhile work in the years following its establishment in 1909. Unlike its American counterpart, which had floundered on the rocks of Congressional opposition, the Canadian body had used its broad and rather vague mandate to involve itself in a wide variety of topics. Led by Sir Clifford Sifton and James White, its energetic permanent secretary, it had inventoried such resources as water power, minerals, fisheries, and forests and had promoted their scientific and efficient utilization. It had produced models of resource legislation and had launched major studies in town planning, public health, rural resettlement, preservation of wildlife, and a host of other questions. Unfettered by constitutional niceties, the Commission undertook a prodigious number of projects and followed these up with attractive, widely distributed reports. The Commission had a very high status, and well-known experts, often academics, did not hesitate to work for it and to support its activities.[16]

The Commission was able to move freely from one level of government within Canada to another, doing studies and projects, making criticisms and publishing them along with recommendations. This freedom from restraint and the high prestige of the Commission were guaranteed to provoke jealous enmity from federal civil servants whose functions and responsibilities overlapped tasks the Commission had taken on for itself. Another source of friction with officials in Departments such as Agriculture, Interior, and Mines was the way in which some of their own reports were republished and distributed by the Commission without their permission.[17] While the Commission considered that it was only fulfilling its mandate to make Canadians aware of the extent and condition of their natural resources, federal public servants fumed about rank opportunism and duplication of effort. They also worried about the Commission's eroding the appropriations given to them. Among the bureaucrats opposed to the Commission, J. P. Challies, Director of the Dominion Water and Power Branch in the Department of the Interior, was probably its most relentless critic, mainly because the independent Commission had almost completely duplicated his own Branch's research efforts.[18] The Forestry Service occasionally criticized the Commission even though it had supported the Service in its battles with the Timber and Grazing Branch. But the situation was brought to a head for Finlayson when the Commission entered into a series of cooperative agreements with the provinces, and with industry, to carry out forest surveys and advise on forest management.[19]

In his report to Campbell about the Empire Forestry Conference, Finlayson first criticized the Commission for the cooperative agreements it had made. He argued these projects rightly belonged to the Forestry Service because it was the national forestry organization, and he was very concerned the Commission would erode the Service's position. The way it had expanded into taking on inventory work for the provinces especially in British Columbia upset Finlayson. Whereas the Service was forced by the British North America Act into negotiating agreements with the provinces, the Commission just acted. Worse, from the point of view of Finlayson, the Commission had not been hampered by manpower shortages during the war. Lacking a permanent staff, it simply contracted for reports and surveys from Canada's forestry academics. This flexible and economic approach was so successful that Finlayson and Campbell had begun to fear that the government might retrench the Service's responsibilities.[20]

The second set of criticisms of Canadian government policy concerned the division of responsibilities between the Timber and Grazing Branch and the Forestry Service within the Department of the Interior. Finlayson termed the way in which the two organizations' responsibilities were divided legislatively, yet united on the ground, "a grave mistake in policy".[21] He pointed to several examples where they shared responsibilities for the same area, where they had different policy objectives and yet were supposed to share staff. Specifically, Finlayson called for a revision of the Forest Reserves Act to give all responsibility for forest and timber management to the Service. He criticized the Timber and Grazing Branch for being dominated by officials in the Lands Office and for having as its sole objective the raising of revenue for the Crown. Finally, Finlayson blasted the Timber and Grazing Branch for corrupt administration and a totally negative attitude toward the introduction of forest management techniques on the forest lands it controlled.[22]

Finlayson's attack on the Commission of Conservation and the Timber and Grazing Branch was typical of his single-minded approach to forestry and conservation. He was a zealot, deeply committed to his cause. Eloquent, a worrier, and dedicated to public service, he forcefully presented his views. At this time, he was not in a position to determine the fate of either the Timber and Grazing Branch or the Commission of Conservation. Only later in the decade, as Director of Forestry, would he attempt to directly influence Forestry organization at the federal level. In the commission's case, however, he was joining a chorus of critics who wished that organization ill.

Bureaucratic infighting would not, on its own, have toppled the publicly popular Commission of Conservation if it had not become politically entangled with the Prime Minister on a sensitive issue. The use of electrical power for industrial purposes had been a major political issue even before World War I, but the war effort led to the expansion of factories using electrical power, creating shortages in parts of southern Ontario and of the United States south of the Great Lakes to such an extent that rationing had been introduced.[23] By 1918 attention was drawn to the St. Lawrence river system as an area that should be more intensively developed for power generation. Plans to develop these waters had existed since 1910, but they were replete with potentially contentious issues. For instance, was a public body or a private agency to carry out and own the development? Did such projects fall under federal or provincial jurisdiction in Canada? The whole issue was full of political pitfalls, and the Unionist government, still under the leadership of Robert Borden, intended to approach it as carefully as possible.[24]

The question was focussed when an application to the International Waterways Joint Commission was renewed by the St. Lawrence River Power Company, a division of the Aluminum Company of America, to develop a power site on the river. The company had made applications before, but they had been opposed by both the Canadian government and the Commission of Conservation. The new application was considerably reduced in size, requesting a weir only on the American side. Nevertheless, the Canadian government disputed the jurisdiction of the Joint Commission, the body which regulated the waterways, to grant power rights and fought the proposal, if somewhat halfheartedly. In the hearing before the Commission, the Canadian government was represented by Solicitor General of Canada Hugh Guthrie and Parliamentary Under Secretary for External Affairs F. H. Keefer. The Commission of Conservation also presented a hastily prepared brief reasserting its belief that all development should be publicly owned. James White represented the body before the Joint Commission, but Sifton, who was out of the country, was aware of the basic contents of the brief. The presentation angered Borden and caused an irreparable rift between Sifton and himself, which led to the Chairman's resignation.[25]

In his presentation, White gave the impression that each member of the board of the Commission of Conservation, including the federal Ministers of Agriculture, Interior and Mines who were board members, supported his intervention. That the Commission had the effrontery to make the intervention, as well as the claims that accompanied it, greatly angered the Canadian member of the Joint Commission, Henry A. Powell. Borden, even though the Commission of Conservation supported the government's position, seemed concerned that the Dominion not be seen to speak with two possibly contradictory voices on what was a difficult case that was probably going to be lost. Also, there may have been some unstated embarrassment that the Commission's Chairman was interested in developing power sites on the Ottawa river, technically part of the St. Lawrence system. White might have been eventually forgiven if the Commission had not then made the major tactical error of publishing documents relating to the company's application. The Prime Minister angrily interpreted this as the equivalent of the Commission's attempting to further set out what was or was not government policy.[26] The issue itself was hardly a major one, but it was blown out of proportion by Borden and Sifton. It was also symptomatic of a declining popularity of the Commission with such leading Tory ministers as Arthur Meighen, George Foster, and Martin Burrell. Thus Sifton's hasty resignation in 1918 in the face of this opposition was really the beginning of the downfall of the Commission of Conservation. Sifton left in his place, as an interim replacement, the elderly Senator W. C. Edwards, an inveterate Laurier Liberal opposed to the government. With no wholehearted Tory support behind the Commission after the falling out with Sir Robert Borden, there was no voice in the government to offer outright support to the organization. When Borden retired in 1920, the Commission was left facing a new Prime Minister, Arthur Meighen, who had openly disliked Sifton and all his works and who believed that the body had outlived its usefulness. Meighen quickly ordered a Committee of Cabinet to be formed under the leadership of the Minister of the Interior, the Hon. Sir James Lougheed, a Senator from Alberta, to compile a case against the Commission and to present a bill to disband it.[27]

In Lougheed's report, all the vitriol and jealousy the federal bureaucracy had stored up against the Commission was allowed to spill forth unrestrained. The duplication of effort with official agencies and departments was discussed at length. It was charged that, except for nominal reporting through the Minister of Agriculture, there was no ministerial or parliamentary control over the body. The blame for this situation was laid, fully and unfairly, on James White. Lougheed charged that White took advantage of the Chairman's long absences from Canada and resulting lack of supervision, to follow issues of interest to himself. Not surprisingly, the Committee of Cabinet recommended the dispersal of the Commission's responsibilities to the appropriate federal departments. This, they concluded, would save the public "further waste of public monies through duplication" and enhance existing programmes through the addition of experienced staff.[28]

None of the arguments against the Commission were telling enough to justify its destruction, but the Prime Minister appeared almost petty in his determination to do away with the body. Compared to the Commission's real achievements, the government's criticisms appeared small and mean. The strangest argument of all was that of fiscal savings. Because it successfully contracted out its work, the Commission's budget was just $99,000 in 1920. Yet, since most of the staff were to be transferred to other departments, the real savings was only $48,000.[29] The Commission was disbanded, as is often the case, because it was activist and got things done and because White, as Secretary, misplayed events politically and gave his enemies the chance they been waiting for. Without the political irritation caused by White's intervention before the Joint Commission, Meighen might have changed things by simply appointing a new Chairman and Secretary.

The first result of the disbandment of the Commission was a rush for the spoils. The Forestry Service was interested in obtaining the services of the three trained foresters employed by the Commission, Roland D. Craig, W. M. Robertson, and G. A. Hulley.[30] Of the three, Craig was the most prestigious because of his experience in forest survey work. The Service wished to take over the Commission's efforts in this direction and expand into a national inventory programme. Craig had worked as a federal forester from 1904 to 1907 when he had resigned to embark on private practice in British Columbia. Before the war, he had worked for the Commission on its cooperative forest survey programmes, starting in British Columbia and moving on to Ontario. During the war, Craig worked for the Imperial Munitions Board as Inspector of Airplane Timber, rejoining the Commission in 1919. By obtaining Craig's services, the Service hoped to use his experience with forest inventories to develop a low-cost, efficient method of conducting surveys of large land areas.[31]

The second benefit accruing to the Service was an expanded role in pure forest research. This involved investigations into methods of securing higher yields and continuous production from the forests. Included was the study of the regeneration of merchantable species, the replacement of nonmerchantable species with merchantable, new uses for waste products, and the silvicultural and economic aspects of reproduction systems.[32] The Petawawa station had already started research in these areas, and the Service took over from the Commission the projects being conducted in cooperation with the Laurentide Company and the Entomological Branch of the Department of Agriculture in Quebec and New Brunswick. The Commission's experimental cutting programmes with the Bathurst Lumber Company and the New Brunswick Forest Service were also absorbed. From this beginning, the Forestry Service was subsequently able to expand into other cooperative agreements, mostly in the eastern half of the country.[33]

With the destruction of the Commission and the acquisition of its forestry programmes, the Forestry Service went a long way toward achieving its goal of becoming the national forestry body. It can be argued this was a continuation of the attempt to emulate Pinchot's successes of the early years of the century. Indeed, Fernow and Pinchot had both made extensive use of cooperative programmes to give their organizations national stature. Because most forestland in the United States was privately owned, these programmes, from the beginning, had concentrated on the private owner; however, in Canada the Crown continued to hold practically all the forest.[34] As will be seen in the next chapter, during the debate over the transfer of Dominion-controlled natural resources to the provinces, the Service attempted to build on this base by promoting a stronger, more activist federal presence in forestry through retention of the western timber reserves. Had it been successful, the Service would have altered the constitutional basis of the British North America Act in regard to provincial control over natural resources. Their interpretation adhered closely to the American model in which the United States Forest Service retained control over large tracts of forestlands. At this stage in its development, the Dominion Forestry Service recognized the need to negotiate with provincial authorities in order to take on forestry programmes in the provinces. Once again, this demonstrates that the control of land is the first necessity for a successful forestry service.

Establishing his Forestry Service as the single national spokesman on forestry and conservation matters was one of Robert Campbell's long-term goals. The Director of Forestry perceived the development of a national forest policy for the Service as being based on four initiatives: (1) improvement, protection, and expansion of the western forest reserves (totaling 9.2 million hectares in 1921); (2) development of a nationwide research programme modelled on that of the Dominion Department of Agriculture and emphasizing cooperation with provincial governments and industry; (3) a national forest inventory; and (4) education of Canadians to the need for a sound forest policy.[35] These were excellent objectives. They can be judged as being, individually and collectively, the necessary foundations for an effective national forest policy. In fact, they comprised more than a policy, representing, as well, the basis for a national attitude toward the nation's forests. The success or failure of Campbell and his foresters in achieving their ideological goals rested, as it had always done, on the ability of the Service to rally public opinion behind it. From this support would come the policy of whatever government was in power.

An element of luck now played a role by providing an opportunity to place before the general public a demonstration of the importance of forestry in Canadian economic and social affairs. The opportunity presented itself in the form of a political embarrassment to the Liberal government of William Lyon Mackenzie King which had taken power following the defeat of Meighen's Unionists in 1921. Like the furor over the Commission of Conservation, the issues that led to King's embarrassment had their roots in much earlier events. It concerned legislation enacted to halt the export to the United States of pulpwood cut from privately owned lands in Canada.

As has been discussed earlier, all the provinces in Canada controlling their own Crown lands had prohibited, since before World War I, the export of unmanufactured logs cut from these lands. Each province, however, had loopholes in its regulations. Nova Scotia, for instance, considered de-barking logs or "rossing" to be sufficient manufacturing to allow export. Ontario allowed fire-killed trees to be salvage cut and exported under ministerial permit. British Columbia habitually eased its regulations whenever the log market became flooded and prices threatened to drop. In addition, logs cut from privately owned land in any province were exportable. This was because the export of privately owned wood fell under the Dominion's jurisdiction, in particular under the provisions in the British North America Act governing international trade.[36]

The privately owned wood was shipped to American newsprint and fine-paper mills concentrated in the northeastern United States. Before the war, these mills had faced shortages in their supplies of wood and had started buying it in Canada. A network of dealers, who were often local merchants, had developed in the marginal farming areas of eastern Canada. Between the dealers and the local farmers or settlers a kind of symbiotic relationship had grown up with the dealer advancing cash or goods to his clients on the promise of pulpwood to be cut and supplied to him. In northern Ontario and Quebec, especially in the clay-belt areas, the relationship between the dealers and settlers was an especially critical one. Here the money received by the settler for the sale of wood cut while clearing his lot was supposed to provide the capital needed for the settler to develop the clearing into an operating farm. By 1923 the money received by settlers for their pulpwood was failing to cover their costs of development. Both settlers and farmers were feeling the hardship which had the effect of increasing the rate of rural depopulation. Canadian mills in northern areas also habitually purchased wood from settlers to diversify their sources of supply. Settlers' wood was convenient, low priced, and free from contractual obligations. Wood purchased under contract from their own jobbers was more expensive and ate into the capital assets of the company as represented by its limits. Canadian companies would have bought more from settlers if it had been available as they used the settlers' prices to set the jobbers' rates, but an average of 48 percent of the settlers' wood was successfully exported annually.[37]

From the point of view of the settlers and farmers, the trick was to get as much of their own wood exported as possible because American mills habitually paid higher prices than Canadian mills. Furthermore, even though the shipper had to pay the freight costs, the farmer received several dollars more per cord for the wood he shipped south. On a personal level these were important matters. The truth, however, was that the total quantities involved were small in relation to the volume of wood cut on Crown land. The importance of the export trade, from an industry standpoint, was that exported wood set prices paid for fibre, and certain mills in northern Ontario and Quebec would definitely have been able to lower the cost of their raw material if this outlet had not existed. Also, given the high proportion of American-based mills relying on Canadian woods, removal of this source of logs would have badly upset these mills. Canadian paper companies, therefore, saw two benefits to be gained from prohibiting the export of all unmanufactured logs from Canada: a probable reduction in fibre costs and the possible closing of competing mills and acquisition of their markets.[38]

Because Canadian settlers and farmers were demonstrably the losers in this game, the Canadian pulp and paper industry, which was eager to steal a march on its American competition, knew it would have to finesse its hand if it hoped to convince the Canadian public that a greater interest was at stake and that the required sacrifice was small and unimportant. What the industry needed was a publicist. Into this role stepped one of the most remarkable and controversial men in the history of the Canadian conservation movement, Frank John Dixie Barnjum.

Frank Barnjum had been born in Montreal in 1859, the son of upper middle-class British immigrants who came from Norfolk. Although his family was impoverished, his parents managed to find him a position as an office boy in a brokerage house in Montreal. Barnjum had an eye for business and at a young age he moved to the Boston, Massachusetts, area and set up business buying and selling tanning bark. Within a few years he had moved into dealing in forestlands in Maine, through the Allagash Land Company, and in Nova Scotia under his own name.[39]

To facilitate this international business, Barnjum acquired houses in Annapolis Royal, near Digby, Nova Scotia, and at Kingfield, a small town in central Maine. Having acquired timber, Barnjum proceeded to cut and sell it. He was closely involved with the McLeod Paper Company of Halifax, Nova Scotia. This small firm purchased quantities of privately cut wood from landowners in the province and used it to produce paper pulp which it shipped to the United States. Barnjum's association with the Allagash Land Company of Maine also meant he was involved with the sale of pulpwood to mills in that state. In addition, Barnjum had owned the rights to the pulpwood growing on the last remaining substantial block of Crown land in Nova Scotia. This was the 1,624 square kilometres of the interior of Cape Breton Island. In 1917, after grossly overestimating the volume of wood on the land, Barnjum successfully sold the rights to the Oxford Paper Company of Rumford, Maine. Barnjum appears to have invested the proceeds from this sale into purchasing Douglas fir land in British Columbia.[40] Clearly, an embargo on the export of private pulpwood was to Barnjum's benefit. His mill in Nova Scotia could purchase wood more cheaply, and the value of the holdings of the Allagash Land Company would increase.

Starting in 1918, Frank Barnjum began a public campaign by writing letters to newspaper editors pointing out how the increasing shortage of pulpwood logs was driving up the price of the raw material for paper, and that, given the then current rates of paper usage, there soon would be no more logs left to cut. In 1920 he began to collect these letters in pamphlet form, had the pamphlets privately printed, and mailed them to anybody he thought would be interested. Increasingly, the theme was the same in each one: An embargo should be placed on the export of pulpwood from Canada; greater education of the public on the importance of Canada's forest resource was required; the Canadian Forestry Association should play a more activist role; forest protection should be increased; and logging should be better supervised to decrease wastage. With the exception of the call for an embargo, the message, which changed little over the years, was strictly conservationist.[41]

The forest industries, and particularly certain companies within the Canadian Pulp and Paper Association led by its President J. A. Bothwell, saw Barnjum's propaganda as a means by which they might achieve their aim of lowering their fibre costs. By trying the old Ontario trick of tying the embargo to the conservationist cause and claiming it would result in greater American investment in Canada, the public might be convinced to push the Dominion government into action. Canada's federal government had, despite enormous pressures, steered clear of the debates surrounding the Dingley tariff on the grounds that overt action would induce American retaliation. This policy was reinforced in 1920 when Senator Underwood of Alabama secured passage of a resolution calling for trade sanctions against Canada if the manufacturing conditions were not removed. Acting on the advice of the State Department whose trade consuls in Canada had said the positive effects of lifting the conditions would be negligible but the effect on public opinion would be harmful, President Wilson accorded the measure a "pocket veto".[42] With the new Liberal federal government in power after the 1921 election and the Underwood controversy a thing of the past, Canadian industry wished to push Mackenzie King into using his authority over international trade. Pressure was therefore applied directly on the government and through the press in Montreal and Toronto for an embargo as a conservation measure because, it was argued on a somewhat suspect basis, Canada was running out of wood.[43] Two magazines, *MacLeans* and *Saturday Night*, joined in broadcasting the arguments. The Rt. Hon. W. S. Fielding, Minister of Finance, pleaded in vain in the cabinet for a more thorough investigation of the matter. He failed to convince his colleagues and was forced to ask the House on 25 June 1923 to give the government power to prohibit the export of pulpwood. Only in the acrimonious debate that followed did the King government begin to realize the size of the hornet's nest it had just kicked. An embargo provision did pass the Commons but it went no further and was never applied.[44]

The public debate on the issue refused to die, and criticism of the government grew. The Prime Minister made an immediate concession by promising that wood cut by farmers on their own land would be exempt from the provisions of the act. This failed to still the clamour. The press rehashed the old question of economic nationalism versus American trade restrictions. American limitholders and owners of timberland pointed out that the government would be cancelling leases and contracts and that this would require the payment of compensation. The debate quickly moved from one over a conservation issue to one of property rights and arrived at the question of whether settlers had the right to use their lands as they saw fit. The provincial governments then became involved, especially those of Ontario and Quebec where northern settlers had specifically been told they could combine agriculture with cutting pulpwood. In Quebec, the supporters of the colonization movement were particularly outraged, eventually causing Premier Sir Lomer Gouin to worry in public about the fate of the colons if pulpwood exports were halted.[45]

In the meantime, representatives of the settlers quickly gained the ear of the federal Conservatives. They contended that Canadian mills wished to create a monopoly for themselves in the purchase of pulpwood and thus lower the price of the commodity. It was rather a mundane and practical issue, but Arthur Meighen successfully elevated it into a debate on the principle of provincial control of natural resources and interference by the federal government in the right of individuals to do what they wished with their own property.[46] As a result, by August, 1923, King and the Liberals were looking for a graceful way out of the difficulties created by their own precipitate action. The solution was the obvious one—the creation of a Royal Commission empowered to investigate the extent of pulpwood supplies on public and private lands in the nation, the quantity of pulpwood produced in Canada in the last decade, the location of its manufacture into paper, and the general question of the pulpwood embargo. The members named to the Commission were Joseph Picard, as chairman, a tobacco manufacturer from Quebec City who had considerable investments in timberlands; Apollos B. Kerr, a Toronto barrister; Robert W. McLellen, a lawyer from Fredericton, New Brunswick; Joseph G. Sutherland, a lumberman from Clyde River, Nova Scotia; and William Anstie, a contractor from Vancouver, British Columbia.[47]

The Secretary named to the Royal Commission was none other than E. H. Finlayson. From the point of view of the Forestry Service, this appointment presented an excellent opportunity for furthering the cause of federal forestry and advertising its expanded agenda. At this point in his career, Finlayson was the rising star of Canadian forestry. His appointment to the Royal Commission came while he was in western Canada supervising the grand tour of the second British Empire Forestry Conference which met in Canada in 1923.[48] Leaving the tour in late August, Finlayson hurried back to Ottawa to assume his new duties. His responsibilities were to be increased a few months later in April, 1924, when Robert Campbell, Director of Forestry, was forced into premature retirement as a result of a head injury he had received in 1918 while inspecting the prairie forest reserves. Finlayson assumed the Director's responsibilities as well at this time and was eventually confirmed as the third of Canada's Directors of Forestry in April, 1925. The strain caused by this extraordinary amount of work, combined with the heavy travel schedule kept by the Commission, affected his health. The difficulties Finlayson was to experience to such an extent in the 1930s date from this period.[49]

Nevertheless, the choice of Finlayson both as Secretary to the Commission and later as Director of Forestry was an excellent one. Enthusiastically he turned the Forestry Service into a research support unit for the Royal Commission, ensuring it took a conservationist stance independent of Barnjum's viewpoint. This was tremendously important because the forest conservation movement as a whole was in danger of becoming tarnished by too close affiliation with the Canadian Pulp and Paper Association and its own particular economic goals. Distance from the Association became more essential as the Commission gathered evidence across the country and as the government's political objectives hardened. The Commission quickly got down to work, holding a series of hearings across Canada but paying particular attention to smaller communities in the Maritimes, Quebec, and Ontario. As a result, the transcripts of the public meetings hold many interesting details about the aspirations and problems of farmers and settlers at this time.[50] The Canadian Pulp and Paper Association was represented by executives from its member companies. American pulp and paper companies exporting wood across the border to the United States hired a Montreal lawyer, Aimé Geoffrion, to follow the hearings and make sure their point of view was represented. In addition, the controversy spawned a new organization, the Canadian Pulpwood Association, based in Halifax, made up of dealers in pulpwood largely from Quebec and the Maritimes. After opening proceedings in Halifax, Nova Scotia, the Commission moved to nearby Digby. Frank Barnjum was invited to appear before it but refused as it appears that Geoffrion, who had been well briefed by officials of the Oxford Paper Company, wished to question him on his land dealings. Barnjum claimed that he was being kept in Montreal by important business. When the Commission reached that city, Barnjum had returned to his home in Annapolis Royal. His apologies were laced with references to the worthlessness of the whole exercise, and, when he made his letter available to the press in Toronto, Chairman Picard lost his patience and ordered Finlayson to have a subpoena issued requiring Barnjum's appearance before the Commission. This action resulted in Barnjum's taking a quick business trip to Boston from whence he wrote yet more letters to the press denouncing the Commission as a waste of public time and money because the government's mind was already decided on the matter.[51] Determined to keep the issue a political one, Barnjum also wrote to Arthur Meighen, rejecting his past association with the Liberals and offering to help the Tories. Later, when the Commission had moved to other locales, he did in fact make speeches for the Conservatives at by-elections in New Brunswick and Nova Scotia. Throughout the 1920s, Barnjum remained a constant critic of Canadian resource management. He also remained a Tory for the rest of his life. In 1930, when the Conservatives were in power under R. B. Bennett, he attended the Imperial Forestry Conference in London, England, as Canada's representative. Many of Barnjum's suggestions were excellently conceived, but his ill-considered associations with various private interests, combined with the fiasco over the Commission, largely destroyed his credibility with the broader conservation cause.[52]

From the point of view of the King government, the Royal Commission did its job well in successfully burying the government's embarrassments over the pulpwood export issue. Its cross-Canada tour let many farmers and settlers vent their views. Thus, the often strongly held opinions landed on the broad shoulders of the Commissioners rather than on the already bowed backs of the politicians. It also collected evidence that called into question the validity of the claims of Barnjum and some members of the Canadian Pulp and Paper Association of a timber shortage, revealing that such estimates were based only on estimates of already accessible forests and did not take into account, for instance, vast areas of unsurveyed timber in northern Quebec. The problem that the Commission did identify was the lack of attention paid to the proper range of forest management techniques which would ensure sustained yields from existing pulpwood stands. Furthermore, the Commission exposed a division within the industry. Not all manufacturers wanted an embargo. The Canadian Pulpwood Association, which opposed the embargo, was led by Angus MacLean, President of the Bathurst Company of New Brunswick, a company which relied primarily on private sources of logs. Combined with official provincial opposition, the King government found it had ample grounds for making a graceful and popular retreat from the whole issue. King showed his political skill when he performed the manoeuvre in such a way as to give the impression he was taking a new and popular initiative by declaring his government would undertake a "new and rigorous campaign" of forest conservation.[53]

This escape hatch for the government can be found in the Royal Commission's *Final Report*, and it is directly traceable to E. H. Finlayson and the Dominion Forestry Service. Practically all the report was written by Finlayson himself. Its first part is largely an analysis of the existing state of the forest resource and the woods industry in Canada. The second part of the report, however, is more analytical and is a direct expression of the author's opinions. It discusses the state of forestry in Canada, looking at each province separately, laying blame and heavy criticism where the author thought necessary. In the pages allotted to the Dominion, there is criticism not only of the lack of funding and manpower made available by the federal government to its forestry service but also of the duplication of effort engendered by having a Parks Branch, the Forestry Service, and the Timber and Grazing Branch all responsible for areas of Dominion forestland. In many ways, the report is a restatement in greater detail, and in tempered terms, of the paper Finlayson had prepared for Campbell after the first Empire Forestry Conference. The same issues are discussed, the same arguments made, and the same solutions proposed.[54]

From the point of view of the Forestry Service, the Royal Commission was a success even if few were prepared to take the time and effort to read the nearly 300 pages of the *Final Report*. Finlayson had made the Service the spokesman for forestry and forest conservation in Canada. He achieved this by skillfully directing all the Commission's research and administrative requirements through the staff of the Forestry Service. The Royal Commission formally recognized the Service's claim, that it had been making since the days of Sifton, that it spoke for forestry in all of Canada.

His confirmation as Dominion Director of Forestry rewarded Finlayson for his work with the Royal Commission, and the Service launched an effort to develop the promised new Liberal initiative in forest conservation. This work was to be overseen by King's Minister of the Interior, Charles Stewart. Born in Strabane, Ontario, in 1868, Stewart was in some ways well suited for his portfolio. He had homesteaded at Killam, Alberta. He had been elected as a Liberal to the Alberta legislature in 1909, where he served as the Minister of Municipal Affairs from 1912 to 1913, the Minister of Public Works from 1913 to 1917, and the provincial Premier and Minister of Railways and Telephones from 1917 to 1921, when he was defeated by the United Farmers of Alberta. In 1922 he ran for the House of Commons in a Quebec by-election and entered King's Cabinet as Minister of the Interior and was therefore, supposedly, the regional spokesman for the western prairies though there is some doubt that he could have been elected in that disaffected region. A low tariff man, Stewart believed in developing Canadian resources and from this grew his interest in, and support for, forestry.[55]

Unfortunately for the conservation program, Stewart did not have an easy relationship with his Prime Minister. By 1923 King would have liked Stewart out of his Cabinet because he felt that his Minister was too uncooperative with the United Farmers of Alberta, the independent farm political protest movement in the area, and not assiduous enough in wooing the Progressive vote back to the Liberals. Ironically, Stewart's main fault seems to have been that he was excessively partisan, which was to be expected since the Progressive party had toppled him from his premiership. Suspect in regard to the western support he could command, only King's failure to lure a suitably prestigious Alberta Progressive into his ranks had saved Stewart for the moment. Unfortunately this political disadvantage denied the Minister much of the Prime Minister's confidence. Thus there developed a situation where the forestry and forest conservation movement benefitted from Stewart's reasonably dynamic political leadership but also suffered somewhat from his uncertain position in the federal Cabinet. The Forestry Service found the Prime Minister was not always eager to support the cause, which created difficulties in the longer term. This was especially evident after 1926 with regard to the natural resource transfer agreements.

The Liberal government had promised action on forest conservation in the report of the Royal Commission and had opened this initiative by convening a forest protection conference. Provincial ministers responsible for forestry matters, and their officials, were invited to meet in Ottawa on 7–11 January 1924.[56] The Prairie Provinces were represented by the federal District Forest Inspectors for each province who were joined by their Minister; the Deputy Minister of the Interior, W. W. Cory; E. H. Finlayson; D. Roy Cameron, who organized the event, and Roland D. Craig. Also present were J. W. Greenway, Commissioner of Dominion Lands; J. B. Harkin, Commissioner of Dominion Parks; B. L. York, Superintendent of the Timber and Grazing Branch; and A. M. Narraway, Controller of Surveys. They were joined by provincial resource Ministers and Chief Foresters. Fire protection was chosen as the subject of the conference because of its noncontroversial nature. All provinces accepted the necessity of carrying out such an activity. As Finlayson pointed out, the problem lay in convincing governments that fire protection was not an end in itself, but rather was a method of securing further investment in the management of timberlands.[57]

Stewart opened the conference with a speech assuring the provinces the federal government was not going to interfere with their jurisdictions. The Minister was able to see "some degree of uniformity" in national public opinion regarding forest "preservation" which apparently the federal officials were now defining to include disease and insect pest control. Besides altering Dominion fire-fighting practices and management policies to more completely meet provincial needs, Stewart suggested that his government could assist the provinces financially in their efforts as well.[58] Essentially this was a proposal to provide a new fiscal foundation for forestry in Canada. It was a rudimentary aid system similar to the American Weeks Act, under which the federal government contributed to state activities. It was, in short, the essential basis and logical next step for the establishment of an effective national forestry programme. There is no evidence available that the provision of financial assistance had been discussed in the cabinet, but one must assume that some discussion had taken place since Stewart's proposals not only had financial implications but also a potential impact on federal-provincial relations, an area to which King paid particular attention.

The press was excluded from the Conference, and the views expressed soon became quite candid and the topics discussed ranged widely beyond fire protection. Soon, basic differences between the provinces and the federal government began to appear. There was agreement on such issues as bogus settlement, but Ontario made it clear that the province could not increase its timber dues to make slash disposal economical on commercial limits and that it had no intention, at the present, of enlarging its forest reserves. Premier Howard Ferguson was apparently opposed to these moves, and the delegation adopted his tough provincial rights view which was typical of the province's attitude until the World War II period. Ontario firmly rejected federal offers of cooperation and declared its intention to retain complete control over its forest surveys and air services. Other provinces, less wealthy than Ontario, were not as quick to reject federal offers although they did wish to maintain their independence. Basically, the differences centred on one set of problems. The provinces were interested in immediate fiscal aid which they would use to purchase fire-fighting equipment, improve trails, and, where appropriate, underwrite air patrols. The federal government seemed willing to provide this kind of aid, especially through the Air Board, which was seeking a role for its equipment and the pilots no longer needed solely for air-defence purposes. In return, the federal government wanted to see more provincial activity in classifying areas as permanent forest and in their proper management. The provinces were willing to commit themselves to this only as a worthy objective to be fulfilled sometime in the distant future.[59]

By the last session of the conference, the provinces were prepared to ask some pretty direct questions of the Minister. Under questioning, the federal officials declined to say whether or not the federal government was actually considering the Canadian equivalent of the Weeks Act. Unable to commit the King government, they indicated that such legislation might be passed if the provinces could unite to bring enough political pressure in the appropriate quarters. Checked here, the provincial officials sought assurance that financial aid would be calculated on total provincial expenditures on forest protection rather than on specific activities, for example, air operations. Here federal officials were more supportive, indicating that this would probably be the case. It was in the area of air operations that the conference made its most significant contribution as the federal government agreed to provide British Columbia with direct assistance. Unfortunately, many other resolutions were rendered meaningless because they were not tied directly to an agreed policy directive and a timetable. The Dominion Forestry Service was asked to move into some new areas by developing a research programme to investigate the relationship between fires and weather and in collecting nationwide data on this topic. The Service was also asked to undertake a publicity campaign and to coordinate the activities for a national "Save the Forest Week" to be inaugurated in 1924.[60]

Charles Stewart was in the chair to receive these resolutions. He suggested the federal government was willing to listen to anything the provinces might propose but held out little hope of federal assistance in areas that were purely provincial in jurisdiction. He was more optimistic in regard to areas of shared responsibility, although he did not define these areas precisely.[61] At any rate, his stance was considerably more conservative than it had been when he had made his opening statement. Clearly, the King government was not about to make a new major initiative in federal-provincial relations without due consideration of all the benefits and problems that might be involved. Despite this political attitude, the Forest Fire Conference was successful in bringing together the two levels of government to define a basis for national cooperation in forestry matters. It appeared to Finlayson and his assistant, Cameron, to be an excellent start in creating the national standards they advocated, and the prospects of future cooperation looked reasonably promising.

As a second thrust in undertaking a new forest and conservation policy, the Dominion government committed itself, at long last, to improving its control over logging on the timber berths in western Canada. The first move was made at the administrative level where the Forestry Service and the Timber and Grazing Branch were instructed to cooperate in establishing sustained yield management on the berths.[62] Wisely, the Service avoided the mistake of trying to institute this practice on berths where cutting was already in progress. Instead, it looked to the relatively untouched forests of central Manitoba where, since 1919, there had been talk of building a large pulp and paper mill. In 1925 the federal government finally granted timber berths north and west of Lake Winnipeg to the Manitoba Pulp and Paper Company. This was backed by the Spanish River Pulp and Paper Company (at that time a subsidiary of Abitibi Power and Paper) and later joined by the Backus interests that had dominated the power and paper industries of northern Minnesota and northwestern Ontario and had played such a nefarious role in timber-stealing in the latter province.[63] The mill, which was completed in 1926, was located at Pine Falls, Manitoba, near the mouth of the Winnipeg river. The Forestry Service was adamant that the exploitation of the forests for this new venture would be properly planned on sustained yield principles. This meant that the resource would be thoroughly inventoried and that cutting of the balsam fir and black spruce forest would be conducted according to working plans. It was also intended that the company would aid settlers in northern Manitoba by purchasing pulpwood directly from them.[64]

In 1926, 35,200 square kilometres of what became known as the Pulpwood Selection Area were surveyed with the aid of aircraft. This survey, the largest that had ever been conducted in Canada, was continued in the following year in an area approximately the size of the province of New Brunswick. In spite of instructions to cooperate with the Service, the Timber and Grazing Branch carried on a tough rearguard action to preserve its mandate, and this hopeful political initiative was largely frustrated by bureaucratic inertia and resistance. The Service was relatively unsuccessful in obtaining control of the management of the forests in which the company was to operate. It managed to control operations only in the parts of the Pulpwood Selection Area outside of the berths essentially under the same conditions under which it operated in the rest of western Canada. Its best gains were made in slash disposal policy where an agreement was reached with the Timber and Grazing Branch that this practice was to be required on the berths. The agreement was worded in such a way that it incorporated all logging operations in the province of Manitoba.[65] Thus, after several years of conferences aimed at getting cooperation between the two agencies, the major accomplishment achieved by 1926 was to get the Timber and Grazing Branch to change its mind about the treatment of logging slash.

Internal negotiated reforms only brought the Service time-consuming difficulties and trivial changes. For these reasons, Finlayson used the government's political difficulties to push on with more wholesale changes to federal forestry policy which would be imposed by the Cabinet rather than arranged by bureaucrats. To accomplish this, the Service returned to the recommendations of the Royal Commission on Pulpwood. The Commission's final report had recommended the institution of forest management across Canada as a solution to the problem of dwindling wood supplies. In 1925 the King government lost many seats in the general election held that year and found itself in a minority position, holding 101 seats to the Tory's 116 and thus dependant upon Progressive and Labour support. King and the Liberals were also trying desperately to find popular issues that would divert public attention from the Customs Scandal then under investigation. Forestry and conservation represented a commitment on the part of the government to positive action and was generally popular with the public. Thus, in early June, 1926, Charles Stewart announced a new federal forestry policy. On the 9.2 million hectares of forest reserve, Stewart stated, the management objective was to achieve natural regeneration following logging as planting was too expensive a proposition. As well, this policy was to be extended to non-reserve timberlands, in other words, to the timber berths.[66] Furthermore, the Minister implied that the Forestry Service was to be given control over all nonagricultural lands held by the Dominion, probably classifying all suitable western timber areas as reserves. For a few short weeks it looked as if the Service had finally won supremacy over its nemesis, the Timber and Grazing Branch, and had also been placed in a supervisory role over the Parks Branch as well. Indeed, it looked as if it had finally achieved the goals set long ago by Stewart and Pinchot. The government's initiative could hardly be interpreted as adventurous, but the press greeted it favourably as emulating European experience and adopting the ideas of "expert foresters".[67]

Unfortunately, the King government was not given a chance to take immediate steps to implement the policy Stewart had announced. In late June, the government was forced to resign because of its minority position in the House, following which Governor-General Lord Byng declined to call a general election as requested by King. Instead, on the grounds that a vote had only recently been taken, he invited the Tories, still led by Arthur Meighen, to attempt to form a government. Meighen's party, however, was in a minority position just as had been the Liberals because the balance of power was held by members of a third party, the western, independently minded, National Progressive party. The political tango, known as the King-Byng Affair, ended in the defeat of the Tories in the House, and another general election was held in September. In this election, King and the Liberals returned to power with a majority, and Stewart once more resumed the Department of the Interior's portfolio on September 25.[68]

Majority government blunted the Minister's and the cabinet's enthusiasm for any review of forest policy especially since it would affect public opinion in western Canada in some way or another. The fiasco in the House and the role played by the small Progressive party since the 1921 general election made King realize that he had to absorb the Progressives into the Liberal fold. One way of achieving this political objective was to implement a policy that was popular with the western provinces with the hope that their Progressive provincial governments would move from an independent stance to one supporting the Liberals. Reaching a settlement with the prairie provinces and British Columbia for transferring to them the control of natural resources, including timber, was one such initiative. As a result, Stewart lost all interest in altering the status quo in the reserves and timber berths of the west. Stewart was content to shift departmental activities to inventory and survey work similar to that being carried out in the Pulpwood Selection Area.[69]

The Dominion Forestry Service felt the alteration in policy immediately. Roland D. Craig expressed concern at this time about the insecurity of the Service's control over reserved lands and the fact that farmers did not hesitate to go through the additional paper work needed to obtain land that was nominally part of a forest reserve. Here too he found little more than sympathy from his Minister. With the possibility of the resource's being transferred, Stewart was not inclined to expand the reserves, now named national forests, especially at the expense of alienating western farmers. Survey work was latched onto by the Minister as a useful alternative programme for the Forestry Service, and Stewart requested that another national conference with provincial ministers and officials be called to discuss this topic. He was aided in making this decision by a new barrage of public criticism from that ever present advocate of forest conservation, Frank J. D. Barnjum, who had been pressing for a Dominion-wide forestry conference to discuss "the need of a thorough investigation of . . . present and future forest resources".[70]

The Conference, called to discuss the possibility of a national inventory of forest resources, met in June, 1929. Once again, Stewart chaired the opening session of the meeting, but his remarks were somewhat the reverse of those he had made in 1924. He emphasized the diversity of Canada's forests; he asserted that he was not seeking to impose uniform regulations; and he stated that the purpose of the Conference was to discuss the coordination and compilation of an inventory of the forest resources of the nation. Stewart drew on the experience of his Forestry Service in its survey of the Pulpwood Selection Area. Here the final results had shown the early cruises to have overestimated the wood available by 50 percent. This experience made a national survey absolutely essential in the opinion of the Minister.[71]

This was a much more limited and immediate proposal than those made at the 1924 Conference. While it was not as creative as some of the ideas for establishing a new basis for forestry in Canada that had been aired earlier, it was still a large project and was necessary for the practice of proper forestry. Each province commented on the inventory proposal. All showed some eagerness to participate, but all wanted some form of long-term financial and policy commitment from the Dominion government.

The important question for most provinces was the timetable for operations and financing. Gustave Piché, head of the Quebec Forest Service, stated it best:

If the federal government should consider the question of subsidizing the provinces in an endeavour to complete the inventory of their forest resources, it seems to me that they should undertake to carry out their efforts to completion, and not confine the work to one year. I make this statement advisedly. In our own province we have begun different undertakings on a few occasions, only to find ourselves shouldered with full responsibility for them after a time, although we started in cooperation with the Dominion.[72]

Finlayson, representing Stewart, was flexible on the length of time taken for the inventory but remained noncommital with regard to financial contributions. It was on this point that the Conference eventually foundered but not before E. H. Finlayson had repeated, a bit piously given the fact that he had not been particularly successful in having the federal government carry out its policy commitments in this area, that forest reserves were the best way of setting aside land for forestry purposes. In this instance, the Director was talking as much to federal authorities, who were in the process of negotiating away the Dominion reserves, as to provincial compatriots. The provinces, for their part, were supportive of greater federal leadership in forestry, urging the continuance and expansion of federally sponsored research into silviculture, reproduction and regeneration, and insect and disease control.[73]

What did the Conference on the National Inventory of Forest Resources accomplish? Little enough, from the point of view of immediate actions. The final resolution which stated that "the delegates evince a keen desire for close co-operation in the forest inventory and pledge the efforts of their respective Services in this direction" was very vague and flexible. The Conference did not move beyond the concept that forest surveys must be conducted by the provincial organization controlling the resource. Arrangements were made to set up a standing committee with representation from each participating province to ensure that inventory standards and procedures were similar, and a commitment was made to complete the project within five years.

Most important from the viewpoint of federal officials, it was agreed that the Dominion Forestry Service would act as the central clearinghouse for the inventory, receiving reports from each province, collating the reports, and forming a forest resource and statistics data base for the nation. Further, it was resolved that

in the formulation of forest policies reliable information is required on the growing stock and the increment accruing under existing conditions or which can be secured by improved methods. Since the field for forest research is so great, it is urged that co-operation between the federal and provincial services be extended to include silvicultural research, especially in regard to reproduction and growth studies. A standing committee similar to the one on forest surveys should be appointed to advise as to standards and methods to be followed in research.[74]

This resolution was to bear fruit in 1935 when a conference on forest research was convened.

Finally, it was agreed to begin reporting insect, storm, and disease damage along with fire losses as factors to be taken into account when determining the inventory of forest resources.

On the whole, these were modest achievements, but, in an era when the concept of Dominion-provincial co-operation was only beginning to emerge, they were substantial enough. Indeed, they bear eloquent witness to the common interests of Canadian forest authorities that they could move so quickly into cooperative arrangements. True, the provinces would have liked definite financial commitments from the federal government, and the Dominion, on its side, might have liked stronger agreements on a forest inventory. Ironically, this was to be the last creative Dominion-provincial forestry initiative for over a decade as first the transfer of the natural resources to the western provinces rocked the Forestry Service to its foundations and then the depression of the 1930s sapped all levels of government of their ability to undertake any dynamic, cooperative activities.

In the short term, both Charles Stewart and the Dominion Forestry Service pinned their hopes for an effective national forestry policy on the opportunities presented by the Conference on the National Inventory of Forest Resources. For the Minister, the meeting became a way in which he could revive his idea of a federal forestry policy. By now, he had begun to appreciate the subtler realities behind the conservationist arguments put forward by his own officials and others prominent in the Canadian forestry movement supporting the development of a national forest policy. It was not that the country would be left a barren, treeless wasteland but rather that merchantable species would be cut out, possibly leaving the forest industries with no room to adapt to new supply species. As Alan Joly de Lotbinière wrote in 1929,

unless immediate steps are taken to effect a change in our forest policy there will be a timber shortage in a few years. Not that every merchantable tree will have disappeared, but that from then on our available industrial supply will diminish, and the output from our forest industries be less from year to year. Indeed indications of shortage are already present as one may see in the small poles that go down the rivers compared with the real logs that went down those same rivers a quarter of a century ago. The public seems to think that, because our cut of pulpwood is increasing from year to year, new supplies of virgin forest are being drawn upon, while as a matter of fact the pulpwood limits are being cut more intensively each year—the smaller trees which really belong to the future are now being taken.[75]

Stewart himself turned to this theme in a speech before the Canadian Lumbermen's Association in Ottawa on 16 January 1930. He pointed out the intense competition in the forest industries for species such as spruce and questioned the common attitude of lumbermen "to disregard the producing power of the soil" and "its treatment of the forest as a mine to be worked out and abandoned". He told the operators that the era of "migration" was over over and that they were "not face to face with the fact that the major forest regions have been or are in the process of being worked over". Stewart asked the lumbermen for their cooperation and support for Dominion and provincial efforts of land classification and forest inventory. He called for forestlands to be set aside "by appropriate legislative action and also boundary demarcation." This would enable both fire protection and inventorying of the resource which would in turn lead to the preparation of management plans based on the principle of sustained yield.[76]

There was absolutely nothing new in the Minister of the Department of the Interior's plan for a national forestry plan. What was new was Stewart's individual political commitment to push these issues and to provide national leadership for forestry measures. In doing so, he was attempting to keep abreast of events in both Ontario and Quebec where forestry principles enjoyed a brief flowering of popularity in the 1920s. Nevertheless, regardless of his motives, Stewart was instrumental in aiding the Forestry Service to continue to advance its national leadership role. It was a role which, by now, went substantially beyond the administration of the western forest reserves— a responsibility which was slipping from its control. It was a role which the Minister responsible for the Forestry Service recognized as an important national task and essential to any continuing influence the organization might have on forest policies.

The survey got under way in the early 1930s when the Dominion Forestry Service was in the midst of dealing with the transfer question which would see it lose all its forestlands in western Canada and when monies were being slashed from its budget because of the Depression. In spite of this apparent setback, the Conference was important because it was one more tentative step on the road to seeking a basis for federal-provincial cooperation in forestry matters. Yet, the Conference on the National Inventory of Forest Reserves is also indicative of the federal government's switch in policy away from emphasis on resource management and toward the transfer of the natural resources to the western provinces. The natural resource question was a problem that had been around for some considerable period. The Liberal party, however, did not view it seriously until after the embarrassments suffered by King in 1925. Political expedience was now to dictate events much more than any dedication to a new federal forestry policy. King was a consummate politician determined to remain in power and to advance the fortunes of the Liberal party. In this light, forestry and forest conservation were issues that could be adopted or, just as quickly, dropped depending on the political needs of the moment. This is the unfortunate truth lying behind the events occurring between 1911 and 1929. The limits of national leadership are clearly revealed. Federal governments, either Liberal or Conservative, were incapable of translating a host of worthwhile ideas about natural resource management into creative policies. The forestry advocates, who had greeted the peace in 1918 with such plans and idealism, found their movement frustrated by a decade of seeming activity but real political drift at the federal level. The Dominion government, despite the efforts of Stewart as Minister of the Interior, was no more willing or able than any of its provincial counterparts, to isolate the true principles of forest conservation from the political considerations of the day. In the resource transfer question, it would deliver the coup de grace to early federal efforts to bring into being an effective national forestry policy.

CHAPTER 9

Retreat and Disaster, 1926–1939

Beginning in the mid–1920s, there was a precipitous decline in interest and activity in the cause of forest conservation in Canada. First noticeable at the federal level, it spread rapidly to the provinces, especially as the Depression deepened in the early 1930s. The cause of this decline is difficult to pinpoint. Some of it was due, as we have seen in previous chapters, to economizing by all levels of government. These pressures were accelerated after the 1929 crash as governments discarded professional forest management staff as a needless frill for administrations cutting expenditures to the bare bone in order to aid economic recovery. In addition, the economic boom of the mid–1920s had tended to reinforce the exploitive ethic within the resource industries, especially as increased competition in the North American market required more attention to cost cutting. The voices supporting forest conservation, always limited in number, were now drowned out by more numerous supporters of unrestrained economic expansion. The fragile position of forestry within the sphere of public administration was exposed and could not be protected.

Gains for forestry had been possible only with support from parts of the forest industries themselves; now these industries became preoccupied with their own problems—pulp and paper with overproduction and intense competition for markets and eastern sawmilling with the very question of survival as timber stocks declined. The difficulties faced by the forest industry should have resulted in the adoption of conservation measures, but after 1926 timber operators feared any change that might bring about a rise in costs. The coalition supporting forest conservation did not recoalesce until after 1935, when governments, industry, and the forestry community began again to cooperate with forestry programmes which, it was agreed, helped economic recovery.

Throughout the 1920s, the Dominion Forestry Service attempted to expand its role and redefine its mandate through a new national forestry policy. At the same time, other events were occurring at the political level which were to impinge dramatically on federal forestry. Incredibly, most of the Service's officials and public supporters seemed blissfully unaware of the implications of the storm brewing on their doorstep. The question of the transfer of the national resources to the Prairie Provinces had been a growing political issue since the end of World War I.[1] Many Canadians felt that the role of the Dominion in settling western Canada had been fulfilled: The land had been settled; the railways had been built, if not actually over built; and the provinces had been created. The western provinces themselves were adamant in wishing equality of status. They found themselves short of money for local improvements and were sure that management of their natural resources would generate the needed revenues.[2] More important pressures festered at the federal political level. National political parties had been shattered in the wake of the conscription crisis and wartime elections. Regionalism was rife in the country, and a general political disillusionment had set in. In the West, the Progressives, a farmers' protest movement that had achieved national prominence in the 1921 federal election, saw the resource issue as vital.

Liberal Prime Minister William Lyon Mackenzie King, who formed the government after 1921, had, as one of his primary tasks, the rebuilding of the Liberal party through the absorption of the Progressives, many of whom were disenchanted members of his party. At various times between 1922 and 1929 King offered to transfer the natural resources to the western provinces as part of a package to gain their support and curtail the cost of government, another of the Prime Minister's preoccupations.[3] However, the Prime Minister's terms did not appear generous enough to the politicians of Manitoba, Saskatchewan, and Alberta. He offered to return the resources and terminate the special subsidy paid to the Prairie Provinces in lieu of resource revenues or, as alternative, account the cost of federal administration of the resources since 1905 and make a payment of any surplus of federal revenues over expenditures. Two conferences were held in 1922, but the federal terms, which included the continuation for three more years of the special federal subsidy, were rejected outright by the governments of Manitoba, Saskatchewan, and Alberta. Only Alberta, in greater financial difficulties than the others and anxious for control over its coal and oil deposits, remained insistent on reaching an agreement. Further conferences were held in 1924, and Alberta finally accepted the federal terms. But a federal election was in the offing in 1925, and King feared that the resource transfer question would reopen the school lands question and with it the thorny issue of support for separate Catholic schools. The Prime Minister, always a great procrastinator, was not prepared to take this chance to sign the agreement and accordingly postponed action.[4]

This controversy over what was popularly known as the natural resource question was obviously of some interest to officials of the Dominion Forestry Service. If the resources were given over to the control of the western provinces, forestlands would most definitely be among the items included in the transfer. This might even include the forest reserves as well and, regardless of the actual extent of the transfer, would have a considerable impact on the mandate of the Service to protect and manage Dominion forest lands. Between 1918 and 1926, Campbell, Finlayson, and other Dominion officials appeared strangely inured to this possibility. This detachment from the issue derived largely, it would seem, from constitutional attitudes or positions generally adopted by the federal government bureaucracy after 1880. The Dominion bureaucrats' position was based on the "purchase" theory of Rupert's Land which likened the administration of the public domain in the Canadian West to that in the United States. Manitoba and the North-West Territories were viewed as having been purchased from the Hudson's Bay Company, like the Louisiana, Gadsden, and Alaska purchases had added territories to the American republic. Thus, it was argued, these western lands became the property of the Dominion and were "really . . . in the same position as lands in the Territories of the United States, which are not given to new States as these new States are created, but remain the property of the United States".[5]

For the Dominion Forestry Service, which drew heavily on American models insofar as reserve lands were concerned, this was an ideal theory. Even if some lands were given away to the western provinces, they argued forcefully that the extensive reserve lands must be retained under federal ownership to accomplish national goals in conservation and forest management policy. In general, foresters and officials in the Department of the Interior were convinced that no settlement of the natural resources question would in the slightest degree affect or limit their national policy mandates. They simply assumed that Canada would develop along the lines of the American model where the federal government took an active leading role in its control of substantial land resources and used their management as an engine for national conservation programmes. World War I, with its experiments in government regulation and the immediate idealism it generated among federal bureaucrats for the accomplishment of national goals, reinforced this view of a major role for Dominion authorities in natural resource management.

An interprovincial conference in November, 1918, had done nothing to dispel these general views. At that meeting all provinces, except Manitoba, Saskatchewan, and Alberta, reinforced the "purchase" theory by declaring that any transfer of natural resources to the Prairie Provinces would infringe on the fiscal arrangements of Confederation and thus in any settlement "a proportionate allowance . . . [should] be granted to each of the other provinces of Confederation". In other words, the prairie west was owned by the Dominion, and in any disposition of property there must be a settlement of money on all the provinces to be contributed to the purchase and upkeep. With this obvious support for the purchase theory, the sporadic nature of the negotiations, and Prime Minister King's seeming lack of concentrated interest in the matter, the Dominion Forestry Service felt reasonably confident in making plans for western Canada with the view that it would remain in control of the existing, if not expanded, forest reserves in the area.[6]

In taking this position, federal forestry officials ignored the actual basis on which the Prime Minister was proposing to settle the natural resources question. He did not subscribe to the purchase theory but rather to the more legally sound argument that, as with the other provinces, Manitoba, Saskatchewan, and Alberta had a constitutional right, based in the British North America Act, to have control over their own natural resources. Therefore, though the 1922 negotiations were to break down over the amount and nature of the compensation to be given to the Prairie Provinces for resources already alienated, there was established an agreement on the principle that any adjustment involving natural resources would be based on "full recognition to the principle that . . . they (the western provinces) are entitled to be placed in a position of equality with the other provinces of Confederation".[7]

The purchase theory and, by implication, the American model had thus been rejected by King, yet this does not seem to have affected the views of the Dominion Forestry Service. It blithely went ahead with its intention to create a national role for itself, which included the control of western forestlands, and, as late as 1925–1926, it requested amendments to legislation to increase the size of the western forest reserves and to gain control over timber cutting operations. This confidence was inadvertently reinforced by the Liberal Minister of the Interior, Charles Stewart. Finlayson and Cameron believed that they would be fully informed by their Minister of any change in the situation. Indeed, the federal government's tough negotiating position with Alberta gave the Forestry Service officials reason for optimism rather than dismay. In negotiations with this government, it was agreed that all national forest reserves in the province, with one exception, would be retained under federal authority. The Forestry Service thereby saw itself moving into a position similar to that of the U.S. Forest Service, controlling vast tracts of western forest as a future timber bank for the nation. As D. Roy Cameron memorialized his Deputy Minister, W. W. Cory,

It is obvious . . . there must be a reserve of young timber protected to bridge the gap between the total depletion of present commercial stands and the systematic management of forest areas on a sustained yield basis which must inevitably come if our timber industries are to be perpetuated.[8]

Unfortunately, Finlayson and Cameron failed to take into account the vagaries of Canadian politics. The federal election of 1925, the resulting political deadlock with Arthur Meighen and his Conservatives, and the spinning out of the constitutional crisis surrounding the King-Byng Affair lent a new urgency to the resource transfer question. King needed western support to effectively consolidate his party's political position in the wake of increasing factionalism among the Progressives. In particular, the Prime Minister wanted a coalition with Premier John Bracken's Progressives in Manitoba. Bracken was also interested in obtaining provincial Liberal support, but he wanted the resource question settled first. He had been upset at the protracted negotiations over the Pulpwood Selection Area and Stewart's inability to comprehend the province's position in water power matters. Since Bracken was determined to obtain control of the natural resources controlled by the Dominion within the province, attention was shifted to Manitoba, while Alberta was left waiting patiently for the first agreement to be signed.[9]

Both a political coalition and a resource agreement were on the table when Bracken arrived in Ottawa in July, 1928. Mackenzie King was thus disposed to be more friendly and reasonable in the terms offered to Manitoba than in those he offered to Alberta. In the provisional agreement that was drawn up, it was proposed that all forestlands be turned over to the province except a very few areas such as Riding Mountain which would become national parks. Bracken left Ottawa with this draft agreement and a commitment that a Royal Commission would be struck to determine a suitable financial settlement between the federal and provincial governments. During the year it was estimated it would take for the Commission to do its work, the Dominion agreed to manage the natural resources of Manitoba in accordance with the province's wishes.[10]

At the political level, the draft agreement was generally greeted with enthusiasm. Difficult questions of federal-provincial relations had been faced in a spirit of cooperation and largely solved. The forestry movement in Canada, however, was left in a desperate situation. The year needed for conducting the Royal Commission gave some time for determined rearguard action, but, for all intents and purposes, the battle was lost. The apparent reversal of political positions occurred quickly, and the loss of the western forest reserves became symptomatic of the decline of the forest conservation movement in the country as a whole and its complete inability to influence the political process. In western Canada, the resources transfer agreement was immensely popular; in Ontario and Quebec, it was largely greeted as a just and proper settlement; in the Maritimes, a desire to press their own provincial claims was expressed. The Dominion Forestry Service, long involved in acrimonious battles to defend its forest reserve boundaries in western Canada, found, as was to be expected, that it had few friends there. One supporter, the *Prince Albert Daily Herald*, with readers in the northern timbered areas of Saskatchewan, was particularly prescient. In an article entitled "Pound Foolish", it accused the federal government of lack of foresight and of crassly attempting to reduce existing federal financial commitments. It judged

this action [as]... abundant indication that the Dominion government, for some ununderstandable [*sic*] reason, contemplates abandoning its forest service, upon which 30 years have been devoted to bring it to his present state of efficiency. Already far behind the United States in this regard, this decision of the federal authorities will leave Canada worse off than she was 30 years ago in the matter of a national forest policy and at least half a century behind her neighbour.[11]

Later, *Saturday Night* excoriated the legislation incorporating the general resource transfer agreements, charging that

the House of Commons... passed the bills in question [on the initiative of the government]... without due [if indeed, any] appreciation of the important factors indicating the unmistakable objections to the transfer of the forestry resources of the provinces concerned as being prejudicial, if not actually inimical, to the development of forestry in Canada.[12]

The same edition indicated that the Canadian Society of Forest Engineers

spoke with no uncertain voice in a resolution which it passed at its last annual meeting whereby it pronounced the transfer of the forest to the jurisdiction of the western provinces to be 'at the present time not in the public interest' and called for a sustained federal forestry effort even if the Department of the Interior was abolished.[13]

This public comment was to no avail; the situation grew even darker for the Dominion Forestry Service. Mackenzie King, happy with his success with Manitoba, moved to play a similar game in British Columbia. There the Railway Belt, actually owned outright by the Dominion government, ran through the heart of the province. Much of the area was largely inaccessible forestland which had not been taken up by the railways or for settlement. Several important forest reserves had been established in the belt, largely in the dry interior. The British Columbian government was interested in the return of the whole area, but a federal Royal Commission on the Reconveyance of Land to British Columbia had pointed out in 1928 that the province had no right to lands in the Railway Belt. King, however, was anxious to steal a march on the new Tory leader, R. B. Bennett. The Prime Minister felt that the federal government had little use for the Railway Belt and that compensation was not a problem since not much land had been alienated. Thus this area and the Peace River Block became, for him, a gift through which he could simultaneously reduce federal expenditures and purchase some political goodwill from the provincial Tory administration of Premier Tolmie.

If the Dominion Forestry Service was to make a stand it would be with the British Columbian lands where there was no doubt of the federal government's legal control of any area it wished to retain. But, the prospects were not good as the political game whirled on. D. Roy Cameron briefed his Deputy Minister, W.W. Cory, in preparation for a trip to British Columbia to discuss possible bases for a transfer agreement. Using the American idea that the reserves could serve as timber banks of young trees which would be available for use in thirty to forty years, Cameron pleaded for areas that would be guaranteed under federal control to be "cropped" and not "mined" for timber. He contended that the primary role of the national forests was to provide a resource base for the future. To drive home the point, Cameron included a document entitled "Statement of Forest Service, Department of Interior re proposed reversion of natural resources in Railway Belt of British Columbia". This document made three points. First, it indicated that both the federal and provincial forest authorities agreed that the present reserves should remain and that turning them over to British Columbia would be placing a considerable burden on a province with a limited population. Second, federal forests were needed for research and demostration purposes if sustained yield of timber was ever to be achieved in the country. Third, an attempt was made to define the national interest in west coast reserves. Cameron pointed out that British Columbia had over half the remaining forest in the nation and thus was richly endowed. Protecting this vast and vital resource was, for the present, beyond the capability of the province, and it should therefore be viewed as a resource of national importance.[14]

These arguments seemed to have had some impact on the process of negotiations. By May, 1929, Cory was requesting from Cameron information about local support for federal forest reserves in British Columbia and exact data on which area or areas it would be deemed essential to preserve. The Service was able to quote from correspondence from both the Hon. Nelson S. Lougheed, then provincial Minister of Public Works, and from the New Westminster Board of Trade to support its cause. In October, 1929, events had moved favourably forward to the point where the departmental Solicitor for the Department of the Interior had been instructed to draw up a special forestry section for the agreement regarding the transfer of the Railway Belt. The basis of this section was that the province of British Columbia would agree to federal control of four national forests: Shuswaps, Niskonlith, and Larch Hills forest reserves and a new area between Harrison Lake and the north arm of Burrard Inlet. These would, in part, contribute to a future timber supply for the western provinces and provide areas for applied silvicultural and other types of research. Just as important, the agreement indicated that the federal government would assume responsibility for forest research in British Columbia, there being an amalgamation of federal and provincial research organizations under an advisory board. Finally, all other forestlands were placed under provincial control subject to Dominion needs for other national forests, the total area not to exceed the original land area of the Railway Belt. This agreement in principle was crucial to the Dominion Forestry Service.[15] When these drafting notes were subsequently incorporated in an actual draft transfer agreement document, there was added to them the responsibility of the federal government for two research stations in British Columbia, one on the coast and the other in the interior.

Once again, all had been done without due regard to the imperatives of Canadian politics. By late 1929 it was evident that the agreement was falling apart. On the broad front, the final negotiations for a resource transfer agreement with Manitoba were completed, and this agreement was signed. The only mention of forestry was a federal admonition that Manitoba provide a proper forestry service for the care of the forest resource. With another federal election expected in 1930, the Prime Minister was showing signs that he had no patience with protracted bureaucratic endeavours at saving the forest reserves, especially if these might, even remotely, upset a province like British Columbia or commit the federal government to new expenditures. The original agreement was clearly not going to be implemented when R. M. Brown, Head of the Forest Products Laboratory in Vancouver, wrote to E. H. Finlayson on 13 January 1930 to offer condolences to him for "recording [his] convictions" on the matter but concluding that "it looks now that our case is hopeless as far as retention of [sic] reserves is concerned". The man coming to Ottawa to complete the transfer agreement, Brown reported, was the same Hon. Nelson Lougheed who had once championed the federal presence in British Columbia.[16]

The federal Liberals moved quickly to consummate the agreement with British Columbia, and King was disappointed only in the fact that Alberta and Saskatchewan still refused to take advantage of the "generous" federal terms. Premier Brownlee of Alberta wished for better terms and thought he could secure them through his own Royal Commission. Thus, settlements with Alberta and Saskatchewan, where the irascible Tory, Dr. W. Anderson, had been elected Premier in 1929, dragged on into R. B. Bennett's new Conservative administration elected 28 July 1930. The final agreements, signed by R. B. Bennett in 1933, did nothing to reverse the dismantling of the western reserves. Mackenzie King took credit for the resource transfer agreements even though he was in opposition when the agreements were signed.[17]

The wisdom of the overall transfer cannot be doubted or criticized. The West had been settled, and there was no reason to treat these provinces on a different constitutional basis than any of the others. Unfortunately, in the case of forestry, there was a lack of vision, understanding, and, it must be added, competence. The example of American initiatives was amply put before the politicians, and the promise of a creative federalism in this area was examined extensively. Both the Forestry Service and the limited public criticism concerning the matter warned that some federal forestland would be needed in the future and that the government was not being responsible in giving it all away. This is, indeed, precisely what had happened by the mid–1930s. In failing to take up the opportunity offered by British Columbia, King walked away from any strong central role for a national forestry policy. In doing so, the Liberal administration immeasurably damaged public forestry in Canada. It was to be twenty years before the damage done in 1930 was begun to be undone.

The major problem facing the Dominion Forestry Service, after the resource transfer agreements became reality, was to satisfactorily redefine its role within fixed constitutional boundaries or face extinction. It was because of this new requirement that D. Roy Cameron detailed one of his staff, W. M. Robertson, to have a closer look at forest research in the United States. Robertson's report was presented in early January, 1930, just as the crisis over the resource transfer agreements was reaching a critical stage. The report indicated that the recently announced American system of forest experiment stations for each important timber growing area "might profitably serve as a guide for a research organization in Canada". Robertson also discussed the McSweeny-McNary Law which he called "the most comprehensive bill dealing with research that has ever been introduced".[18] Basically, the legislation underwrote a long-term programme of forest research which included soil, silvicultural, economic, and product research. Most important, however, the law confirmed the leadership of the United States federal government in forest research in cooperation with the individual states and, through advisory councils, private industry. Robertson called for seven experimental stations roughly matching both provincial areas and forest boundaries: Acadian, Quebec, Ontario, Manitoba, Saskatchewan, Alberta, and British Columbia. Building on this base, Charles Stewart announced in mid-February, 1930, that forestry research would indeed form an important part of the altered mandate of the Dominion Forestry Service after the transfer of the natural resources to the western provinces. Stewart evoked great hope in the forestry community in Canada when he compared the new federal role to that given to agricultural matters, where the Dominion offered research support and various subsidies to provincial agriculture.[19]

This alteration in mandate elicited from E. H. Finlayson a detailed paper entitled "Federal Forestry Functions after Transfer of the Natural Resources". The Director was careful to compare the proposed future functions with the current role of the Agriculture and Mines Departments in their fields. The mandate was broken into seven areas. The first area was silvicultural research which Finlayson contended his organization was already carrying out on a limited scale throughout the country. He pointed out that this was a natural field for federal forestry because the provinces had to, by necessity, engage primarily in forest protection and administration. It was pointed out that the only province to engage in silvicultural research was British Columbia which did not have the resources to undertake proper work in this field and now "emphasizes the need for the conduct of such work by the federal authority [while] . . . [o]ther provinces, also, have urged an extension of federal activities within their domain".[20]

The second item was a logical extension of the first—the establishment of forest experiment stations and demonstration forests. These stations, located in representative forest types, would carry on field work concerning unique regional forestry problems. Only one station actually existed at that time, at Petawawa.

The third item was forest products research. Long recognized as a federal responsibility, the existing laboratories were to be continued to benefit the development of the country's forest industries.

The fourth field of activity was the national inventory of forest resources. This project originated with the Dominion-Provincial Forestry Conference held in 1929. As it stood, it was a cooperative effort with the older provinces undertaking the surveys and the Dominion compiling and maintaining the statistics and setting standards. The Service had, however, promised to survey the prairie provinces and was obligated to complete it. Further, Finlayson pointed out, the Service had been involved in cooperative studies of growth and yield, and, thus, the inventory was an essential practical base for forestry to develop in Canada.[21]

The next three responsibilities were of a more technical nature. They included forest protection (investigation into fire-fighting standards, weather forecasting, and insect and disease prevention) where the role was to spur on the provinces and provide support. Studies on forest mensuration, working plans, and forest economics and utilization were intended to aid industry, help ease shortages in raw materials so that declining sectors could be improved, and promote private forestry to encourage better care of farm woodlots and continued farm tree planting especially on the prairies. Finally, the Forestry Service saw itself performing a policy role for the federal government in regard to forestry affairs, including conservation methods, welfare of the forest industries, and implementation in Canada of international scientific ideas and standards in the field.[22]

Unfortunately, Stewart's influence with the government was no greater than it been earlier, and Finlayson once again found there was a great deal of difference between planning and execution in defining a new federal forestry programme. The resources transfer had largely eliminated the Service's field force in western Canada. This occasioned the Deputy Minister of the Department of the Interior, Cory, who was eager to serve the Liberal's cost-cutting objectives, to suggest that headquarters staff be reduced as well. Finlayson, as Director, countered that his organization had been decentralized and that the field staff received only limited support from headquarters. As well, he pointed out, all headquarters staff were needed to carry out the new duties involved with the research function, particularly silvicultural research and economic investigations which had not been given a high enough priority in the past because of the lack of time of the existing staff. This argument was useless in any case because the reality was that the government intended to cut the Service, to halve its original staff if possible. Federal forestry was in deep trouble.[23]

It was this staff matter, behind which Finlayson perceived the hand of Liberal politics grooming conditions for the July, 1930, election, which brought to the surface the tension and brittleness that sapped the morale of the Service in the wake of the resource transfer agreements. The Liberals' decision had cut to the quick one of the most idealistic and professional services within the federal bureaucracy. As well, there was an immense amount of work to be done, particularly by Finlayson, as the Natural Resources Royal Commission delved into a myriad of transactions, activities, and policies stretching back to 1905. This involved days of testimony before the Commissioners and provincial counsellors as well as detailed written defences of federal policies. It fell most often to the Service to defend the whole of federal timber administration, including that of the Timber, Mines and Grazing Branch which the Service had so often condemned as inept, unenlightened, and, at times, outrightly corrupt. What Finlayson found most infuriating was the way in which former Dominion Crown Timber Agents, taken on by the various provincial forest administrations in western Canada, fed the provincial counsel questions drawn from their own experience. The steady questioning proved to be a difficult and acrimonious experience for Finlayson, who had a quick temper and had by this time completely run out of patience.[24]

Under this type of pressure, senior officials in the Forestry Service were not disposed to react positively to political procrastination by Cory on behalf of the King government. As early as 25 April 1930, Finlayson had pointed out that in Manitoba, Saskatchewan, and Alberta it was necessary to retain two forest rangers each for his proposed research station projects. He was shocked to find out that, in Manitoba at least, the formation of a provincial forest service under the direction of Col. H. I. Stevenson, an old foe, was being helped by his staff while they were still being paid out of the Dominion accounts. Finlayson's anger at this state of affairs was increased by Cory's suggestion that "perhaps it would be better to leave the matter until after the election". Prevented from acting, Finlayson fully documented his case then lashed out at his Deputy Minister immediately after the 1930 federal election which Mackenzie King lost. In this memorandum, Finlayson went beyond the bounds of decorum, lecturing his superior:

I have, of course, assumed that in the protection of the interests of the Department of the Interior, there would be a strong personal desire on your part to conserve the interests of the Forest Service which is a constituent of the Department. I sincerely hope, however, that your desire goes farther than that. I hope that it goes to the extent of desiring to conserve the interests of the Forest Service because of the work for which it stands, the work which it has done, and the work it still has to do if it be given but a fair opportunity.[25]

This outburst allowed Finlayson to vent his frustrations, but it did little to save his staff or to promote the research programme planned by the Service. Finlayson charged in July, 1930, that he still had not received "official indication of your attitude or the attitude of the Minister, other than numerous expressions of the Minister that we were to carry on with our research and investigative work".[26] Cory made no move. He was now moribund, sure to be replaced by a Tory appointee and unwilling to push any policies with vigour.

In order to gain for the Service a continuing role in forestry in Canada, Finlayson realized that he must influence the new Conservative government of R. B. Bennett. He had connections with the Tory establishment in Ontario through his half-brother William Finlayson, who was provincial Minister of Lands and Forests. Further, both the Director and Cameron saw some hope in the positive attitude of the new government toward research into the "economic life" of the nation.[27] This attitude certainly permeated meetings with the new Minister of the Interior, the Hon. Thomas Murphy, Member of Parliament for the Manitoba riding of Neepawa. By January suggestions were being made that, if approached, the Prairie Provinces would welcome federal support of forest research in their region. Robertson's plan for research stations was quickly revived, and the Service suggested in early 1931 that letters be sent, by Murphy, to the western provinces calling for a conference on the matter.[28]

Early 1931 was not a suitable time to propose an expansion of services. The Bennett government was bent on reducing government expenditures, and a new Deputy Minister, H. H. Rowatt, had been promoted to carry out this specific task. This policy was followed despite the Service's contention that the federal government budgeted $905,981 in 1931–1932 for forestry while the vote for agriculture was $9,802,985 and for mines, $1,435,810. At a bare minimum, the Service pleaded, their appropriation should at least equal the status given to agriculture and mines because of the economic importance of the woods industry to the nation. Despite the amassing of an impressive array of statistics to support this claim, expansion was not allowed. Forestry's estimates were scaled downward but, in spite of closing offices in Winnipeg, Calgary, and Kamloops, there was hope that agreements might be signed with Saskatchewan and British Columbia to open experimental stations in these provinces. The first session of Parliament under the Bennett administration passed without Murphy's making any decision on this matter. The priority of the government remained fiscal restraint and reduction of the civil service. Regardless, Finlayson sensed that the Tories would soon have to create employment programmes to counter the searing disaster of the depression. He saw forestry and general conservation work as one possible type of relief measure and was wise enough to remind Rowatt and Murphy that "the Forestry Service absorbed all of the forestry functions of the Conservation Commission, and has enlarged, improved and consolidated that work". Politic as such a reminder might be, its time had not yet come. Rowatt took the Department of the Interior through one more round of budget cutting in the financial year 1932, and an additional 54.5 person years were forced out of the Dominion Forestry Service. This serious reduction removed twenty permanent positions from the staff and seemed to indicate that the plans made since the transfer of the natural resources had come to naught. By the end of 1932, the Service had been reduced to about 30 percent of its 1924 level and was performing a minimal caretaker role.[29]

The severity of this cutback of the federal Service prompted several provincial foresters, the Canadian Society of Forest Engineers, and a number of university foresters, including Dr. Clifton D. Howe, Dean of Forestry at the University of Toronto, to urge the Minister of the Department of the Interior to "advocate better support for the Dominion Forest [sic] Service" and to seek national leaderhip in the field.[30] The effort, surprisingly, had a salutary effect showing that broad representation was the key to preserving and promoting initiatives in forest conservation. The Bennett government was ready, in early 1932, to commence some consideration of new programmes, especially when they might be classified as relief work. But the government was still very constitutionalist in its approach and did not wish to encroach on provincial rights. The idea of a conservationist programme, as suggested by Finlayson, appealed to Murphy but he was not sure of the scope of federal jurisdiction in this area. Throughout 1932, therefore, the senior officials at the Department of the Interior conducted a detailed review of federal powers in the field of conservation.[31]

When queried on the matter, Finlayson had no doubt about a federal role in forestry and, in a policy paper entitled "Forestry as a National Problem," emphasized Sir Robert Borden's views, expressed in 1909, of "the necessity for consistent steps to take stock of the timber situation in this country . . . [and] the absolute necessity of thoroughly investigating the forest resources of the Dominion with a view to the development and application of rational methods of management".[32] Further, the Director referred to the twelve years of work done by the Commission of Conservation to "enlighten public opinion with respect to forests and natural resources and the fact that, upon the abolition of the Commission, its responsibilities had been transferred to various government departments, including Interior". Considerable progress had been made in the past twenty years at both the provincial and federal levels in placing the forest services on a footing that emphasized more careful and conservative approaches to timber harvesting, but, Finlayson contended, fire protection and timber sales operations had been emphasized and little staff or money had been left over for investigative work. The Depression and the efforts of governments to balance budgets had blunted even this work when support was absolutely necessary to "the evolution of better methods of forest management". Naturally, the Director ended his missive with a plea that

the Dominion's forestry business cannot be left entirely to the highly individualistic efforts of some eight provincial services. . . . The acquisition and practical application of basic data regarding the extent, growth, utilization and wastage of Canada's forest resources are absolutely essential to the prosperity of the Dominion, and there is no manner in which this requirement can be met other than through the operation of a strong and well-supported forest service in the federal administration.[33]

In this document, Finlayson stressed the work of the Forestry Service outside of administering federal forests. The work of the forest laboratories, the initiation and development of silvicultural research, the launching of the National Inventory of Forest Resources, and the assumption of the work of the Commission of Conservation were marshalled to justify an expanded role for the Service in forest research to replace forest protection and timber administration, responsibilities it no longer had. It was the question of which responsibilities had been taken over from the Commission by the Service that most intrigued Rowatt and Murphy. They wanted to know if a research role in forestry could legally be attached to a federal body. While this seems stilted and overly cautious today, the question of constitutional authority was less fluid and more formal in the 1920s and 1930s than after World War II. At any rate, the long-serving Roy Gibson, Assistant Deputy Minister of the Interior, who seemed able to survive every political turn of events, asked his departmental solicitor for advice on federal responsibilities toward conservation. A positive reply came in the fall of 1932, which was reasonably unequivocal and was based on the powers that had enabled the creation of the Commission of Conservation itself.[34]

Further, the solicitor was of the opinion that the National Research Council Act of 1924 was meant to extend the scientific research being carried on federally and not to subsume research responsibilities already being carried out. Thus, neither the British North America Act nor other laws restricted forest research by the Department of the Interior if it chose to do any. This legal opinion served as the basis for a major departmental policy paper entitled "Conservation in Canada" which called for expansion of the federal role in the conservation and utilization of natural resources. In this instance, the ultimate objective was to enable economic recovery with a thorough knowledge of the country's resource base and, more important, knowledge about proper management. The paper also suggested that an extensive publicity campaign be undertaken to mould public opinion in support of conservation measures much as had been done in the United States since Pinchot's time.[35] The objective of the departmental policy effort was to secure federal-provincial cooperation in conservation through a National Conservation Council which would be similar to the National Research Council, embracing the university community and serving as an advisory body. The actual work was to be performed by federal and provincial departments until a formal organization was established. Nothing appears to have come from this idea of the National Conservation Council as a tool in the recovery and refurbishing of the Canadian economy in the 1930s. Nevertheless, the seeds sown by these ideas were to bear fruit during and after World War II. For the moment, however, the only example the Bennett administration gave to the provinces was one of fiscal restraint.

While it is not correct to suggest that the provinces slavishly followed the federal lead in paring back their forestry administrations, it is fair to say that neglect and underfunding led to the same end. As we have seen in previous chapters, Quebec, New Brunswick, and British Columbia all ceased to expand their forestry services in the late 1920s. Staff was spread more thinly, and, as early as 1924, all these provinces were looking to the federal government for some sort of financial support for forestry endeavours.

In 1933 the Bennett government first showed signs of breathing new life into federal forestry. The Minister of the Interior accepted the idea of a research role for the Forestry Service. During 1933, the same year that the Civilian Conservation Corps was set up in the United States, a new start was made in federal forestry work, basing its rationale on the need to carry on investigations of a "broadly regional", "extra-provincial", or "Dominion-wide" scope similar to that occurring in agriculture and mining. An experimental silvicultural research area was established near Fredericton, New Brunswick, with the cooperation of the provincial government. At the same time, agreement was reached with the Department of National Defence for a portion of the Valcartier military reserve in Quebec to be used for similar purposes, and the Province of Manitoba assigned part of the Duck Mountain Forest Reserve to the federal government for similar purposes. Finally, negotiations were opened with the British Columbian government for establishment of a similar base station in the coastal forest area. These were completed in 1934.[36]

In developing these stations full advantage was taken of unemployment relief projects operated by the Department of National Defence. Labour from this source was used to build roads, trails, buildings, and other improvements and also to undertake tree planting and experimental logging work. The defence camps had become odious to many workers by the time of the "On to Ottawa Trek" in 1935, and cooperative federal-provincial forestry camps in British Columbia were cancelled by mutual agreement between Pattullo and King in 1938. Nevertheless, in the same year, recommendations from the National Employment Commission concerning forest conservation projects were implemented by the federal government. This programme continued through to the beginning of World War II, emerging eventually with the title of the National Forestry Programme. Beginning purely as relief work on the various stations, the Service soon realized that if it was going to get the best use out of the men sent to them, especially in silvicultural and other experimental areas, some training would be required. Consequently, short courses were organized; by 1939, these courses had evolved into a youth training programme, run by the National Parks and the Dominion Forestry Service.[37]

At the same time, some progress was again made on the National Inventory of Forest Resources. During 1933 a special bulletin on the forests of Manitoba was published and some additional survey work was done, especially in New Brunswick.[38] Unfortunately, even this limited progress was not continued because of government restraint and no more activity was undertaken until after World War II. The same constraints were placed on a number of other projects. Limited amounts of work were done on silvicultural research at Petawawa and also in the provinces through cooperation with provincial forest services. These research projects had been protected and maintained by the Service through the budget-cutting exercise, but in 1933 there was only a faint glimmer of hope for any growth in these areas.

Finlayson started 1934 in a less than optimistic mood. In reality, time was passing him by. He had weathered a tremendous storm with the transfer of natural resources and the budget-cutting exercise under the new Bennett administration. The Director's stance was now at once both defensive and aggressive. In early 1934 he recorded his own thoughts on the state of forestry in Canada. It was to be his last major statement on the matter before his presumed suicide in February, 1936. The statement was made with the conviction that always pervaded Finlayson's writing, but now it also exuded a heightened radicalism with regard to proposed solutions. Finlayson could not comprehend why lumbermen in Canada did not see that it was to their advantage to maintain an adequate and accessible supply of timber close to their mills. The "destructive logging" that was the norm in Canada was both an economic and social detriment to the country. He claimed that

sawmills have to some extent followed the timber, leaving behind deserted villages, impoverished settlements and devastated lands. Pulp and paper mills . . . cannot be so readily moved to new locations, and the pulpwood must be transported for increasing distances. If Canadian forest industries are to continue as an important factor in world trade, adequate timber supplies must be readily available; the more accessible forests must be kept permanently in a state of systematic and continuous production. In Canada, we are prone to boast of the wisdom of our forefathers in having retained to such great extent in public control the ownership of forest lands. Probably in no other country had this feature so strongly characterized the administration of timber lands. Nowhere in the world were opportunities so favourable for a reasonable and orderly regulation of the development of forest industry. The debacle of the last ten years (it was well under way before even a thought was given to the depression) is of itself abundant evidence of the extent to which real opportunities were lost.[39]

Finlayson blamed much of the problem on overdevelopment of the forest sector by the "ingenious promoter whose most alluring argument was that capital outlay would be amortized within a relatively short period of years". Finlayson charged that speculation and mass overproduction in most regions pulled mills—old and new—into bankruptcy. Nothing was done either in the expansionary state or at the time of collapse to safeguard the essential forest resource.[40] He contended that ownership of the forest resource implied a "public trust" to use it "wisely and providentially", but in casting his eye across Canada Finlayson saw little to praise in "regulative control by government authority". Rather he charged that

The past generation has shown all too clearly what can happen to a highly destructible resource, and to the industry founded upon it, when private endeavour is allowed almost untrammelled way. The ownership of timberlands remains still with the people, and it is greatly to be desired that the present generation will witness the calling into legitimate play the regulative functions which are reserved to the State. For thirty, forty or even fifty years, timber licences and leases have contained clauses which imply at least the elements of forest conservation, but all too rarely have they been enforced.[41]

Finlayson, never reticent about publicizing his views, had this article published in *Saturday Night* in late 1933, but it accomplished little.

The challenge now facing the Forestry Service was not to embark on plans to reform the Canadian capitalist system but rather to find the forebearance to practice conciliation. Finlayson's ideas were born of desperation and a sense of powerlessness. He no longer had the mental resources and patience to begin over again the mammoth task of reestablishing the essential axis between forest conservation and industrial development. It had become unstuck in the late 1920s, and there were only vague signs in the mid–1930s that the axis might be rebuilt. For that matter, the Bennett government itself was running out of momentum. Its members were frustrated by the Prime Minister's egotistical domination of all affairs and the simple inability of traditional remedies to have any effect on economic conditions. As Bennett himself turned to his "New Deal" in preparation for the 1935 federal election, forestry officials took a much lower profile and attempted to consolidate the few gains that they had made to that date.

The Service's position was that the key to successful Dominion-provincial cooperation had been amply demonstrated in the Forest Protection Conference of 1924 and the Conference on the National Inventory of Forest Resources held in 1929. They contended that any federal forestry and forestry research programme should build from this base. Officially, the Service advocated a government policy which entailed

(1) the urgent need of the collection and coordination of [inventory and research] data; (2) investigation and research in various phases of forest activities; (3) the standardization of methods of handling and utilizing the timber resources of the Dominion; and (4) that for the attainment of these objectives, a strong and virile Forest Service in the Federal Administration was a paramount necessity.[42]

To secure support for this proposal, the Dominion Forestry Service sponsored, at the official and political levels, a campaign to secure general agreement on their programme. This was initiated under the Bennett administration, and Minister of the Interior Murphy began to contact provincial ministers responsible for forest resources, promoting new federal initiatives in forest research. Such approaches supported the existing Conservative initiative with the new experimental stations.[43]

The defeat of the Bennett government in the summer election of 1935 threw all these carefully laid plans into limbo. Mackenzie King was returned to power, and Thomas A. Crerar became the minister responsible for the Forestry Service. Crerar, a Winnipeg businessman and a former Progressive, was laissez-faire in both his economic and social views and, perhaps most important, a strict constitutionalist as far as federal and provincial rights and powers were concerned. Potentially, this boded ill for the Forestry Service's quiet efforts to garner support for federal-provincial cooperation in the forestry field. Crerar became preoccupied with the King administration's reorganization plan, which included abolishing the Department of the Interior and replacing it with a proposed Ministry of Mines, Resources and Colonization. This appeared to make the Minister, at least at first, more pragmatic toward the forestry efforts of his department. He contacted his provincial compatriots and received an enthusiastic response in January, 1936, from W. F. Kerr, Saskatchewan's Minister of National Resources. Kerr saw no hinderances at all to Dominion-provincial cooperation in forestry.[44]

Not all provinces were as enthusiastic as Saskatchewan. The Western and Maritime provinces basically welcomed federal initiatives, although British Columbia was most supportive at the official level but more ambivalent at the political level. The same was true of Quebec, but it grew to be much less cooperative when Maurice Duplessis was elected in 1936. Ontario, under Mitch Hepburn, adamantly refused to even correspond on the matter and simply added this to the other list of grievances it was compiling against the King government.

Normally, Crerar might have been discouraged from pursuing the forestry issue with this mixture of support, but another vital element came into play which made the King government more persistent in its efforts. The Liberals had no magic solution for the Depression any more than had the Tories. Their election slogan had been "King or chaos", but they had not produced any detailed plan on how Liberal policy would pull the country back to prosperity. They simply let Bennett destroy himself and, after achieving power, submitted most of the former Primer Minister's "New Deal" legislation to the Supreme Court to determine its constitutionality.

From this basis then, it did not appear that the King government was a powerful instrument for exploring new cooperative federal-provincial initiatives. First appearances were somewhat deceiving. The reason for the cabinet's interest appears to have been based on the fact that the forest industries, after several years of neglect and economic catastrophe, began to interest themselves once more in forestry policy, linking it to a recovery strategy.[45] When the Woodlands Section of the Canadian Pulp and Paper Association and the Canadian Society of Forest Engineers met in their annual meeting at the Petawawa Experimental Station in July, 1935, several members of the Lumbermen's Association and the provincial forest services were included. At this meeting, earnest consideration was given to holding a conference to be attended by representatives of all interests concerned. This suggestion was brought to the attention of the National Research Council under the presidency of Major General A. G. L. McNaughton. The Council took a lead in the matter on behalf of the federal government.[46]

The Conference on Forestry Research was convened in Ottawa on 26–27 November 1935 under the general auspices of the National Research Council and with the sponsorship of the Hon. W. D. Euler, the Minister of Trade and Commerce and the Chairman of the Cabinet Committee on Scientific Research, and Crerar's as Minister of the Interior. The federal delegation to the conference included representatives from the Departments of the Interior and Agriculture and, of course, from the Council itself. Finlayson and Cameron were present, along with R. D. Craig, Roy Gibson, and J. D. B. Harrison. Also present were chiefs of the provincial forest services, representatives of the universities with forestry schools, and men from the lumber, pulp and paper, and allied industries.[47] A number of papers were read, including a lively presentation by A. Koroleff, forester and manager of the Woodlands Section of the Canadian Pulp and Paper Association. This highly critical piece charged that, because European forestry traditions were not strong in Canada and because forest research, particularly soils research, was virtually nonexistent, there was little, if any, hope of setting up an effective forest management system on anything approaching a sustained yield basis. Koroleff contended that research was the basis of all true forestry and that this superstructure had to be developed before the latter discipline could hope for success. Both Cameron and Finlayson jumped to defend the forest research work undertaken up to that point by the Dominion Forestry Service and stressed that silvicultural work should not be suspended until other research caught up. Both agreed that not enough was being done: Cameron pointed out that the Service had had its budget slashed from $1,500,000 in 1929 to about $325,000 after 1930 as a consequence of the

transfer of the natural resources and budget cutting by the Bennett government; Finlayson urged cooperation among federal and provincial forestry
programmes to pool research already completed and to plan new projects.[48]

In this manner, the problems and future needs for forest research were
probed. The Conference eventually unanimously adopted a resolution urging
the establishment of an Advisory Committee on Forestry under the National
Research Council. The Service seemed to accept this leadership from the
Council because of its higher profile and because, rather than undertaking
the research, the Associate Committee would serve as a coordinating body
through which the activities of the various agencies engaged in forest research
could be coordinated. The Council's role was to give all researchers access
to a wider variety of opinion from different sources and to identify problems
that should be tackled.

The Committee, set up by the Council at the close of 1935, met annually
thereafter. It had an executive body which guided its overall activities. In
its early days, this body consisted of McNaughton, Cameron, D. A. and
J. A. Gillies (lumbermen from Braeside, Ontario), Dr. C. D. Howe of the
University of Toronto, Howard Kennedy of the E. B. Eddy Company,
Koroleff, W. A. E. Pepler of Canadian International Paper, Ellwood Wilson
of Laurentide Paper, and Dr. J. M. Swaine, Director of Research, in the
Department of Agriculture. These gentlemen had an Ottawa and an Ottawa
valley bias, but their living close to one another enabled efficient and economical guidance of the larger committee, which had more than thirty members. It was the membership of this committee that gave it a more national
character.[49]

One of the Committee's main efforts during 1936 and 1937 was to promote
a Canadian Forestry Congress similar to the one sponsored by Sir Wilfrid
Laurier in 1906. This did not come to fruition, but important gains were
made on the research front, where subcommittees kept track of and promoted
research on such diverse topics as cut-over and burned-over lands, logging
methods, regeneration of Douglas fir, the training of forest soil experts, the
use of chemicals in fire prevention, water bombs, and the utilization of
hardwoods. The National Research Council also sponsored the publication
of such major forest research studies as K. M. Mayall's "White Pine Succession As Influenced by Fire", which finally began to explore the need for fire
in the regeneration of this species in eastern Canada. E. D. Euler later
claimed that the Associate Committee served the essential function of providing critical analysis of the practice of forestry in Canada, making suggestions for its improvement and recommending the appropriate agencies to
undertake particular research. It was also a unique instrument for teaching
Dominion, provincial, and industry officials the benefits of communication
and cooperation. For these reasons, it gave forestry in Canada a much needed

boost in the late 1930s and served as the foundation for the meetings and negotiations that eventually led to the Canada Forestry Act of 1949.[50]

While the Associate Committee was assisting in the continuation of federal forestry, elsewhere much was happening to keep supporters of forest conservation from becoming too optimistic. The King government was not about to accede completely to the wishes of the forest industries. It was determined to keep forestry in its place by adopting a strictly constitutionalist interpretation of the British North America Act. This attitude was best illustrated by the abolition of the Department of the Interior and the creation of a new Department of Mines and Resources in 1936. A major and long-held contention of both the Dominion Forestry Service and the forest industries was that the federal government should pay as much attention to forestry as to agriculture and more than to mining. In the organization of this new agency, Crerar proposed a number of branches, one of which was to be a Forestry and Water Power Branch. The Canadian Lumbermen's Association, for one, objected to this. It bluntly told the Minister that "the Dominion Government in the past has not done for the forest industries what might have been expected in view of their importance in Canadian domestic and export trade". The Association praised the assistance given them by the Forestry Service and pointed out that this should be upgraded into a national effort especially in forest research. In closing, the Association declared it wished to see the Service upgraded to divisional status.[51]

Crerar was unmoved. Neither he nor King had any intention of increasing the importance of forestry within the federal government, in spite of pressure from the powerful forest industries. The Service might be a useful research group, but it lacked credibility with men like Crerar, who saw forestry as an almost exclusively provincial responsibility. The apparently irrevocable decision to reduce the Service to subbranch status was taken early in 1936. Before it was made public, the decision had an immediate and terrible effect on the one man in Canada who cared most deeply and personally and who had worked the hardest for the health of the cause. On the morning of 26 February 1936, E. H. Finlayson, dressed as usual for a day's work in his office, left his house after saying farewell to his family and was never seen again.[52]

There are few people in Canada who have had as great a commitment to a cause as Finlayson had to forestry and forest conservation. It is therefore extremely hard to appreciate the strain and stress under which he had lived since the early 1920s. He was in the throes of a nervous collapse which was directly attributable to the reorganization. His health had been broken during 1923 when he had worked as Secretary to the Royal Commission on Pulpwood. Senior officials in the Department of the Interior admitted that exceptional strains had been placed on him during the crisis over the transfer of natural resources and the hours of testimony, justifying federal policies, that he had been required to give before the Natural Resources Commission. For fifteen years, Finlayson was the leading spokesman for forestry and forest conservation in Canada. His outspoken nature and strong leadership made him the closest equivalent Canada has had to Gifford Pinchot. It is a sad commentary on the nation and on its leaders that the high ideals Finlayson had brought to the Director's office in 1925, as a relatively young man, were to be cruelly dashed by the reality of Canadian politics, ending in a disappearance classed as a suspected suicide.

Finlayson's disappearance proved to be the low point in the modern history of forestry and conservation in Canada. Even as the cold, short days of February, 1936, lengthened into March, the King Liberals were slowly, very slowly beginning to tackle the problem of federal-provincial relations which lay at the base of many forestry problems in Canada. The commencement of the process of reorienting federal-provincial relations, which was to lead to the Rowell-Sirois Commission of 1937–1940, did not mean that the King government was about to embark on the elaborate cooperative arrangements that had marked forestry in the United States since the mid–1920s. Though the Service had major ambitions in this direction, the period leading to the events of February, 1936, had left it deeply scarred. The resources transfer question had forced a major redefinition of its mandate, and the budget restraints of the Depression period had significantly weakened its remaining programmes. Only the development of a skeletal group of experimental stations and the impetus toward coordination of research in the late 1930s coloured an otherwise unmitigated disaster. In the provinces, as well, forestry policy was in disarray and despair. The epitaph to Canadian forestry in the late 1920s and the 1930s belongs, perhaps appropriately, to the European-trained forester, Alexander Koroleff, and to the long-suffering D. Roy Cameron. Koroleff wrote in 1935 that

it would be difficult and probably even impossible to find another country with forests of such great economic importance as *ours* [Canada's], and a country standing on as high a level of civilization where generally available evidence of intelligent attention being given by those in high command to the problems of forest management and to a sound forest policy for the whole country, were so meagre.[53]

In a similar vein, Cameron reminded his political superiors in 1936:

There is undoubtedly a great need for real leadership in forestry affairs in this country. That leadership, to be effective, must come from sources much higher than any departmental officer . . . it is equally true that the remedy [to conflicting jurisdictions] can be alone in coordination and/or operation under Dominion auspices.[54]

A world war lay between the Canadian forestry and even a glimmer of hope for solutions to the problems described by Koroleff and Cameron.

CHAPTER 10

Optimism, Progress, and Misgivings: The Modern Era

The declaration of war in Europe in the fall of 1939 ended for a period the Forestry Service's campaign for a coordinated federal-provincial program in forestry and the King government's efforts at achieving a new federal-provincial constitutional balance. Instead, attention was switched to mobilization plans and organizing the country's economy so that vital strategic materials, including timber, could be produced. Production was the watchword, and, when the western front collapsed in June, 1940, a Timber Control Branch was set up in the Department of Munitions and Supply. It was a unit of the Wartime Industries Control Board of which the Timber Controller was a member. Its role was "to forestall chaos in the home timber market and to ensure that the flow of lumber urgently needed for war purposes in the United Kingdom would not be interrupted".[1]

The first Timber Controller, Harvey MacMillan, staffed his office with twenty-seven prominent members of the lumber industry, two members from the Dominion Forestry Service, and one member from the Department of Lands and Forests of British Columbia. The objective was to have men of broad practical experience, who could deal with matters without unnecessary friction and delays. This headquarters staff was supplemented by regional committees in Vancouver, British Columbia; Edmonton, Alberta; Winnipeg, Manitoba; and Saint John, New Brunswick. The most pressing issues facing the Controller were the maintenance of lumber shipments to the United Kingdom; the distribution of timber to Canada's own war building programmes, including the British Commonwealth Air Training Plan; and, finally, the promotion of timber exports to non-sterling countries to acquire urgently needed foreign exchange.[2]

Liaison was set up with agents of the British Timber Control to ensure that supplies and transport across the Atlantic were available. Canadian war building programmes were supervised directly by the Department of Munitions and Supply; the Timber Control Branch purchased the lumber. This meant that contractors bought supplies directly from the Branch and obtained delivery without delay. To maintain supplies, increasingly tight export restrictions were placed on west coast Douglas fir and hemlock. In spite of these precautions, acute shortages for fir plywood occurred during the war years. At the end of 1941, pulpwood operations were also brought under the Timber Control Branch with an Assistant Controller supervising this field. Eventually, exports of pulpwood to non-Empire countries was placed under a permit system.[3]

Up to 1942 the prime concerns of the Branch were the production and allocation of forest products. Shortages of materials meant that massive over-cutting of easily accessible forest stands occurred while the drain of manpower into the armed services and government emphasis on war financing bled already stretched provincial forest services of yet more manpower restricting their ability to carry on even rudimentary forest protection work. During 1942 MacMillan moved his Branch into managing wood exports and prices, having largely overcome the problems of procurement of timber. This raised the old question of federal support for provincial forestry programmes which was projected into discussions on the overall war effort and planning for post-war reconstruction.

Though war work had eaten greatly into the operations of the Dominion Forestry Service, especially into the time of Finlayson's successor as Director, Roy Cameron, its contacts with the provincial forest authorities made federal officials keenly aware of these problems. Having spent much of his time, since the mid–1920s, attempting to establish federal support of provincial forestry programmes, Cameron saw the opportunity and, as early as December, 1940, had his staff restate to senior officials within the Department of Mines and Resources, examples of federal-state cooperation in the United States. In particular, he had them refer to various pieces of American legislation, including the Weeks Law, the Clarke-McNary Act, and the McSweeny-McNary Act. Early in 1941, as the situation grew more desperate in provinces like British Columbia, the Prime Minister's own words issued in October, 1939, were used to introduce the question of federal aid. The Prime Minister had declared that forest utilization was an important part of the war effort but that it must take account of the fragile nature of the resource.[4]

On this basis, it was contended that British Columbia's forests were essential to the well-being of the national economy. It was estimated that the Dominion secured a total of $10,600,000 in tax revenue from this source and that the timber supply from the province was vital to Canada's and the United Kingdom's war effort. Further, Service officials argued that these supplies would continue to be tremendously important to national and world reconstruction in the wake of the war and that reforestation itself was vital to soil and river conservation in the West. Finally, it was pointed out that the Dominion had a direct interest in the national economy, and the "social security in British Columbia, based very largely on her forest industry, . . . is of value and importance to the Dominion as a whole".[5]

This missive was prepared in expectation of a letter from A. Wells Gray, Minister of Lands and Forests in British Columbia, to Thomas A. Crerar, the federal Minister of Mines and Resources, concerning possible assistance from the federal government for "the protection of the mature and growing forests from fire". The bottom line for Gray was that $1,000,000 per year was needed to provide the type of protection required and that the province was able to provide only $750,000. His proposal was that the Dominion government make a contribution of $250,000 to the forest protection fund of British Columbia "in view of the vital and diversified interest of the whole of Canada in this great resource".[6] This seemingly modest proposal was bolstered by a detailed memorandum from Denis Orchard, Provincial Forester. The most interesting part of Gray's letter was his statement that

the Federal interest in the forests of the individual states of the Union to the south has long been recognized by the well known "Clarke-McNary Act" under which contributions to state and private forestry are authorized up to fifty percent (50%) of the total expenditures. Our Federal Government has no less an interest and the case is here presented for your consideration.[7]

The letter also confirmed that federal and British Columbia officials had been in close contact on the proposal in an effort to infuse the politicians with a degree of cooperation. While British Columbia's request was to be rejected by the King government, the principles set out in Gray's letter were to have a tremendous impact when reconstruction planning began, and the federal government at last reassessed its role in resource development. British Columbia, itself, set about raising support for its cause by writing to other provincial forest authorities to solicit their help in getting federal contributions to forest protection activities using American examples of cooperative legislation. The whole was orchestrated in the limelight of the Liberal government's attempts to organize a Dominion-provincial conference to discuss the recommendations of the Rowell-Sirois Commission, released in 1940, for rebuilding the fiscal and constitutional basis of Confederation. A certain immediacy hung over this proposed meeting since the government had been informed that a number of provinces, especially on the prairies, were on the verge of defaulting on the interest payments covering their loans in spite of the fact that war was easing the nation's economic problems left over from the Depression. A reluctant Prime Minister was convinced by his Finance Minister, J. L. Ilsley, to go ahead with the conference assuring himself that "it will serve the advantage itself to the government at this time of war. It will lay the ground for such action as may shortly become imperative, and it should help to advance the necessary reforms by at least a step".[8]

King, convinced that a conference was going to accomplish little, was not prepared to commit his government to action by endorsing the recommendations of the Rowell-Sirois Commission. Surprisingly, T. A. Crerar was much more enthusiastic. He wanted the federal government to adopt an active stance rather than the "take it or leave it" position favoured by the majority of the cabinet. He feared that the Dominion would be blamed for any lack of progress. But, the Prime Minister stuck to his political instincts, which told him that Premiers Mitchell Hepburn of Ontario and William Aberhart of Alberta would attack him unmercifully if he adopted an interventionist position. Despite this uneasiness and reluctance, there did seem to be some hope for the conference. Premiers Bracken of Manitoba, Patterson of Saskatchewan, MacMillan of Nova Scotia, and Campbell of Prince Edward Island could be counted on to support the Dominion's efforts; Premiers Godbout of Quebec and McNair of New Brunswick were noncommital. Premier T. D. Pattullo of British Columbia was less enthusiastic than some of his ministers and officials, but he appeared to be willing to accept financial changes for the duration of the war if not of a permanent altering of constitutional powers. Thus, at the start of the Conference, only Hepburn and Aberhart were adamantly opposed to considering federal proposals.[9]

Once the federal and provincial politicians assembled in Ottawa, politics jumped to centre stage. Pattullo, wooed by Hepburn and Aberhart, joined the opposition to the Rowell-Sirois Commission report. Then Hepburn put on a one-man display characterized by one observer as "the god damnest exhibition and circus you can imagine". The Ontario Premier accused the federal government of foisting the Commission's report on the country to protect "certain bonds held largely by financial houses" and a day later accused the federal government of attempting to ram through changes "dressed...up with the garments of patriotism and cloaked...with the exigencies of war". These outbursts and Hepburn's refusal to meet in private, lest this signal an acceptance of the Commission report, led to incessant delays and difficulties.

At last, the conference called on Ilsley to address it in an initial preparation for any discussion of tax reform. King consented to this, and the Finance Minister discussed the financial distortions created by the war and the necessity to have a new fiscal arrangement so that economic prosperity could be assured in peacetime. He concluded bluntly, but with no hint of a threat, that, as Armstrong has paraphrased, "unless the report or some variant of it were adopted, the federal government would certainly take action which would reduce provincial revenues, such as raising the income tax or bringing in succession duties. Ottawa would no longer meet 40 percent of the cost of unemployment relief, and there would be no more advances to help the provinces meet bond maturities or cover declining revenues from liquor and gas taxes". In closing, the Finance Minister defended the federal government's method of proceeding; it had power to impose the new taxes uni-laterally but preferred to seek an agreement with the provinces.[10]

Ontario's strenuous objections to Ilsley's stand abruptly ended the Do-minion-Provincial Conference of 1941 for all practical purposes. With it went much hope of gaining any federal-provincial cooperation in forestry matters for some time. As E. H. Roberts, Saskatchewan Director of Forests, informed Dennis Orchard, "Since the collapse of the . . . Conference early this week in Ottawa, where there might have been a possibility of presenting the forest protection picture, it is apparent that the opportunity has passed or at least been postponed indefinitely".[11] The Prime Minister, publicly appearing to be distressed at the turn of events at the Conference, was secretly pleased. As he noted privately, "Far from being a failure, the conference has resulted in achieving beyond expectation the principle aim for which it was called, namely the avoidance of any excuse for protest on the part of provincial governments once the Dominion government begins, as it will be obliged very soon to do, to invade fields of taxation which up to the present have been monopolized in whole or in part by some of the provinces."[12] He might have added that an excellent excuse was created for the federal government to delay in underwriting any provincial programs.[13]

Despite its support for the British Columbia proposal, it is fair to say that the Forestry Service was not unhappy about the demise of action based on the Rowell-Sirois Commission's report. It was the opinion of D. Roy Cam-eron, in particular, that the Commission had put too much emphasis on forestry as primarily a provincial responsibility and that, as a consequence, any new arrangement might again delay cooperative action in managing the resource. In preparing for the Dominion-Provincial Conference of 1941, Cameron stressed to Roy Gibson, Director of the Lands, Parks and Forests Branch, and to Crerar that the "question should be handled on a cooperative basis" and had hoped that the conference would present an opportunity for a start.[14] Now that the conference had ended in a shambles, Cameron's main concern was that continued pressure be kept up for a general forestry policy based on federal-provincial cooperation. Cameron reminded his superior, Gibson, that Manitoba, as well as British Columbia, had had a proposal for financial assistance for forest protection. The Dominion Forester's recom-mendation was that the amount of $250,000 be placed in the supplementary estimates as the basis of a forest protection fund which would be disbursed through agreements with the provinces with Forest Service approval.[15]

When he sent this advice to Roy Gibson, the Dominion Forester sent along a paper entitled "Dominion Assistance in Forestry" which detailed how the cost-cutting of the Depression decade and now the war effort had, by several provinces' own admission, pushed forest protection, let alone forest regeneration plans, back to pre–1920 standards. He stressed the need for a simple forest protection contribution by the federal government which would be based on arrangements and agreements similar to those of the Clarke-McNary Act in the United States. In addition, Cameron was not loathe to promote a few potential federal projects like fire fighting on the eastern slopes of the Rockies where Alberta could not undertake the work and was asking the Dominion to assume responsibility since the watersheds being preserved affected all three Prairie Provinces.

Unfortunately, the King government felt that the failure of the conference discharged it of any obligation to aid the provinces in any way, especially in forestry which it contended was clearly their own responsibility. The Forestry Service soon received the political direction it had been seeking in the form of a copy of a reply from T. A. Crerar to A. Wells Gray in Victoria. The letter, drafted in the Minister's office, was a blunt statement of the current constitutional point of view from a government still smarting from Pattullo's defection to Hepburn in Ottawa. As Gibson laconically observed to Cameron, upon transmitting this letter to him, though the matter of federal aid had been taken up fully with Mr. Jackson, the Assistant Deputy Minister, the "whole situation has been complicated by the outcome of the discussion of the provincial authorities here on the subject of the report of the Sirois Commission". Gibson, ever the master of the obvious, also added that with the minister's present attitude he saw little opportunity of the matter's being taken up in the near future.[16] The Dominion Forester was, however, visibly angered by this blatant playing of politics and the outright neglect of his numerous submissions. He criticized both the tone of the letter and its twisting of the facts, pointing out that the Dominion had not run a Save-the-Forest campaign since 1928 though the letter indicated otherwise. "To turn around at this late date", Cameron lamented, "and tell the provinces we have been doing our part in this phase of forestry work would be humourous if it were not tragic". He further suggested rather strongly that "there is no question of the right of the Minister's Office to make decisions in matters of policy. However, this office is supposed to fill the role of technical adviser to the government on forestry matters. Is it too much to expect that we be allowed to check over important outgoing rulings to be sure that they accord with the facts?"[17] The Dominion Forestry Service did not expect the King government to accede to British Columbia's request, but Cameron feared a rupture in the careful relationship he had developed with provincial authorities in the hope that it might develop into a cooperative system.

Fortunately, for the future of Canadian forestry, Mr. Gray was neither to be so easily put off nor so ready to declare war on Ottawa. Writing to Crerar, he reviewed the efforts of British Columbia in forest protection. The Minister further informed his federal counterpart that "it was not until we had reached that limit that we approached the Dominion in the hope of securing some assistance to provide more adequate protection" and left the door open by urging Crerar to agree "in principle at least, that the matter is worthy of our joint consideration".[18] The federal Liberals, however, were not prepared in 1941 to be lured further into support for forestry. More than a year was to pass before the seeds sown by British Columbia were to bear fruit. The catalyst for action was the Canadian Forestry Association. The key to getting federal-provincial cooperation was paradoxically, Ontario.

On 5 March 1943 Robson Black, secretary to the Canadian Forestry Association, led a delegation to meet N. O. Hipel, Ontario's Minister of Lands and Forests. He suggested to Hipel that there was a tremendous need for an interprovincial conference on forestry and that Ontario should sponsor such a meeting. Three objectives were stated: (1) To clearly define federal and provincial responsibilities for forestry in Canada, (2) to have each level of government make a fair contribution toward a long-term policy, and (3) to lay down broad lines of a national forestry policy.[19] The Ontario Minister, who had been given his portfolio by Hepburn in order that he could bring effective forest administration to the province, picked up the suggestion of the Association and, quickly moving beyond the Premier's usually antifederal stance, invited all his provincial colleagues and their forestry advisors to convene in Toronto in mid-April. The intent of the gathering was to discuss problems and then move on to Ottawa with a "provincial" brief that would be presented to T. A. Crerar in an interview. Crerar was informed by Hipel that "the thought [was] that the federal government be asked to assist financing in forest protection and forest management along somewhat similar lines to the co-operative agreements now in force in the United States".[20] Once this Ontario initiative was presented, pressure from the forest industries began to mount on Ottawa; the Canadian Pulp and Paper Association and the Newsprint Association wrote to Crerar to support the calling of the conference and advocated "subventions from the Dominion Government" in "active cooperation with the Provinces in the essential task of protecting the forests from fire, insect infestation and similar hazards".[21]

Fate now took over just as arrangements for the conference seemed to be jelling. Crerar became ill and was hospitalized for an operation. Dr. Charles Camsell, Deputy Minister of Mines and Resources, informed Hipel that nothing was possible until early May. Hipel, himself, suggested Thursday, May 6, for an interview and on that date the provincial forest resources ministers gathered in Ottawa with their brief in hand. The interim period permitted the Dominion Forestry Service to marshall its plans for federal-provincial cooperation. These were crucial since they laid the basis for the forestry agreements which were signed in the postwar period. At long last, Crerar, himself, gave to the Dominion officials the framework from which to plan federal activities which had been missing since early in the Bennett years. Roy Gibson summarized this in the following way:

From what the Minister has said on the subject of forest conservation we know that he believes that it is the Dominion's responsibility to give leadership in forest conservation, which, after all, means that by the best known methods trees should be grown on lands best suited for that purpose, that they should be protected from fire, insects and disease, that these trees should serve for the protection of watersheds and to give shade and recreation to our people, that in due course they should be harvested and that the products derived therefrom should be utilized to the fullest possible extent and marketed to best advantage in the public interest so that work may be provided and our balance of trade maintained.[22]

It was motherhood but it was the closest Canada had, and perhaps has, ever come to a full-blown forestry policy, and it was infinitely better than Crerar's constitutionalist approach of 1941.

The Forestry Service used this framework to develop both a jurisdictional position for the upcoming meeting and a projects list for postwar forestry. There was a reaffirmation that the solution of forestry problems lay in co-operation among three parties: the federal and provincial governments and the private forest industries. Further, it was contended that continuous or sustained production required proper regulation of security of tenure of forest holdings, taxes, and stumpage and proper forestry principles. As was to be expected, the Dominion marked out for itself silvicultural research common to two or more provinces; research in forest products, entomology and pathology; market extension; and statistical and economic investigations. It also appropriated the old problem of watershed protection where two or more provinces were involved. A tremendously important new twist was added, however, with the proviso that, if the forest industry of a province was of outstanding importance to the country's export trade, Dominion assistance might be forthcoming. Finally, it was declared that a "national interest" existed in aiding all provinces with forest protection, inventory, and public education because they did not have "sufficient financial resources to make adequate provision". The end result was to have a plan that could be agreed to by both levels of government and the industry—a plan that would "operate continuously over a term of years" for the protection and management of the forest resource.[23]

In practical terms this would require strengthening the Dominion Forestry Service to carry out federal activities, starting with restaffing and equipping existing silvicultural research stations; adding new stations in Nova Scotia, Ontario, Saskatchewan, and British Columbia; and extending cooperative work with the provinces and industry on other lands. It also meant meeting Alberta's standing demand of over a decade for the Dominion to reassume forest protection and management on the eastern slope of the Rockies. There was also an immediate need to improve the techniques for producing inventory information. These and other projects were expected to demand a federal forestry appropriation of $1,960,000, of which $690,000 would go to the Service and $840,000 would be used to assist the provinces.[24]

This planning did not, however, signal a federal acceptance of the provincial point of view. Crerar was careful on 6 May 1943 to indicate that, while he did not disagree with the provincial brief, it would be impossible to divert funds from the war effort in "the immediate future". Instead, he stressed that now was the time for planning so that measures would be ready for implementation immediately on the cessation of hostilities. In regard to fire protection, Crerar promised aircraft and other war material after victory over the Axis had been secured. The Minister went on, nevertheless, to specify some conditions for federal participation. He thought that forestry projects in which the Dominion participated should be approved by the Dominion. Further, he indicated that such projects must be attached to an integrated approach with the reconstruction effort and mentioned reforestation and the eastern slopes conservation effort as suitable cooperative projects. Both he and Hipel agreed that it would be appropriate to carry out a joint federal-provincial planning effort to propose one overall scheme. Ontario was also anxious to entrench such a programme in legislation.[25]

Most provinces were insistent, however, that they needed essential fire protection assistance immediately. J. S. McDiarmid from Manitoba stated "The provinces are interested in the situation *now* as well as post-war— Manitoba does not like the idea of working out Dominion-provincial arrangements phase by phase". Saskatchewan, New Brunswick, and, of course, British Columbia, which was represented by a new Minister, Mr. Melrose, supported Manitoba, at least on the need for some immediate assistance.[26] Crerar, however, remained obdurate, insisting that money, equipment and personnel were in short supply thereby living up to King's determination not to move on anything approaching the Rowell-Sirois recommendations until after the war. The most the Minister would promise his provincial counterparts was that he would approach J. L. Ilsley, the Minister of Finance, concerning the possibility of immediate assistance in fire protection. As Crerar had been sure he would, Ilsley turned down any possibility of doing anything for forestry in 1943, using as the basis of his argument a strict constitutional approach, but promised reconsideration after the war.[27]

The problem, however, would not go away. The Canadian Society of Forest Engineers, the Canadian Pulp and Paper Association, and the Canadian Forestry Association kept up a barrage of criticism that manpower was in short supply for forest protection work, that there was a scarcity of trained leaders, and that wartime priorities cut the supply of necessary equipment. An added problem was the elimination of alternative service workers in British Columbia and growing budworm infestations in eastern Canada, especially in Ontario. Furthermore, these groups were anxious to know Ottawa's long range plans for forestry. This representation from the industrial and professional associations was tremendously important in bringing action. It marked the first time since the 1920s that this type of support was forthcoming in force to forestry. At last, it created a public lobby which was difficult for the government to ignore.[28]

The King government was interested in tackling the problem of forestry under the wider field of Conservation and Development of Natural Resources which was an agenda item for the proposed Dominion-Provincial Conference scheduled for the fall of 1944. In late July, 1944, the cabinet asked for detailed plans for the "financial and constitutional adjustments . . . necessary to carry out a desirable program" in this and in other resource development areas. These were to be broken down into those which were entirely a federal responsibility and those in which, over the years, the Dominion had carried out functions even though there had been some encroachment or overlapping with the provincial field.[29]

The conference was postponed until after the federal election of 1944, but preparation for it generated a number of off-the-shelf plans which were brought into operation in the period up to 1950. The Dominion government was finally recognizing that it benefitted greatly in tax revenues from the forest industries, that these industries contributed tremendously to the country's balance of trade, and that the federal government had a responsibility to maintain the health of Canadian forests for both their economic and their social values. When the conference was finally held in August, 1945, the government declared that:

It has been learned through experience that forests, far from being inexhaustible, are being seriously depleted. There is growing realization of the fact that if our forest industries are to exist and expand, the forest must be handled as a crop and not as a mine, in other words, must be managed on a sustained yield basis.[30]

The federal role was defined as promotion of forest conservation and better utilization and expansion of trade. Reference was also made to the report of the Subcommittee on the Conservation and Development of Natural Resources of the Advisory Committee on Reconstruction (Wallace Subcommittee) which had called for greater federal activity in forestry. This was particularly important because it recommended the passage of a Dominion Forest Act to give legislative authority to these activities and to the Dominion Forestry Service.

The Forestry Service, of course, was lobbying for increased appropriations for those areas that it considered to be largely under federal jurisdiction: silvicultural research, forest inventory compilation, products research, and fire protection research. These areas were viewed as complementary activities with the provinces which would lead to the development of a truly national forest policy—the Dominion meeting general needs and the provinces concentrating on local problems. All these programmes could be expanded from the restraint levels imposed by the Depression of the 1930s and the war effort. Also, the Service wished to resume the forest inventory project launched in 1929 but abandoned in 1931 because of lack of funds. Finally, the Service wanted to move into other fields, forgotten since the 1920s, including watershed conservation, soil classification, increased activities in promoting forest colonies in northern regions, and establishment of forest apprenticeships to train men for work in the forest industries and in forestry itself. This was really a revival of the National Forestry Policy that had been proposed two decades before with some modern facets added to suit the circumstances.[31]

These projects, to be carried out in cooperation with the Departments of Agriculture and Labour, reflected the broad social and economic approach of the reconstruction planning process. In addition to these projects were the other existing proposals to offer assistance to the provinces. The Wallace Subcommittee proposed a Forest Resources Rehabilitation Act to authorize financial assistance to the provinces for forest protection, insect and disease control, recreational developments, woodlot improvement, reforestation, publicity and education, and improvement of woodlands management. This proposal, which closely followed American examples first presented during the 1920s, was supported by the recommendations of the provincial ministers' conference of May, 1943.

No concrete action occurred, however, even for Dominion-controlled capital expenditure programmes, until 1945. The postponed Dominion-Provincial Conference was rescheduled for that year, and one topic to be emphasized was increased federal-provincial cooperation. In the ensuing negotiations, which lasted a considerable period of time, D. Roy Cameron, who had been seconded to the Department of Reconstruction and Supply, took a prominent part. Basically, the Dominion stated that it now wished to underwrite work in such areas as surveying, mapping, and forest inventories as it had in the years before the Depression. In the area of forestry, it was at last accepted "that no province . . . had an adequate forestry programme" and that wholesale reform was needed in all jurisdictions.[32]

Whereas Ontario had traditionally frustrated federal attempts at cooperation, after 1945 this mantle passed to Quebec which had to be repeatedly reassured that the Dominion proposals did not encroach on the province's rights to levy any taxation on resources that it might choose. Quebec, under Premier Maurice Duplessis, took a nationalist, pro-provincial rights stance and remained skeptical of federal suggestions throughout the Dominion-Provincial Conference, claiming that much of the work should be done by the provinces alone from their own tax-base. Nevertheless, the situation slowly progressed from the point of view of most provinces despite Quebec's doubts and refusals to cooperate. Great faith was placed by federal, and most provincial, authorities in a new Canada Forestry Act which would provide a clear definition of responsibility in forestry matters between the two levels of government.[33]

In late 1949, after a quarter century of debate and often thankless labour, an "Act Respecting Forest Conservation" was passed. Its common title was the Canada Forestry Act, and its cryptic nature gave little indication of what all the debate had been about. Yet, it sanctioned for the Dominion Forestry Service many of the responsibilities that Finlayson and Cameron had fought for over the years. It provided for national forests and forest experimental areas; it sanctioned the forest products laboratories; it enabled the federal government to offer assistance to provinces and private owners in protection and development of forestlands with a view to the conservation and advantageous utilization of forest resources; and, finally, the Act authorized negotiation of agreements with provinces for forest protection activities, inventories, silvicultural research and other forestry work. In short, the Canada Forestry Act was a high-water mark in the struggle for forestry and conservation in Canada.[34]

In spite of the Act, federal forestry initiatives remained dependent on the two other players in the field, the provincial authorities and the forest industries. Fortunately, various provinces were attempting to put their forestry houses in order in cooperation with their private sectors. The reasons behind this renewed interest in forestry were threefold and related. First, the depression years had resulted in personnel reductions and the deterioration of equipment. Second, these trends had been accompanied by severe overcutting of timber to support the war effort. Provincial reconstruction studies had commented on the fragility of the forest resource base and the need for its careful management if it was to support new industrial and economic growth in the postwar years. In turn, the forest industries were becoming concerned that wood shortages might curtail business expansion. Thus, a third factor, industry, began to pressure provincial governments to support forest management and to ensure that adequate planning was applied to the forest resource problem. Provincial foresters suddenly saw the neglect they had experienced through the 1930s evaporating and found themselves surrounded by politicians and businessmen who seemed to have been converted to the idea of sustained yield management. In fact it was a chimera, a new aspect of the old corporate-political game to gain access under secure tenure arrangements to new timber supplies in return for substantial increases in the revenues paid to provincial governments. But in the 1940s the commitment appeared to be real, and it seemed that true forestry and forest conservation would come of age in Canada.

It was, in fact, this support for new, progressive forestry measures from the forest industries that disposed provincial governments to treat forest resource management more generously. Lambert and Pross speculate that timber management controls were successfully implemented in Ontario during this period because both the provincial government and its foresters were sure they could move forward "without fear of disrupting the forest industries".[35] Indeed, such controls were welcomed by the woodlands corporations as part of a management package underwritten by tax dollars to ensure a continuous supply of trees for their mills. The forest industries were plagued after 1945 by their traditional fears about timber supplies and stability of tenure. Looking abroad to other jurisdictions and listening to the arguments made by forestry experts since 1900, they began to better comprehend that forestry and lumbering or pulping were not mutually exclusive occupations, indeed, the former could be used to improve the business conditions and efficiency of the latter. It was a lesson that a portion of their industrial forebears had understood earlier in the century but which had been lost in the tangled political and business paths of the 1920s and 1930s.

Of course, the support of the forest industries for forestry measures forced upon provincial politicians in New Brunswick, Quebec, Ontario, and British Columbia, in particular, hard decisions about how to regulate the use of the forest resource, promote desired industrial growth, and plan for sustained yield, all at the same time. In this period, most provinces adopted some form of public or Crown working circle combined with long-term licences or agreements. The first type of arrangement is pure public forestry. The government service assumes responsibility for all protection and management activities and costs. Such leasing of timber is usually for a short period of time, usually with an annual renewal. In theory, public maintenance costs are included in the upset price for the lease. Under these arrangements the government theoretically retains full authority to control the use of the forest and the land on which it is located. This system is an outgrowth of the traditional nineteenth century timber berth but has, in modern times, been largely restricted to smaller operators usually as a flexible timber allocation tool for situations where mills are suffering from timber shortages. Large forest operations have tended to dislike this public leasing system because they feel it does not answer their concerns about the acquisition of wood supplies obtained through long-term stable prices negotiated in advance. During the postwar period, the larger, politically influential forest corporations approached provincial governments for special areas to be assigned to their firms. In a sense, it was a return to the old Gatineau privilege granted to George Hamilton and his associates in the 1830s, though it must be said that governments attempted to impose forestry requirements on the new arrangements.

These long-term leases, such as the forest management licence (tree farm licence) recommended by the Sloan Commission in British Columbia in 1945 and enacted by the provincial government and the long-term agreements more recently introduced by Ontario, have been aimed at consolidating supplies of raw material. At the same time, the agreements generally demanded, through government regulation and inspection, that the corporation assume the responsibility for sustained yield management since it was the corporation which would benefit from the resulting continuous supply of wood. The forest industries have welcomed this type of licence system because it has given them virtual control over huge areas of forest for long periods of time (usually twenty-one years). Provincial governments also have favoured the system because, while the public purse was sometimes relieved of much of the costly responsibility of carrying out intensive forestry work over huge areas, the province maintained a regulatory role through inspection and approval of working plans. It should be noted, however, that in 1962 in Ontario and in 1973 in Quebec a modified approach was adopted. These provinces chose to retain responsibility for all forest management on Crown lands to ensure the work was done and, perhaps, as an incentive for forest industries to expand or locate in those provinces. The policy of separating forestry practice from timber harvesting proved a failure, and has been largely abandoned. While it probably did serve to retain existing industries and lure a few new ventures to deteriorating eastern forests, the policy also encouraged companies to cut in a reckless fashion which made regeneration more difficult. Ontario, at least, put an amount nearly equal to its timber revenues back into forestry measures during this period but still found itself slipping behind. It therefore moved in the late 1970s to shift some substantial responsibility back to the forest industry through the general type of forest management agreements described here, though this shift may not be any-more successful in solving regeneration problems.[36]

Therefore, because of its attraction to both industry and government, the long-term licence or agreement had been the preferred method of disposing of forestlands throughout Canada since World War II. Under such arrangements, vast tracts of the best commercial forest in the country have been leased and operated under private-public auspices which were supposed to impose an enlightened regime of sustained yield management. It is also worthy of note that, despite some interest in management of Canadian forests by independent commission or Crown corporation as suggested by the Ontario Tories in 1941 and formally recommended by the Royal Commission on Forestry of 1945 in Ontario, which was chaired by the former president of the old Ottawa valley firm, E. B. Eddy Company, Howard Kennedy, the rule has been to keep the minister responsible for forests completely in control of leasing arrangements and timber allocation. This remains the ultimate pressure point for the forest industries in obtaining altered harvesting and management conditions and, as was witnessed in the case of government forester Donald MacAlpine in Ontario, during 1981–1982, politics can still override professional opinions in any forestry authority anywhere in the country.[37]

Thus one major trend in forestry in the postwar decades has been the provinces' and industry's acceptance and promotion of sustained yield and timber conservation goals under suitable leasing conditions. Another equally important trend, largely inspired by industry support, was the renewal of forest inventories conducted to enable better planning of resource management processes and also to discover and open up new commercial stands to exploitation. New markets made industry hungry for new, accessible wood supplies which could be brought under the long-term leasing agreements. It was admitted by all interests, private and public, that existing stands had been overcut and that some relief was necessary for both conservation and business reasons. Lured by the promise of new mills, virtually every province began to count its trees and build forest access roads. It was in this area that federal assistance through the Canada Forestry Act and later the forestry agreements was to play its most dynamic role.

After the passage of the Canada Forestry Act in 1949, the provinces began to send forestry assistance proposals to Ottawa which went far beyond the research role defined for the Dominion Forestry Service in the late 1920s and 1930s. Led by British Columbia and a much more cooperative Ontario, under the Tory government of George Drew and later Leslie Frost, the provinces asked for money to carry out forest protection improvements (roads, trails, telephones, and lookout towers) and soon assistance in spraying for spruce budworm and other insect pests; improvements in silvicultural practices (investigation of better extraction techniques, cultural treatment, purchase of abandoned lands and reforestation); and industrial bonuses for sustained yield harvesting. Most important, however, the provinces asked for both financial and personnel assistance in carrying out forest inventories and later for direct monetary contributions to build forest access roads.[38]

It was from this basis that federal forestry grew during the late 1950s and early 1960s into an important national programme. Indeed, by 1959, pressure had become intense from several quarters, especially from the forest industries, that the programme itself be given departmental status with a minister who could represent forestry interests directly to the federal cabinet. Hearings were held that year before the House of Commons Standing Committee on Mines, Forests and Waters. Briefs were presented before the Committee not only by the professional forestry associations and the academic community, but also by a number of prominent industrial and business associations.[39]

Perhaps the most interesting testimony came from Professor D. V. Love of the Faculty of Forestry at the University of Toronto and from the Woodlands Section of the Canadian Pulp and Paper Association. Love prophetically expressed the need for federal leadership in developing proper techniques for the growing and regeneration of forests because, as he noted, "the growing of timber holds no incentive for the investment of private capital and, therefore, is clearly a government responsibility". Professor Love had, perhaps, put his finger on a fatal flaw in the implementation of public forestry as it was developing in Canada.[40] In a sense, he was supported by the Woodlands Section of the Canadian Pulp and Paper Association. It too called for federal leadership in moving to technical solutions necessary to obtain greater yields from the forests. But these were bright spots in a host of industry briefs which took the normal corporate approach of protecting standing, merchantable timber as the prime goal of forestry and called for dramatic increases in federal assistance for fire protection which reached beyond capital expenditures to the costs of actual fire fighting in the provinces.[41]

The report of the House of Commons Committee emphasized that the Dominion Forestry Service lacked the necessary status to aid forestry adequately in the provinces or to represent the interests of the forest industries. It was critical of federal officials for not using the powers of the Canada Forestry Act to a greater extent and suggested the establishment of a National Forestry Development Advisory Board. Also, the Committee took the forest industry's advice and recommended increased federal assistance in forest fire prevention and protection. On 11 July 1960, the federal Conservative government of John Diefenbaker, acting on the Committee's report, introduced an act to create a Department of Forestry. Besides setting up this new government agency, the act included an expanded forestry agreements clause which permitted the Minister to enter into arrangements with any province or individual for forest protection, management, or utilization and related research, or for publicity or education.[42] The Diefenbaker administration was to continue to show its commitment to federal forestry in a variety of ways which included giving increased support to the concept of federal-provincial agreements, convening the Resources for Tomorrow Conference, and securing Quebec's cooperation through the government of Premier Jean Lesage in a new federal-provincial coordinating body, the Canadian Council of Resource Ministers.

Thus by 1960 there were in Canada provincial forest authorities who were supposedly working in cooperation with the forest industries to develop the forestry sector of the economy on sustained yield policies. Their aim was to perpetuate supplies of wood, which was underwriting industrial expansion and social stability in the forested areas of the country. Overlaid on this system was a federal assistance plan designed to support the provinces and industry with research facilities, technical developments, and financial assistance. But, in spite of these facilities for government-industry cooperation, two decades later, such widely diverse sources as the *Globe and Mail* and the Science Council of Canada were reporting that management of Canada's commercial forests was nearing a point of crisis and that the country might well face a shortage of supplies in some softwood species in the near future.[43] Both federal and provincial forestry officials have substantiated these reports, and the forest industries have been quick to concur with the analysis.

Canadians cannot be blamed for asking what has gone wrong with a system designed to ensure our country commercially viable and vibrant forests in perpetuity. The answers, of course, are myriad. The advent of mechanized harvesting equipment, which destroys young trees and creates a more difficult environment in which to carry on regeneration; a lack of adequate silvicultural research and a lack of trained foresters to determine specific techniques for individual forest sites, both resulting from the fact that although forestry as a profession has had a long history in Canada, it has had only limited stature; naive attachment to the hope of natural regeneration; simple over-cutting to maintain vulnerable one-industry communities that would sink into ghost towns if the mills closed; and the lack of investment in viable reforestation projects by both government and industry are only a few of the answers offered by experts in the field. But it can also be said that all these factors fit into the themes of this book concerning the failure of Canadian public policy to deal adequately with forestry and forest conservation. Basically, the failures of the political policies of the 1920s have been translated to our own day. Refusing to view effective forestry as an absolute necessity, Canadian governments have too often settled for the minimum acceptable solution, rather than enact effective measures that would go beyond the exploitive ethic.

It can be argued that public forest administrations fell into a trap after World War II. It was a trap dictated by the very tradition governing the development of the woods industries in Canada. In relying on past experience and trying to serve the dictates of their political masters for increased industrial growth in the forestry sector, foresters surveyed and opened up vast new tracts of timber for exploitation on generous long-term arrangements. Indeed, it made sense to do so since many of the older licenced areas needed relief from cutting, and much of the timber elsewhere was becoming overmature and, it was argued, was going to waste. It was common to claim in the 1960s that there were lots of trees in Canada and that with basic forest management there always would be. But by opening the new areas, forestry officials, perhaps unwittingly, reinforced the industry pattern of migrating to new stands when they had cut out the species needed for production in an existing area.

Investigation of any long-established lumber or pulp and paper mill confirms this fact. Cutting starts close to the production site and moves out farther from it year by year until the transportation costs become immense.[44] True, the long-term leases contained sustained yield commitments, but areas are large, silvicultural methods are both expensive and imperfect, and thus too much faith is placed in natural regeneration. There is, as well, another factor. Most large timber leases are connected to equally large mill facilities, and, all too often, the sole criterion of forestry becomes finding wood to maintain the jobs in the mill. Perhaps D. V. Love, who testified before the Commons Select Committee in 1959, described the situation best in a paper presented at the Resources for Tomorrow Conference in 1961. Love believed that there was much surplus timber in Canada but that wood utilization was suffering. He contended that

Canadian expenditures on the maintenance of the resource are preponderantly for protection, road construction, road maintenance, inventory and planning. These things, though desirable and often essential in sustaining revenue from the forest, do not contribute directly to a better recovery of the productive capacity of those accessible fruitful lands which should provide raw materials for expansion on industry. The policy of industry and provincial governments of applying a thin veneer of forest management in the form of protection and low-intensity silviculture over an extended area cannot provide, at competitive prices, the quality of wood needed to encourage the growth of the wood-using industries. Our tremendous unused allowable cut has apparently created the impression amongst forest administrators in both government and industry that expenditures for intensive forest management are rarely justified until all of the potential allowable cut within the reach of extensive forestry methods is accounted for.[45]

In essence, what occurred during the postwar decades was a continuation of the exploitive ethic in timber harvesting only slightly moderated from that of the nineteenth century and disguised by some forestry regulations and practices. No better example of this can be found than in the white paper "Suggestions for a Program of Renewable Resources Development" placed before the Ontario Legislature by the Conservative Minister of Lands and Forests, the Hon. W. S. Gemmell, in 1954.[46] The document discussed the use of the Forest Resources Inventory as a base for planning land use for forests and recreation; at the same time, it honestly described the plight of the sawmilling industry in Ontario and its need for new sources of supply. Government policy developed after the presentation of this white paper was oriented toward shifting sawmilling's "centre of gravity" to find new sources of wood and new species to exploit. On this basis, white and red pine mills operating in the Ottawa valley turned north to other areas like the Temagami forest for jackpine timber. The white paper also claimed that there were "many indications that the cut of spruce pulpwood in Ontario may soon reach its peak or a position similar to that reached by the white pine saw log industry in 1908. Almost the same forces are at work with respect to the pulp and paper industry and spruce pulpwood as caused the decline of the white pine saw-log industry".[47] These were grim words, and the government promised that the policies it had put in place since 1946 were designed to ease the forest industries over any temporary wood shortages and to rebuild the forest on a perpetual supply basis. But, in fact, that policy, other than the extensive inventorying already mentioned, really was to move forest utilization north into new areas of older timber. The theory behind the policy was correct because, as the white paper pointed out, "in forest operations an over-cut in one section cannot be wholly made up by an under-cut in other sections. It is important, in order to realize the full allowable cut, that operations be uniformly distributed over the entire forest area". But government forest administrators were candid in admitting that by moving the forest industries into new stands of timber they could still only underwrite "present requirements and normal expansion" for valuable softwood species including spruce for only twenty years. The document further stated, "After this period, industry will become increasingly dependent on presently immature stands and regrowth on cut-over areas and, therefore, the need for improved silvicultural methods in our forest is self-evident".[48]

This is the crux of the question. The forest industries were being moved to new timber areas just the same as in the past. They had undertaken to institute some sustained yield techniques, but they reasoned that the government would relocate them again if the areas failed. On the administration's part, effective forestry measures depended on sufficient regulation of industry practices and improved silvicultural practices to arrest the replacement of harvested softwoods by inferior species such as poplar. If even one of these factors failed, Ontario's forests would sink to a precarious state. In fact, neither was implemented in a particularly successful fashion, and, just as predicted by the authors of the white paper, twenty years later Ontario finds itself with a wood supply crisis.

The reasons behind such failures, not only in Ontario but also in such other provinces as British Columbia and New Brunswick, lie in a basic reluctance on the part of provincial governments either to pay the costs of effective management or to force the industries to live up to their commitments. Despite more knowledge of the problems involved, forest authorities and their political overlords have progressed only infinitesimally toward sustained yield management in their various jurisdictions since 1945. As a rule, they still refuse to press home public policy going beyond the exploitive use of the forest resource for industrial purposes and the collection of revenues for the public coffers.

W. A. E. Pepler, manager of the Woodlands Section of the Canadian Pulp and Paper Association, suggested to the Resources for Tomorrow Conference of 1961 that there are three stages of development in forest policies. The first stage is exploitation, during which the government draws its profits from direct revenues. Pepler characterized the policies at this stage as protective— designed to prevent damage or loss to a source of revenue. The second stage, the supervisory stage, encompasses the period when the renewable nature of the forest is realized, and supervisory policies are set up and inspection is carried out to ensure that renewal measures are taken. Pepler characterized this stage as extensive management—where policies are aimed at protection, sustained yield and improved utilization. His third stage, termed intensive management, is characterized by pressures on the resource forcing more productive use if industries are to survive. Cooperation is the basis for this type of policy, and, in forestry, silviculture and research become important activities.[49] If we accept Pepler's subdivisions, the rhetoric surrounding forest policy in Canada during the postwar years was at the intensive level, but, in reality, what was occurring in the woods had advanced only a little beyond exploitation to a minor supervisory role.

This is, perhaps, the crucial point. The reforms of the 1940s and early 1950s required an active supervisory and regulatory role by the various forest authorities. But, if they were empowered to carry out these activities, the forest authorities were not always funded to do so. Indeed, provincial governments have constantly voiced their desire to keep control of forest royalties as part of general revenues and to continue to use them to finance other public services. In 1945 Frank MacDougall, Deputy Minister of the Ontario Department of Lands and Forests, advised his Minister that installation of a proper forestry programme in Ontario would require an annual expenditure of from $10 million to $16 million. His request for resources was restricted to annual increases for five years to bring budgetary expenditures to his minimum base of $10 million.[50] If money was difficult to get when programmes were young and vibrant, increases were harder to obtain when a system was in place and appeared to be functioning without major complaint by the public. When insufficient resources were made available, it was usually the silvicultural, reforestation, and research projects that were curtailed and postponed. As Jamie Swift has pointed out, recent British Columbia Royal Commissions on forestry have found the government more assiduous in drafting and enforcing regulations concerning revenues than those governing harvesting practices and resource use.[51]

Forestry measures also suffered a status reduction in the wake of the antipollution movement of the mid–1960s. Indeed, after the Canadian Council of Resource Ministers convened its conference, entitled Pollution and Our Environment, in the fall of 1966, the political tide began to flow away from administrative operations such as forestry which seemed overly preoccupied with serving the needs of business. In a very direct sense, forestry was still identified with the old conservation of renewable resources through efficient utilization by big business. The new antipollution advocates were interested in the quality of the environment and were somewhat out of sympathy with those who would use the forest environment and attempt to alter its natural qualities in the process, though they did find considerable merit in preserving the forest ecology.

The general decline of the postwar forestry initiative in Canada was most evident at the federal level. In 1966 a major forestry conference was held in Montebello, Quebec, but the lack of action as a result of this meeting was a sign that the Liberal government of Lester Pearson had little new in mind in this field. In the same year the Department of Forestry was merged with the Department of Rural Development, resulting in a reduction of federal forestry's influence because it became submerged in regional development programmes. A more serious event occurred in 1968, however, when the federal-provincial forestry agreements were discontinued. The basis for a national forestry programme, for which E. H. Finlayson and D. Roy Cameron had worked so hard and long, was abandoned. Under a new prime minister, Pierre Elliot Trudeau, the Liberal government did not appear disposed to reverse the trend. This does not mean that considerable federal monies were not spent on forestry. By the end of the Trudeau era, some $200 million dollars annually found its way to aid the provinces, but not in a particularly coordinated manner, and less than half went to regeneration and stand tending. Indeed, most of the funds were spent on industrial incentives. Forestry was again moved and merged with the Department of Fisheries under a British Columbian, Jack Davis, in 1968, who busied himself with fisheries and the new environmental problems, and phased out such forestry programmes as the Forest Economics Research Institute. Finally, the federal service was swallowed up in the federal government's answer to the environmental crisis—the Department of Environment. In this large institution, the newly titled Canadian Forestry Service became lost and lacked positive political direction. After 1973, the General Regional Development Agreements under the Department of Regional Economic Expansion became more important as a method of giving forestry aid to provinces like New Brunswick. These stressed immediate infrastructure development and gave the Forestry Service concerns, such as regeneration and silviculture, a less prominent role. It should be noted, however, that the new agreements did give support to a pilot project in the province for removal of Crown land from licence and the placing of complete control of the extraction and re-generation of the forest resource with a government agency on an experimental basis. This harked back somewhat to the objectives of the Kennedy Royal Commission in Ontario, which had recommended that this type of public commission take forest management responsibilities away from industry. This experiment, however, was only one bright spot in a sea of darkness, and it was not expanded by New Brunswick. The coup de grace was delivered in 1978 when steps were taken by the government to privatize the federal forest products laboratories and, at the same time, to close the Petawawa Forest Experiment Station.[52]

In essence, the government wished to return federal forestry to the position it had enjoyed before 1913. The Petawawa station was saved after a public outcry, and it was merged with the Forest Management Institute and the Forest Fire Research Institute into the Petawawa National Forestry Institute. Nevertheless, the Canadian Forestry Service was left moribund and demoralized. It was a crisis similar to those caused by the Natural Resource Transfer Agreements and the depression. Indeed, across the country at both the provincial and federal levels, the political drive had gone out of forestry and forest conservation.

As had happened so often in the past, the nadir of modern Canadian forestry was accompanied by some rays of hope. The fate of the country's woodlands and their unique relationship with the industries, which are the nation's leading employers and export earners, have remained too important for politicians to ignore for very long. Even in the mid–1970s, there were signs of a reversal of the trend of events. A major report in Ontario and another Royal Commission in British Columbia were reviewing forest management problems in those provinces, prescribing ways to bring sustained yield closer to reality and to face the forest regeneration crisis. The Social

Credit government in British Columbia enacted a new Forest Act in 1977, but a slump in the province's economy in the early 1980s and the administration's dedication to deficit slashing and small government has retarded progress there. Ontario has embarked on a plan of revamping its forestry programme in conjunction with a major land planning exercise. For its part too, New Brunswick has begun the process of reform in the allocation of timber holdings to provide a more rational basis for wood utilization and better reproductive capacity.

Also, the federal government has reversed its policies and has begun to support forestry initiatives once more. Recognizing the magnitude of the problems facing Canadian forests and their crucial importance to the national economy, the Liberal government has upgraded the Canadian Forestry Service, pledging to increase its size and making its head an assistant deputy minister; it has revived cooperative agreements with the provinces, particularly in the field of research and forest renewal; and it has announced a forest strategy to improve the collection of statistics, to train workers, and to promote international markets. With regard to the forest renewal agreements, each participating province was asked to design a long-term plan outlining goals related to timber production, forest renewal and protection, and better utilization and productivity in wood manufacturing. Once again, however, provincial governments have not all agreed to this approach. Ontario, by way of example, originally asked that its agreement cover only the construction of new forest roads. The new federal Conservative government, elected in 1984, had, as part of its campaign platform, more aid to forestry. The new government has established a Ministry of State for Forestry and has committed new funding for forest renewal in Canada on an immediate basis. It has also moved the Service to the Department of Agriculture. This move may give federal forestry more political support, but the success of this experiment must await future judgement. Too often, public forestry in Canada has been treated only as a science to reclaim waste farmland, supporting unviable farm/forest communities, rather than as an essential basis for underpinning an important industrial sector. It would appear that the ideas first put forward by E. H. Finlayson and by D. Roy Cameron in the early 1920s could become a permanent fixture of the national forest conservation policy in Canada, but political stamina is still required at the federal level and, most particularly, in the provinces.[53] Accomplishing this goal requires a major reorientation in the way that both government and industry approach the forest resource. The pessimism entailed in the title of this book derives from the ultimate failure over the period of a century of any political party to come to terms, in a public policy sense, with the requirements that must underlie any intensive, sustained yield forest management programme. Since 1900 politicians and businessmen have talked increasingly about the possibilities of renewing the forest, but, in the end, it is impossible not to conclude that, for the most part, this has been mere rhetoric.

This may seem a harsh judgement, but this book has ranged over a wide field of historical events, and it reveals a common theme of failure. By the mid-nineteenth century, there had developed in British North America a symbiotic relationship between the lumbermen and the colonial governments of that period. The lumbermen sought security of tenure for stands of timber which was necessary for use as collateral to finance their operations and for providing the desired products for established markets. In return, these entrepreneurs were willing to pay to the Crown, who controlled the forest-lands, revenues for cutting wood and leasing timber areas. It is this close relationship which endures to this day. In order to ensure provincial revenues, to promote industrial expansion in hinterland areas, and, more recently, to serve the socioeconomic purpose of maintaining employment in one-industry towns, provincial governments have allowed and even encouraged the forest industries to roam over the vast expanse of the country's woodlands to pick off the species they needed.

Appearing at first sight as a client of government and totally dependent on the Crown for wood supplies, the reverse is actually true of these indus-tries. Entrenched in the tradition of receiving guarantees of tenure and wood supply from the public sector, they can wield tremendous economic influence which provincial governments find hard to resist. The closing of one large mill can send shock waves crashing through a local legislature. But ironically, it is not this economic power that has been primarily responsible for the migrant nature of Canadian cutting operations. Rather, the real reason behind this policy lies in the nature of Canadian attitudes toward the forest itself. Within the general public, there exists a view, undiminished by the years, that there are plenty of forestlands to be exploited and that technology will somehow keep on improving accessibility, growing methods, and utilization. While the latter trends may well occur, there are no more virgin stands to offer on the altar of increased industrial expansion. Yet, it is this older view which continues to permeate forest policy in Canada. It is based on an exploitive ethic, a naive liberal-democratic myth of an ever open northern frontier and the consequent belief that the forest may be nibbled away at like a mine to pay for or underwrite other government programs. It is a popularly held view, which makes it very difficult to come to grips with serious management issues within the political process.

Illustrations that these two factors exist in combination as part of today's forest scene are not hard to find. For a demonstration of extensive harvesting operations, one need only visit an older paper mill like that at Dryden, a kraft plant built during World War I. Cutting has taken place in ever-ex-panding circles around the mill as the centre. As a result, logs must be hauled more than 200 miles over a network of all-weather gravel roads. Designed to keep fuel and maintenance costs low, these roads are expensive to build and maintain. They represent the fact that the operating company is essen-tially a prisoner of the cost of getting the wood to its mill. The message is clear. If the cut-overs had been properly regenerated beginning in the 1920s, rather than being virtually abandoned, they would now be able to supply at least some of the current wood fibre needed for operations. We are, in fact, now paying for our past shortsightedness, and present-day neglect will cost Canadians even more in the future.

In another context, Ontario, the province of Howard Ferguson and the Tory timber scandal, can provide evidence of the lack of dedication by modern Canadian political leadership to genuine forest management. This was perhaps most poignantly displayed by George Drew's successor, Leslie Frost. The Kalamazoo Vegetable Parchment (KVP) Company had been lured to Espanola, Ontario, by the Tories to take over the old Spruce Falls mill in the late 1940s. The KVP purchase was the highlight of the new forest policy put forward by the Drew government. Unfortunately, the facilities were quite ancient and spewed all manner of matter into the Spanish river in contravention of the Lakes and Rivers Improvement Act. Landowners in the area obtained an injunction to stop the pollution and were successful in maintaining it through company appeals to the Ontario Supreme Court. The company then turned to the government of Leslie Frost, successor to George Drew, who first amended the Act to force the courts to consider the economic impact before issuing injunctions and, when this amendment was determined not to be retroactive, moved to simply dissolve the original statute, thus removing the grounds for the complaint. On his retirement, Premier Frost assumed a directorship with KVP.[54]

This disregard for the environment has been repeated many times when business investment in resource extraction is at stake. The close relationship between the forest industries and the government, which was first investigated with George Hamilton and the British colonial government of the Canadas has persisted to this day.[55] It is in a context of migrating cutting operations and a political climate more supportive of industrial exploitation than sound management and development practices, that the forest conservation movement has developed since 1880. Perhaps, given the odds, Canadians should be thankful that the movement and the consequent rise of the discipline of forestry accomplished as much as it has in the intervening century. The original forest conservation movement grew out of the concerns of a small group of individuals that Canadian forests were being overexploited in reckless and wasteful ways. They foresaw the consequences of overexploitation as a diminished forest resource, erosion of valuable land due to destruction of tree cover on watersheds, and elimination of an important aesthetic component in the natural environment. This small group was composed mostly of scientists, scientific farmers, public servants, and lumbermen.

It was the lumbermen, with the most direct economic interest in the forest, who were essential in promoting the movement. Wealthy and politically influential, these entrepreneurs tended to foist their own agenda on the early conservationists. This agenda was really an extension of their business concerns about securing access to the resource to produce timber for existing markets. They were attracted by progressive ideas about employing modern planning techniques to resource extraction and the improvement of forest utilization as the basis for long-term economic growth. These ideas were complemented in eastern Canada where timber stocks, mostly pine and spruce, were already reduced in quantity and quality by general overexploitation. Both factors led businessmen to find in the forest conservation movement a means to advocate the further protection of timberlands.

There was little to criticize in this enlightened self-interest. It posed a worthwhile challenge to the prevalent liberal-democratic attitude of mining the forest resource without any visible controls or long-range economic planning. Advocating the conservation movement's stated ideals of efficient and planned use of resources to engineer economic growth, the lumbermen, through organizations like the Canadian Forestry Association, supported enhanced fire protection measures, the classification of land, the creation of forest reserves, the inventorying of forest resources, and a host of other measures. Their economic position and political standing meant that most of these measures were eventually adopted by the various provincial governments controlling major timber areas and by the federal government on western lands.

The fact remained, however, that these were ideas put forward by a specific business community to accomplish particular ends. It is through forest protection that the forest industries first approached conservation ideas, and it has remained a prime factor in their support for forestry measures. They remained much more ambivalent in the period up to 1950 about the virtues of control of lumbering practices and the requirements for management and regeneration plans. Industry has not been averse to applying pressure to ensure that government restricted itself to protection and investigatory work and did not become involved in actual lumbering activities. It was the case western lumbermen made to the federal government when the Dominion controlled western lands, and, only when they were convinced of the advantages to their businesses, did timber operators initially accept control over lumbering in Quebec, British Columbia, and New Brunswick.

This self-interested support of forestry and forest conservation measures would have been highly beneficial had there been a strong public interest to direct it toward proper forest management. The lack of such an interest is, perhaps, the greatest tragedy of the period surveyed in this book. The analysis of events at both the provincial and federal levels since 1900 reveals that forest resource utilization questions have been fought out in the political sphere between those who would champion the right of the individual and smaller interests to use the forest virtually untrammelled by regulation and larger interests, who, under the guise of efficient but conservation-oriented use, would monopolize the commercial woodlands to their own corporate ends. From the very beginnings of the forest conservation movement in Canada, the voicing of a wider public interest has been extremely weak. The movement appears to have had a popular base only between 1898 and 1918, when events with the United States impinged on similar issues in Canada, creating a popular support among the new urban middle class for conservation policies that would preserve the country's forests.

The definition of a broader public interest divorced from strict business economics was best demonstrated by European foresters like Bernhard Fernow who came to teach in Canada and inculcated a pride in public service in many of his graduates from the University of Toronto. Of this generation, Finlayson is the best example. Almost invariably these men went into government service where they were muted by the political process and could express themselves only through their professional organizations. Some were conspicuous in their efforts to create an independent public interest which could look beyond the business proposition of forest conservation to the broader social implications of regenerating the forest. These were best represented at the federal level by such men as Roland Craig, D. Roy Cameron, and, of course, E. H. Finlayson, who was driven to probable suicide by the very frustrations of the effort. Gustave Piché in Quebec and P. Z. Caverhill in British Columbia also fall into this category as do Dean C. D. Howe, of the Faculty of Forestry at Toronto, and Judson F. Clark. The point is that these public servants and a few other individuals were virtually alone in fostering this cause.

At the political level, it is almost possible to count the ardent supporters of consistent, independent, and effective forestry and forest conservation policies on one hand. Certainly, Henri Joly is one of them. Perhaps Alexander Campbell, the last Commissioner of Crown Lands in the United Canadas, falls into this category; perhaps also Clifford Sifton at the federal level although his deeds sometimes fell far short of his words on the subject; perhaps Sir Lomer Gouin and Honoré Mercier, Minister of Lands and Forests in Quebec during the early 1920s; and, of course, William Ross in British Columbia and Norman Hipel in Ontario. Beyond those few, however, there has been little political leadership in this country which has endeavoured to create in an imaginative way a policy framework, taking into account the needs of the forest industries, but going beyond these to ensuring regeneration of Canadian woodlands on a rational basis for future generations. Rather, our politicians have remained preoccupied with the more immediate issues of raising revenues and ensuring that enough forestland is given to the forest industries to satisfy their needs and to promote industrial stability and expansion.

That fault can be laid right at the door of the Canadian public, which seems to expect little more from its governments. Locked in their own exploitive bonanza from colonial times, Canadians have rarely brought to bear any sustained critique of how their resources have been used and abused.

They have been aroused over the years by opposition jibes in a few electoral campaigns when outright fraud and corruption in resource dealings have been revealed, but the anger has died quickly. Basically, until the last two decades, there has been no discernible public interest lobbying for political solutions to the forest resource problem which have gone beyond the demands of the forest industries themselves.[56]

This lack of a discernible public interest involving public representatives willing to advocate forest conservation within the political system has gravely misled forestry in the decades following World War II. Recognizing their dependence on industry support, public forest authorities appear to have largely abandoned a more neutral position and have moved over to support the forest corporations in securing large areas under long-term tenures. Forest engineers and foresters have become preoccupied with lowering extraction costs while increasing utilization standards—all laudable goals, but timber harvests have spiralled upward and stocks of desirable species have declined, and the application of sustained yield forestry has retreated from the long-term objective of regulating the growing stock on a proper silvicultural basis. Sustained yield was replaced by the more immediate objective of providing an even supply of timber so that mills could meet market quotas and communities would not face mill closings and unemployment. Adoption of a system that relies on a corporate-public regulatory axis removed regeneration as a primary aim of forestry policy and perpetuated the traditional Canadian system where cutting does not destroy the forest but rather alters its composition. Thus, over time, the white pine forest became one of spruce and balsam fir, and further cutting will result in forests of only balsam fir or, worse, perhaps a mixture of broad-leaved shrubs and poplar. The result of this and similar forest successions in other areas has created the crisis in the Canadian forestry sector which is now the subject of so much comment.

That crisis is now clearly visible. Governments at both the provincial and federal levels have announced plans to deal with it, and, although the success of these efforts cannot yet be judged the view can not be one of total optimism. An old enemy, government expenditure retrenchment, has reared its head once more. Yet, on the bright side, the pollution issues of the 1960s have generated a general concern for the deterioration of our environment, and this, combined with the perception that we may live in an energy scarce world, has finally, in the last two decades, created that large-scale public support for forest conservation that has been lacking for so long. In the end, what we have witnessed in Canada in regard to the management of forests is a colossal failure of public policy. It is a failure of which Canadians should feel particularly ashamed given their dedication to professional and technical excellence in other management and engineering spheres. In the depth of that failure lies both the hope of a new beginning and the threat of unparalleled social and economic catastrophe.

Notes

List of Abbreviations

PAC   Public Archives of Canada

PAO   Public Archives of Ontario

OA   Ontario Department of Public Records and Archives

QA   National Archives of Quebec

RG   Record group

MG   Manuscript group

Chapter 1

1. The best discussion of the early North American timber trade remains A.R.M. Lower's two books: *The North American Assault on the Canadian Forest, A History of the Lumber Trade between Canada and the United States* (Toronto; 1938) and *Great Britain's Woodyard: British America and the Timber Trade, 1763–1867* (Montreal; 1973). Attention should also be paid to Graeme Wynn, *Timber Colony: A historical geography of early nineteenth century New Brunswick* (Toronto, 1981).

2. See PAC, The Bronsons and Weston Company Records, MG28 III 26 vol. 816, Notes on the firm.

3. R. G. Albion, *Forests and Seapower: The timber problems of the Royal Navy, 1652–1862* (Cambridge, Mass., 1926); W. T. Easterbrook and H. G. J. Aitken, *Canadian Economic History* (Toronto, 1956), pp. 188–189; and Sandra J. Gillis, *The Timber Trade in the Ottawa Valley, 1806–1854*, Parks Canada Manuscript Report Number 153 (Ottawa, 1975), pp. 1–6.

4. See S. Gillis, *Ottawa Valley*, pp. 5–10; and Wynn, *New Brunswick*, pp. 28–33.

5. The establishment of the timber trade and its impact on British North America is discussed in detail in: Lower, *Great Britain's Woodyard*, chap.6; F. Ouellet, *Histoire économique et social du Québec* (Montreal, 1966) pp. 190–216; Donald Creighton, *The Empire of the St. Lawrence* (Toronto, 1956), chaps. 5–6; L. Dechêne, "William Price:

1810–1850" (unpublished thèse de maitrise, Univ. of Laval, 1964), pp. 141–143; S. Gillis, *Ottawa Valley*, pp. 6–12. See also: PAO, Hamilton Brothers Records, George Hamilton Letterbook no. 2, George Hamilton to Palton Harton, 27 May 1809.

6. Albion, *Forests and Seapower*, pp. 354; and S. Gillis, *Ottawa Valley*, pp. 210–213.

7. Dechêne, "William Price": 141–143; and PAC, MG11 Colonial Office 42, Q Series, vol. 126, pp. 162–163, John Inglis to the Earl of Bathurst, 6 Dec. 1813.

8. Creighton, *Empire of the St. Lawrence*, p. 150.

9. *Quebec Gazette*, 6 July 1828.

10. PAO, Hamilton Brothers Records, esp. Letterbook no. 2, George Hamilton to William Hackney, 5 April 1810, William Hamilton to Robert Hamilton, 9 June 1812, and George Hamilton to Robert Hamilton, 17 Oct. 1813. PAC, MG24 B7 no. 10: 62–63, Memorandum by George Hamilton, 12 Sept. 1828. M. S. Cross, "Dark Druidical Groves: The Lumber Community and the Commercial Frontiers in British North America to 1854" (unpublished doctoral dissertation, Univ. of Toronto, 1968): pp. 227–230.

11. A red herring if ever there was one as the timbers were generally sawn into lumber once in England.

12. Lower, *Great Britain's Woodyard*, chap. 12; Thomas J. Stobart, *The Timber Trade in the United Kingdom* (London, 1927), vol. II, Hardwoods. Squared hardwood timbers were also imported from the United States. The trade was handled by a Canadian broker who supplied skilled French Canadian timber-makers to the logging companies mainly in the southern states. See John Keyes, "The Dunn Family: Two Generations of Timber Merchants at Quebec, 1850–1914" (unpublished manuscript, Dept. of History, Univ. of Laval, May 1984).

13. Ibid.; and Wynn, *New Brunswick*, chap. 3.

14. Much of this section is drawn from Wynn, *New Brunswick;* chap. 6. A fuller explanation of early timber regulations in New Brunswick can be found there.

15. Wynn, *New Brunswick*, pp. 142–146.

16. Ibid.; and W. S. MacNutt, "The Politics of the Timber Trade in Colonial New Brunswick, 1825–40," *Canadian Historical Review* 30 (1949): 133.

17. MacNutt, "Colonial New Brunswick", 139.

18. For sources on the Hamiltons see: note 10 above; S. Gillis, *Ottawa Valley*, pp. 71–72; and Peter Gillis, "George Hamilton," in *Dictionary of Canadian Biography*, forthcoming.

19. Almost certainly of the gate, gang saw variety powered by waterwheels.

20. S. Gillis, *Ottawa Valley*, pp. 71–72.

21. For an analysis of George Hamilton's interaction with this community see Peter Gillis, "David Pattee," in *Dictionary of Canadian Biography*, forthcoming, and also PAC, RG5 A1 Civil Secretary's Correspondence, Upper Canada, vol. 14, file 39235–8, George Hamilton to Charles Shireff, 13 Sept. 1825.

22. Great Britain, House of Lords, *First Report*, p. 64, Evidence, John Hamilton.

23. Hamilton came to these conclusions after he had been intimately involved in the violence plaguing the early timber trade, earning him the title "the greatest Black-guard" in the Ottawa valley from his business competitors. In the period from 1818 to 1823, his firm was in desperate financial straits, and Hamilton had not hesitated to use violence and intimidation to reach his goal of financial stability. See PAC, RG5 A1, vol. 14: 25157–25158C, Charges of George Hamilton.

24. S. Gillis, *Ottawa Valley*, pp. 212–219.

25. In the Shiners' War, fellow lumberman Peter Aylen used ethnic hatred and economic desperation in the Irish-Catholic immigrants of the Valley to seize a substantial part of the trade. Irish lumberjacks, employed and directed by Aylen, intimidated their French-Canadian co-religionists and drove them away from their camps and rafts of logs in order to seize their jobs for members of the Irish community. Hamilton was imbued with a Protestant Scots-Irish disdain for his Catholic countrymen but his greatest scorn was saved for the businessmen who promoted economic and racial war to obtain their ends. He could see nothing but financial ruin resulting from the violence and its unsettling effects, as well as an eventual rise in wages and costs. To Hamilton, the only explanation for the difficulties between the various groups of lumbermen was the "immediate gratification of some jealousy or pique (originally about boundaries) against other employers having Canadian labourers." PAC, RG4 A1 Civil Secretary's Correspondence, Lower Canada, vol. 213, p. 57, Opinion of law officers of the Crown on the petition of Walter Beckwith, 20 Oct. 1824 and RG5 A1 vol. 14. The best discussion of the Shiners' War appears in M. S. Cross, "The Shiners' War: Social Violence in the Ottawa Valley in the 1830's," *Canadian Historical Review* 54 (1973): 1–26.

26. An explanation of these developments is given in H. V. Nelles, *The Politics of Development: Forests, Mines and Hydro-Electric Power in Ontario, 1849–1941* (Toronto, 1974), pp. 1–17.

27. Not more than 56 cubic metres per licence. Cross, "Druidical Groves"; pp. 271–272; S. Gillis, *Ottawa Valley*, pp. 216–219.

28. QA, QBC13 vol. 18, file E–65, J. B. Robinson to John Davidson, Aug., 1828. OA, F–1–8 vol. 57, A. J. Russell, "Historical Memorandum on the Management of Crown Timber Forest and of Crown Timber Lands and Connexions Therewith," p. 13. PAC, RG5 A1 vol 124: 68315–18, George Hamilton to Lord Aylmer, 16 Dec. 1832.

29. The Gatineau Privilege is discussed in S. Gillis, *Ottawa Valley*, pp. 269–273.

30. OA, RG1 series F vol. 16, p. 4.

31. Buller's comments were based on the *Report of the Select Committee on Timber Duties* (Upper Canada, Journals of the Assembly, 1836), app. 54. See also R. S. Lambert with Paul Pross, *Renewing Nature's Wealth* (Toronto, 1967), p. 43.

32. The only sensible regulation issued during this period imposed double duty on undersized timber and thus acted as a crude form of minimum size limit.

33. Canada, *Journals of the Assembly* (1853), app. NNNN. *Ottawa Packet*, 10 Oct. 1846. QA, QBC13 vol. 2, extract of a letter, 2 Dec. 1845. PAO, RG1 series F vol. 11, Timber Agencies Letterbook, James Stevenson to Commission, 25 May 1846.

34. S. Gillis, *Ottawa Valley*, pp. 248–249.

35. Ibid.; Province of Canada, Legislative Assembly, *Journals of the Legislative Assembly of the Province of Canada* (1849).

36. Ibid.

37. Thomas Southworth and Aubrey White, *A History of Crown Timber Regulations from the Date of the French Occupation to the Year 1899* (Toronto, 1899).

38. S. Gillis, *Ottawa Valley*, pp. 251–252.

39. Province of Canada, *Journals*.

40. It was about this period that Britain started importing quantities of hardwoods, especially squared oak logs, from Canada. Much of this was re-sawn and used to

build the frames for railway carriages. British imports of large quantities of tropical hardwoods came later, at the end of the Victorian period. Keyes, "Dunn Family."

41. Wynn, *New Brunswick*, p. 144.

42. Peter Gillis, "Samuel Dickson," *Dictionary of Canadian Biography*, vol. XX (Toronto, 1976), pp. 205–206.

43. J. H. Morgan, *The Dominion Annual Register, 1884* (Toronto, 1884), p. 200; PAC, MG30 B62, F. J. Audet's Biographical Notes, vol. 9, p. 396; Lower, *North American Assault*, p. 123.

44. PAC, RG1 E1, Minutes of the Executive Council of the Province of Canada, 30 June 1852, book M, p. 264; PAC, MG27 II B 14, Hon. R. W. Scott Papers, vol. 5, "Recollections of Bytown".

45. Clarence F. Coons, "The John R. Booth Story," *Your Forests* II 2 (Summer 1978): 8–26.

46. S. Gillis, *Ottawa Valley*, pp. 55–64;. and S. A. Saunders, "The Maritime Provinces and the Reciprocity Treaty," *Dalhousie Review*, Oct. 1934: pp. 355–371.

47. The effect of the Reciprocity Treaty on the Canadian forest industry is best discussed in Lower, *North American Assault*, pp. 123–147. He contends that, although the Treaty did not benefit Canadian lumbermen in economic terms, it did stimulate production. In fact, it probably led to overproduction.

48. J. W. Hughson and C. C. J. Bond, *Hurling down the Pine* (Old Chelsea, Quebec, 1964) gives an excellent analysis of the Gilmours' switch to sawn lumber. See also Peter Gillis, "Ottawa and Early Sawmilling," *Proceedings of the Conference of the Institute for History and Research on the Outaouais Region* (Ottawa, 1981).

49. Nelles, *Politics*, pp. 14–15.

50. PAC, RG31 A1, Statistics Canada, Census of 1871, vol. 893, sched. 7, Ottawa Industrial.

51. John Langton, "On the Age of Timber Trees and the Prospects of a Continuous Supply of Timber in Canada", *Transactions of the Literary and Historical Society of Quebec* 1 (May 1862): pp. 61–79.

52. PAC, Sir John A. Macdonald Papers, MG26A, vol. 518, pt. 4, L.B. 15, p. 963; Macdonald to John Sandfield Macdonald, 23 June 1871.

53. Quoted in Province of Canada, *Annual Report of the Commissioner of Crown Lands* (1865); Lambert with Pross, *Renewing*, p. 157.

Chapter 2

1. The origins of the early conservation movement are discussed in a number of works, notably: H. Cheer, ed., *Origins of American Conservation* (New York, 1966); Samuel P. Hays, *Conservation and the Gospel of Efficiency* (Cambridge, Mass., 1959); Roderick Nash, *Wilderness and the American Mind* (New Haven and London, 1967); John R. Ross, "Man over Nature: Origins of the Conservation Movement," *American Studies* 16, 1 (Spring 1975): 49–60. George Marsh is best recorded in D. Lowenthal, *George Perkins Marsh: Versatile Vermonter* (New York: 1958). The Canadian movement is mentioned in R. S. Lambert with Paul Pross, *Renewing Nature's Wealth* (Toronto, 1967), pp. 162 and 167. Interesting and controversial commentaries can be found in Gabriel Kolko, *The Triumph of Conservatism* (New York, 1963) and Anthony Scott, *Natural Resources: The Economics of Conservation* (Toronto, 1955 and Ottawa, 1983).

2. The urban and preservationist wing of the early Canadian conservation move-

ment is analyzed to some extent in H. V. Nelles, *Politics of Development* (Toronto, 1973), pp. 184–214, and Janet Foster, *Working for Wildlife: The Beginning of Preservation in Canada* (Toronto, 1978), chap. 3. The lumbermen's influence on the conservation movement is discussed in Peter Gillis, "The Ottawa Lumber Barons and the Conservation Movement, 1880–1914", *Journal of Canadian Studies* (February 1974): pp. 14–31.

3. Lambert with Pross, *Renewing*, p. 162.

4. Ontario, Department of Agriculture and Arts, "Report of the Fruit Growers' Association of Ontario," *Annual Report, 1878–1883*, A. D.

5. See Gillis, "Ottawa Lumber Barons."

6. Little's career is discussed by P. Gillis, "James Little", *Dictionary of Canadian Biography*, vol. XI (Toronto and Quebec City, 1982), pp. 521–522, and Donald Mackay, *Heritage Lost: The Crisis in Canada's Forests* (Toronto, 1985), pp. 29–36.

7. James Little, *The Lumber Trade in the Ottawa Valley*, 3rd ed. (Ottawa, 1872). James Little, *The Timber Supply Question of the Dominion of Canada and the United States of America* (Montreal, 1876).

8. The Cincinnati meeting is discussed in Lambert with Pross, *Renewing*, pp. 162–163; Mackay, *Heritage Lost*, pp. 29–31; and, more fully, A. D. Rodgers, *Bernhard Eduard Fernow* (Princeton, 1950), pp. 31, 38–39.

9. Ibid.

10. Rodgers, *Fernow*, pp. 38–39.

11. American Forestry Congress, Proceedings of the American Forestry Congress at its Sessions held at Cincinnati, Ohio, April 1882 and Montreal, Canada, August 1882 (Washington, D.C., 1883).

12. P. Gillis, "Ottawa Lumber Barons," p. 19; D. McCalla, "The Rise of Forestry" (unpublished research manuscript, Ontario Department of Lands and Forests, 1966), pp. 1–4; PAC MG28 III 26, Bronsons and Weston Company Records, E. H. Bronson to Peter White, M.P., 21 June 1882.

13. Bruce W. Hodgins, Jamie Benidickson, and Peter Gillis, "The Ontario and Quebec Experiments in Forest Reserves, 1883–1930", *Journal of Forest History* 26, 1 (January 1982): 20–23. Hon. Ruggles Church, *Report of Argument Submitted to the Honourable the Executive Council for the Province of Quebec On Presentation of a Memorial Respecting the Vested Rights of Limitholders In Their Limits, March 16th 1880*. The contract issue was multidimensional and complex. Besides the question of whether or not stumpage and ground rents should be fixed for the life of any future contract issued by the Quebec government, there was a major problem over the terms of renewal. Contracts were nominally renewable annually for a stated number of years. Quebec lumbermen expected that, on expiry, a new contract would be issued to them for their limits following a mutual agreement over terms. Some politicians, on the other hand, considered the government had the right and duty to place the limit up for auction with open bids once the contract had expired. In contrast, timber berths in Ontario at this time were leased for as long as the operator worked them and were returned to the Crown or sold to other operators to rework for a different product until they were completely cut out.

14. H. G. Joly is a Canadian who has too long been neglected by biographers considering the excellence of his family papers (PAC, MG27 II C2 M794). Some published sources include: J. K. Johnson ed., *The Canadian Directory of Parliament* (Ottawa, 1968), p. 295. Brian Young, "Federalism in Quebec: The First Years after

Confederation," in Bruce W. Hodgins, D. Wright and W. H. Heick, eds, *Federalism in Canada and Australia: The Early Years* (Waterloo, 1978), pp. 97–108; Mason Wade, *The French Canadians*, vol. 1 (Toronto, 1968), pp. 331–392.

15. P. Gillis, "Ottawa Lumber Barons," p. 20; and *Canadian Parliamentary Companion* (1887), p. 234.

16. Ontario Legislature, "Report of the Delegation appointed to Attend the American Forestry Congress Held in Montreal, Province of Quebec," *Sessional Paper No. 3* (1883), pp. 21–37.

17. Ibid.; Rodgers, *Fernow*; PAC, RG15 vol. 298, file 6241; *Montreal Gazette* 23 August 1882, p. 5.

18. Ibid.; and Ontario Legislature, "Report," pp. 34–36. See editions of *The Montreal Herald*, 21 August 1882 to 30 August 1882, and *Montreal Gazette*, 21 August 1882 to 23 August 1882.

19. Ibid.

20. Ibid.; Rodgers, *Fernow*, p. 39

21. Rodgers, *Fernow*, p. 39.

22. PAC, MG28 III 26 vol. 103, Bronsons and Weston Company to W. W. Lynch, Quebec Commissioner of Crown Lands; P. Gillis, "Ottawa Lumber Barons," p. 20; Province of Quebec, Legislature, *Sessional Paper No. 4* (1883–1884), p. viii; Bruce W. Hodgins, *Paradis of Temagami* (Cobalt, Ontario, 1976), pp. 13–24.

23. Quebec's colonization movement was made up of societies that were themselves the outgrowth of agricultural clubs devoted to farming improvement and dating from around 1869–70. Backed by some members of the clergy, the societies encouraged the movement of colons into areas of Quebec until then untouched by settlement. This was promoted as an alternative to emigration to the northeastern United States, as a lure to those who had already left, as a means of extending French-Canadian influence northward and westward across northern Ontario and into Manitoba, and as a means of perpetuating the agrarian roots of French-Canadian culture and thus ensuring its survival. The movement started to settle people in the area of the Laurentian mountains from about 1875 on. Many of the lots chosen by the settlers of the northern forest were located on land already leased to lumbermen. The colons, under Quebec law, had the right to cut and sell the timber on this land as long as they paid Crown dues on the volume. Conflict with the limitholder resulted as soon as the settlers cleared land not only for the obvious reason of ownership of the logs, but also because the settlers were a source of wildfires. Colons habitually piled and burnt their brush and slash with little concern to the safety of the surrounding forest. The forest fires that resulted often got out of control, financially hurting the lumbermen. Due to these problems, at the time of the Montreal meeting, the Quebec lumbermen were already promoting the cause of forest reserves and land classification systems as well as organization of fire prevention and suppression efforts. For a summary of the motivations behind this movement, see: Jack Little, "La Patrie: Quebec's Repatriation Colony, 1875–1880," *Historical Papers* (Ottawa, 1977), pp. 66–85. G. Vattier, *Esquisse Historique de la Colonisation de la Province de Quebec* (Paris, 1928).

24. Lambert with Pross, *Renewing*, pp. 164–165.

25. Ibid.

26. Ibid., p. 163; and Gillis, "Ottawa Lumber Barons," p. 20.

27. Ibid.; and PAC, RG15, Department of the Interior, vol. 298, file 62441.

28. Ibid.

29. PAC, RG15, Department of the Interior, vol. 317, file 72369. The treelessness of the prairies had worried successive Dominion governments since at least 1871. In this year, Great Britain's west coast colony of British Columbia had joined the Canadian Confederation. One of the terms of the union was that the Dominion government would guarantee the construction of a transcontinental railway. Settlement of the prairies would speed this construction as well as lower its cost. To encourage settlement, the Liberal government of Alexander MacKenzie established a forestation program in 1876. Western settlers could file for a "Forest Tree Culture Claim" and obtain an extra 160 acres of land as long as they planted a proportion of their total holding with trees. Many settlers took advantage of this program and planted nursery stock obtained from Ontario only to see it die of winter-kill. By the mid-1880s, the word was rapidly spreading that trees could not be grown on the prairies. Farmers who tried soon came to be considered faddists and, according to a later report, were subjected to "local ridicule." Imported stock was used not only because Ontario was the only nearby source of young trees, but also settlers keen on tree planting generally came from eastern Canada or western Europe and looked to familiar trees for solace in their new land. See Norman M. Ross, *The Tree-Planting Division: Its History and Work*, Canada, Department of the Interior, Forestry Branch, 1923; and Peter Murphy, *History of Forest and Prairie Fire Control Policy in Alberta* (Edmonton, 1985), pp. 70–71. During speeches in the House of Commons, Macdonald referred to European experiments with tree nurseries as an example to be investigated for the west.

30. PAC, RG2, Records of the Privy Council, Order in Council no. 640, 23 May 1882. The head of the Branch was given the title "Chief Clerk." This title was retained until the Branch was disbanded in 1935. During all these years, the Branch successfully avoided employing professional foresters to manage the lands it was responsible for. In fact, college graduates were a rarity among its employees. PAC, RG15 vol. 15, book 9, pp. 195–199, Saskatchewan and Alberta Resources Commission, memo: George W. Payton to J. Lorne Turner, 9 March 1934.

31. PAC, RG15 file 62441.

32. Ibid.; and Murphy, *Prairie Fire Control*, pp. 82–83. Burgess was convinced that Morgan's work was properly the responsibility of the Department of Agriculture and may also have been apprehensive over Forestry recommendations that would expose Tory patronage activities in giving away a large number of (up to 50) timber berths in western Canada without fees being charged.

33. PAC, RG15 vol. 311, file 69113.

34. Murphy, *Prairie Fire Control*, p. 132; PAC, RG15 vol. 311, file 69113 and vol. 630, file 235667, pt.2; Canada, *Statutes* 47 Vict, cap 25 and Senate, *Debates* (28 March 1884), pp. 358–364.

35. These events are recorded in Hodgins, *Paradis*, pp. 13–24. See Province of Quebec, "An Act Respecting Public Lands," *Statutes* (1887) pp. 51–52 Vict, cap 15.

36. Lambert with Pross, *Renewing*, pp. 165–168; and P. Gillis, "Ottawa Lumber Barons," p. 21.

37. Province of Quebec, *Statutes* (1894), 58 Vict, cap 22 and cap 23. One reason

for establishing northern parks in Quebec was to try to save the caribou from extinction.

Chapter 3

1. For biographical details on Sifton, see Pierre Berton, *The Promised Land: Settling the West 1896–1914* (Toronto, 1984); David J. Hall, *Clifford Sifton*, (Vancouver: 1981 and 1985), vol. 1, *The Young Napoleon 1861–1900*, and vol. 2, *The Lonely Eminence 1901–1929*.

2. For an idea of the looseness of Sifton's dealings with favoured timbermen, see Berton, *Promised Land*, pp. 235–240.

3. Canada, Department of the Interior, *Annual Report* (1898).

4. PAC, RG15 vol. 772, file 523278, Privy Council (PC) 1762, 29 July 1899.

5. Canada, Department of the Interior, *Annual Report* (1900); Peter Murphy, *History of Forest and Prairie Fire Control Policy in Alberta* (Edmonton; 1985), pp. 102–105; and Carl Alwin Schenck, *Birth of Forestry in America* (Santa Cruz, Ca., 1974).

6. PAC, RG39 vol. 1, file 18374, "Policy resolutions". Canada, Department of the Interior, *Annual Report* (1901); RG39 vol. 417, PC1913, 22 Oct. 1901; Norman M. Ross, *The Tree-planting Division* (Ottawa, 1923).

7. PAC, RG39 vol. 267, file 39766-I, "Policy, National Forest Policy."

8. PAC, RG39 vol. 19, file 383, "Policy, U.S. Forest Service"; Stewart to Pinchot, 23 August 1899; Pinchot to Stewart, 26 August 1899; Stewart to Pinchot, 29 Nov. 1899; Pinchot to Stewart, 16 Dec. 1899.

9. PAC, RG39 vol. 232, file 349, "Head Office, Publicity, Canadian Forestry Association"; James A. Smart to E. Stewart, 20 Dec. 1899; reply, 22 Dec. 1899; Stewart to Smart, 3 Jan. 1900. Henri Joly had been knighted on 25 May 1895 and earlier, in 1888, had added his wife's family name to his. PAC, MG27 II C2.

10. Ibid., Sydney Fisher to Stewart, 16 Jan. 1900; Thomas Southworth to Stewart, 24 Jan. 1900; Joly to Stewart, 13 March 1900; Stewart to H. L. Patmore of Brandon, Manitoba, 13 March 1900. PAC, MG28, I, 188, vol. 1, Canadian Forestry Association, *Minute Book*, Minutes for 15 Jan. 1900.

11. Ibid., RG39, Thomas Southworth to E. Stewart, 24 Jan. 1900.

12. Canadian Forestry Association, *Report of the First Annual Meeting* (Ottawa, 1900); "Formation of the Canadian Forestry Association," *Rod and Gun in Canada* 1, 10 (March 1900): 192, 202–204, 239–241. As noted above, the Department of the Interior paid for all the printing and office costs in the early years, and the Association's business files are mixed up with those of the Forestry Branch. After the meeting, Elihu Stewart continued as Secretary assisted by a young clerk in the Timber and Grazing Branch, Robert H. Campbell.

13. Berton, *Promised Land*, pp. 226–249; and Hall, *Clifford Sifton*, vol. 2, pp. 162–182.

14. A biography of this colorful and lively westerner has yet to be written. See: References in Hall, *Clifford Sifton*, vols. 1 and 2; and Berton, *Promised Land*.

15. Gifford Pinchot, *Breaking New Ground* (Seattle, 1972), pp. 254–262; and Canadian Forestry Association, *Report of the Canadian Forestry Convention* (Ottawa, 1906). Of interest is the comparatively radical paper given by Judson F. Clark which eventually led to his resignation from the employ of the Ontario government.

16. Canadian Forestry Association, *Report* (1906).

17. Pinchot, *Breaking New Ground*, p. 254.

18. Ibid.

19. Canadian Forestry Association, *Report* (1906).

20. Canada, House of Commons, *Debates* (1906), vol. I, p. 559.

21. PAC, RG39 vol. 259, file 3805–1–2, "Head Office Supervision, Forest Reserves Act"; Stewart to Southworth, 28 Nov. 1904; Southworth to Stewart, 19 Nov. 1904; Sifton to T. G. Rothwell, 19 Dec. 1904; R. G. Keys, Secretary to the Department of the Interior, to E. L. Newcombe, Deputy Minister of Justice, 20 Jan. 1905; Ernest Lemaire, Private Secretary to the Prime Minister, to Stewart, 21 Feb. 1905; Rothwell to Sifton, 1 March 1905; Stewart to Laurier, 23 Feb. 1906.

22. Ibid., W. W. Cory, deputy minister, Department of the Interior, to Rothwell, 5 March 1906; Rothwell to W. W. Cory, 16 March 1906; Cory to Rothwell, 9 March 1906 to 17 March 1906; J. B. Naskin to Stewart, 22 March 1906. See supporting correspondence from Southworth to Oliver and Laurier during the months of March and April, 1906.

23. R. H. Coats, *Wholesale Prices in Canada, 1890–1909 (Inclusive)* (Ottawa, 1910), p. 393, chart 78; and Wilson Compton, *The Organization of the Lumber Industry* (Chicago, 1916), pp. 80–82.

24. Hall, *Clifford Sifton*, vol. 2, p. 96. Kenneth H. Norrie, "The National Policy and the Rate of Prairie Settlement: A Review", *Journal of Canadian Studies* 14, 3 (Fall 1979): 63–76; Compton, *Lumber Industry*, pp. 79–80.

25. Canada, House of Commons, "Proceedings of the Select Committee Appointed for the Purpose of Inquiring into the Prices Charged for Lumber in the Provinces of Manitoba, Alberta and Saskatchewan," *Journals of the House of Commons of Canada* 42, 2, app. 6 (Ottawa, 1907) (hereafter referred to as "Select Committee"). For a more detailed discussion, see Chapter 6, "A Touch of Pinchotism: Forestry in British Columbia".

26. Ibid.

27. Canada, House of Commons, *Debates* (1906), vol. II, pp. 2832, 3318, 3412; vol. III, pp. 5416, 5537, 5556. See correspondence in RG39, vol. 259, file 3805–1 cited above.

28. Ibid., vol. III, pp. 5538, 5543.

29. House of Commons, *Debates* (1911), vol. V, pp. 8085, 8606–8023, 8650–8659.

30. Ibid.

31. Ross, *Tree Planting*. See testimonials in RG39 vol. 1, file 18374, "Policy Resolutions."

32. PAC, RG39 vol. 259, file 3805–1–2; Owen Ritchie to Frank Oliver, 16 Nov. 1910; L. Pereira, Assistant Secretary of the Department the Interior, to E. L. Newcombe, 27 Dec. 1910; P. G. Keyes to Owen Ritchie, 1 August 1911.

33. Ibid.

34. Canada, House of Commons, *Debates* (1911).

35. Ibid, p. 8610; and Sylvia Van Kirk, "The Development of National Park Policy in Canada's Mountain National Parks, 1885 to 1930," (unpublished masters thesis, Univ. of Alberta, 1969), chap. I.

36. Canada, House of Commons, *Debates* (1911), p. 8612.

37. Canada, Department of the Interior, Forestry Service, *Timber Disposal Manual* (Ottawa, 1929), pp. 54–57. The accompanying explanatory text makes it clear that the phrase "non-competitive rates" means below market value. In particular, settlers

were to receive all the wood they wanted free and when surpluses were sold non-commercially, the objective was to keep small, local concerns in business and help ease unemployment. The forestry officers were thus fulfilling political roles rather than silvicultural roles.

38. Canada, House of Commons, *Debates* (1911), pp. 8619–8623.

39. Ibid.

40. F. G. Fensom, *Expanding Forestry Horizons* (Montreal, 1972), p. 404; and PAC, RG 2 PC51–399, 28 Feb. 1907.

41. PAC, RG32 C2 vol. 40, Frederick H. Byshe, "Robert Henry Campbell"; PAC, RG2 PC51–399, 28 Feb. 1907.

42. PAC, RG39 vol. 1, file 18374, "Policy Resolutions"; RG39 vol. 267, file 39766–1, Charles McCormick, general merchant, Kenville, Manitoba to Minister of Agriculture, 10 March 1914; vol. 448, file 34238, H. R. Duchane (letter and petition), Plamondville, Alberta, to Minister of the Interior, 29 Sept. 1915. Others can be found in file 38067 of the same volume. This presented Oliver with a chance to profit. He had some friends file fraudulent squatter's claims and supervised their processing himself. When the claims were paid, the money was divided between the parties involved. Berton, *Settling the West*, p. 207.

43. Chester Martin, *Dominion Lands Policy* (Toronto, 1973), p. 189; and Canada, House of Commons, "Select Committee". The returns were made to the Timber and Grazing Branch in the form of sworn statement by the mill's owner which was rarely checked by the Branch's officers. The reduction of volume was up to 50 percent of that actually sold as lumber and was actually higher in some cases: one enviable mill in Winnipeg had no waste whatsoever. What it did not burn to produce its own steam, it sold as firewood. The new regulations compromised on the choice of rule, requiring the use of Scribners instead of the Doyle rule desired by the mill owners or the new International rule pushed by the Forestry Branch.

44. PAC, RG39 vol. 268, file 39770–1, "Forestry, Head Office, Brush Disposal"; especially a report by R. H. Palmer, Chief Fire Ranger, Edmonton, June 1913, sent to W. W. Cory by R. H. Campbell on 11 June 1913; memo by F. K. Hershmeir, District Inspector, Manitoba, 11 Jan. 1914; Campbell to Cory, 5 Sept. 1917; as well as various petitions from operators and their answering letters in this file until 1923 and then in file 39980.

45. PAC, RG39 vol. 267, file 39766–1; W. J. Roche, Minister of the Interior, to James White, Secretary, Commission of Conservation, 22 April 1915. See the briefs and submissions made by the Dominion Forestry Service to the Royal Commission on Transfer of Natural Resources to Alberta and Saskatchewan in PAC, RG15 vols. 15 and 16.

46. Pinchot, *Breaking New Ground*, p. 437.

47. Ibid., pp. 344–345, 355–360, 421–422; PAC, RG15 vol. 1038, file 1711511, PC2561, Report of the Committee of the Privy Council, 21 Nov. 1908; "Preservation of the Forest," *Ottawa Citizen*, 15 Dec. 1908, p. 9.

48. Ibid.

49. Ibid.

50. Pinchot, *Breaking New Ground*, pp. 361–366; "Resources of North America", *Ottawa Citizen*, 28 Dec. 1908, p. 3. "Mr Gifford Pinchot", 30 Dec. 1908, p.3. "International Conservation," 31 Dec. 1908, p. 3. The problem was that Pinchot lacked formal diplomatic status. How was he to present his letter without upsetting Roo-

sevelt's appointed ambassador to the British Empire based in London, England? An ingenious solution was quickly devised. That Saturday, on the thirty-first, the President of the Republic of Honduras was to address the Ottawa Canadian Club. As a result, the Prime Minister, the Leader of the Opposition, the Governor-General and the diplomatic corps would be in the city, and a special luncheon meeting of the Canadian Club was quickly organized. See also C. R. Smith and D. R. Witty, "Conservation, Resources and Environment: An Explanation and Critical Evaluation of the Commission of Conservation," *Plan Canada* 11, 1 (1970): 55–71; and D. M. Calnan, "Businessmen, Forestry and the Gospel of Efficiency: The Canadian Conservation Commission, 1909–1921", (unpublished Masters thesis, Univ. of Western Ontario, 1976); S. Renfrew, "Commission of Conservation", *Douglas Library Notes* (Spring 1971): 17–26.

51. *Ottawa Citizen*, 30 Dec. 1908.

52. Ibid.

53. Hall, *Clifford Sifton*, vol. 2, chap. 2.

54. Pinchot, *Breaking New Ground*, pp. 366–372.

55. Harold T. Pinkett, *Gifford Pinchot: Private and Public Forester* (Chicago, 1970), pp. 114–115.

56. Canada, House of Commons, *Debates* (1909), vol. 1, pp. 355–356; vol. 4, pp. 4988, 5249, 6363, 6375–6376, 6379–6380.

57. See Canada, Commission of Conservation, *First Annual Report, 1910* (Ottawa, 1910).

58. Canada, *Statutes*, 8–9 Edw. III, cap. 27. On the work of the Commission, especially urban planning see A. F. J. Artibise and G. A. Stelter, "Conservation Planning and Urban Planning: The Canadian Commission of Conservation in Historical Perspective," in R. Kain, ed., *Planning for Conservation* (New York, 1981), 17–36.

59. PAC, RG39 vol. 267, file 39766–1; W. J. Roche, Minister of the Interior, to James White, Secretary of the Commission of Conservation, 22 April 1915 in response to a letter White wrote to Borden on 23 March "asking for a change in organization re cutting regulations on timber berths". Clyde Leavitt to R. H. Campbell, 15 May 1915; reply, 19 May 1915. Canada, House of Commons, "Report of the Select Standing Committee on Forests, Waterways and Waterpowers," *Journals of the House of Commons* (9 Edw. VII, 1909, app. IV–4, pp. 3–4.

Chapter 4

1. Wilson Compton, *The Organization of the Lumber Industry* (Chicago, 1916), p. 3. Ronald N. Johnson and Gary D. Libecap, "Efficient Markets and Great Lakes Timber: A Conservation Issue Reexamined," *Explorations in Economic History* 17, 4 (October 1980): 372–385; Arthur R. M. Lower, *The North American Assault on the Canadian Forest* (Toronto, 1938), pp. 148–184.

2. Robert F. Fries, *Empire in Pine* (Madison, Wis., 1951), pp. 239–251; Michael Frome, *Whose Woods These Are* (New York, 1962), pp. 163–167; Mark E. Neithercut and Graeme Wynn, "Logging the Hemlock–White Pine–Northern Hardwood Forest: Geographical Perspectives," paper presented at the annual meeting of the American Historical Association, Chicago, 1984; Johnson and Libecap, "Efficient Markets."

3. H. V. Nelles, *The Politics of Development* (Toronto, 1975), pp. 48–107; Peter

Gillis, "The Ottawa Valley Lumber Barons and the Conservation Movement, 1880–1914," *Journal of Canadian Studies* 1 (1974): 14–30. See Ontario, *Sessional Papers* 58(1898) which contains correspondence from various milling interests.

4. Ibid.

5. Nelles, *Politics of Development*, pp. 182–183. Ontario, Bureau of Colonization, *Report of the Director of Colonization, 1900* (Toronto, 1901); Richard S. Lambert with Paul Pross, *Renewing Nature's Wealth* (Toronto, 1967), pp. 164–173. Ontario, *Report of the Commission on Forest Reservation and National Park* (Toronto, 1893); Peter W. Sinclair, "Strategies of Development on an Agricultural Frontier: The Great Clay Belt, 1900–1950," (unpublished doctoral dissertation, Univ. of Toronto, 1980).

6. Gillis, "Lumber Barons". In 1889, one company had 55 percent cull lumber in its daily mill output. Ronald Brown, "Depot Harbor, Busy Great Lakes Port, 1900–1928," *Canadian Geographical Journal* 95, 3(1977/1978): 56–61; Clarence F. Coons, *The John R. Booth Story* (Toronto, 1978); Duncan Johnston, *Canada Atlantic Railway, Old Boys' Reunion, August 19–24, 1935* (Ottawa, Donald H. Legate, 1935). G. R. Stevens, *The Canadian National Railways*, vol. 1 (Toronto, 1960); Lower, *North American Assault*, map on p. 184.

7. Ibid.

8. Gillis, "Lumber Barons"; Nelles, *Politics of Development*, pp. 42–43; Lower, *North American Assault*, pp. 157–159.

9. Gillis, "Lumber Barons"; Nelles, *Politics of Development*; Lambert with Pross, *Renewing*, pp. 142–145.

10. Ibid.; Compton, *Lumber Industry*, pp. 32–35; United States Department of Commerce, Bureau of Corporations, *The Lumber Industry* vol. 4 (Washington, D.C., 1914), pp. 490–492.

11. Nelles, *Politics of Development*, pp. 66–67.

12. In 1885, the two sections of the industry were about equal in production, contributing about 42 percent each to the total income from "Woods and Forests." In 1889, the west was to the fore, 50 percent to 31 percent and, in 1894, 64 percent to 25 percent. Nelles, *Politics of Development*. W. C. Edwards, one of the leading Ottawa men, expressed his disdain for the men of western Ontario when he termed them a "hairbrained lot of jingoes . . . who do not lumber on a scale to make lumbering profitable at all." PAC, MG26 G, Sir Wilfrid Laurier Papers, p. 17706; W. C. Edwards to Laurier, 21 Nov. 1897 and 181964–181965, W. C. Edwards to B. E. Walker. Ontario was the only province involved in open competition with United States lumber. At this time, British Columbia's industry was not developed enough to enter the California market. The products of Quebec were sold in the United States but also a significant portion, there and in eastern Canada, was sold locally or exported to Britain.

13. Gillis, "Lumber Barons".

14. Lewis L. Gould, "The Republicans Under Roosevelt and Taft," in Lewis L. Gould, ed., *The Progressive Era* (Syracuse, 1974), p. 55.

15. For the Joint High Commission, see J. M. V. Foster, "Reciprocity and the Joint High Commission of 1898–99," *Canadian Historical Association Annual Report*, 1939, pp. 87–98.

16. Gillis, "Lumber Barons"; Nelles, *Politics of Development*.

17. Ibid.; and E. W. Rathbun, *Shall We Place An Export Duty on Sawlogs and Pulpwood?* (Deseronto, 1897.)

18. Ibid. See Ontario, *Sessional Papers* 58; and PAC, Bronson Company Records, MG28 III vol. 724, J. M. Gibson to Levi Crannell, 1 Oct. 1897 and R. W. Scott Papers, MG27 II B14 vol. 4, A. S. Hardy to Scott, 1 August 1898.

19. Nelles, *Politics of Development*, p. 51.

20. Gillis, "Lumber Barons."

21. Like the first holder of the position, Robert Phipps, Southworth was a former journalist with little experience in forestry matters. P. Gillis and T. Roach, "Early European and North American Forestry in Canada: The Ontario Example, 1890–1940" in Harold K. Steen, ed., *History of Sustained-Yield Forestry: A Symposium* (Santa Cruz, Calif., 1984), pp. 211–219. Lambert with Pross, *Renewing*, pp. 137–140. Gillis, "Lumber Barons".

22. Ontario, *Annual Report of the Clerk of Forestry, 1896* (Toronto, 1896), p. 25.

23. Ontario, *Report of the Royal Commission on Forestry Protection in Ontario, 1899* (Toronto, 1899), pp. 5–8.

24. Ibid.

25. Gillis and Roach, "European and American Forestry."

26. Ibid.

27. Ontario, *Report, 1896*, pp. 23, 26. Gillis, "Lumber Barons."

28. Andrew Denny Rodgers, *Bernhard Eduard Fernow, A Story of North American Forestry* (Princeton, 1951), pp. 394–395, B. M. Winegar, "Fire Protection in Ontario, Quebec and New Brunswick along the Canadian Pacific Railway, Season of 1914," in Canada, Commission of Conservation, *Forest Protection in Canada, 1913–1914* (Toronto, 1915), pp. 67–69; Ontario, Commission on Forest Reservation, *Report*, pp. 39–43; William Schlich, *A Manual of Forestry* (London, 1889).

29. Gillis and Roach, "European and American Forestry".

30. Gillis, "Lumber Barons"; Lambert with Pross, *Renewing*, pp. 185, 255; Bruce W. Hodgins, Jamie Benidickson, and Peter Gillis, "The Ontario and Quebec Experiments in Forest Reserves, 1883–1930," *Journal of Forest History* 26, 1 (1982): 20–33. Both these reserves contained licences and the holders were given five years to cut the remaining pine before their licences were revoked. The intention with these two relatively small reserves was that they should become regeneration projects in regions that had once contained rich pineries.

31. Hodgins, et. al., "Reserves"; and Nelles, *Politics of Development*, pp. 182–214. Subsequent to the establishment of the Temagami Forest Reserve, a belt of reserves was established across northern Ontario including Mississagi, an area of virgin pine created in 1903 (7,800 square kilometres) and enlarged in 1913 (to 13,000 square kilometres; Nipigon, a pulpwood area of 19,700 square kilometres laid aside in 1905; and the Quetico Boundary Reserve of 4,660 square kilometres created in 1909.

32. Gillis and Roach, "European and American Forestry." See also, Austin Cary, "White Pine and Fire," *Journal of Forestry* 35 (1936): 62–65; J. André Linteau, "Le feu, régénerateur de la fôret," *La Fôret Quebecoise* 3, 8 (1941): 40–49 and 3, 9 (1941): 35–48; D. K. Maissurow, "Fire as a Necessary Factor in the Perpetuation of White Pine," *Journal of Forestry* 33 (1935): 373–378; K. M. Mayall, *White Pine Succession as Influenced By Fire* (Ottawa, 1941); Gillis and Roach, "European and American Forestry"; Neithercut and Wynn, "Logging"; Lower, *North American Assault*; Lower, *Great Britain's Woodyard* (Montreal, 1973); Compton, *Lumber Industry*; Coons, *John R. Booth*.

33. Roland D. Craig, "The Present State of Canada's Pulpwood Resources," *The Paper Mill and Woodpulp News* (13 Feb. 1926): 14, 16.

34. Coons, *John R. Booth*; Gillis, "Lumber Barons"; Nelles, *Politics of Development*, pp. 56–62, 82–83. See Alfred D. Chandler, *The Visible Hand* (Cambridge, 1977).

35. For a discussion of the role of the chemist and chemical engineer in the pulp and paper industry at about this period, see R. W. MacKenzie, "The Chemical Engineer and the News Print Industry", *Canadian Chemistry and Metallurgy* 5, 3 (1921): 75–76 and subsequent articles by the same author in the following three issues.

36. Nelles, *Politics of Development*, pp. 56–62.

37. Ibid.

38. Nelles, *Politics of Development*, pp. 102–107.

39. Ibid.

40. Hodgins, et. al., "Reserves". In particular, the colonization societies feared that any type of export restriction would eventually affect the harvesting of pulpwood by the colons from their lots. Nelles, *Politics of Development*, p. 336.

41. Gillis, "Lumber Barons."

42. Lambert with Pross, *Renewing*, pp. 250–258; and Nelles, *Politics of Development*, pp. 116, 205–206.

43. Lambert with Pross, *Renewing*, pp. 186–189.

44. Ibid.

45. Lambert with Pross, *Renewing*; and Nelles, *Politics of Development*.

46. Lambert with Pross, *Renewing*, pp. 259–260; Nelles, *Politics of Development*, pp. 205–206; C. W. Humphries, *Honest Enough to Be Bold: The Life and Times of Sir James Pliny Whitney* (Toronto, 1985), pp. 100–101.

47. Lambert with Pross, *Renewing*, pp. 259–260.

48. Ibid., p. 187; and Nelles, *Politics of Development*, p. 211.

49. Ibid.

50. Quoted by Rodgers, *Fernow*, p. 398.

51. Thomas R. Roach, "Stewards of the People's Wealth," *Journal of Forest History* 28, 1 (1984): 14–23; Rodgers, *Fernow*, pp. 394–398.

52. Lambert with Pross, *Renewing*, pp. 187–188, 260–264. The major problem with the Doyle rule was that it estimated the volume of first-grade lumber in a given log. This was fine when the rule was defined, but, by this period, the standard of what was a salable plank had dropped, and mills were able to dispose of a much greater proportion of each log than had previously been possible.

53. Lambert with Pross, *Renewing*; Nelles, *Politics of Development*; Thomas R. Roach, "The Pulpwood Trade and the Settlers of New Ontario," paper presented at the 1981 annual meeting of the Ontario Historical Association; Hodgins, et. al., "Reserves"; J. W. B. Sisam, *Forestry Education at Toronto* (Toronto; 1961), chap. 2.

54. Trevor J. O. Dick, "Canadian Newsprint, 1913–1930: National Policies and the North American Economy," *Journal of Economic History* 42, 3 (1982): 659–687; Herbert Marshall, Frank Southard, Jr., and Kenneth W. Taylor, *Canadian American Industry* (Toronto; 1976); Tom Traves, *The State and Enterprise* (Toronto; 1979), pp. 30, 47–54.

55. Lewis Ethan Ellis, *Reciprocity 1911, A Study in Canadian American Relations* (New Haven; 1939); Lewis Ethan Ellis, "The Newsprint Paper Pendulum" in *Newsprint, Producers, Publishers, Political Pressures* (New Brunswick; 1960); Dick, "Canadian Newsprint". Dick argues that the removal of the tariff was not a factor in the

growth of the industry in Canada since, at the time the tariff was removed, the industry in the United States had only enough extra capacity for about six months more of growth. He estimates that the removal of the tariff advanced the growth of the industry in Canada by about two years.

56. P. Oliver, *Public and Private Persons: The Ontario Political Culture 1914–1934*, (Toronto; 1975), chap. 2.

57. Lambert with Pross, *Renewing*, p. 263; Nelles, *Politics of Development*, pp. 376–393; "Death of Mr. Aubrey White C.M.G.," *Canadian Forestry Journal* 11 (July 1915): 134–135.

58. American Paper and Pulp Association, *The Paper and Pulp Industry*, vol. 1, 1 (1920); Canadian Pulp and Paper Association, *The Underwood Resolution, Committee Hearings*, C.P.P.A. Bulletin no. 24 (1 May 1920); Ellis, *Reciprocity 1911*; Traves, *State and Enterprise*; United States, Federal Trade Commission, *Report on the News-Print Paper Industry* (Washington, D.C., 13 June 1917).

59. Lambert with Pross, *Renewing*, pp. 263–267; Nelles, *Politics of Development*, pp. 386–391; P. Oliver, *G. Howard Ferguson: Ontario Tory* (Toronto; 1977), chap. 6.

60. Nelles, *Politics of Development*; Rodgers, *Fernow*, pp. 435–439.

61. Craig, "Canada's Pulpwood Resources"; Clifton D. Howe, "The Forest Problems of Ontario," *Illustrated Canadian Forests and Outdoors* 21, 1 (January 1924): 852–854, W. N. Millar, "Sustained Yield, Its Legislative Basis in Canada," *Forestry Chronicle* 2, 4 (1926): 3–16; Rodgers, *Fernow*, p. 439; Lambert with Pross, *Renewing*, pp. 190–194.

62. Lambert with Pross, *Renewing*, pp. 190–194.

63. Ibid.; Yale University Forest School, Biographical Record of the Graduates and Students of the Yale Forest School (New Haven, 1913), p. 121.

64. Lambert with Pross, *Renewing*, pp. 314–316, 321–323.

65. Gillis and Roach, "European and American Forestry"; Howe, "Forest Problems"; Millar, "Sustained Yield."

66. Marshall et al., *Canadian American Industry*, pp. 35–56; Ellis, "The Newsprint Paper Pendulum"; pp. 125–127; John A. Guthrie, *The Newsprint Paper Industry: An Economic Analysis* (Cambridge, 1941), pp. 130–145; Roach, "The Pulpwood Trade and the Settlers of New Ontario".

67. Howe, "Forest Problems"; Millar, "Sustained Yield"; Gillis and Roach, "European and American Forestry."

68. Wilson Compton, *Conservation: the Form or the Substance, Which?* (Chicago, 1919). These are arguments from an ongoing debate in the period discussed here. See "Who Should Pay Forest Conservation Costs," *Illustrated Canadian Forestry and Outdoors* 20, 12 (1924): 751–752; Frank D. Adams, "Our National Heritage" in J. O. Miller, ed., *The New Era in Canada* (Toronto; 1917), p. 98; Robson Black, "A Lumber Yard Without Lumber," *Canada Lumberman* 64, 18 (1922): 156–158; William Brown, "The Application of Scientific and Practical Arborculture to Canada" in British Association for the Advancement of Science, *Canadian Economics* (Montreal; 1885), pp. 119–130; Austin Cary, "Unprofessional Forestry," *Forestry Quarterly* 4, 3 (1906): 183–187; Roland D. Craig, "Canada's Pulpwood Resources"; Bernhard E. Fernow, "The Result of Systematic Forest Management," *Forestry Quarterly* 6, 3 (1908): 229–233; Alfred Gaskill, "How Shall the Forests Be Taxed?" paper presented at the Society of American Foresters, 8 December 1904, P.A.C. Library, pamphlet coll. 2–2993; Robert B. Goodman, "The Problems of Our Raw Wood Supply," *Forest*

Management (Marinette, Wis.; 1927), 3–11; J.E. Rhodes, "Lumbermen and Forestry". *Can. Jour. For.* 11, 12(1915): 16–20. Carl A. Schenck, *The Art of Second Growth* (Albany; 1912), 11, 107–110; Ellwood Wilson, "The Forest from an Investor's Point of View," *Illustrated Canadian Forests and Outdoors*, 19, 10 (1923): 651–652, 670; E. H. Finlayson, "Control of Timber Cutting," *Illustrated Canadian Forestry and Outdoors* 20, 10 (1924): 585–586, 628–629 and 20, 11 (1924): 665–668.

69. Ibid., PAO, E. C. Drury Papers, R. Black to E. C. Drury, CFA file, 15–19 December 1919.

70. Lambert with Pross, *Renewing*, pp. 263–267; Nelles, *Politics of Development*, pp. 386–391; Oliver, *Howard Ferguson*.

71. Ibid.; PAO, E. C. Drury Papers, R. Black to E. C. Drury, CFA file, 15–19 December 1919.

72. Ibid.

73. Ibid.; Judson F. Clark, "A Plan to Improve Ontario's Forest Management," *Illustrated Canadian Forestry and Outdoors* 18, 10 (1922): 1109–1112.

74. Ibid.; "Lumbermen Protest Judson Clark Report," *Illustrated Canadian Forestry and Outdoors* 19, 1 (1923): 27, 54–55, 57. The lumbermen's criticisms revolved around the now familiar theme that any change in their operating conditions would automatically so increase their costs that they would be forced out of business. Further, they argued, their leases represented unbreakable contracts, and this meant that the government could make no alterations without their complete consent. Drury accepted this position.

75. Oliver, *Howard Ferguson*; Lambert with Pross, *Renewing*, pp. 500–502; Ontario, *Statues* (1927) Forest Act, 17 Geo. V, cap 41.

76. Lambert with Pross, *Renewing*, p. 199.

Chapter 5

1. Bruce W. Hodgins, Jamie Benidickson, and Peter Gillis, "The Ontario and Quebec Experiments in Forest Reserves, 1883–1930," *Journal of Forest History* 26, 1 (January 1982): 23–32; E. T. O. Chambers, "The Province of Quebec," *Canada and Its Provinces* (Toronto, 1914–17), vol. 16, pp. 541–544.

2. John A. Guthrie, *An Economic Analysis of the Pulp and Paper Industry* (Seattle, 1972), pp. 1–8.

3. Canada, *Report of the Royal Commission on Pulpwood* (Ottawa; 1924), pp. 39–49, 144–145; Thomas A. Roach, "Farm Woodlots and Pulpwood Exports from Eastern Canada" in H. K. Steen, ed., *History of Sustained Yield Forestry* (Santa Cruz, Calif., 1984), pp. 202–210.

4. See Quebec, *Report of the Colonization Commission of the Province of Quebec, 1904* (Quebec City, 1904).

5. Ibid.; Roach, "Farm Woodlots."

6. See R. Peter Gillis, "The Ottawa Lumber Barons and the Conservation Movement, 1880–1914," *Journal of Canadian Studies* 9 (February 1974): 14–30; Quebec, *Sessional Papers* (1883–1884), no. 4; PAC, Bronsons and Weston Lumber Co. Records, MG 28 III 26, E. H. Bronson to Hon. W. W. Lynch, Quebec Commissioners of Crown Lands, 12 June 1883; Hodgins et al., "Reserves."

7. Ibid.; Chambers, "The Province"; Quebec, *Sessional Paper* no. 4.

8. Chambers, "The Province"; Quebec Commissioners of Crown Lands, *Annual*

Reports (1872–1900; M. Hamelin, *Les Premières Annés du Parlimentarisme Québecois, 1867–1878* (Quebec City; 1974), pp. 183–190.

9. Hodgins et. al., "Reserves"; Quebec, "An Act Respecting Public Lands," *Statutes* (1888), 51–52 Vict, cap 15, see chap. 2.

10. See Robert Rumilly, *Histoire de la Province de Québec* (Montreal; 1940), vol. 5, pp. 258–266; Gillis, "Ottawa Lumber Barons"; Bruce W. Hodgins, *Paradis of Temagami* (Cobalt; Ontario, 1976), pp. 13–24.

11. Ibid.

12. Hodgins et al., "Reserves"; Quebec, *Statutes* (1894), 58 Vict., cap. 22 and cap. 23.

13. Quebec, *Report of the Colonization Commission*.

14. Ibid.

15. Rumilly, vol. 10, pp. 58–67; vol. 11, pp. 110–118. Bourassa linked any alienation of the province's resources to attempts to sell the resources to English and American capitalists.

16. Ibid., vol. 11, p. 64.

17. Ibid., vol. 10, pp. 135–137.

18. Ibid., vol. 11, pp. 63–65. Langelier's brothers were the Hon. Charles Langelier, who had been President of the Council and Provincial Secretary in the Mercier government and the Hon. Sir F. C. S. Langelier, who had been Commissioner of Crown Lands and then Treasurer in the Joly government (1878–1879) and later became Lieutenant-Governor of the province.

19. Ibid., pp. 114–117.

20. Ibid.

21. Ibid., p. 117.

22. Ibid.

23. Quebec, *Report of the Colonization Commission*.

24. Ibid.

25. Ibid.

26. C. A. Hopkins, *Canadian Annual Review, 1905* (Toronto; 1905), p. 601 contains a report of the Quebec City meeting.

27. Ibid.; Hodgins et al., "Reserves"; Paul-Andre Linteau, Réné Durocher, and Jean-Claude Robert, *Quebec: A History 1867–1929* (Toronto; 1983), pp. 505. Gouin felt continued pressure to reform forest management policy because of charges of maladministration by Baron Lepine, a Belgian emigre, concerning lands in the Abitibi.

28. Chambers, "The Province"; Quebec, *Sesssional Paper No. 5, Report of the Minister of Lands, Mines and Fisheries* (1908), pp. 95, 141–152. See B. Weilbrenner, "Les idées fôret politiques de Lomer Gouin"; in J. P. Heisler and F. Ouellet, eds., *Canadian Historical Association Report* (Ottawa; 1966), pp. 46–57.

29. Ibid. The reservations included the immense Labrador, St. Maurice, and Ottawa reserves (276,000, 55,000, and 72,000 square kilometres, respectively), the Bonaventure Reserve (885 square kilometres), the Riviere Ouelle Reserve (885 square kilometres), and the Barachois Reserve (294 square kilometres), as well as the Laurentides, Mont Tremblant and Gaspesian Parks.

30. Quebec, "Department of Lands and Forests and Matters Connected Therewith," *Revised Statutes* (1909) cap. 6, sec. 1633. The effect of this revision was to

give the licencee time to remove merchantable timber from a lot located on an already granted licence or berth.

31. Hodgins et al., "Reserves"; Rumilly, vol. 14, p. 67, vol. 15, p. 10, vol. 19, p. 20. Chambers, "The Province," pp. 550–551.

32. Ibid.; Hodgins et al., "Reserves."

33. Quebec, *Report of the Minister of Lands, Mines and Fisheries* (1910). "Forestry Methods in the Province of Quebec," *Canada Lumberman and Woodworker* 17 (1 Sept. 1912): 67–68.

34. Hodgins et al., "Reserves."

35. Ibid.

36. Ibid.

37. Ibid.

38. Ellwood Wilson, "Reforestation in Canada," *Forestry Chronicle* 5 (June) 1929: 14–18; Hodgins et al., "Reserves"; Quebec, *Annual Reports of the Forestry Service* (1921–1926).

39. Quebec, *Report of the Forestry Service* (1921), pp. 38–40; Hodgins et al., "Reserves"; P. Asselin, "L'Administration de Domaine Forestier" in E. Minville, ed., *La fôret* (Montreal); 1944, pp. 80–82.

40. Quebec, *Report of the Minister of Lands, Mines and Fisheries* (1910). *Report of the Forestry Service* (1921), pp. 38–88; (1924–1925), pp. 19–37.

41. See Canada, Department of the Interior, Canadian Forestry Service, *The Forests of Canada* (Ottawa; 1928) and Rumilly, vol. 25, pp. 32–34, vol. 27, pp. 79 and 147.

42. Quebec, *Report of the Minister of Lands and Forests* (1924–1925), 37.

43. Ibid., *Report of the Minister of Lands, Forests and Fisheries* (1913–1914), pp. 59–60 and (1917–1918), pp. 29–30; Asselin, "L'Administration," pp. 80–82.

44. Rumilly, vol. 16, pp. 75–76.

45. Quebec, *Report of the Minister of Lands, Forests and Fisheries* (1917–1918), p. 30. Quebec, *Statutes* (1918), 8–9 Geo. V, cap. 30.

46. Ibid., *Report* (1924–1925), p. 37.

47. Hodgins et al., "Reserves"; Rumilly, vol. 25, pp. 32–34, vol. 27, p. 147.

48. See Quebec, Department of Lands and Forests, *Annual Reports* for these years; Canada, Department of the Interior, Canadian Forestry Service, *Proceedings of the Forest Fire Conference, Parliament Buildings, Ottawa, January 7–11, 1924* (mss. 1924).

49. Minville, *La fôret*; virtually all articles make this point.

50. Herbert Marshall, Frank Southard, and Kenneth W. Taylor, *Canadian-American Industry* (Toronto, 1976), pp. 39–49.

51. Ibid., 49–52.

52. Quebec, *Report of the Chief of the Forestry Service* (1924–1925); Avila Bédard, "Forestry in Quebec," *Canadian Geographical Journal* 28 (June 1944): 258–280.

53. Hodgins et al., "Reserves."

54. L. Z. Rousseau, "La fôret Quebecoise" in Minville, *La fôret*, p. 76.

55. Ibid.

Chapter 6

1. Portions of this chapter appeared in Thomas R. Roach, "Stewards of the People's Wealth," *Journal of Forest History* 28, 1 (January 1984): 14–23.

2. The best contemporary descriptions of the forests are J. R. Anderson, "Pres-

ervation of Our Forests," *Report of the Third Annual Meeting of the Canadian Forestry Association* (Ottawa, 1902), pp. 120–122; H. N. Whitford and Roland D. Craig, *The Forests of British Columbia*, (Ottawa, 1918); T. C. Whyte, "British Columbia's Forests," *Rod and Gun in Canada* 3 (June, 1901): 7. See also Graeme Wynn, "Prolegomena to a History of the Forest Industries in British Columbia," unpublished ms provided by the author, 1985.

3. See Robert E. Cail, *Land, Man and Law* (Vancouver, 1974); Margaret A. Ormsby, *British Columbia, a History* (Vancouver, 1958); Martin Robin, *The Rush for Spoils: The Company Province, 1871–1933* (Toronto, 1972).

4. Ibid., especially Cail, *Land*, pp. 1–97.

5. Ibid.; Walter G. Hardwick, *Geography of the Forest Industry of Coastal British Columbia* (Vancouver, 1963); Joseph Collins Lawrence, "Markets and Capital: A History of the Lumber Industry of British Columbia" (unpublished masters thesis, University of British Columbia, 1957); Richard M. Yerburgh, "An Economic History of Forestry in British Columbia" (unpublished masters thesis, Univ. of British Columbia, 1931).

6. Cail, *Land*, pp. 92–98. W. A. Carrothers, "Forest Industries of British Columbia" in A. R. M. Lower, *The North American Assault on the Canadian Forest* (Toronto, 1938), pp. 233–243, 259. See also, Hardwick, *Geography*, pp. 122–124; Lawrence, "Markets"; Yerburgh, "Economic History," p. 32.

7. L. D. McCann, "Urban Growth in a Staple Economy: The Emergence of Vancouver as a Regional Metropolis, 1886–1914" in L. J. Evenden ed., *Vancouver: Western Metropolis* (Victoria, 1978), pp. 17–41. See also, Robert A. J. McDonald, "Victoria, Vancouver and the Economic Development of British Columbia, 1886–1914" in Peter Ward ed., *British Columbia: Historical Readings* (Vancouver, 1981), pp. 369–395; Norbett MacDonald, "The Canadian Pacific Railway and Vancouver's Development to 1900" in ibid., pp. 396–425; A. H. MacDonald, "Population Growth and Change in Seattle and Vancouver, 1880–1960" in J. Friesen and H. K. Ralston, eds., *Historical Essays on British Columbia* (Toronto, 1976).

8. Lawrence, "Markets;" pp. 11–14; Carrothers, "Forest Industries," pp. 263–269; Hardwick, *Geography*, pp. 22–25.

9. McCann, "Urban Growth," p. 19; MacDonald, "Population Growth," Hardwick, *Geography*, pp. 22–30; Lawrence, "Markets," pp. 38–39.

10. Hardwick, *Geography*, pp. 1–25; Lawrence, "Markets;" pp. 48–60; Carrothers, "Forest Industries"; Yerburgh, "Economic History;" pp. 58, 63–68.

11. Hardwick, *Geography*; and McCann, "Urban Growth."

12. An analysis of the reports of mill activity and the arrival of booms at Burrard Inlet in the *Vancouver Daily Province* during these years reveals this. See also Yerburgh, "Economic History."

13. William H. Mercer, *Growth of Ghost Towns* (Victoria, 1944); Lawrence, "Markets;" pp. 38–39.

14. See British Columbia, Department of Lands, "Report of the Timber Inspection" in *Sessional Papers* for these years.

15. Lawrence, "Markets;" pp. 65–68; T. F. Patterson, "Review of the Lumber Trade," *Vancouver Daily Province*, 13 Jan. 1906, p. 22; "Anxious to Favour Farmers," ibid. 20 Oct. 1905, p. 1.

16. "Northwest a Hungry Market," *Vancouver Daily Province*, 8 Oct. 1902; Editorial, *Pacific Coast Lumberman*, 22 Oct. 1902; Kenneth H. Norrie, "The National

Policy and the Rate of Prairie Settlement: A Review," *Journal of Canadian Studies* 14, 3 (1979): 63–76.

17. Great Britain, Dominions Royal Commission, *Minutes of Evidence taken in the Central and Western Provinces of Canada in 1916* (H. M. S. O., 1912, pt. II app. C, pp. 181–190, evidence of H. R. MacMillan.

18. Carrothers, "Forest Industries," pp. 246–249.

19. Ibid., pp. 234–247; Cail, *Land*, pp. 90–105.

20. Ibid.; British Columbia, Royal Commission on Timber and Forestry, *Final Report* (Victoria, 1910), pp. 11–13, 45. For impressions of the American reaction to the measure, see PAC, MG27 II C2, H. G. Joly Papers, Mr. Pencier, Manager, North Pacific Lumber Co., Garnet, B. C. to J. R. Anderson, Deputy Minister of Agriculture, Victoria, B. C., (22 Jan. 1902): 7723–4; P. D. Roe, Manager, Canadian Pacific Lumber Company Limited, Port Moody, B.C. to J. R. Anderson, (19 Nov. 1902): 7721–2; James D. McNair, Hastings Manufacturing Company, Vancouver, B.C., to J. R. Anderson, (17 Nov. 1902).

21. Carrothers, "Forest Industries," p.236, British Columbia, *Statutes* (1901) cap. 30; Patterson, "Review"; "Lumber Prices To Be Advanced," *Vancouver Daily Province*, 28 Feb. 1906; p. 1.

22. "Is Government Order Evaded?" *Vancouver Daily Province* 29 Oct. 1904, p. 1. "Would Shut Out All B.C. Logs," ibid. 1 Dec. 1904, p. 1. "Why Loggers Wish to Export," ibid., 22 Jan. 1906, p. 13. "Commission May End Forestry Enquiry Here," ibid., 26 Aug. 1909, p. 7.

23. "The Loggers State Their Case," *Vancouver Daily Province* 29 June 1904, p. 4. "Is New Timber Bill Ultra Vires," ibid., 20 Jan. 1906, p. 3. "Timber Question is Discussed," ibid., p. 7. "Will Start Suit to Recover His Logs," ibid. *Vancouver Daily Province*, 25 March, 1906, p. 1.

24. "Logs Released on Heavy Cash Bond," *Vancouver Daily Province*, 30 March 1906, p. 1. "Mr. Skinner Himself or the Crown," ibid. 31 March 1906 p. 1. "Attempt to Steal Seized Logs Failed," ibid. 9 April 1906, p. 1. "Government Fears Raids on Logs," ibid. 17 April 1906, p. 1. "Confiscation of Logs Postponed," ibid. 24 April 1906, p. 1. "J. S. Emerson to Turn Pursuer," ibid. 30 May, 1906, p. 1. "Why Emerson Wins in Logging Case," ibid., p. 2.

25. "To Demand Logs for Export," ibid., 2 June 1906, p. 1. "No Judgement in Emerson Case," ibid., 19 June 1906, p. 1. "Emerson Right, Skinner Wrong," ibid., 2 July 1906,: p. 1. "To Take Emerson to Privy Council," ibid., 14 July 1906, p. 1. "Says More Logs Are Threatened," ibid., 18 July 1906, p. 1. "Too Late to Seize Boom," ibid., 14 July 1906, p. 1. "Four Judges Against the Crown," ibid., p. 9.

26. "Illegal Export of Logs Must Stop," *Vancouver Daily Province*, 13 Sept. 1902, p. 1. "Warned Loggers Against Exporting," ibid., 16 Sept. 1902, p. 1. "Another Row Over Timber Regulations," ibid., 22 June 1906, p. 1. "Legal Opinion with Objections," ibid., 22 June 1906, p. 1. "Loggers Support Scaling Bill," ibid., 26 June 1906, p. 9. "Supervision of Scalers at Work," ibid., 4 July 1906, p. 1. "May Deal in Logs Without Scaling," ibid., 6 July 1906, p. 1. "Scalers Are to Grade All Logs," ibid., 20 Aug. 1906, p. 2. "Log Grading Agreed Upon," ibid., 24 Aug 1906, p. 1.

27. See British Columbia, Timber Inspectors Report, *Sessional Papers* for the years 1881–1900.

28. Roach, "Stewards"; British Columbia, *Statutes* (1903–1904), cap. 30, sec. 8

and (1905), cap. 33, sec. 3; Royal Commission on Timber and Forestry, *Report*, pp. 11–14, 48–49. The amendment of 1905 caused some political dissension in the hurried way it was introduced. Cloture had to be used to get it passed. "House Prorogued on Saturday," *Vancouver Daily Province* 10 April 1905, p. 1.

29. Royal Commission, *Report*; Carrothers, "Forest Industries", pp.236–237.

30. British Columbia Timber and Forestry Chamber of Commerce, *Programme of Inaugural Meeting* (n.p., n.d.), "Practical Forester Will Come to the Coast," *Vancouver Daily Province*, 19 Nov. 1907, p. 7.

31. Royal Commission, *Report*, pp. 42, 55; Wilson Compton, *The Organization of the Lumber Industry* (Chicago, 1916), p. 11. Compton cites changes in transportation rates for west to east carriage of lumber as a major contributing factor as well as the destruction of the city. In British Columbia, disruption of normal trade was considerable. See "Proceedings of the Select Committee Appointed for the Purpose of Inquiring into the Prices Charged for Lumber in the Provinces of Manitoba, Alberta and Saskatchewan," *Journals of the House of Commons of Canada* (Ottawa, 1907), vol. 62, pt. 2, app. 6. The expansion of the industry in this period was very well reported by the Vancouver newspapers. Articles of particular interest include T. F. Patterson, "Review of the Lumber Trade," *Vancouver Daily Province*, 13 Jan. 1906, p. 22. "Lumber Prices Will Go Up As Result of Fire," ibid., 25 April 1906, p. 1. "United States Removes $2 Duty on Lumber," ibid., 26 April 1906, p. 1. "Lumber Has Another Jump in Price Today," ibid., 29 Sept. 1906, p. 1. "Logs So Scarce That No Price Is Quoted," ibid., 3 Dec. 1906, p. 1. "Wonderful Growth of Traffic in Timber," ibid., 11 May 1907, p. 26. "Forty Million Feet of Timber Cut," ibid., 8 June 1907, p. 1. "Demand For Lumber Was Never So Great," ibid., 6 August 1907, p. 1. "Expect Great Lumber Business In the Spring," ibid., 24 Oct 1907, p. 13. The Provincial Government placed all unlicenced and unleased Crown land under reserve on 22 December 1907 by an Order in Council, a move that had been rumoured for some time: "Timber Not To Be Taken Off the Market," *Vancouver Daily Province*, 8 July 1907, p. 13. "Timber Reserve Meets with Very General Approval," *Vancouver Daily Province*, p. 1.

32. Whitford and Craig, *Forests*, pp. 87–96; "To Ask Increase of Life of Timber Licences," *Vancouver Daily Province* 28 Nov. 1907, p. 1; "To Discuss Life of Timber Leases," ibid., p. 1. "Equity in Timber Is Claimed by the Licencees," ibid., 20 Dec. 1907, p. 5. "Asked Government To Amend Timber Laws," ibid., 4 Feb. 1908, p. 4. "Legislature Day by Day," ibid., 24 Feb. 1908, p. 6. "Wish Timber Titles Made More Perfect," ibid., 7 Oct. 1908, p. 1. "Loggers and Millmen Seek Government Protection," ibid., 23 Dec. 1908, p. 1. "Lumbermen Will Meet Government," ibid., 15 Feb. 1909, p. 1. "Invasion by The Timbermen," *Victoria Daily Times*, vol. 47, no. 40, 17 Feb 1909, p. 2. Millmen, Loggers and Timbermen Are Organizing," *Vancouver Daily Province*, 19 Feb. 1909, p. 1.

33. Roach, "Stewards."

34. Ibid.

35. Ibid.

36. Ibid.

37. Ibid., *Vancouver News-Advertiser*, Sept 29, 1909, pp. 1–3; *Vancouver Daily Province*, 29, Sept 1909, p. 7.

38. Roach, "Stewards."

39. Ibid. See Compton, *Lumber Industry*, pp. 65–70, for a discussion of factors affecting stumpage values at this time.

40. Roach, "Stewards."

41. Ibid. See H. R. MacMillan, "The Late Overton Price," *Canadian Forestry Journal* 10, 6 (1914): 67; Jean Pablo, "Overton Westfeldt Price," *Encyclopedia of American Forestry and Conservation History* (New York: 1983), vol. 2, p. 547; Carl Alwin Schenck, *The Birth of Forestry in America* (Santa Cruz, Calif. 1974), pp. 43, 80.

42. Roach, "Stewards"; Andrew D. Rodgers, *Bernhard Eduard Fernow: A Story of North American Forestry* (Princeton, N.J., 1951), pp. 340–341, 489, 495–498, 503, 505; Lawrence, "Markets," pp. 158–160. See also early chapters of Donald MacKay, *Empire of Wood: The MacMillan Bloedel Story* (Vancouver; 1982).

43. Roach, "Stewards"; J. Castell Hopkins, *Canadian Annual Review* (1912), p. 604. Rodgers, *Fernow*, p. 518.

44. Roach, "Stewards"; *Vancouver News-Advertiser*, 31 Jan.1912, p. 2.

45. Roach, "Stewards." See Hon. William R. Ross, *British Columbia's Forestry Policy, Speech to Legislature Assembly of B.C. on the 2nd Reading of the Forest Bill, 1912* (n.d., n.p.), PAC Library pamphlet.

46. Ibid.

47. Roach "Stewards." See British Columbia, "Forest Act," *Statutes* (27 Feb. 1912), 2 Geo V. cap. 81–132.

48. Roach, "Stewards."

49. Ibid., Stephen Gray, "Forest Policy and Administration in British Columbia, 1912–1928" (unpublished masters thesis, Simon Fraser Univ., 1982), pp. 62–65; Patricia Marchak, *Green Gold: The Forest Industry in British Columbia* (Vancouver, 1983) chap. p. 1.

50. Roach, "Stewards." John Lafon was a graduate of Schenck's Biltmore Forest School and subsequently worked with Schenck on consulting projects and as a forester for American west coast lumber companies. R. E. Benedict was a graduate of the Yale School of Forestry where he had taught before joining the U.S. Forest Service as Supervisor of the Olympic National Forest. Gray, "Forest Policy," pp. 59–60; Schenck, *Birth*, pp. 114, 194.

51. Roach, "Stewards." See Robert E. Ficken, "Gifford Pinchot Men: Pacific Northwest Lumbermen and the Conservation Movement, 1902–1920," *Western Historical Quarterly* 13 (April 1982): 165–178.

52. British Columbia, Department of Lands, *Report of the Forest Branch, 1912* (Victoria, 1912), p. 19.

53. British Columbia, *Statutes* (1913), cap. 26 and (1914), cap. 76; William R. Ross, *Speech by the Hon. Wm. R. Ross, Minister of Lands on the Timber Royalty Bill in the British Columbia Legislature, 13 February, 1914* (p.p. 1914); Overton W. Price, "Progress in British Columbia," *American Forestry* (April 1914): 273; Gray, "Forest Policy."

54. Ibid., *Report of the Forest Branch* (1913), pp. 18–19. "Profit Sharing With Lumbermen," *Daily News Advertiser* 52 (14 Feb. 1914): 1, 4.

55. Patricia E. Roy, "Progress, Prosperity and Politics: The Railway Policies of Richard McBride," *B.C. Studies* 47 (Autumn 1980): 3–28; Eleanor A. Bartlett, "Real Wages and the Standard of Living in Vancouver, 1901–1929," *B.C. Studies* 55 (Autumn 1981): 3–63.

56. Ibid. See *Reports of the Forest Branch* for the years 1914, 1915.

57. Gray, "Forest Policy," pp. 104–105. See also Donald McKay, *Empire of Wood*

(Vancouver, 1982), chaps. 1 and 2; British Columbia, *The Forest Resources of British Columbia* (Victoria; 1945), pp. 104–118 especially graph on p. 12.

58. Ibid.

59. Ibid., *Reports of the Forest Branch* (1916–1920).

60. Gray, "Forest Policy," pp. 62–65; Yerburgh, "Economic History," pp. 63–68. See the later chapters in this book for a discussion of the return of the railway belt.

61. Gray, "Forest Policy," pp. 163–164.

62. Ibid., pp. 105–110. Yerburgh, "Economic History," pp. 50–55.

63. Gray, "Forest Policy," pp. 29–48; C. D. Orchard, "Forest Administration in British Columbia: A Brief for Presentation to the Royal "Commisson on Forestry" PAC, RG39 vol. 405, file 50063, January 1945.

64. Ibid., pp. 66–79.

65. Martin Robin, *The Company Province.* See Margaret Ormsby, "T. Dufferin Pattullo and the Little New Deal," in Ward, *Historical Readings,* pp. 533–554, British Columbia, *Reports of the Forest Branch,* 1930 and 1935.

66. *Vancouver Sun* (1937.

67. British Columbia, *Reports of the Forest Branch,* 1938 and 1939.

68. Compare the Forest Branch *Annual Reports* for these years.

69. Orchard, "Forest Administration;" F. G. Fensom, *Expanding Forestry's Horizons* (Montreal, 1982).

70. British Columbia, *Annual Report of the Forest Branch* 1941.

71. Robin, *Company Province*; Ken Drushka, *Stumped: The Forest Industry in Transition* (Vancouver, 1985), pp. 42–45.

72. Ibid. British Columbia, *The Forest Resources of British Columbia* (Victoria, 1965) Orchard, "Forest Administration" J. Swift, *Cut and Run* (Toronto, 1983), 84–87; J. A. Gray, "Royal Commission and Forest Policy in British Columbia: A Review of the Pearse Report," *Canadian Public Policy* 3, 2 (Spring 1977): 219–223.

73. Ibid.

74. Ibid., Drushka, *Stumped,* pp. 70–90.

75. Ibid.

Chapter 7

1. G. H. Prince, "Planning for Post-War Reconstruction in New Brunswick," *The Canadian Forestry Situation in 1944. Reports and Papers Presented to the 36th Annual Meeting of the Canadian Society of Forest Engineers* (Toronto, 1944), p. 15.

2. Hugh G. Thorburn, *Politics in New Brunswick* (Toronto, 1961), p. 8.

3. Ibid., p. 9.

4. The Hon. Charles Connel, quoted in J. Miles Gibson, *The History of Forest Management in New Brunswick: An H. R. MacMillan Lectureship Address Delivered at the University of British Columbia, Tuesday, April 7th, 1953* (Vancouver, 1953), p. 4.

5. New Brunswick, *Forests and Forestry in New Brunswick: A Special Report to the Second Imperial Forestry Conference, 1923* (Fredericton, 1923), p. 12.

6. Ibid., p. 13.

7. An early discussion of this process is found in K. B. Brown, "Memorandum Regarding Progress Made Toward Forest Management by the Department of Lands and Mines of New Brunswick in the Administration of Crown Lands, August 1943," Environment Canada Library, PB9.40 N.B.

8. S. A. Saunders, "The Maritime Provinces and the Reciprocity Treaty," *Dalhousie Review* (October 1934): 355–371.

9. W. S. MacNutt, *New Brunswick, A History: 1784–1867* (Toronto, 1963), pp. 268–270.

10. Ibid., and R. Rice, "The Wrights of Saint John: A Study of Shipbuilding and Shipowning in the Maritimes, 1839–1855," in D. J. Macmillan, ed. *Canadian Business History: Selected Studies, 1497–1971* (Toronto, 1972), pp. 317–337.

11. Saunders, "Maritime Provinces"; and E. R. Forbes, *The Maritime Rights Movement, 1919–1927: A Study in Canadian Regionalism* (Montreal, 1979).

12. Graeme Wynn, *Timber Colony* (Toronto, 1981), pp. 146–147.

13. Ibid.

14. Ibid.; and New Brunswick, *Second Imperial Conference*, pp. 12–13.

15. Wynn, *Timber Colony*, p. 149.

16. New Brunswick, *Second Imperial Conference*, pp. 12–13. The only major new regulation brought into force before 1900 was a diameter limit in 1883 and some ineffective fire regulations which will be discussed later in this chapter. New Brunswick, Crown Lands Department, *Annual Report, 1893* (Fredericton; 1894).

17. R. B. Miller, "Forest Resources of the Maritime Provinces: New Brunswick," *Canada and Its Provinces*, vol. 14, *The Atlantic Provinces*, pt. II (Toronto, 1913), p. 597.

18. Saunders, "Maritime Provinces."

19. F. Phillips, "The Main John Glasier," Saint John *Telegraph Journal*, 27 Feb. 1937, p. 3.

20. Ibid., 6 Mar 1937, p.3.

21. *The Wood Industries of New Brunswick in 1897* (reprint of the *New Brunswick Section of the Wood Industries of Canada*) in *The Timber Trades Journal* (London, 1897), pp. 4–10; David C. Smith, *A History of Lumbering in Maine, 1861–1960* (Orono, Maine, 1972), pp. 300–304.

22. *The Wood Industries of New Brunswick*, p. 11.

23. Ibid.

24. J. F. Gregory, "Lumbering on the Saint John River Years Ago and At The Present Time," Saint John *Globe*, 23 April 1913.

25. Fred Phillips, "The Frasers," Saint John *Telegraph Journal*, 5 April 1937, p. 3.

26. *The Wood Industries of New Brunswick*, p. 15.

27. Fred Phillips, "Alexander 'Boss' Gibson," Saint John *Telegraph Journal*, 15 March 1937, p. 3. *The Wood Industries of New Brunswick*, p.15. J. Rankin, *A History of Our Firm* (Liverpool, U. K., 1921), p. 66.

28. Phillips, "Gibson"; and New Brunswick, *Second Imperial Conference*, p. 12.

29. Ibid.; and J. K. Johnson, ed., *Canadian Directory of Parliament 1867–1967* (Ottawa, 1967), pp. 541–542.

30. C. A. Woodward, *The History of New Brunswick Provincial Election Campaigns and Platforms, 1866–1974* (Micromedia, 1976), pp. 17–20.

31. Andrew George Blair was a Fredericton lawyer, who served as Premier from 1883 to 1896 and then went to Ottawa as Laurier's Minister of Railway and Canals. Ironically, given his small government attitudes early in his career (he advocated abolishing the upper house, reducing the size of the executive, and cutting government expenditures), he resigned from the federal cabinet in 1903 when Sir Wilfrid

Laurier ignored his suggestion over public ownership of the new transcontinental railway. See Johnson, *Canadian Directory of Parliament*, pp. 48–49.

32. New Brunswick, *Second Imperial Conference*, p. 13.

33. PAC, RG15, Saskatchewan Resources Commission 1934, "Additional Information," p. 9.

34. K. B. Brown, "Forests and Forestry in New Brunswick," *Forestry Chronicle* 17 (December 1941), p. 140.

35. Gibson, "Forest Management in New Brunswick," p. 4.

36. R. B. Miller, "The Atlantic Provinces," p. 6. *Canadian Annual Review* (1920), p. 570 and (1924–1925), p.363.

37. Miller, "The Atlantic Provinces," pp. 3–4.

38. New Brunswick Resources Development Board, "The Utilization of Wood" in *The Development of the Forests and Forest Industries of New Brunswick*, pt. 2 (Fredericton, 1951), p. 14.

39. Ibid.

40. "New Brunswick Timberland Situation," *Canada Lumberman and Woodworker* 32, 15 (April 1912).

41. *Canadian Directory of Parliament*, p. 542; *Canadian Annual Review* (1908), pp. 125–127; and Canadian Commission of Conservation, *Annual Reports* (1910–1911). Snowball served as president of the Canadian Forestry Association in 1908 and was appointed to the Advisory Council of the Commission in 1909.

42. Woodward, *N.B. Elections*, pp. 30–36.

43. PAC, RG39 vol. 409, file 39884, New Brunswick.

44. Ibid.

45. *Canadian Annual Review* (1907), pp. 235–236.

46. Ibid.

47. Woodward, *N.B. Elections*, pp. 36–37. Tweedie became Lieutenant-Governor in 1907 on J.B. Snowball's death. He was replaced by William Pugsley, who almost immediately was called to Ottawa to join the Laurier cabinet, and who was replaced by Clifford W. Robinson. It was no wonder then that the Liberal government presented such a ripe target for the opposition.

48. *Canadian Directory of Parliament*, p. 265.

49. PAC, RG15, Saskatchewan Resources Commission; *Canadian Annual Review* (1911), pp. 519–520; New Brunswick, *Second Imperial Conference*, p. 14.

50. Gibson, "Forest Management in New Brunswick."

51. Woodward, *N.B. Elections*, p. 39; Arthur T. Doyle, *Front Benches and Back Rooms: A Story of Corruption, Muckraking, Raw Partisanship and Intrigue in New Brunswick* (Toronto, 1976), pp. 27–28.

52. *Canadian Annual Review* (1912), pp. 460–463; Doyle, *Front Benches*, p. 28.

53. See "New Brunswick Timberland Situation," p. 29–31.

54. Miller, "The Atlantic Provinces;" p. 615.

55. *Canadian Annual Review* (1913), p. 517; New Brunswick, *Second Imperial Conference*, p.13; PAC, RG15, Saskatchewan Resources Commission, p. 8.

56. *Canadian Directory of Parliament*, p. 103.

57. *Canadian Annual Review* (1914), pp. 559–562; Doyle, *Front Benches*, p. 37.

58. Doyle, *Front Benches*, p. 38.

59. Other members of the Royal Commission were Sir Frederic E. Barker and W. S. Fisher, a Saint John businessman.

60. Doyle, *Front Benches*, pp. 48–49.

61. *Canadian Annual Review* (1914), p. 559.

62. Gibson, "Forest Management in New Brunswick."

63. There were scandals over the financing and construction of the Saint John Valley Railway and a particularly odious affair involving the South Hampton Railway where a Tory bagman was sued by the government for collecting far more in subsidies than the railway actually cost. Doyle, *Front Benches* p. 66

64. Doyle, *Front Benches*, p. 179.

65. *Canadian Annual Review* (1918), p. 658; and Doyle, *Front Benches*, p. 178.

66. *Canadian Annual Review* (1918), p. 658; and PAC, RD15, Saskatchewan Resources Commission.

67. PAC, RG39, vol. 409, file 39884.

68. *Canadian Annual Review* (1923), p. 332.

69. Ibid.; and (1924–1930).

70. Ibid.; (1923).

71. Canada, *Report of the Royal Commission on Pulpwood*, (Ottawa, 1924), p. 30.

72. J. F. Hamilton, "The Pulp and Paper Industry of New Brunswick, Canada" (unpublished masters thesis, Indiana University, 1950), p. 44.

73. Doyle, *Front Benches*, p. 242. The Bathurst Lumber Company had been incorporated in 1907 to take over existing interests in the Bathurst area. It involved American capital and was organized by two Canadians, Senator W. C. Edwards and Angus MacLean, who had run a lumber business in Buffalo, New York. The company eventually came to monopolize holdings in the Bathurst area and also had holdings in Bonaventure County, Quebec. In 1913, Bathurst moved into pulping and was one of the leaders in pressuring the Fleming government into extending leases before the 1918 expiry date in order to secure pulpwood areas on a long-term basis. The company's connection with the Ottawa valley operators made it a natural conduit for ideas concerning the use of conservation as a corporate planning mechanism.

74. *Canadian Annual Review* (1924–1925), p. 388; Doyle, *Front Benches*, p. 246.

75. Ibid.

76. A. Lagace, *How Grand Falls Grew* (n.p., 1946).

77. *Canadian Annual Review* (1923), p. 332.

78. *Canadian Annual Review* (1924–1925), p. 365.

79. Brown, "Forests and Forestry," pp. 143, 145.

80. Gibson, "Forest Management in New Brunswick."

81. *Canadian Annual Review* (1927–1929), p. 463.

82. Brown, "Memorandum," pp. 2-4.

83. Ibid., p. 1.

84. J. Swift, *Cut and Run: The Assault on Canada's Forests* (Toronto, 1983), p. 180.

85. Brown, "Forests and Forestry," pp. 142-143.

86. *Canadian Annual Review* (1933), pp. 219-220.

87. Ibid.

88. *Canadian Annual Review* (1934), pp. 262-263.

89. Brown, "Forests and Forestry."

Chapter 8

1. This chapter is based almost entirely on new primary research in the Records of the Canadian Forestry Service, PAC RG39; scattered records of the Canadian

Commission of Conservation, especially PAC, Records of the Department of Indian Affairs and National Development, RG22, vol. 6, legal files; the Royal Commission on Pulpwood, PAC RG33 no. 13, and the Commission's *Proceedings* in RG39, new acquisition.

2. Canada, Commission of Conservation *Forest Protection in Canada, 1913–1914* (Toronto: 1915), 67–75.

3. Ibid., Commission of Conservation, *Annual Report* (1913).

4. PAC RG32 C2 Historical Personnel Files, vol 608, E.H. Finlayson file, E.F. Drake to W.W. Cory, Deputy Minister of Interior, Reports on Fire Inspection, Board of Railway Commissioners.

5. PAC RG39, vol 20, file 43335, particularly letter W.H. Goodwin, Dean, School of Mining, Queen's University, Kingston to R.H. Campbell, 22 Jan. 30 and 7 Feb 1914. Goodwin wished the federal government to put money into experiments in his school but Campbell indicated all federal monies were going into facilities at McGill University "to establish a forest products laboratory for this purpose on the lines of that established in the United States Forest Service". See also Department of the Interior, *Annual Report* (1914) Part VI and *Annual Report* (1915) Part VI.

6. PAC RG 39 vol 4 file 43746 and Interior, *Annual Report* (1919) Part III,11.

7. Ibid. vol 20 file 43335 and *Annual Report* (1919) Part III,10–11.

8. Ibid. RG39 vol 271 file 40129 Part I. This includes an exchange of correspondence between H.S. Graves, United States Forester, and R.H. Campbell, May-July 1919 in which a proper basis for forestry policies in a federal system are discussed. In a letter of 9 July 1919, Campbell sets out the Forest Service's policy creed for the 1920's.

9. Ibid. Finlayson Report, 30th September 1920.

10. Ibid.: 10–13, 25–26, 28–30.

11. PAC R632 C2 vol. 608 E.H. Finlayson File Part I.

12. Ibid. RG39 file 40129 Part I Finlayson Report,1–3.

13. Ibid. Canada, Department of the Environment, *Progress Report, 1966–1972, for Tenth Commonwealth Forestry Conference* (Ottawa: 1974.

14. Ibid. Finlayson Report: 4.

15. Ibid.: 25–39.

16. See: Commission of Conservation, *Forest Protection in Canada, 1913–1914*, *Annual Reports* (1910–1920); B.E. Fernow, C.D. Howe, and J.H. White, *Forest Conditions of Nova Scotia* (Ottawa: 1912); C.D. Howe, and J.H. White, *Trent Watershed Survey: A Reconnaissance* (Toronto: 1913).

17. PAC RG22, vol. 6, Report of the Sub-Committee of Council on the Commission of Conservation (1920): 4.

18. Ibid.

19. Ibid. RG 39. Finlayson Report: 29–30 and letters W.J. Roche, Minister of the Interior to James White, Secretary of the Commission of Conservation, 22 April 1915 and R.H. Campbell to Clyde Leavitt, Forester, Conservation Commission, 19 May 1915. The Commission had begun cooperative forest inventory projects with Nova Scotia, Ontario and British Columbia. At first the D.F.S. had supported this work but became increasingly miffed as the Commission openly trespassed on its mandate after the war. The most major of these were silvicultural experiments with New Brunswick, and an American firm, the Pejepescot Paper Company, based in Maine but owning extensive timber lands in Canada. The Commission also entered into

an agreement with the Laurentide Company to establish cooperative research plots on its limits near Grand Mère in Quebec.

20. Ibid. and RG22 vol 16 Report to Council.

21. Ibid. RG39 Finlayson Report: 35–39.

22. Ibid.

23. Ibid. RG22 vol. 6 Report to Council: 2–3. See also C. Armstrong, *The Politics of Federalism: Ontario's Relations with the Federal Government, 1867–1942* (Toronto: 1981), Chapter 8, "Waterpower and the Constitution". See: D.J. Hall, *Cifford Sifton*, vol. 2, 258–263. Foster, *Working For Wildlife*, 210–216.

24. Ibid.

25. Ibid. PAC RG22, vol. 6, Report to Council: 2–3.

26. Ibid; Armstrong, *Politics of Federalism*, 178–80, and Canada, House of Commons, "Speech from the Throne," *Debates* (1 Feb. 1921, 2. "Speech by Right Hon. Arthur Meighen," Ibid. (26 May, 1921), 3959.

27. Ibid. RG 22, vol. 6, Report to Council.

28. Ibid. esp. p.10.

29. Ibid.

30. PAC RG39, vol. 131 file 45672 Memorandum T.W. Dwight, Dominion Forestry Service, to W.W. Cory, Deputy Minister of the Interior, 27 May 1921, with attachments. It also took most of the Commission's library holdings.

31. Ibid.

32. Ibid. Memorandum E.H. Finlayson to W.W. Cory, Deputy Minister of the Interior, 13 Sept. 1922.

33. Ibid.

34. Ibid. vol. 271, file 40139 Part I. Correspondence H.S. Graves and R.H. Campbell, May-July 1919. William G. Robbins, "Federal Forestry Co-operation: The Fernow-Pinchot Years," *Journal of Forest History* 28 4(Oct 1984): 164–173.

35. Ibid.

36. Castell Hopkins, *Canadian Annual Review, 1923* (Toronto: 1923), 79–81.

37. Thomas R. Roach, "The Pulpwood Trade and the Settlers of New Ontario, 1919–1939," Paper read to the 1981 Annual Meeting of the Ontario Historical Association.

38. Ibid.

39. Harvey H. Black, "Pulpwood Policy for Canada" in *Canadian Annual Review* (1924–1925), 718–732. For details of Barnjum's life, see, the collection of his pamphlets deposited in the Public Archives Library and Floyd S. Chalmers, *Frank J.D. Barnjum, an Appreciation of Canada's Most Practical Propagandist* (Toronto: 1924); "Death of Noted Canadian Conservationist," *Canada Lumbermen* 52 5(March 1933): 14. And, the papers regarding the settlement of his estate held in the Probate Office, Provincial Court, Annapolis Royal, N.S. Barnjum will be discussed more fully inThomas R. Roach and Richard Judd, "Frank John Dixie Barnjum, Conservationist or Opportunist," presented the 1986 Annual Meeting of the Forest History Society.

40. Ibid.

41. Ibid. See for instance Frank J.D. Barnjum, *Some Startling Facts About Canada's Forests* (p.p. 1920), and *Startling Facts and Fallacies About Canada's Forests* (Montreal: 1930.

42. *Canadian Annual Review* (1923), 79–81; (1924–25), 82–83. L.H. Dennison, U.S. Consul, Quebec City, to U.S. Secretary of State, Washington, D.C.,22 June

1920, United States Forest Service Records, Forest History Society, Duke University, N.C.

43. *Canadian Annual Review* (1923), 78–79. For an example of Barnjum's methods, see PAC MG27 III B6 vol 25, Sir Lomer Gouin papers, Barnjum to Gouin letters and pamphlets, 26 May 1920 to 22 March 1924.

44. Ibid.,80. "The Front Page," *Saturday Night* (24 Nov. 1923).

45. Ibid. Lomer Gouin, "Sir Lomer Gouin on Pulpwood Embargo," *Ill. Can. For. and Outdoors* 20 3(March, 1924): 177–178.

46. *Canadian Annual Review* (1923); Roach and Judd, "Barnjum."

47. PAC RG33 no 13.

48. PAC RG32 C2 vol 608, E.H. Finlayson File, "Statement Re E.H. Finlayson," 4 May 1936.

49. Ibid.

50. PAC RG39 new acquisition, *Proceedings of the Royal Commission on Pulpwood.*

51. *Canadian Annual Review* (1923), 79–81.

52. Ibid.

53. *Canadian Annual Review* (1924–25), 83.

54. Canada, Royal Commission on Pulpwood, *Final Report* (Ottawa: 1924.

55. J.K. Johnson; ed, *Canadian Directory of Parliament, 1867–1967* (Ottawa: 1967), 551. H. Blair Neatby, *William Lyon Mackenzie King*, vol. 2, *The Lonely Heights 1924–1934*, (Toronto: 1963), 64.

56. PAC RG39 no file number, *Proceedings of the Dominion-Provincial Conference on Forest Fire Protection.*

57. Ibid., 3–4.

58. Ibid.

59. Ibid., 162–171.

60. Ibid., 408–414, Resolutions.

61. Ibid.

62. Ibid. vol 248 file 28829, Report on Staff Conferences, (20 Oct 1928).

63. Canada, Dept. of the Interior. *Annual Reports* (1925–1926), "Dominion Forestry Service."

64. Ibid. John Kendle, *John Bracken: A Political Biography* (Toronto: 1980, chapt 5.

65. Ibid. PAC RG39 vol 248 file 28829.

66. Ibid. vol 271 file 40139-II, Clippings of Hon. Charles Stewart's Announcement, 16 June 1926; Canada, House of Commons, *Debates* (1926, 2915.

67. Ibid. file 40139-II.

68. See; Rodger Graham, ed. *King-Byng Affair, 1926: A Question of Responsible Government* (Toronto: 1967).

69. PAC RG39, vol. 248 file 22829; Neatby, *The Lonely Heights.*

70. PAC RG39, vol. 238 file 28820, R.D. Craig to E.H. Finlayson, 30 August 1929.

71. PAC RG39, vol. 418, *Proceedings of the Conference on National Inventory of Forest Resources* (1929), 1–5, "Speech of Hon. Charles Stewart."

72. Ibid.,78.

73. Ibid.,79–80 and "Reports of Special Committees."

74. *Proceedings*, Forest Resources Conference, Appendix "A."

75. Alan Joly de Lotbinière, "A National Forest Policy." *Can. Woodlands Review*

(1929). Alan Joly de Lotbinière was the grandson of the great patron of Canadian forestry, Sir Henri Joly de Lotbinière, and had a B.Sc. in Forestry from the University of Toronto.

76. Toronto *Globe* (17 January 1930).

Chapter 9

1. For basic information on the natural resources transfer issue see Chester Martin, *Dominion Lands Policy* (Toronto: 1973) and H. Blair Neatby, *William Lyon Mackenzie King* vol 2, *The Lonely Heights* (Toronto 1963).

2. Chester Martin, *Lands Policy*, 204–226.

3. Neatby, *The Lonely Heights*, 101.

4. Ibid., 102.

5. Martin, *Lands Policy*. For an academic defense of this interpretation, see, Lionel L. Rubin, "The Transfer of Natural Resources to the Prairie Provinces," (unpublished M.A. Thesis, McGill U., 1931).

6. Ibid., 214–15.

7. Ibid.

8. PAC RG39 vol 95 file 48183, Memorandum, D. Roy Cameron, 12 March 1929.

9. Bracken's difficulties with federal authorities over timber limits and water power development at the Seven Sisters site on the Winnipeg River are discussed in John Kendle, *John Bracken: A Political Biography* (Toronto: 1980), chapts, 5 and 8.

10. Neatby, *The Lonely Heights*, 253–255.

11. Prince Albert, Saskatchewan, *Daily Herald* (13 December 1929).

12. *Saturday Night* (17 May 1930).

13. Ibid.

14. PAC RG39 vol 95 file 48183, Memorandum 12 March 1929.

15. Ibid. Memorandum D. Roy Cameron, 4 May 1929. See, the discussion papers, "The Objects and Administration of the National Forests of the Railway Belt of British Columbia," "Suggested Draft for Forestry Section of Agreement Re Transfer of Railway Belt" and draft "Agreement between the Dominion of Canada and the Province of British Columbia on the Subject of the Transfer to the Province of the Railway Belt and the Peace River Block".

16. Ibid., Letter R.M. Brown to E.H. Finlayson, 13 Jan 1930 and Neatby, *The Lonely Heights*, 295.

17. Neatby, *The Lonely Heights*, 298.

18. PAC RG39, vol.248 file 28829-II, Memorandum and Report, W.M. Robertson to D. Roy Cameron, 10 Jan 1930.

19. Regina, Saskatchewan, *Leader* (18 Feb 1930).

20. PAC RG39, vols. 267–8 file 39766.

21. Ibid.

22. Ibid.

23. Ibid. vol 95 file 48143, Memorandum E.H. Finlayson to W.W. Cory, Deputy Minister of the Interior, 25 April 1930, Letter P.Z. Caverhill, Provincial Forester of British Columbia, to E.H. Finlayson, 21 July 1930. Memorandum E.H. Finlayson to W.W. Cory, 31 July 1930.

24. Ibid., especially Finlayson to Cory, 31 July 1930, and Day Letter E.H. Fin-

layson to G. Turnstell, District Forest Inspector's Office, Winnipeg, 30 July 1930. Details regarding Finlayson's appearances before the Royal Commissions are found in the federal records relating to the Saskatchewan and Alberta Resource Commissions, Records of the Department of the Interior, RG15, vols. 13–81. The actual records of the Prairie Natural Resource Royal Commissions are found in PAC RG33, No's 50, 51 and 52.

25. PAC RG39 vol 95 file 48143.

26. Ibid.

27. Ibid. vols 267–8 file 39766, Letter E.H. Finlayson to G.H. Prince, Deputy Minister, Department of Lands and Mines, New Brunswick.

28. Ibid. Memorandum D. Roy Cameron to W.W. Cory, 31 Jan 1931.

29. Ibid. See major policy papers "Forest Policy Considerations" and "Functions of Continuing Forest Service". See Also Memorandum R.A. Gibson, Assistant Deputy Minister of the Interior, to E.H. Finlayson, 20 April 1931 indicating that the Minister had not considered the D.F.S. proposals; Memorandum E.H. Finlayson to H.H. Rowatt, Deputy Minister of the Interior, 5 Aug 1931 containing renewed proposals; and Memorandum H.H. Rowatt to Finlayson, 2 March 1932 asking for a plan for staff reductions and Finlayson's reply 3 March 1932.

30. Ibid. Letters G. Piché, Provincial Forester of Quebec, to E.H. Finlayson, 25 Aug 1931 and Dr. C.D. Howe to G. Piché, 21 June 1932.

31. Ibid. Memorandum E.H. Finlayson to R.A. Gibson, Assistant Deputy Minister, 15 Feb 1932. Also vol. 411 file 40765, Policy Paper "Forestry as a National Problem" and RG22 vol. 6 Legal File Oct-Nov 1932, "The Responsibility of the Department of the Interior with Respect to Conservation".

32. Ibid., "Forestry as a National Problem".

33. Ibid.

34. Ibid., RG22, vol. 6.

35. Ibid., specifically the paper entitled "Conservation in Canada".

36. PAC RG39, vols. 267–68 file 39766. Memorandum E.H. Finlayson to H.H. Rowatt, Deputy Minister of the Interior, 5 Aug 1931 and Department of the Interior *Annual Reports* (1933–34).

37. Ibid., RG39, vol. 28 file 49209 Part I, National Employment Commission, 1935–1939.

38. Department of the Interior, *Annual Report* (1934) and PAC RG39, vols. 267–68 file 39766, Memorandum re Inventory of Forest Resources, 27 Oct 1932.

39. Canada, Department of the Interior, *Annual Report* (1934), "Report of the Director of Forestry".

40. Ibid.

41. Ibid.

42. PAC RG39, vols. 267–68 file 39766; especially "Federal Functions and Obligations in Conservation as Defined and Implied by the British North America Act and Subsequent Legislation" and extract of letter Hon. T.G. Murphy to Premier R.G. Reid, Alberta, 28 Sept 1934 and G. Piché, Provincial Forester, Quebec to E.H. Finlayson, 25 Aug 1931.

43. Ibid.

44. Ibid. Letter Hon. W.F. Kerr, Minister of Natural Resources, Saskatchewan to Hon. T.A. Crerar, 20 Jan 1936. At the same time, similar letters were received from Hon. J.S. McDiarmid, Minister of Lands and Mines, Manitoba, 2 Mar. 1936;

the Hon J.D. MacQuarrie, Minister of Lands and Forests, Nova Scotia, 8 Jan. 1936 and the Hon. F.W. Pirie, Minister of Lands and Mines, New Brunswick, 30 Dec. 1935.

45. Ibid. Resolution Passed by Canadian Lumbermen's Association at Annual Meeting 1933.

46. See Department of the Interior, *Annual Report* (1935–36);43 and Canada, National Research Council, *Proceedings of the Conference on Forestry Research, November, 1935* (Ottawa: 1936).

47. Ibid., *Proceedings*.

48. Ibid., App. E, Alexander Koroleff, "Fundamental Cause Of Our Failure in Forestry and the Remedy."

49. PAC RG39, vols. 267–68 file 39766, Letter Hon. W.D. Euler, Minister of Trade and Commerce to Hon. J.S. McDiarmid, Minister of Mines and Natural Resources, Manitoba, 2 March 1936 and Department of the Interior, *Annual Report* (1935–36).

50. K.M. Mayall, *White Pine Succession As Influenced by Fire* (Ottawa: 1941)

51. PAC RG39, vols. 267–68 file 39766, Letter, Canadian Lumbermen's Association to Hon. T.A. Crerar, 10 June 1936.

52. Ibid., RG 32 C2 vol. 608, E.H. Finlayson File.

53. Canada National Research Council, Proceedings, Nov. 1935.

54. PAC RG39, vols.267–68 file 39766, Memorandum D. Roy Cameron to J.M. Wardle, Deputy Minister of the Interior, 1 Sept, 1936.

Chapter 10

1. PAC RG39, vol. 399 file 47625, History of Timber Control published in John de N. Kennedy, *History of the Department of Munitions and Supply Canada in the Second World War* (Ottawa: 1950), vol 2, 243–269.

2. Ibid.

3. Ibid. See Frank H. House comp., *Timber At War* (London: 1965), for the British side of the story.

4. Ibid. vol. 2 file 49785, Memorandum re the Dominion's Contribution to Forestry, 4 Jan 1941.

5. Ibid.

6. Ibid., Letter Hon. A. Wells Gray to Hon. T.A. Crerar, 8 Jan 1941.

7. Ibid. and Memorandum D. Roy Cameron to R.A. Gibson, Director, Lands, Parks and Forests Branch, 20 Jan. 1941.

8. C. Armstrong, *The Politics of Federalism: Ontario's Relations with the Federal Government, 1867–1942* (Toronto: 1981), 220–232.

9. Ibid.

10. Ibid.

11. PAC RG39, vol 399 file 44625, Letter E.H. Roberts to C.D. Orchard, Forest Branch, Department of Lands, British Columbia, 17 Jan. 1941.

12. Armstrong, *Politics of Federalism*, 224–232.

13. PAC RG39, vol 2 file 49785, "Dominion Assistance in Forestry" by D. Roy Cameron, 22 Jan 1941.

14. Ibid., Memorandum re Request of British Columbia for assistance in Forest

Protection, R.A. Gibson, Director, Lands, Parks and Forests Branch to D. Roy Cameron, 7 Feb 1941.

15. Ibid., and Letter Hon. T.A. Crerar to Hon. A. Wells Gray, 4 Feb 1941.

16. Ibid., Memorandum D. Roy Cameron to R.A. Gibson, Director, Lands, Parks and Forests Branch, 8 Feb 1941.

17. Ibid.

18. Ibid. Letter Hon. O. Wells Gray to Hon. T.A. Crerar, 18 Feb 1941.

19. Ibid., Letter Hon. N.O. Hipel, Minister of Lands and Forests, Ontario to Hon. A. Wells Gray, Hon. N.E. Toner, Hon. W.F. Kerr, Hon. J.S. McDiarmid, Hon. W. Hamel, Hon. F.W. Pirie and Hon J.H. MacQuarrie and letter Hon. N.O. Hipel to Hon T.A. Crerar, 26 March 1943.

20. Hepburn's various efforts to deal with the problems of the forest sector through the later 1930's are too lengthy to discuss here. These involved various pieces of legislation including the Woodsmen's Employment Act to regulate wages and health conditions in the camps; the Settlers' Pulpwood Protection Act to regulate the prices paid for pulp cut by settlers; and the Forest Resources Regulation Act, through which the Premier attempted to reallocate limits from bankrupt firms to companies which would use them and thus create employment. The Premier also reduced timber dues and bonuses and prorated pulp and paper sales to prop up pulp and paper production. It was the Forest Resources Regulations Act which got the government in trouble. The Tories had removed the manufacturing condition on pulp in 1933 to stimulate employment. Now the Hepburn government reallocated timber limits at will, often in secret and to firms exporting logs. Despite the Depression it became open to charges that it was betraying the time-honoured provincial development policy and trading away the province's future. The collapse in 1938 of the Lake Sulphite Company, the pride of Hepburn's new forest recovery programme led to an assault by the Opposition on the ineptness of the policies of the Department of Lands and Forests and its Minister, Peter Heenan. The result of hearings by a Legislative Committee was the resignation of Heenan and his Deputy Minister Walter Cain and the appointment of N.O. Hipel to reform forest policy in Ontario in order to save the Hepburn government. These efforts are masterfully analyzed in H.V. Nelles, *The Politics of Development* (Toronto: 1976), Chapter 11 and R.S. Lambert with P. Pross, *Renewing Nature's Wealth* (Toronto: 1967), Chapter 17.

21. PAC RG39, vol 2 file 49785, Memorandum W.S. Pratt, Private Secretary to Hon. T.A. Crerar, to Deputy Minister, 31 March 1943. A.E. Cadman, Canadian Pulp and Paper Association to Hon. T.A. Crerar, 31 March 1943. W.J. Pratt to Deputy Minister, 1 April 1943.

22. Ibid., Noted on Memorandum A.E. Cadman to Crerar.

23. Ibid., Letter Charles Camsell, Deputy Minister to Hon. N.O. Hipel, 1 April 1943 and Hipel's reply 6 April 1943; R.A. Gibson, Director, Lands, Parks and Forests Branch, to Mr. Jackson, Chief Executive Assistant, 4 May 1943.

24. Ibid., Memorandum R.A. Gibson, Director, Lands, Parks and Forests Branch to D. Roy Cameron, 5 May 1943 including policy paper "The Dominion Role in Post-War Forestry" and "Notes of Conference of Provincial Ministers, 6 May 1943.

25. Ibid., "Notes."

26. Ibid.

27. Ibid.

28. Ibid., Memorandum D. Roy Cameron to R.A. Gibson, Director, Lands, Parks

and Forests Branch, 8 Feb. 1944. Letter Hon. J.L. Ilsey to Hon. F.W. Pirie, Minister of Lands and Forests, New Brunswick, 12 May 1943.

29. Ibid.

30. Ibid., Memorandum Re: Dominion-Provincial Conference, C.W. Jackson, Chief Executive Assistant, to R.A. Gibson, Director, Lands, Parks and Forests Branch, 27 July 1944 and vol 17 file 49953, Letter Hon. W. Hamel, Minister of Lands and Forests, Quebec to Hon. T.A. Crerar, 30 June 1944.

31. Ibid.

32. Ibid.

33. Ibid., vol 405 file 50063, "Memorandum to the Dominion-Provincial Conference by the Hon. Maurice L. Duplessis K.C., LL.D., Prime Minister of the Province of Quebec, Ottawa, 25 April 1946."

34. Ibid., vol 2 file 49785, "Notes on the Clarke-McNary Act", 19 Dec 1949 and Canada, *Statutes* (1949), "An Act Respecting Forest Conservation," 13 Geo VI, cap. 8.

35. Lambert with Pross, *Renewing*, 404–407.

36. For an overview of Canadian forest policies see Canadian Council of Resource and Environment Ministers, *Forest Policies in Canada*, 2 vols. (Ottawa:June, 1976. D. Mackay, *Heritage Lost* (Toronto: 1985),157–160.

37. Jamie Swift, *Cut and Run: The Assault on Canada's Forests* (Toronto:1983), 231–34.

38. PAC RG39, vol 405 file 50063, "Papers in Preparation for Federal-Provincial Conference, 1950", especially "Statements of Proposals,"

39. L. Sayn-Wittgenstein, "Forestry: From Branch to Department." *Canadian Public Administration* 4 (Dec., 1963): 434–452.

40. Canada, House of Commons, Standing Committee on Mines, Forests and Waters, *Minutes and Proceedings* (May 14–21, 1959), esp. May 18, 607 and May 19, 658, 669 and 673.

41. Ibid.

42. Canada, *Statutes (1960*, "An Act Respecting the Department of Forestry," 8–9 Elizabeth II.

43. Numerous articles have appeared in Canadian newspapers over the last few years decrying the fate of Canada's forests. By way of example see M. Keating, "Vanishing Forests," *Globe and Mail* Dec 1982. See also Canada Science Council, *Canada's Threatened Forests: A Statement by the Science Council, March, 1983* (Ottawa: 1983.

44. As witnessed by T.R. Roach.

45. D.V. Love, "Potentialities of the Forest Resource Base," *Proceedings of the Resources for Tomorrow Conference, Conference Background Papers*, vol 2 (Ottawa: 1961), 654.

46. Ontario, Department of Lands and Forests, *Suggestions for Program of Renewable Resources Development* White Paper (Toronto: 1954).

47. Ibid.

48. Ibid.

49. W.A.E. Pepler, "Review and Assessment of Present Forest Policies," in *Proceedings, Resources for Tomorrow* vol 2, 731–736.

50. Lambert with Pross, *Renewing*, 402–408.

51. Swift, *Cut and Run*, Chapter 4.

52. F.L.C. Reed, *The Role of the Federal Government in Forestry* (Edmonton: 1978). and *Forest Management in Canada* (Ottawa: 1978). Reed is a forestry consultant in British Columbia who was brought in during the early 1980's on an executive interchange to head the CFS and to try to turn around federal forestry. He was only partially successful in his objectives. See: Canada, House of Commons, "Debate on the Forest Industry," *Debates* (30 May 1983):25815–25869, and D.J. Savoie, *Federal-Provincial Collaboration: The Canada-New Brunswick General Development Agreement.* (Montreal: 1981), 48–52.

53. Progressive Conservative Party of Canada, "Campaign Platform" and Canada, Prime Minister's Office, *News Release* (17 Sept 1984).

54. H. Winsor, "Is There a Softer Touch," *Globe and Mail* 20 April 1981.

55. Ibid. One of the most recent manifestations of the relationship was the hiring of the Hon. Rene Brunelle, a former provincial Tory resources minister and general political czar of northwestern Ontario, upon his retirement from government, as an "external relations consultant" with a large pulp and paper company in order to handle its dealings with the provincial government. But lest it be thought that Ontario is the only culprit, let it be said that similar events have occurred in other provinces as well, many with much more venial results such as the acceptance by Robert Sommers, B.C. Minister of Lands, of money from forest firms in return for tree farm licence arrangements during the mid–1950's.

56. The rise of the modern conservation movement and its relationship with such movements in the Canadian past is discussed to a very limited extent in T.L. Burton, *Natural Resource Policy in Canada: Issues and Perspectives* (Toronto: 1972), 139–41.

Bibliographical Essay

There has been a neglect in the historical analysis of the forest industries, forest policy, and forest conservation in Canada as profound as the failure in public policy chronicled by this book. Unlike the specialities of social, ethnic, labour, and women's history which have complemented traditional political and diplomatic studies since World War II, themes dealing with lumbering and forestry have, with a few notable exceptions, been studiously ignored. This has made it difficult to present a coherent national analysis. Where good monographs or articles do exist, they have been eagerly seized on to complement primary research materials. Outlined below, by theme, is a selection of the source materials, primary and secondary, which are of major importance in documenting this volume.

List of Abbreviations

PAC	Public Archives of Canada
PAO	Public Archives of Ontario
OA	Ontario Department of Public Records and Archives
QA	National Archives of Quebec
RG	Record group
MG	Manuscript group

British North America

Lumbering and government regulation in the Pre-Confederation period is documented in a vast array of archival sources. The most important are listed below.

PAC: Timber Policy and Trade, 1762–1831, MG11, Colonial Office 323, vols. 17, 24, 27, and 30; Q series, MG11, Colonial Office, 42; George Hamilton Papers, 1803–1888, MG24, D 7; Wright Family Papers, 1792–1864, MG24, D 8; James Maclaren Company Papers, 1866–1920, MG24, D 39; Archibald Campbell Collection,

MG24, D 61, vols. 1–4; James Stevenson Papers, MG24, D 66; Hill Collection, MG24, I 9; Nicholas Sparks Papers, MG24, I 40; Gatineau River, Quebec, Diary of a Lumberman, MG24, I 89; Richard William Scott Papers, MG27, II D 14; Bronsons and Weston Company Records, MG28 III 26; Commissioner of Crown Land's Correspondence RG1, 16E, vol. 5; Civil and Provincial Secretary's Correspondence, Lower Canada, 1760–1840, RG4 A 1; Lands Records, Lower Canada, Report of the Commissioner the Crown Lands Department, 1846, RG4, B 15, vol. 17; Civil and Provincial Secretary's Correspondence, Upper Canada, RG5, A 1; Executive Council, Upper Canada, Petitions and Addresses, 1792–1849, RG5, B 3, vols 6–15; Statistics Canada, Census of 1871, RG31 A 1, vol 893, schedule 7; F. J. Audet's Biographical Notes, MG30, B 62; Sir John A. Macdonald Papers, MG26 A.

PAO: A.J. Russell, "Historical Memorandum on the Management of the Crown Timber Forests and of Crown Lands Connexions therewith," F–1–1, vol. 57; Department of Lands and Forests, Timber Branch Records, RG1, series E; Crown Lands Department, Timber Agencies, Bytown, RG1, series F; Hamilton Brothers Company Records, 1797–1888; McLachlin Family Papers, 1834–1941.

QA: series QBC 13, vols. 1–5.

A number of primary published sources were also consulted. The most informative among these include Great Britain, Parliament, House of Lords, *Minutes of Evidence Taken before the Select Committee of the House of Lords Appointed to Enquire into the Means of Extending and Securing the Foreign Trade of the Country and to Report to the House*, Sessional Paper No. 59 (London; HMSO, 1820); Upper Canada and Province of Canada, Legislative Assembly, *Journals 1836–1853*; J. H. Morgan, *The Dominion Annual Register, 1884* (Toronto; 1884; Province of Canada, Commissioner of Crown Lands, *Annual Reports, 1842–1867*; and John Langton, "On the Age of Timber Trees and the Prospects of a Continuous Supply of Timber in Canada," *Transactions of the Literary and Historical Society of Quebec* 5 (1862).

By far the best secondary source on the growth and development of the British North American lumber industry remains Arthur R. M. Lower, *The North American Assault on the Canadian Forest: A History of the Lumber Trade Between Canada and the United States . . . with Studies of the Forest Industries of British Columbia by W. A. Carrothers and the Forest Industries of the Maritimes by S. A. Saunders* (Toronto, 1938). This should be read in tandem with Lower's more modern but less satisfactory rendition of the early timber trade entitled *Great Britain's Woodyard: British North America and Timber Trade, 1763–1867* (Montreal, 1973), which is drawn from the first part of his 1928 Harvard doctoral dissertation. Reference should also be made to an earlier work by J. E. Defebaugh, *The History of the Lumber Industry of America*, 2 vols. (Chicago, 1906–1907), vol. I.

The imperial and staple themes of the early timber trade are explored in a number of works and essays such as R. G. Albion, *Forests and Sea Power: The Timber Problem of the Royal Navy, 1652–1862* (Cambridge, Mass., 1926); G. S. Graham, *Sea Power and British North America, 1783–1820: A Study in British Colonial Policy* (Cambridge, Mass., 1941); T. J. Stobart, *The Timber Trade in the United Kingdom* (London, 1927); Donald Creighton, *The Empire of the St. Lawrence* (Toronto, 1956); and W. T. Easterbrook and M. H. Watkins, eds., *Approaches to Canadian Economic History: A Selection of Essays* (Toronto, 1967), especially those essays by W. A. Mackintosh, H. A. Innis and A. R. M. Lower. Useful economic overviews of the period are provided in W. T. Easterbrook and H. G. J. Aitken, *Canadian Economic History* (Toronto, 1956); and W. L. Marr and D. G. Paterson, *Canada: An Economic History* (Toronto, 1980). The best economic study of the early timber trade is, however, Fernand Ouellet's classic *Histoire économique et social du Québec, 1760–1860: structures et conjonctures* (Montreal, 1966).

The violent social conditions of the early timber trade and the search for order are discussed best by M. S. Cross in his brilliant doctoral dissertation "The Dark Druidical Groves: The Lumber Community and the Commercial Frontier in British North America to 1854" (unpublished doctoral dissertation, Univ. of Toronto, 1968) and his two articles, "The Lumber Community of Upper Canada, 1815–1867," *Ontario History* 52, 4 (Autumn 1960) and "The Shiner's War: Social Violence in the Ottawa Valley in the 1830's," *Canadian Historical Review* 54 (1973). Cross has also edited an interesting volume entitled *The Frontier Thesis and the Canadas: The Debate on the Impact of the Canadian Environment* (Toronto, 1970); this should be read in conjunction with Cole Harris, "Of Poverty and Helplessness in Petite-Nation," *Canadian Historical Review* 25 (March 1971). Other more limited but informative works about the early timber trade are C. H. Craigie, "The Influence of the Timber Trade and Philemon Wright on the Social and Economic Development of Hull Township, 1800 to 1850" (unpublished masters thesis, Carleton University, 1969). Louise Dechêne, "Les enterprises de William Price," *Histoire Sociale*, vol. 1 (1968); R. P. Gillis, "The Ottawa Valley Timber Industry and the Algonquin Park Area, 1850–1920," and "The Square Timber Era in the Ottawa Valley," unpublished manuscripts, 1968, Ontario Department of Natural Resources; J. W. Hughson and C. C. J. Bond, *Hurling Down the Pine: The Story of the Wright, Gilmour and Hughson Families, Timber and Lumber Manufacturers in the Hull and Ottawa Region and on the Gatineau River, 1820–1920* (Old Chelsea, Quebec, 1965); and C. C. Kennedy, *The Upper Ottawa Valley* (Pembroke: 1970).

Canadian commercial developments and the Reciprocity Treaty are discussed in D. C. Masters, *Reciprocity Treaty of 1854: Its History, Its Relation to British Colonial and Foreign Policy, and to the Development of Canadian Fiscal Autonomy* (Toronto, 1963). G. N. Tucker, *The Canadian Commercial Revolution, 1845–1851* (New Haven, Conn.; 1936); and S. A. Saunders, "The Maritime Provinces and the Reciprocity Treaty", *Dalhousie Review* (Oct. 1934). The main theme of the chapter concerning the forest industries and government regulations is analyzed in five outstanding works: Sandra J. Gillis, *The Timber Trade in the Ottawa Valley, 1806–1854*, manuscript report no. 153, Parks Canada, 1975; Graeme Wynn, *Timber Colony: A Historical Geography of Early Nineteenth Century New Brunswick* (Toronto, 1981); W. S. MacNutt, "The Politics of the Timber Trade in Colonial New Brunswick, 1825–40," *Canadian Historical Review* 30 (1949); H. V. Nelles, *The Politics of Development: Forests, Mines and Hydro-electric in Ontario, 1849–1941* (Toronto, 1974), chap. 1; and R. S. Lambert with P. Pross, *Renewing Nature's Wealth: A Centennial History of the Public Management of Lands, Forests and Wildlife in Ontario, 1763–1967* (Toronto: 1967).

Finally two sources should be mentioned: the novel by Ralph Connor [pseud.] entitled *The Man from Glengarry; a Tale of the Ottawa* (Toronto, 1901), which captures the flavour of the early timber industry, and D. MacKay's popular history of the forest industries, *The Lumberjacks* (Toronto, 1978).

Early Conservation Movement

Major primary archival sources consulted at the PAC were the Bronsons and Weston Company Records, MG28 III 26; the Lotbinière Family Papers, MG27 II C2; the Records of the Department of the Interior, RG15, vol. 298, file 624411; and Records of the Privy Council, RG2. In addition, James Little's two pamphlets, *The Lumber Trade in the Ottawa Valley* (Ottawa, 1872) and *The Timber Supply Question of the Dominion of Canada and the United States of America* (Montreal, 1876) are found in the PAC pamphlet collection.

Reference was also made to the Ontario Department of Agriculture and Arts, *Report of the Fruit Growers' Association*, 1878–1883 and Ontario, *Sessional Papers*, 1883. Official documents of the Province of Quebec included the *Statutes* 1883–1894; *Sessional Papers* 1893; *Report of Argument Submitted to the Honourable the Executive Council for the Province of Quebec on Presentation of a Memorial Respecting the Vested Rights of Limitholders in Their Limits* (March 16, 1880); and for both Ontario and Quebec the *Annual Reports* 1881–1896 of the Commissioners of Crown Lands.

The original reports of the Cincinnati and Montreal conferences can be found in *Proceedings of the American Forestry Congress at Its Sessions Held at Cincinnati, Ohio, April 1882 and Montreal, Canada, August 1882* (Washington, D.C., 1883); the editions of the *Montreal Herald* and the *Montreal Gazette* for August 1882. Three other valuable sources were Lambert and Pross, *Renewing Nature's Wealth*; D. MacKay, *Heritage Lost: The Crisis in Canada's Forests* (Toronto, 1985); and Norman Ross, *The Tree-Planting Division: Its History and Work* (Ottawa, 1923).

George Marsh's influential book, *Man and Nature*, was edited by D. Lowenthal and reissued by Harvard University Press in 1965, and Lowenthal also published a biography entitled *George Perkins Marsh: Versatile Vermonter* (New York, 1958). Other historical texts dealing with the rise of the conservation ethic in North America are H. Clepper, ed., *Origins of American Conservation* (New York, 1966); S. P. Hays, *Conservation and the Gospel of Efficiency: The Progressive Conservatism Movement, 1890–1920* (Cambridge, Mass. 1959); R. Nash, *Wilderness and the American Mind* (New Haven and London, 1967); and J. R. Ross, "Man Over Nature: Origins of the Conservation Movement," *American Studies* 16, 1 (Spring 1975). Two other interesting and controversial commentaries are found in Gabriel Kolko, *The Triumph of Conservatism* (New York, 1963); and Anthony Scott, *Natural Resources: The Economics of Conservation* (Toronto, 1955 and Ottawa, 1983).

The origins of the Canadian conservation movement are analyzed in Nelles, *The Politics of Development*; and J. Foster, *Working for Wildlife: The Beginning of Preservation in Canada* (Toronto, 1978). A somewhat different perspective on this movement is given in R. Peter Gillis, "The Ottawa Lumber Barons and the Conservation Movement, 1880–1914," *Journal of Canadian Studies* 9 (February 1974); and B. W. Hodgins, J. Benidickson, and R. P. Gillis, "The Ontario and Quebec Experiments in Forest Reserves, 1883–1930," *Journal of Forest History* 26 (January 1982).

Three other books should also be mentioned in regard to the early conservation movement: A. D. Rodger's biography entitled *Bernhard Eduard Fernow* (Princeton, 1951); the second edition of Gifford Pinchot's autobiography, *Breaking New Ground* (Seattle, 1972); and C. A. Schenck, *The Birth of Forestry in America: Biltmore Forest School, 1898–1913* (Santa Cruz, Calif., 1974).

The colonization movement in Quebec and northern Ontario is dealt with in Jack

Little, "La Patrie: Quebec's Repatriation Colony, 1875–1880," in Canadian Historical Association, *Historical Papers* (Ottawa, 1977); B. W. Hodgins, *Paradis of Temagami* (Cobalt, Ont. 1976); P-A. Linteau, R. Durocher, and J-C. Robert, *Quebec; A History, 1867–1929* (Toronto, 1983); G. Vartier, *Esquisse Historique*; and G. C. Brandt, "The Development of French-Canadian Social Institutions in Sudbury, Ontario, 1883–1928", *Laurentian University Review* 11 (February 1979). The settlement effort through land grants in the shield area of Ontario is discussed to some extent in L. F. Gates, *Land Policies of Upper Canada* (Toronto; 1968).

Major sources on politics in Quebec are R. Rumilly, *Histoire de la Province de Québec* (Montreal; 1940), vols. 4–6; B. Young, "Federalism in Quebec: The First Years After Confederation," in B. W. Hodgins, D. Wright and W. H. Heick, eds., *Federalism in Canada and Australia: The Early Years* (Waterloo, 1978); and M. Wade, *The French Canadians*, vol. 1 (Toronto, 1968).

The only useful secondary work on early federal forestry administration in western Canada is Peter Murphy, *History of Forest and Prairie Fire Control Policy in Alberta* (Edmonton, 1985).

The Laurier Liberals and Conservation

Most of the primary source material for this chapter comes from the PAC. They include the Records of the Department of the Interior, RG15; the Records of the Department of National Resources and Development, RG22; Legal files relating to the Commission of Conservation, 1909–1921; Records of the Canadian Forestry Service, RG39, Head Office Policy Files; the Governor-General's Records, RG7 and Sir Wilfrid Laurier Papers, MG26 G, regarding correspondence on Canadian representation at Theodore Roosevelt's conservation congresses. Also Records of the Canadian Forestry Association, MG28 I 188; and Lotbinière Family Papers, MG27 II C2.

Use was also made of the published *Annual Reports* of 1896–1912 of the federal Department of the Interior; *The Dominion Forest Reserves and Parks Act: An Indexed Summary of Regulations Relating to Dominion Parks as Approved by Order-in-Council Consolidated for Office Purposes Only* (Ottawa, 1912 and 1928); the *Annual Reports* 1910–1920 of the Commission of Conservation; Canada, House of Commons, *Sessional Papers and Journals*, 1895–1911; Canada, House of Commons, *Debates*, Sessions of 1906, 1909 and 1910–1911; and Canadian Forestry Association, *The Forests and the People* (Toronto, 1906) and *Proceedings* of annual meetings, 1901–1911; Department of the Interior, *Timber Disposal Manual* (Ottawa, 1929); N. Ross, *Tree-planting Division*; and Canada, *Statutes*, 1906–1911; *Rod and Gun in Canada*, 1901–1911; and the *Ottawa Citizen*, 1900–1911.

Much has been written about the administration of Wilfrid Laurier but a full-scale historical work is sadly lacking. Many articles and short books deal with the period, but there has been very little analysis of a substantial nature fixing the attitudes of the government and the various policies it pursued. Prof. Blair Neatby's thesis, "Laurier and a Liberal Quebec: A Study in Political Management", published in the Carleton Library Series in 1973, remains the best readily available source. There is also Paul Stevens "Laurier and the Liberal Party in Ontario, 1887–1911" (unpublished doctoral dissertation, Univ. of Toronto), and, of course, J. Schull, *Laurier* (Toronto, 1966).

In regard to resource policies, the Laurier government has received proportionately less attention. D. J. Hall has produced a two-volume biography of Clifford Sifton, *The Young Napoleon, 1861–1900* and *The Lonely Eminence, 1901–1929* (Vancouver, 1981 and 1985), but it is an avowedly political biography in the older style. A somewhat more controversial effort in the same general vein is Pierre Berton, *The Promised Land: Settling the West 1896–1914* (Toronto: 1984). This leaves Chester Martin's study from the 1930s, "Dominion Lands Policy," as the standard work. Reprinted in 1973 by the Carleton Library Series, it provides an overview of resource policy in a very dry manner devoid of the political debate that surrounded its formation. The only bright exceptions to this rather sad tale are Janet Foster, *Working for Wildlife*, which looks at the origins of federal preservationist policies and Peter Murphy, *History of Forest and Prairie Fire Control*, which deals with some early forestry policy.

These few works can be supplemented by R. C. Brown, "The Doctrine of Usefulness: Natural Resources and National Parks Policy, 1887–1914" in J. G. Nelson, ed., *Canadian National Parks: Today and Tomorrow* (Calgary; 1958); M. Zaslow, *The Opening of the Canadian North, 1870–1914* (Toronto, 1971); K. H. Norrie, "The National Policy and the Rate of Prairie Settlement: A Review," *Journal of Canadian Studies* 14, 3 (Fall 1979); Sylvia Van Kirk, "The Development of National Park Policy in Canada's Mountain National Parks, 1885–1930," (unpublished masters thesis, Univ. of Alberta, 1969), chap. 1; R. Haig-Brown, "The Land's Wealth" in *The Canadians* pt. II (Toronto, 1967); E. A. Mitchner, "William Pearce and Federal Government Activity in Western Canada, 1882–1904," (unpublished doctoral dissertation, Univ. of Alberta, 1971); and D. H. Breen, *The Canadian Prairie West and the Ranching Frontier, 1874–1924* (Toronto, 1983).

References to C. A. Schenck and Gifford Pinchot are found in C. A. Schenck, *Birth of Forestry in America*; G. Pinchot, *Breaking New Ground*; and H. T. Pinkett, *Gifford Pinchot: Private and Public Forester* (Chicago, 1970). The origins of the Canadian Commission of Conservation and its work are dealt with in C. R. Smith and D. R. Witty, "Conservation Resources and Environment: An Explanation and Critical Evaluation of the Commission of Conservation," *Plan Canada* 11, 1 (1970); D. M. Calnan, "Businessmen, Forestry and the Gospel of Efficiency: The Canadian Conservation Commission, 1909–1921," (unpublished masters thesis, Univ. of Western Ontario, 1976); S. Renfrew, "Commission of Conservation", *Douglas Library Notes* (Spring 1971); and A. F. J. Artibise and G. A. Stelter, "Conservation Planning and Urban Planning: The Canadian Commission of Conservation in Historical Perspective," in R. Kain, ed., *Planning for Conservation* (New York, 1981).

Ontario

Primary sources for this chapter are drawn mostly from the PAO, including the Department of Lands and Forests, Timber Branch Records, RG1, series E; the Ontario Lumbermen's Association, Minute Book; the James Pliny Whitney Papers; the E. C. Drury Papers, particularly the Canadian Forestry Association file; and the unpublished manuscript by J. P. Bertrand entitled "Timber Wolves" in manuscript no. 124.

Major primary sources from the PAC are the Bronsons and Weston Company Records, MG28 III 26; the Sir Wilfrid Laurier Papers, especially correspondence with E. W. Rathbun, John Bertram. A. S. Hardy, and W. C. Edwards, MG26 G;

the Sir John Willison Papers, MG30 D 29; and the Sir R. W. Scott Papers, MG27 II D 14.

Published primary materials are found in Ontario, *Sessional Papers*, particularly no. 58, 1898; Ontario, *Statutes*, 1896–1934; the *Interim Report* of 1921 and *Final Report* of 1922 of the Timber Commission; Ontario, Director of Forestry (formerly Clerk of Forestry) *Annual Reports* 1896–1906; Ontario, Bureau of Colonization, *Report of the Director of Colonization*, 1900; Ontario, *Report of the Commission on Forestry Reservation and National Parks, 1893*; Ontario, *Report of the Royal Commission on Forestry Protection in Ontario, 1899*; Ontario, Commission on Forest Reservation, *Report, 1905*; Canada, Commission of Conservation, *Forest Protection in Canada, 1913–1914* (Toronto, 1915); E. W. Rathbun, *Shall We Place An Export Duty on Sawlogs and Pulpwood?* (Deseronto, 1897); and William Schlick, *A Manual of Forestry* (London, 1889). Reference was also made to *The Paper Mill and Woodpulp News*; the *Canadian Forestry Journal*; the American Paper and Pulp Association, *Paper and Pulp Industry*; the Canadian Pulp and Paper Association, *The Underwood Resolution Committee Hearings*, C.P.P.A. bulletin no. 24 (1 May 1920); United States, Federal Trade Commission, *Report on the News-Print Paper Industry* (Washington, D.C., 1917); *Illustrated Canadian Forests and Outdoors*, 1920–1926; W. Compton, *Conservation the Form or the Substance Which?* (Chicago, 1919), and *The Organization of the Lumber Industry* (Chicago, 1916); J. O. Miller ed., *The Progressive Era in Canada* (Toronto, 1917); *Canada Lumberman*, 1920–1926; *Canadian Economics* (Montreal: 1885); *The Forestry Quarterly*, 1906–1909; A. Gaskill, "How Shall the Forests Be Taxed," *Society of American Foresters*, 1904, PAC, pamphlet collection no. 2–2993; and C. A. Schenck, *The Art of Second Growth* (Albany, 1912).

The basic secondary works are Lambert with Pross, *Renewing Nature's Wealth* and H. V. Nelles, *The Politics of Development*. Both deal with the events leading up to the declaration of the manufacturing condition and the rise of the pulp and paper industry. A somewhat different viewpoint is given by R. P. Gillis, "The Ottawa Lumber Barons and Conservation", and special mention should also be made of R.C. Brown, *Canada's National Policy: A Study in Canadian-American Relations* (Toronto, 1964); J. M. Bliss, *A Living Profit: Studies in the Social History of Canadian Business, 1883–1911* (Toronto, 1972); and Paul Stevens, "Laurier and the Liberal Party in Ontario, 1887–1911."

The history of the Canada Atlantic Railway is detailed in R. P. Gillis' biography of William Goodhue Perly in vol. XI of the *Dictionary of Canadian Biography*; R. Brown, "Depot Harbour, Busy Great Lakes Port, 1900–1928," *Canadian Geographical Journal* 95, 3 (1977/78); C. F. Coons, "The John R. Booth Story," *Your Forests* 11, 2 (Summer 1978); D. Johnston, *Canada Atlantic Railway, Old Boys Reunion, August 19–24, 1935* (Ottawa, 1935); A. R. M. Lower, *North American Assault*; G. R. Stevens, *Canadian National Railways: Towards the Inevitable, 1896–1927* (Toronto, 1962), vol. II; and R. P. Gillis, "E. H. Bronson and Corporate Capitalism, 1880–1910" (unpublished masters thesis, Queen's University, 1975.

John Charlton's career is covered in L. J. Curnoe, "John Charlton and Canadian-American Relations" (unpublished masters thesis, Univ. of Toronto, 1939); and the Joint High Commission is dealt with in J. M. V. Foster, "Reciprocity and the Joint High Commission," Canadian Historical Association, *Annual Report* (1939). Conditions in the United States are described in R. F. Fries, *Empire in Pine* (Madison, Wis., 1951); M. Frome, *Whose Woods These Are* (New York, 1962); R. N. Johnson and G. D. Libecap, "Efficient Markets and Great Lakes Timber: A Conservation

Issue Re-examined," *Explorations in Economic History* 17, 4 (October 1980); A. R. M. Lower, *North American Assault*; M. E. Neithercut and G. Wynn, "Logging the Hemlocks–White Pine–Northern Hardwood Forest: Geographical Perspectives," American Historical Association, Chicago, 1984; and L. L. Gould, ed., *The Progressive Era* (Syracuse, 1974).

The origin of the Ontario forest reserve system is covered in detail in Hodgins, Benidickson and Gillis, "Ontario and Quebec Experiments in Forest Reserves." Reference should also be made to B. E. Fernow, "Forest Resources and Forestry," in A. Shortt and A. G. Doughty, eds., *Canada and Its Provinces: A History of the Canadian People and Their Institutions*, vol. 18, *The Province of Ontario* (Toronto, 1914–1917); B. W. Hodgins and J. Benidickson, "Resource Management Conflict in the Temagami Forest, 1898–1914," Canadian Historical Association, *Historical Papers* (1978); P. W. Sinclair, "Strategies of Development on an Agricultural Frontier: The Great Clay Belt, 1900–1950," (unpublished doctoral dissertation, Univ. of Toronto, 1980); R. P. Gillis and T. Roach, "Early European and North American Forestry in Canada: The Ontario Example, 1890–1940," in H. K. Steen, ed., *History of Sustained-Yield Forestry: A Symposium* (Santa Cruz, Calif. 1984; A. D. Rodgers, *Fernow*; J. A. Linteau, "Le feu, regenerateur de la fôret," *La Fôret Québecoise* 3 8 (1941) and K. M. Mayall, *White Pine Succession as Influenced By Fire* (Ottawa, 1941).

The pulp and paper industry in Ontario is discussed in the ghost-written volume *Paper in the Making* (Toronto, 1947) by George Carruthers, then President of Interlake Tissue Mills. Reference should also be made to J. A. Guthrie, *The Newsprint Paper Industry: An Economic Analysis* (Cambridge, Mass., 1941); L. E. Ellis, *The Print Paper Pendulum: Group Pressures and the Price of Newsprint* (New Brunswick, N.J., 1960); and *Reciprocity 1911: A Study in Canadian American Relations* (New Haven, Conn., 1934); N. Reich, *The Pulp and Paper Industry in Canada* (Toronto, circa 1926); T. Traves, *The State and Enterprise* (Toronto: 1979); H. Marshall, F. Southard, and K. W. Taylor, *Canadian-American Industry: A Study of International Investment* (Carleton Library Edition, Toronto, 1976); R. W. Mackenzie, "The Chemical Engineers and the News Print Industry," *Canadian Chemistry and Metallurgy* 5, 3 (1921); and Trevor J. O. Dick, "Canadian Newsprint, 1913–1930: National Policies and the North American Economy," *Journal of Economic History* 42, 3 (1982). Francis Clergue's career may be followed in H. V. Nelles, *The Politics of Development*; and M. Van Every, "Francis Hector Clergue and the Rise of Sault Ste. Marie as an Industrial Centre," *Ontario History* 56 (September 1964). Harvesting of pulpwood by settlers on private lands is investigated in A. R. M. Lower, *Settlement and the Forest Frontier in Eastern Canada* (Toronto, 1936); T. Roach, "Farm Woodlots and Pulpwood Exports from Eastern Canada, 1900–1930," in Steen, ed., *History of Sustained-Yield Forestry*, pp. 202–210; and "The Pulpwood Trade and the Settlers of New Ontario," paper presented to the 1982 annual meeting of the Ontario History Association.

James Pliny Whitney has generally been given a fairly favourable review by historians because of his experiments with public ownership of hydroelectric power. This is covered in Nelles, *Politics of Development*, but, most particularly, in C. W. Humphries, *Honest Enough to Be Bold: The Life and Times of Sir James Pliny Whitney* (Toronto, 1985); and "The Sources of Ontario 'Progressive Conservatism', 1900–1914," Canadian Historical Association, *Historical Papers* (Ottawa, 1967). This section develops the theme that Tory forestry policy under Whitney and his successors was not particularly enlightened. This draws on R. P. Gillis, "The Ottawa Lumber Barons and Conservation"; and reference should also be made to B. D. Tennyson, "The Succession of William H. Hearst to the Ontario Premiership, September, 1914," *Ontario History* (September 1964); P. Oliver, *Public and Private Persons: The Ontario Political Culture, 1914–1934* (Toronto, 1975), and, by the same author, *G. Howard Ferguson: Ontario Tory* (Toronto, 1977).

Quebec

Very little has been written about forestry policy and the woods industries in Quebec. The main primary sources used here are PAC, the Lotbinière Family Papers, MG27 II C2; Records of the Canadian Forestry Service, RG39, especially files 3–2–0 and 50063 I-II relating to Quebec's participation in the National Conferences on Forest Protection (1924) and Forest Inventory (1929) and Maurice Duplessis' position at the federal-provincial negotiations in 1946; and Bronsons and Weston Company Records, MG28 II I26.

Reference was also made to Quebec, Minister of Lands and Forests (earlier Commissioner of Crown Lands), *Annual Reports* 1883–1946, including after 1910 reports by the Quebec Forest Service; Quebec, *Statutes*, 1883–1946; Quebec, *Sessional Papers*, 1893–1930; *Report of the Colonization Commission of the Province of Quebec, 1904* (Quebec City, 1904); C. Hopkins, ed., *The Canadian Annual Review* (Toronto, 1903–1910); Canada, Department of the Interior, Canadian Forestry Service, *The Forests of Canada* (Ottawa, 1928), and Canada, *Report of the Royal Commission on Pulpwood* (Ottawa, 1924); as well as the *Canada Lumberman and Woodworker*; and the *Forestry Chronicle*.

The best modern secondary survey of Quebec history is Linteau et al., *Quebec: A History, 1867–1929*. This must be supplemented, however, by R. Rumilly, *Histoire de la Province de Québec*; and E. T. O. Chambers, "The Province of Quebec," in *Canada and Its Provinces*, vol. 16. Other useful works are M. Zaslow, *The Opening of the Canadian North*, chap. 7; Hodgins, Benidickson, and Gillis, "The Ontario and Quebec Experiments in Forest Reserves"; R. P. Gillis, "The Ottawa Lumber Barons and Conservation"; T. Roach, "Farm Woodlots and Pulpwood Exports from Eastern Canada," in Steen, ed., *History of Sustained-Yield*; E. Minville ed., *La Forêt* (Montreal, 1944), which is an excellent but forgotten survey of forest law, policy and conditions in the province; and A. Bédard, "Forestry in Quebec," in the *Canadian Geographical Journal* 28 (June 1944). Reference should also be made to M. Hamelin, *Les Premières Années du Parlementairisme Québecois, 1867–1878* (Quebec City: 1974); R. Comeau, ed., *Economie Québecoise* (Quebec City, 1969); and J. Hamelin and Y. Roby, *Histoire Economique du Québec, 1851–1896* (Montreal, 1976), chap. III. Also important to this chapter are B. Weilbrenner, "Les idées politiques de Lomer Gouin," Canadian Historical Association, *Historical Papers* (Ottawa, 1965); M. Wade, *The French Canadians, 1760–1967*, 2 vols. (Toronto, 1968), vol. II; W. F. Ryan, *The Clergy and Economic Growth in Quebec, 1896–1914* (Quebec City, 1966); and J. Levitt, *Henri Bourassa and the Golden Calf: The Social Program of the Nationalists of Quebec, 1900–1914* (Ottawa, 1969). The pulp and paper industry is specifically dealt with in John A. Guthrie, *An Economic Analysis of the Pulp and Paper Industry* (Seattle, 1972); and H. Marshall, F. Southard, and K. W. Taylor, *Canadian-American Industry*.

As pointed out above, Jack Little, "La Patrie"; and Hodgins, *Paradis of Temagami* deal to some extent with the French Canadian colonization movement. These works should be supplemented with S. Vattier, *Equisse Historique de la Colonization de la*

Province de Québec (Paris, 1928); E. J. Auclair, *Le Curé Labelle, Sa Vie et Son Oeuvre* (Montreal, 1930); B. A. Testard de Montigny, *La Colonization—Le Nord de Montréal ou la Région Labelle* (Montreal, 1896); I. Caron, *Un Nouveau Centre de Colonization, l'Abitibi* (Quebec City, 1915); and M. Brunet, "Trois Dominates de la Pensée Canadienne-Française," *Ecrits du Canada Français* 3 (1957).

British Columbia

British Columbia forest history is largely in the same state as that of Quebec. Given the importance of the wood industries to the province, there has been a strange reluctance on the part of the historians to investigate them.

Extensive use was made of the *Vancouver Daily Province*, the *Vancouver Daily News Advertiser*, and the *Victoria Daily Times*, as well as *Rod and Gun in Canada* and the *Canadian Forestry Journal* in researching this chapter. Other primary sources consulted were Province of British Columbia, *The Forests of British Columbia* (Victoria, 1965); the *Final Report of the Royal Commission on Timber and Forestry* (Victoria, 1910); British Columbia, *Statutes*, 1912–1920; British Columbia, Timber Inspectors Report, *Sessional Papers*, 1881–1900; British Columbia, *Gazette* (1912); British Columbia, Minister of Lands, *Annual Reports*, 1912–1952; Canada, House of Commons, *Journals*, 1900–1912; Canada, Commission of Conservation, *The Forests of British Columbia* (Ottawa, 1918); Canadian Forestry Association, *Proceedings of Annual Meetings*, 1901–1914; a pamphlet by Hon. William R. Ross, "British Columbia's Forest Policy, Speech to the Legislative Assembly of British Columbia on the 2nd Reading of the Forest Bill"; and British Columbia Timber and Forestry Chamber of Commerce, *Programme of Inaugural Meeting* (n.p., n.d).

There is a host of semipopular literature on British Columbia logging, of which G. Taylor, *Timber: The History of the Forest Industry in British Columbia* (Vancouver, 1975) is the best. Of course, forestry is covered in M. A. Ormsby, *British Columbia: A History* (Toronto, 1964); Martin Robin, *The Rush for Spoils: The Company Province, 1871–1933* (Toronto, 1972), and *Pillars of Profit: The Company Province, 1934–1972* (Toronto, 1973).

Books and articles which bear more directly on the development of the forest industries in the province are R. E. Cail, *Land, Man and Law* (Vancouver, 1974); W. G. Hardwick, *Geography of the Forest Industry of Coastal British Columbia* (Vancouver, 1963); W. A. Carrothers, "Forest Industries of British Columbia," in A. R. M. Lower, *The North American Assault on the Canadian Forest* (Toronto, 1938); L. A. McCann, "Urban Growth in a Staple Economy: The Emergence of Vancouver as a Regional Metropolis, 1886–1914" in L. J. Evenden, ed., *Vancouver: Western Metropolis* (Victoria, 1978); T. R. Roach, "Stewards of the People's Wealth," *Journal of Forest History* 28, 1 (January 1984); K. Drushka, *Stumped: The Forest Industry in Transition* (Vancouver, 1985); P. Marchak, *Green Gold: The Forest Industry in British Columbia* (Vancouver, 1983; J. Swift, *Cut and Run: The Assault on Canada's Forests* (Toronto, 1983); and J. A. Gray, "Royal Commissions and Forest Policy in British Columbia: A Review of the Pearse Report," *Canadian Public Policy* 3, 2 (Spring 1977).

Several excellent graduate theses also cover the development of the industry and forest policy. These include J. C. Lawrence, "Markets and Capital: A History of the Lumber Industry of British Columbia" (unpublished masters thesis, Univ. of British Columbia, 1957), which provides a good overview of the topic; R. H. Marris,

"Pretty Sleek and Fat: The Genesis of Forest Policy in B.C., 1903–1914" (unpublished masters thesis, Univ. of British Columbia, 1979), which gives a somewhat left-wing interpretation of the Fulton Commission and the founding of the Forest Service; S. Gray, "Forest Policy and Administration in British Columbia, 1912–1928," (unpublished masters thesis, Simon Fraser Univ. 1982); and R. M. Yerburgh, "An Economic History of Forestry in British Columbia" (unpublished masters thesis, Univ. of British Columbia, 1931). Mention should also be made of M. A. Grainger's novel, *Woodsmen of the West* (Toronto reprint, 1964); and D. Mackay's *Empire of Wood: A History of the MacMillan-Bloedel Company* (Toronto, 1982). Perspectives on Gifford Pinchot and the American conservation movement relevant to this chapter come from G. Pinchot, *Breaking New Ground*; C. A. Schenck, *The Birth of Forestry*; A. D. Rodgers, *Fernow*; and H. T. Pinkett, *Gifford Pinchot*. Information was also derived from P. E. Roy, "Progress, Prosperity and Politics: The Railway Policies of Richard McBride," *British Columbia Studies* 47 (Autumn 1980); E. A. Bartlett, "Real Wages and the Standard of Living in Vancouver, 1901–1929", *British Columbia Studies* 55 (Autumn 1981); J. R. Jeanneney, "The Impact of World War I on French Timber Resources," *Journal of Forest History* 22, 4 (October 1978); R. A. J. McDonald, "Victoria, Vancouver and the Economic Development of British Columbia, 1886–1914", N. MacDonald, "The Canadian Pacific Railway and Vancouver's Development to 1900", and M. A. Ormsby, "T. Dufferin Patullo and the Little New Deal," all in Peter Ward, ed., *British Columbia: Historical Readings* (Vancouver, 1981); A. H. Macdonald, "Population Growth and Change in Seattle and Vancouver, 1880–1960," in J. Friesen and H. K. Ralston, eds., *Historical Essays on British Columbia* (Toronto, 1976); and R. E. Ficken, "Gifford Pinchot Men: Pacific Northwest Lumbermen and the Conservation Movement, 1902–1920," *Western Historical Quarterly* 13 (April, 1982).

New Brunswick

Two newspapers were used in the preparation of this chapter: the *Saint John Telegraph Journal*, 1910–1939, and the *Saint John Globe*, 1900–1913. These were supplemented by C. Hopkins, ed., *The Canadian Annual Review*, 1903–1939; and the *Canada Lumberman and Woodworker*, 1906–1912. Primary source materials that were invaluable to the analysis were New Brunswick, Crown Land Department, *Annual Reports*, 1889–1910; *Canadian Forestry Situation in 1944: Reports and Papers Presented to the 36th Annual Meeting of the Canadian Society of Forest Engineers* (Toronto: 1944); Province of New Brunswick, *Forests and Forestry in New Brunswick: A Special Report to the Second Imperial Forestry Conference, 1923* (Fredericton: 1923); K. B. Brown, "Memorandum Regarding Progress Made Toward Forest Management by the Department of Lands and Mines of New Brunswick in the Administration of Crown Lands, August, 1943," Environment Canada Library, PB9.40 N.B.; *The Wood Industries of New Brunswick* a reprint of the New Brunswick Section of the *Wood Industries of Canada* in *The Timber Trades Journal* (London: 1897); New Brunswick Resources Development Board, "The Utilization of Wood," in *The Development of the Forests and Forest Industries of New Brunswick*, pt. 2 (Fredericton, 1951); PAC, Records of the Department of the Interior, RG15, Saskatchewan Resources Commission, 1934, Additional Information; Canadian Forestry Service, RG39 vol. 409, file 39884, New Brunswick Regulation; and Canada, *Report of the Royal Commission on Pulpwood* (Ottawa, 1924).

New Brunswick is reasonably well-served with secondary material concerning the history of its forest industries up to 1850. Graeme Wynn's excellent book, *Timber Colony*, is a major source, which can be supplemented by W. S. MacNutt, *New Brunswick: A History, 1784–1867* (Toronto, 1963); and the article by the same author, "The Politics of the Timber Trade in Colonial New Brunswick, 1825–40." Also of interest are R. Rice, "The Wrights of Saint John: A Study of Shipbuilding and Ship-Owning in the Maritimes, 1839–1855," in D. J. Macmillan, ed., *Canadian Business History: Selected Studies, 1497–1971* (Toronto, 1972); and S. A. Saunders, "The Maritime Provinces and the Reciprocity Treaty," *Dalhousie Review* (October 1934).

The period after 1850 has, however, been written about only infrequently. An important work is R. B. Miller, "Forest Resources of the Maritime Provinces: New Brunswick," in *Canada and Its Provinces*, vol. 14, *The Atlantic Provinces, Part II* (Toronto, 1913). This can be complemented with J. M. Gibson, *The History of Forest Management in New Brunswick: H. R. MacMillan Lectureship Address Delivered at the University of British Columbia, Tuesday, April 7th, 1953*; and K. B. Brown, "Forests and Forestry in New Brunswick," *Forestry Chronicle* 17 (December 1941). Additional information can be drawn on the politics of the province from H. G. Thorburn, *Politics in New Brunswick* (Toronto, 1961); E. R. Forbes, *The Maritime Rights Movement, 1919–1927: A Study in Canadian Regionalism* (Montreal, 1979); D. C. Smith, *A History of Lumbering in Maine, 1861–1960* (Orono, Maine, 1972); J. Rankin, *A History of Our Firm* (Liverpool, U.K., 1921); C. A. Woodward, *The History of New Brunswick Provincial Election Campaigns and Platforms, 1866–1974* (Micromedia, 1976); and J. F. Hamilton, "The Pulp and Paper Industry of New Brunswick, Canada" (unpublished masters thesis, Indiana Univ., 1950).

Two recent works have looked critically at the relationship between the forest industries and politics in New Brunswick: J. Swift, *Cut and Run*; and A. T. Doyle, *Front Benches and Back Rooms: A Story of Corruption, Muckraking, Raw Partisanship and Intrigue in New Brunswick* (Toronto, 1976). Additional information on the Grand Falls project can be found in A. Legace, *How Grand Falls Grew* (n.p., 1946). Reference should also be made to S. Cote, *Origins of the Owners of the First Pulp and Paper Mills in New Brunswick* (Saint John, N.B.; 1978).

Federal Forestry between the Wars

The analysis of this period is based almost entirely on primary archival materials. These include from the PAC, the Records of the Canadian Forestry Service, RG39; Historical Personnel Files of the Canadian Government, RG32, C 2; the Records of the Department of Northern Affairs and National Resources, legal series, RG22; Proceedings of the Royal Commission on Pulpwood, RG 39, New Acquisition and RG33, Royal Commission No. 13; Sir Lomer Gouin Papers, MG27 III B4; and the Arthur Meighen Papers, MG26 I, particularly for correspondence with F. J. D. Barnjum.

Published primary materials, which were of great assistance, were C. Leavitt, C. D. Howe and J. H. White, *Forest Protection in Canada* (Toronto, 1915); Canada, Department of the Interior, *Annual Reports*, 1913–1920; Canada, Commission of Conservation, *Annual Reports*, 1910–1920; B. E. Fernow, C. D. Howe, and J. H. White, *Trent Watershed Survey* (Toronto, 1913) and, by the same authors, *Forest Conditions of Nova Scotia* (Ottawa, 1912); Canada, House of Commons, *Debates*, 1918–

1929; Canada, Royal Commission on Pulpwood, *Final Report* (Ottawa, 1924); and the long-term relationship of the Canadian Forestry Service with the Imperial (Commonwealth) Forestry Conference is reflected in Canada, Department of the Environment, *Progress Report, 1966–1972, for Tenth Commonwealth Forestry Conference* (Ottawa, 1974). F. J. D. Barnjum was a prolific writer and pamphleteer whose writings may be sampled in the Pamphlet Collection at the PAC. Reference should also be made to F. S. Chalmers, *Frank J. D. Barnjum, an Appreciation of Canada's Most Practical Propagandist* (Toronto, 1924). Newspapers and journals which were consulted for this period include the Toronto *Globe*; *Saturday Night*; *Canadian Lumberman*; *Illustrated Canadian Forests and Outdoors*; and *Canadian Woodlands Review*. The *Canadian Annual Review* documents the relationship of forestry matters to political events such as the Pulpwood Commission and Barnjum's propaganda activities.

Events surrounding the demise of the Commission of Conservation are dealt with, to some extent, in C. Armstrong, *The Politics of Federalism: Ontario's Relations with the Federal Government, 1867–1942* (Toronto, 1981), chap. 8; D. J. Hall, *Clifford Sifton*, vol. 2; and J. Foster, *Working for Wildlife*. William G. Robbins' interesting article "Federal Forestry Co-operation: The Fernow-Pinchot Years," *Journal of Forest History* 28, 4 (October 1984) outlines the type of programme which Canadian federal foresters were attempting to emulate. The pulpwood trade in eastern Canada is described in Roach, "The Pulpwood Trade and the Settlers of New Ontario." The government of W. L. M. King is described in detail in H. Blair Neatby, *William Lyon Mackenzie King*, vol. 2, *The Lonely Heights: 1924–1934* (Toronto; 1963) the King-Byng Affair is analyzed in R. Graham, ed., *The King-Byng Affair, 1926: A Question of Responsible Government* (Toronto, 1967). Pulpwood developments and politics in Manitoba are well covered in J. Kendle, *John Bracken: A Political Biography* (Toronto: 1980).

The Modern Era

A major feature of forestry policy of this period were the attempts, during and after World War II, to obtain a federal-provincial basis for pursuing the forestry objectives of conservation and renewal. The primary archival source used is PAC, Records of the Canadian Forestry Service. This is supplemented by Canada, *Statutes*, 1939–1970; and the report of the Rowell-Sirois Royal Commission, which has been reprinted in the Carleton Library Series (Toronto, 1963) edited by D. V. Smiley. Primary material for the post–1950 era has been drawn from *The Proceedings of the Resources for Tomorrow Conference, Conference Background Papers* (Ottawa, 1961); Ontario Department of Lands and Forests, "Suggestions for Program of Renewable Resources Development," (white paper) (Toronto, 1954); *Report of the Ontario Royal Commission on Forestry, 1947* (Toronto, 1947); K. Armson, *Forest Management in Ontario, 1976* (ministerial report, Toronto, 1976); Province of British Columbia, *The Report of the Commissioner Relating to the Forest Resources of British Columbia* (Victoria, 1945) and the same for 1956, as well as, *Timber Rights and Forest Policy in British Columbia. A Report of the Royal Commission on Forest Resources* (Victoria, 1976); Canada, House of Commons, *Debates*, 1950–1980, and Standing Committee on Mines, Forests and Waters, *Minutes and Proceedings*, 1958–1963; Canada, Science Council, *Canada's Threatened Forests: A Statement by the Science Council, March 1983* (Ottawa 1983); the *Globe and Mail* 1964–1983; Conservative Party of Canada, *Campaign Platform, 1984*; Canada, Prime Minister's Office, *News Release* (17 September 1984); and Canadian Council of Resource and Environment Ministers, *Forest Policies in Canada*, 2 vols. (Ottawa, 1976).

There is a wide variety of secondary works that deal with the period. The history of timber control during World War II is analyzed in J. de N. Kennedy, *History of the Department of Munitions and Supply Canada in the Second World War* (Ottawa, 1950), vol. 2; and F. H. House, comp., *Timber at War* (London, 1965). Federal-provincial relations up to 1942 are described in C. Armstrong, *Politics of Federalism: Ontario's Relations with the Federal Government, 1867–1942*; and the later period is dealt with in R. Bothwell, I. Drummond, and J. English, *Canada Since 1945: Power, Politics and Provincialism* (Toronto, 1981). Reference was also made to H.V. Nelles, *The Politics of Development*; R.S. Lambert with P. Pross, *Renewing Nature's Wealth*; P. Pross, "The Development of a Forest Policy: A Study of the Ontario Department of Lands and Forests" (unpublished doctoral dissertation, Univ. of Toronto; 1967); J. Swift, *Cut and Run*; K. Drushka, *Stumped*; and L. Sayn-Wittgenstein, "Forestry: From Branch to Department," *Canadian Public Administration* 4 (Dec. 1963).

The "Conclusions" portion of this book was drawn from a reading of a wide selection of current materials. The most important of these, not already mentioned, are K. Armson, "Introducing Options in the Forest: Renewing the forest instead of mining it is a policy change requiring new attitudes and implementation mechanisms," *Policy Options* 2, 6 (November/December 1981); and A. Zimmerman, "Investment in Foresters" and Jack Munro, "The Land for Better Trees," both in *Policy Options* 3, 1 (January/February 1982); F. J. Anderson, "Resource Allocation Issues in the North American Forest Sector", and J. A. Zwnuska, "Public Policy, Timber Supplies and the Canadian—U.S. Forest Products Trade," both in P. Nemetz, ed., *Resource Policy: International Perspectives* (Montreal; 1980); D. Mackay, *Heritage Lost*; D. J. Savoie, *Federal-Provincial Collaboration: The Canada–New Brunswick General Development Agreement* (Montreal; 1981); and T. L. Burton, *Natural Resource Policy in Canada: Issues and Perspectives* (Toronto, 1972). Finally, three extremely valuable works that cannot be ignored when discussing the modern era are F. L. C. Reed, *The Role of the Federal Government in Forestry* (Edmonton, 1978), and, by the same author, *Forest Management in Canada* (Ottawa, 1978); and an American article by B. T. Parry, H. J. Vaux, and N. Dennis, "Changing Conceptions of Sustained-Yield Policy on the National Forests", *American Journal of Forestry* (March 1983).

Index

About the Authors

R. PETER GILLIS has written widely on the themes of lumbering, conservation, and progressive reform in Canada. His articles have appeared in *Alternatives: Perspectives on Society and Environment*, *Urban History Review*, *Journal of Canadian Studies*, and *Journal of Forest History*. Mr. Gillis also served as Executive Editor of the Canadian Historical Association from 1973 to 1978 and is a director of the Forest History Society. He is currently employed as a senior public servant with the Treasury Board Secretariat of the Canadian Government.

THOMAS R. ROACH is a writer and researcher in resource and conservation history and policy. He has had practical experience in the forestry and forest industry and has analyzed many aspects of the industry's present performance and history in articles published in the *Journal of Forest History*, *History of Sustained Yield Forestry*, the *Beaver*, and *Northward Journal*.